SACRED SPACE

Sacred Space

Shrine, City, Land

Edited by

Benjamin Z. Kedar

and

R. J. Zwi Werblowsky

NEW YORK UNIVERSITY PRESS
Washington Square, New York

First published in the U.S.A. in 1998 by
NEW YORK UNIVERSITY PRESS
Washington Square
New York, N.Y. 10003

This book is printed on paper suitable for recycling and
made from fully managed and sustained forest sources.

Library of Congress Cataloging-in-Publication Data
Sacred space : shrine, city, land / edited by Benjamin Z. Kedar and
R. J. Zwi Werblowsky.
p. cm.
Proceedings from the international conference in memory of Joshua
Prawer held in Jerusalem, June 8–13, 1992.
Includes indexes.
ISBN 0–8147–4680–2
1. Sacred space—Congresses. I. Prawer, Joshua. II. Werblowsky,
R. J. Zwi (Raphael Jehudah Zwi), 1924– . III. Kedar-Kopfstein,
Benjamin.
BL580.S25 1997
291.3'5—dc21 97–23137
CIP

Printed in Great Britain

Contents

Preface

Joshua Prawer (1917–1990), whose studies have profoundly affected the understanding of the legal, constitutional and social history of the Crusading Kingdom of Jerusalem, was also keenly interested in the idea of the crusade and in the role of Jerusalem in the genesis of crusader spirituality. The perceptions of Jerusalem's sanctity by Christians — and Jews — from the early Middle Ages to the eruption of the First Crusade, and from the establishment of the Crusading Kingdom in 1099 to its final downfall in 1291, was a major theme of his work, especially in its later stages.

When the Israel Academy of Sciences and Humanities and the Hebrew University of Jerusalem decided to mark the second anniversary of Prawer's death by convening an international conference, his colleagues and friends agreed that rather than hold still another convention dedicated to crusader studies as such, the conference should relate to Jerusalem's sanctity, the subject that was a focus of Prawer's scholarly work in the closing years of his life. Hence the conference on Sacred Space: Shrine, City, Land that took place in Jerusalem on 8–13 June 1992; most of the papers read there are printed herein.

The space dealt with in the articles that follow ranges from the lands of the Fertile Crescent to Europe, India, Japan and Mexico, and from mountains and seas to temples, cities and countries; the issues treated extend from the construction, perception and functioning of sacred sites to the psychotic breakdowns they bring on some visitors. Apart from Jonathan Z. Smith's discussion of the transposition of spaces that are marked as sacred, each of the articles concentrates on a specific, temporally delimited subject, with only an occasional macro-comparative remark or hunch. We have therefore decided to dispense with grouping the articles into artificial thematic clusters, and present them in a rough chronological order. Thus, in a book dedicated to space, time has emerged once again as the superior organizing principle.

The editors are deeply indebted to a number of individuals who have been involved in this project at one stage or another of its protracted progress: to the late Professor Nathan Rotenstreich of the Israel Academy of Sciences and Humanities, who chaired the organizing committee of the 1992 conference and, as chairperson of the Academy's Publications Committee, gave the initial backing to the publication of its proceedings; to Dr. Lea Zivoni, the secretary of the organizing committee, who assembled the articles; and to Deborah Greniman, the Academy's editor, who prepared the volume for press. A rush proofreading job was accomplished by Evelyn Katrak and Eliyahu Green, who prepared the Index. Yehudit Sternberg undertook the complex task of setting a volume rife with unusual diacritical marks, and the setting of the final copy was completed by Marek Lasman. Niko Pfund of New York University Press initiated the cooperation between the Academy and Macmillan, and T.M. Farmiloe of Macmillan brought it to fruition. We would like to thank them all.

Benjamin Z. Kedar
R.J. Zwi Werblowsky
July 1996

1
Introduction: Mindscape and Landscape

R.J. Zwi Werblowsky

Looking at the programme of our conference, I could not help feeling overwhelmed by an almost numinously threatening sense of erudition evoked by both the names of the participants and the titles of their papers. Where you cannot hope to compete, you had better stick to your own modest game. My opening presentation, intended to sketch some of the parameters of this week's deliberations, will therefore be, unabashedly, a string of plagiarisms, quotations and references to the work of others. Already my title is a monumental plagiarism, as will soon become apparent. And, going from bad to worse, I shall begin by rushing in as a *religionswissenschaftlicher* fool where angels and philosophers fear to tread. For it surely seems odd for an historian of religion to begin his reflections on the theme of our conference with Kant. But his three a priori categories — time, space and causality — happen to be, in a way, the three a prioris of religion. There are, of course, ever so many subcategories of causality underlying (*pace* Frazer) not merely magic but all ritual and mythology. Commemorating a great historian, our late lamented colleague Joshua Prawer, one might be tempted to make a beeline for time as the framework of history and historicity. We have, however, opted for space — or, more precisely, for "Sacred Space: Shrine, City, Land" — to honour the memory of the great authority on the crusades, the Latin Kingdom of Jerusalem and the history of the Holy Land in general.

Indeed, being in a plagiarizing mood anyway, I wondered whether we should not have chosen Samuel Alexander's title "Time, Space and Deity" as the title of our conference as well. But hiding behind my presentation, essentially, are Merleau-Ponty's reflections on the primacy of perception, that is, of the ways we construct what we perceive, including our perceptions of the difference between "sacred" and "profane." As Bardieu put it: "la vision du monde est une di-vision du monde." Eliade spoke of "Sacred Space and Making the World Sacred," and a conference on related themes held in Italy five years ago spoke of *La Sacralizzazione dello spazio naturale*, a formula which seems to assume that there is such a thing as *spazio naturale* in the first place.

Landscape — whether macro-cosmography or local geography — is shaped, in the very act of our perceiving it, by our mindscape. The copyright on this particularly felicitous and catchy phrase belongs to our colleague Allan Grapard, whom we are happy to count among our participants. I shall have occasion to plagiarize Grapard even more in the sequel. Perceiving the space separating Santa Barbara from Chicago as non-existent, we might associate the aforementioned pair with the map/territory distinction. Jonathan Smith, whom we are also happy to count herein, borrowed the wording of the title of his book, *Map is not Territory*, from Korzybski. My concern here is with Smith's significant addition: "but maps are all we possess" — even when we are not at school learning geography by staring at a Mercator-projection atlas.

On our mental as well as physical pilgrimages we traverse territory transformed into maps, or, if you prefer, maps identified as territory. Our images and spiritual constructs of inner and outer, mental and cosmic space, best exemplified in Asia by the mandala (I do not distinguish here, for brevity's sake, between the very different uses of the term from Tibet to Japan), have therefore been well described by Grapard as the "mandalization of geography." Had I provided myself with illustrations, I would have shown Chinese drawings of "their" geographical space, structured as it is around the five or more holy peaks or mountains: Tai Shan (to which Chavannes devoted a monograph as far back as 1910), Mt. Wu-i, Mao Shan, Sung Shan, Mt. Wu-t'ai and others. We shall return to the mountains at a later stage. Meanwhile, suffice it to say that throughout history people have not only perceived and constructed space in many different ways, but have also crystallised their experience of the sacred in their view of space.

There are holy lands (and you are undoubtedly aware that we

are actually assembling in one) — a subject on which I do not wish to dwell. It may suffice to remind you of the temple in Benares in which the object of worship is not a divine effigy but a map of Mother India, *Bande Mataram*. There are holy places, as distinct from holy lands, places which confer blessing because the divine became manifest there in one way or another, in experiences or traditions of theophanies or hierophanies, in miracles, or in the lives of saintly men. As a matter of fact, the latter in particular — not only tombs and relics, but even mere association with a charismatic person who passed there — seem to have generated a very high percentage of pilgrimage sites. Surely the pilgrimages to holy mountains (Mt. Fuji, Ontako, Yoshino or any other) and the *yama-no-kami* dwelling there, or to the *saigoku sanju san-sho* (the 33 sanctuaries of the Bodhisattva Kannon in Western Japan) are neither less nor more meaningful than the Shikoku pilgrimage to the 88 sites visited by St. Kukai. In fact, in this particular case even the solitary pilgrim is never alone because he is accompanied, invisibly, by Kukai himself: *dogyo nin-nin*.

There are holy cities, as distinct from holy places. Some of them acquired their holiness as a result of historical circumstances or events, or because either in theory or in actual fact they were constructed so as to reflect cosmic reality — a kind of microcosmic spatial reflection of the macrocosm and its divine ground. Other cities are holy because they harbour or possess a holy object, a shrine or a tomb. Others again exhibit all these qualities in various combinations. We think of Benares (and of Diana Eck's fine study of this fascinating instance of *geographia sacra*), of Mecca, Lhasa, Angkor, or Rome (I am referring here to the ancient *Roma quadrata*). As a modern example we may instance Tenri (near Nara, in Japan), which is sacred not only because it is built around the sacred *kanrodai*, the navel of the earth, but also because it is constructed according to a divine plan.

My random selection of examples of "sacralized" spaces, and hence mostly also goals of pilgrimages, has been thrown together somewhat helter-skelter in order to illustrate the wide range of possibilities, ranging from "concentric" centres (socio-political or *axis mundi* type) such as Jeruslem — both "the kingly sanctuary and city of royalty" and, cosmologically, the site of the *'eben shetiyah* — to excentric centres "out there," such as Lourdes, Fatima or Shikoku. No doubt my listeners will automatically think of Mircea Eliade and Victor Turner. The latter has indeed significantly enriched our terminology and our view of the scope of the phenomenon, though his valuable insights are clearly inadequate and even misleading as a general theory.

Several of the modalities indicated are exemplified by the city in which we are meeting. Some 25 years ago, Krister Stendahl wrote:

> For Christians and Muslims the term "holy sites" is an adequate expression of what matters. Here are sacred places, hallowed by the most holy events, here are the places for pilgrimage, the very focus of highest devotion. ... But Judaism is different. ... The sites sacred to Judaism have no shrines. Its religion is not tied to "sites" but to the land, not to what happened in Jerusalem, but to Jerusalem itself.

Of course, this statement needs some careful qualifications, but its basic insight seems correct. A whole chapter in the history of religions could be written on the progression of Christianity from an original rejection of, or at least eloquent indifference towards, Jerusalem, to the fourth-century revolution in its attitude under Constantine and his mother Helena. More recently, Peter Walker (*Holy Cities, Holy Places?* Oxford 1990) has drawn attention to the insistence with which Eusebius distinguishes between holy city (negative) and holy place (positive). Jerusalem also exemplifies the political dimensions of the sacrality of holy space as well as the gradual mythologization — in both cosmogonic and eschatological directions — of original data of a different kind. Readers of these papers will be treated to yet further variations on the political role of holy cities and of sanctuaries.

Some scholars have distinguished between cities evincing a basic "temple culture" (e.g., ancient Greece), a "palace culture" (e.g., Minoan Crete or seventeenth–eighteenth century Europe) or an amphitheatre and thermae culture (as in late antiquity). These distinctions seem to have seduced Walter Burkert to identify our age as a "highway culture," coining this very apt phrase long before the publication of W. Schivelbusch's fascinating book *Railway Journey: The Industrialisation of Time and Space in the Nineteenth Century* (1986).

Talking about sacred space, whether shrines, cities or lands, means breaking up the homogeneity of space. We might formulate this thesis, known today mainly through the writings of Eliade, by proposing a variation on the title of a book by the historian Bernard Lewis. We might metamorphose his title *History Remembered, Recovered, Invented* (1976) to "Geography Perceived, Constructed, Invented." Marcel Granet, one of the founding fathers of the modern study of Chinese religion, spoke of space as complex and unstable, a "hierarchical federation of heterogeneous expanses." Homogeneity might be achieved by radical pan-secularization — viz., desacralization — on the one hand, or equally, by radical pan-sacramentalization. But where everything is sacred, nothing is sacred, for the sacred exists by dint of a binary opposition. Perhaps Durkheim learned this truth from the Jewish *habdalah* formula that he heard spoken by his rabbinic forebears.

The dilemmas to which the homogeneous option can give rise are illustrated by hasidism, or rather by certain anti-hasidic polemics, no less than by certain admittedly elitist (as opposed to folk-piety) Zen doctrines. If the pure Dharmakaya of the Buddha is a limitless and empty inner space — to be contrasted, as Bernard Faure has pointed out, to the densely populated realm of the Taoist body — then we can sympathize with the quandary of the Ch'an monk who complained: "Since the Dharmakaya fills all space, where in the entire universe can I find a place to shit?" These dilemmas have been addressed by Jonathan Smith in his enlightening distinction between the *locative* and the *utopian* vision of space. The distinction is helpful, although, together with Faure, I am not sure about the correlation of these two types with, respectively, normative-imperial and peripheral-disruptive space. Very possibly it is the other way round. At any rate, we may ponder the difference between the spatial orientation of the pilgrim moving from place to place, and the total annihilation of space represented by the immobility of sitting in the *za-zen* lotus position.

Had we but world enough and time, to quote a seventeenth-century poet, I would link space and time by means of the connecting concept of movement, which, for our purposes, means pilgrimage and its wide range of spiritual and social functions: piety and recreation, devotion and desire for adventure, release from the interruption of the yoke of routine and hierarchy (Turner's liminality), asceticism and tourism, plus all the the other elements that have been pointed out by Erik Cohen. But my concern is mainly not with the psycho-social aspects of pilgrimage, but rather with the correlation between outer space and inner space. In fact, the latter can be used as a kind of homologizing justification of the former. Commenting on the words of Jesus, "If any man thirst, let him come unto me and drink" (John 7:37), St. Augustine wrote:

> When we thirst, then we should come — not with our feet but rather with our feelings; we should come not by wandering but by loving. In an inward way to live is to wander. It is one thing to wander with the body, and a different thing to wander with the heart. He who wanders with the body, changes his place by the motion of the body; he who wanders with the heart, changes his feelings by the motion of the heart.

From here it is but a small step to the more radical conclusion of Ibn al-Arabi: if the circumambulation of the Ka'abah means that the heart revolves around Allah, then one might conceivably dispense with the pilgrimage. But neither of the two movements would make sense to a Zen monk.

I have already hinted at the ways in which pilgrimage illustrates the homogeneous/heterogeneous polarity. The Ch'an Buddhist desacralizes — at least in theory — the naturally sacred Chinese mountains, substituting for them the abstract space of temple and meditation hall. Similarly, though for very different reasons, the Puritan poet mocked the superstitious "popish" belief in the merit of pilgrimages by peopling his Paradise of Fools with pilgrims:

> Here pilgrims roam, that stray'd so far to seek
> In Golgotha him dead, who lives in Heav'n.

There can be no doubt that John Milton figures on the Israeli Tourism Ministry's blacklist of anti-Zionist enemies.

One might usefully compare the orientation to space of religions in which normative monotheistic doctrine recognizes only one centre of required pilgrimage — whether three times a year or once in a lifetime, whether as a major commandment or even as one of the "pillars" of the religion concerned — to that of polytheistic religions with their inbuilt multiplicity of pilgrimage centres. Needless to say, this mechanical distinction is meaningless in practice. There may be only one god, but the associated saints, tombs, relics, and places of supernatural appearances are many, and the irrepressible need for contact with sacred sites makes pilgrimage a feature of every religion and turns every pilgrim — to use a Homeric phrase — into a *hos mala polla plankte*. I shall leave it at that and resist the temptation to discuss the dialectic, or rather the two-way traffic, between what have been called great and little traditions. Suffice it to say that even when there is actual or potential conflict between the two, folk-devotion always wins out.

But let me return, in conclusion, to the mountains with which I began. With your permission, I shall stay in East Asia rather than bother you with the nearly one hundred pre-Hispanic cultic sites that have been found by an enterprising and amazingly tough archaeologist on top of the Andean mountains at altitudes between 5,000 and 7,000 metres. Unfortunately, I do not possess a Japanese translation of the Bible, and hence I could not check whether the statement of the Aramaean king (1 Kings 20:23) that the god of the Israelites was a god of the hills (and that is why the Aramaeans had better fight the Israelites in the valleys next time) is translated, in good Shinto fashion, as *yama-no-kami* (mountain deity). But if a mountain is, as one scholar has put it, "a text to be deciphered" (by means of its mythological toponymy, or of the hagiography of the saints and ascetics said to have lived there, or of the ritual practices associated with it — including the many mountains in Japan that are so sacred that women are denied access to them), then, like every text, this text, too, can be "translated." In other words, geographical perception can be the starting point for series of homologies and correspondences.

A most telling example is the Taoist landscape, where mountains, grottos and caves, rivers, wells and gardens can be homologized with houses, tombs, temples and, above all, the human body. A similar point was made long ago by Stella Kramrisch in her analysis of the Hindu temple as an analogue of the body. Mountaintops can be locations of or passages to paradises; grottos and caves can be (and in China and Japan often are) entrances to hells or, alternatively, wombs for rebirth. They can be the preferred locus of revelations. Elijah (1 Kings 19:9 ff.) experienced one of the most moving and impressive theophanies on record at the mouth of a cave, and it was in a cave that R. Simeon b. Yohai wrote the *Zohar*. The Taoist holy scriptures (known as the *Tao Tsang*) are, of course, all descended from heaven, but an important portion is known as the *San-tung*, so called after Master Lu (fifth century C.E.), who signed himself "Disciple of the Three Caverns." Most of these caves and caverns are thought to be connected by a network of underground passages, providing us with another instance of landscape, though underground, being shaped by mindscape. (I might add here that one of the standard bibliographies on Chinese religions has a special section on "Caves and Mountains.") The literature on caves as wombs is immense, and I shall restrict myself, by way of homage to a recently deceased dear colleague and friend, to the account by the late Anna Seidel. In her last publication before her premature death, she relates how she volunteered to help her revered teacher Rolf Stein collect material for the revised edition of his 1942 study, which subsequently appeared in 1980 as *Grottes-matrices et lieux saints*. As a result, she found herself creeping through a grotto on Mount Fuji called *tainai* ("inside the womb"):

> Bent double in the dark and narrow interior, I wriggled through sections called "Small Intestine," "Large Intestine" and "Five Viscera." My feet got soaked in a pond of "Spermatic Liquid," I ducked under "Nipple" stalactites and felt truly reborn after squeezing through a "Birth Canal" that was narrow indeed.

Raoul Birnbaum's experiences on Wu-t'ai Shan were not much different. Hence, Stein's conclusion comes as no surprise: the "imagery and practice is never automatically derived from the site: the images precede the sight, and the rituals can be enacted just as well without a natural grotto, using instead an edifice symbolizing the womb."

Stein could also have mentioned the Japanese miniature mountains erected nearer home for those unable to undertake the long journey or arduous climb. You do not even have to erect a homologous edifice. The Taoist homologue to a geographical site can simply be a *fu* or a *chen hsing* (a talisman in the form of a "true shape") diagram. Persevering climbers to the top of the holy mountain Tateyama near Toyama City in Japan (today also a booming ski resort) are nowadays greeted on arrival at the high summit of Oyama by a priest who gets there by helicopter. A well-known Benten shrine used to be reached by pious pilgrims after climbing several hundred steps. Today a moving staircase provides a less ascetic alternative.

Didn't I, earlier on, say something about the contemporary industrialization, or perhaps we should say mechanization, also of sacred space?

2
Constructing a Small Place

Jonathan Z. Smith

The activity of *transposition* is one of the basic building blocks of ritual and a central object of ritual thought. The capacity to alter common denotations in order to enlarge potential connotations within the boundaries of ritual is one of the features that marks off its space as "sacred." Transposition is a paradigmatic process set within the largely syntagmatic series of actions which characterize ritual. The respects in which a "this" might, under some circumstances, also be a "that" gives rise to thought which plays across the gaps of like and unlike (to give the most famous example, how do the Nuer think of a cucumber as an ox in sacrificial contexts?). Seen in this light, ritual is a prime mode of exploring the systematics of difference in relation to processes of transformation and identification.

There is, however, one mode of transposition that is most difficult for ritual praxis and thought — the transposition of space marked as sacred. This is most pressing when the ritual is tied to a specific locale, where the gap between "this" and "that" or "here" and "there" seems unbridgeable — can the rite for consecrating the waters of the Nile, in either its archaic Egyptian or later Christian forms, be performed anywhere else? But the difficulty occurs in a far wider range of phenomena, including that of the shifting of the locus for religious activity. In many of these cases, historical change has challenged or perturbed the ritual system, giving rise to new ritual activities and thoughts concerning the relations of "this" to "that," as modes of dis-placement and re-placement.

I should like to think about these sorts of transpositions by revisiting, with both new materials and new conceptual assists, two topics studied previously. The first, in honour of Professor Prawer's memory, concerns the Church of the Holy Sepulchre, while the second treats an aspect of the characteristic Late Antique domestication of temple activities expressed in the so-called Greek Magical Papyri. I wish to approach these topics with an eye towards a particular technique, that of *miniaturization*.

i

The Church of the Holy Sepulchre, the Anastasis, could not have been built anywhere else and still be the same. Its locus in Jerusalem had to correspond fully to the *topos* of the Gospel narratives — leaving aside the problem that the location is by no means clear in these narratives, the precise place having been determined later on by a miraculous self-disclosure. It is the Church's locative specificity and thick associative content that guarantees the site's power and religious functions. There can be no two ways about it. For all the commonsense charm of the formulation, it cannot be, as Dean A.P. Stanley would have it, that the Church of the Holy Sepulchre is:

> the most sacred of all the holy places, in comparison of which, *if genuine,* all the rest sink into insignificance; the interest of which, *even if not genuine,* stands absolutely alone in the world.[1]

The latter option would render the site a mere historical or folkloristic curiosity. The site's power depends on its *praesentia*. In Christian Jerusalem of the fourth century, gesture, story, emotion and re-presentation coalesced. For example, any homiletician of modest accomplishment and learning could develop the typology: "after these things you were led to the holy pool of divine baptism as Christ was carried from the Cross to the Sepulchre," but only a Cyril in Jerusalem could add, "from the Cross to the Sepulchre *which is before our eyes*."[2] It is only from her presence at the site that Flora could experience the sort of emotions, prompted by sight, reported by her brother, Jerome: "like a thirsty man who has waited long and at last comes to water, she faithfully kissed *the very shelf* on which the Lord's body had lain."[3]

What if such a site becomes inaccessible, because of distance or the vicissitudes of conquest? In *To Take Place*, I focussed on one ritual solution to this problem with respect to the Sepulchre, through the Christian liturgical structuring of time. Temporal sequence, story, the festal calendar allowed a supercession of place by creating a new systematics of time.[4] I noted, in passing, two other strategies of transposition.[5] The first is a metonymical project of exchanging parts for wholes. The second is a metaphoric project of exchanging relations of equivalence for those of identity.

The substitution of *pars pro toto* — in this case, the exportation of the Holy Sepulchre by means of relics — is most familiar and continues to this day. One type of relic consists of pieces of the site itself, small portions of earth and chips of the rock of the tomb that were carried off by pious pilgrims.[6] As these were not infinitely renewable resources, a second form developed: objects that were placed in contact with or had a functional relationship to the site. Already, the Anonymous Pilgrim of Piacenza (c. 570) reports that "earth is brought to the tomb and put inside, and those who go in take some as a blessing."[7] Even more economical, notes E.D. Hurt, and "eventually the most popular ... were small flasks of the oil which kept alight the lamps at the Holy Sepulchre. The collections dating from the sixth century at Manza and Bobbio in north Italy ... are the most celebrated examples."[8]

The second strategy, the metaphoric project of replacing relations of identity (the Holy Sepulchre is Christ's tomb) with those of equivalence, finds its most literal form in the construction, in Europe, of scaled architectural copies of the Anastasis, each serving as a miniaturized reproduction.[9] In addition to free-standing churches and chapels which replicate the prestigious prototype — most common in Germany[10] — five functional types may be distinguished.

(I) In the first and earliest type, the replicas, of fairly large scale, serve either as tombs or as chapels located within cemetery complexes, and range in date from the Apostoleion, Constantine's fourth-century grave-church in Constantinople, to the mausoleum constructed for Emperor Frederick III at Potsdam in 1888.[11] These monuments are governed by analogy, based on the equivalence of copy to prototype, the relation between Christ's resurrection and the future resurrection of the entombed, as is made plain by a verse written by Hrabanus Maurus for the dedication in 822 of a chapel replicating the Church of the Holy Sepulchre in St. Michael at Fulda, constructed in a cemetery as an ossuary for the bones of monks:

"This altar to God is dedicated most especially to Christ, whose tomb *here* helps our graves."[12]

(II) The second type of replica consisted of churches built especially to house relics from Holy Land pilgrimages, especially those associated with Christ's death and resurrection, such as the eleventh century Neuvy Holy Sepulchre, which displayed in its rotunda a fragment of Jesus's tomb and earth from Calvary.[13] This type of construction is essentially a large-scale reliquary, no different in intent from the small, two-dimensional representations of the Sepulchre found on the common lead ampullae containing oil from the Anastasis, or on pilgrim's boxes like the one preserved in the Vatican Museum which is "filled with pebbles and earth from five sites" depicted on its cover, marking the "nativity, baptism, crucifixion, resurrection and ascension."[14]

(III) In the third type, which begins to occur in the eleventh century, the Sepulchre is incorporated within a larger church building, and is so reduced in size as to resemble a play house. Or, in the more dignified description by Pamela Sheingorn:

> Although such a Holy Sepulchre still replicates the architecture of the Holy Sepulchre in Jerusalem, its architectural form loses its functional meaning when it is seen within another building. The object begins to strike the eye more like a large piece of sculpture than a small piece of architecture. It is as if the entire Holy Sepulchre had been reduced in size, shrunk to a model.[15]

For example, a mid-eleventh century replica of this type, in the cathedral at Aquileia, is 2 metres high and 3.8 metres in diameter, dimensions that are approximated in a number of other surviving replicas of the third type.[16]

This type, and types IV and V, represent a major shift in ritual logic. The large-scale replicas (types I and II) serve to reproduce and/or replace the Jerusalem site as *memoria*. They either house Christian dead, awaiting their resurrection, or house relics of Christ's paradigmatic death and resurrection. They are, therefore, located between the "not yet" and the "no longer," and are, as well, *sancta* in and of themselves. The smaller replicas (types III–V) are no such thing.However, their miniaturization produces a kind of clarity missing from both the original and the large-scale copies. As Lévi-Strauss has shrewdly observed in his meditation on miniaturization,the "reduction of scale seems to result from a sort of reversal in the process of understanding." As he elaborates the point:

> To understand a real object in its totality we always tend to work from its parts. The resistance it offers us is overcome by dividing it. Reduction in scale reverses this situation. ... By being quantitatively diminished, it seems to us to be qualitatively simplified. ... In the case of miniatures, in contrast to what happens when we try to understand an object ... of real dimensions, knowledge of the whole precedes knowledge of its parts. ... The intrinsic value of a small scale model is that it compensates for the renunciation of sensible dimensions by the acquisition of intelligible dimensions.[17]

For an understanding of what is clarified, what whole is being grasped in the miniaturized Sepulchre, we must turn to the final two types, which became especially common in Europe in the fourteenth through sixteenth centuries.

(IV) The fourth type is no longer a free-standing object, but rather a niche, usually set in the north wall of the chancel near the high altar, containing a selection of architectural details replicating the Church of the Holy Sepulchre.[18]

(V) The fifth type exhibits little concern for verisimilitude. Small temporary structures of wood and fabric, called "sepulchres," would be fashioned and placed on or in front of altars of European churches as representations of *the* Holy Sepulchre.[19] Sheingorn notes that bequests for their construction, repair and maintenance (often undertaken by a "Sepulchral" or "Resurrection" Guild) appear in many testaments, "in some areas [of England] appearing virtually a part of the standard language of the will."[20]

In types III, IV and V, there is an increasing tendency towards abstraction, which grows greater as the overall size of the replica decreases. The metaphoric reduction becomes increasingly emblematic. If the large-scale replicas (types I and II) relate the Christian mythos of death and resurrection, the small-scale miniatures, through their sharp focus, serve to make this mythos mimetically present in ritual activity. In such a project, verisimilitude would constitute a distraction, overemphasizing the "then" and "there" of Jerusalem at the expense of the European "now" and "here." The whole that is grasped through miniaturization is that of the foundation myth of the resurrection, removed from the sort of reduplication, elaboration, and potential confusion that surrounds the composite of competing Easter rituals in the "actual" Church of the Holy Sepulchre — all the more so since 1757.

To this end, beginning perhaps as early as the late tenth century in Western Europe, a new Christian ritual complex was fashioned for which the sepulchres of types III, IV, and V served as settings. Indeed, a distinguished line of theatre historians, from K. Young to O.B. Hardison, Jr., have seen in these little constructions, along with their attendant ritual dramas, the origin of the European stage.[21]

The new ritual had four parts: (1) the Burial (*Depositio*), in which a cross and/or wafer was ritually entombed within the replica on Good Friday; (2) the forty-hour Easter Vigil, during which the replica was sealed, watched and guarded; (3) the Raising (*Elevatio*), in which the previously entombed cross and/or host was ritually resurrected — either it was taken out of the replica, held up and displayed on Easter morning, or it was secretly removed, so that the replica was shown to be empty; (4) the Visit to the Tomb (*Visitatio Sepulchri*), in which the Gospel narrative of the witness of the women to the empty tomb was dramatically re-enacted later on Easter day.

The chief function of the new ritual complex appears to have been a recovery of the sense of *praesentia* characteristic of Christian Jerusalem by an appeal to sight.[22] Not only was the Christian mythos narrated and proclaimed, but it was witnessed, it was seen. In its simplest form, the little sepulchre was empty. In the more complex forms, rather than the entombed object being secretly removed, it would secretly be switched: a wounded Christ figurine for the *Depositio* would be exchanged with a triumphant, royal Christ figurine for the *Elevatio*; a dark cross for the Burial would be exchanged with a green cross for the Raising. Some churches, especially in England, employed a jointed "resurrection puppet," stiff when first placed in the sepulchre for the *Depositio* and mobile when removed for the *Elevatio*. In some instances, this puppet was raised out of the sepulchre by mechanical means.[23]

The monumental replicas (types I and II) of the Church of the Holy Sepulchre sought to assimilate themselves to the prototype in Jerusalem, thereby erasing distance. The more miniaturized and, ultimately, more stylized replicas of the Sepulchre (types III–V), along with their attendant ritual, sought to simulate the prototypical experience which lay behind the monument, thereby creating a utopia, a theatre of the mind and imagination, in which there was no distance because the specific locality in Jerusalem was, in the ritual process, erased.

ii

In an article published a number of years ago, I used the second-century (?) autobiographical (?) text of Thessalos the Magician to explore a shift in the locus of religious experience from a permanent sacred centre, the archaic temple, to a place of temporary sacrality created and sanctified by the magician's rituals.[24] As the second part of this essay, I should like to enlarge on this theme, focussing particularly on the strategy of miniaturization.

As part of a larger pattern of religious persistence and change in late antiquity, and for a diversity of reasons ranging from the economic to the aesthetic and from the political and demographic to the ethical and theological, temple sacrifice, especially that requiring animal victims, declined in a number of traditions. As sacrifice was the *raison d'être* of the archaic temple, the chief currency of both its divine and its human economies, this meant that temples must be either revalorized or abandoned. A temple or altar without sacrifice is a mere monument (see, already, the admittedly polemic account in Josh. 22:10–34). This meant, as well, that sacrifice would have to be either dis-placed or re-placed.

The rationales and strategies for these latter processes were varied. Sometimes, as in the case of Orphic, Neoplatonic and Neopythagorean traditions, a moral cast — no bloodshed — was given to older cultic rules prohibiting pollution by dead animal products, corpses and blood, with a consequent recovery and refocus on archaic practices of cereal and incense offerings (see, for example, the fumigation recipes which form part of the titula of seventy-eight of the eighty-seven late third-century "Orphic" Hymns).

In the case of the emergent Judaisms and Christianities, spurred only in part by the destruction of the Temple in Jerusalem, the locus of sacrifice was shifted from Temple to domicile, and the act of sacrifice was wholly replaced by narrative and discourse. Early rabbinic traditions talked endlessly about sacrifices no longer performed and in many cases never experienced, substituting speech for deed in its ritual praxis. The best-known example is the dictum attributed to Rabbi Gamliel: "Whoever does not say these three things on Passover has not fullfilled his obligations," with the first of the three being the sacrifice of the Paschal lamb (M. *Pesahim* 10:5). This is a sentence about ritual speech which, by virtue of its inclusion in the later Passover Haggadah has itself *become* ritual speech.

Some early Christians developed the utterly rhetorical metaphor of sacrifice as an important component of their narrative understanding of Jesus's death. Over time, the Christian use of the sacrificial analogy was extended, by traditions that never "actually" sacrificed, to characterize a whole host of human phenomena, including the sacrament of marriage, post-Vatican II.

Christian liturgy maintained the language of "altar," of "smoke," and of the sacrificial elements, now wholly metaphorized; the eucharistic flesh and blood was subsumed to a narrative of paradigmatic institution which was set in a domestic, non-sacrifical context.

Of all the documents from late antiquity, I know of none more filled with the general and technical terminology and the praxis of sacrifice than those texts collected by modern scholars under the title Greek Magical Papyri. They are all the more important because they display, as well, a throughly domesticated understanding of sacrifice.

In the papyri,[25] while a small number of the ritual *topoi* are outside — in an open place, a deserted place, a tomb, or by a river[26] — the vast majority of rituals which give a locale are set in domestic space, in the practioner's house,[27] or, more rarely, in the client's place of business or home.[28] As a substantial number of rituals are for procuring some sort of dream oracle, "your bedroom" predominates.[29] There are, as well, a number of references to rituals performed on "your housetop," "lofty roof," or upper room,[30] chiefly as a place for receiving a celestial power who is then conducted to "the room in which you reside."[31] Within this domestic space, there is an intense concern for purity in the rituals of preparation and reception. The practioner is to abstain from sexual relations, from animal foods (including fish), and from "all uncleanness."[32] The ritual site is to be a "clean room," a "pure room" — "let your place be cleaned of all pollution."[33]

Within the "clean" domestic place, the chief ritual is that of sacrifice, most commonly of generic incense, with frankincense the most frequently specified. Some dozen other aromatic plant substances, from gums to spices, were also employed.[34] Other vegetable offerings include: roses, sumac, mulberries, beets, moss, cakes and fruits, along with libations of wine and/or milk.[35]

In contrast to these common vegetable offerings, sacrifices *wholly* made up of animal victims or products are rare. The largest group requires the sacrifice of a white cock.[36] The only instance of the whole offering of a mammal remains an editorial conjecture.[37]

More common than purely animal sacrifices, though less common than purely vegetable offerings, are sacrifices of mixed animal and plant substances. Their usual form is a series of plants plus one animal part, usually its dung or an organ. If it is a vegetable series plus a whole animal, the latter is invariably a bird.[38] Some of the animal *materia* (for example, dung, eggs, a snake's shed skin) do not require the killing of the animal, while other *materia* — like "wolf's eye" and "frog's tongue" — may well be code names for plants, as is certainly the case for the ingredient "pig's snout."[39] Other texts appear to place differing valences on animal and plant offerings, for example:

> For doing good, offer storax, myrrh, sage, frankincense, a fruit pit. But for doing harm, offer magical material of a dog and dappled goat [(gloss:) or, in a similar way, of a virgin untimely dead].[40]

The impression that animal offerings were not the central focus is strengthened by the fact that a sharp knife — the one indispensable requirement of animal sacrifice — is mentioned as an implement just three times in the corpus.[41]

The other ritual implements mentioned introduce another important and highly characteristic element. They are not only highly portable, but appear to be miniaturized. The table, the throne, the tripod, and the censer seem, themselves, to be small and to hold relatively small objects. The sacrificial altar — most often constructed of two or more (unbaked) bricks, but never more than seven — seems especially so. What must be the scale of an altar on which is sacrificed "on grapevine charcoal, one sesame seed and [one] black cumin seed?"[42]

In addition to these common, though miniaturized, implements, we find a set of small wooden shrines. Eight appear to be mentioned in the corpus: a juniper wood shrine that holds a mummified falcon; a small wooden shrine, set up on a table covered with pure linen, enclosing a tripod, censer and small figurine; a lime wood shrine in which lies a small figurine of Hermes made of dough; a shrine of olive wood containing a statuette of Selene; a small temple, standing on a table, into which a small dish is placed in which the first morsels of food from a meal are offered; two small (?) temples connected by a single sheet of papyrus;[43] and, most suggestive of all, we find a ritual for fashioning a phylactery which will cause any "place or temple" (apparently the shop of the ritual's patron[44]) to flourish, to become a "marvel," and to be "talked about throughout the whole world"[45] The ritual involves the construction of a small, three-headed wax statue, "three handbreadths high," which is deified by animal(?) sacrifice and placed within a "little juniper wood temple" wreathed with olive branches. The practioner is enjoined, "Now feast [with the god], singing to him all night long."

As this last text makes plain, the "little" temples and shrines, in the last case housing a figure 30 cm high, are treated as if they were major edifices housing a divine image and a cult table. Sacrifice is held before them and a cultic meal follows, accompanied by a chanted liturgy. In other cases, incubation practiced before the miniature[46] replaces sleeping within the large temple precincts. In still other rituals, the divine being is conducted to a small throne, in an ordinary but purified room, from which it gives oracles or provides a powerful guiding presence,[47] just as in the throne room of a major temple complex. These quite typical procedures within the Magical Papyri suggest that the practioner's "clean room" and the rituals performed therein are to be understood, to no small degree, as *replacements* of (and for) temple space and rituals.

Alternatively, the small shrines resemble the portable *naiskoi* commonly carried in religious processions, and the ritual implements, small statues and ritual practices have their closest parallels, as Fritz Graf has convincingly argued, in small-scale, private, domestic rituals conducted by ordinary householders for their household deities and/or ancestors[48] (a comparison that deserves further detailed study). From this point of view, the domestication of ritual has already occurred. What is different about the Magical Papyri is that these practices have been divorced from a familial setting, becoming both highly mobile and professionalized.

In either case, the sacrality of the place is established, *temporarily*, through ritual activities, and by virtue of the direct experience of a mobile, professional ritualist (the 'magician') with an equally mobile deity.

One further matter. If one reads through the entire corpus with an eye towards ritual activities, it is not purification, or incubation, or even sacrifice that predominates. Rather, the chief ritual activity within the Magical Papyri appears to be *the act of writing itself*. The vocabulary of inscription constitutes one of the larger groups. Alongside the evident concern for the accurate transmission of a professional literature, marked, among other features, by scribal glosses and annotations, is an overwhelming belief in the efficacy of writing, especially in the recipes which focus on the fashioning of amulets and phylacteries—themselves miniaturized, portable, powerful written texts of papyrus, metal, stone and bone.

The most common writing material is a sheet of papyrus, often described as "clean," "pure," "choice," or "hieratic." While blood and other *magica materia* occasionally function as writing fluids,[49] most of the inks, some of which are quite complex, are variants of the common, everyday combination of a burnt substance for pigment (e.g. charcoal, soot, lamp black) and a gum as a fixative. The most frequent combination is "myrrh ink" (*smurnomelan*, or *zmurnomelan*). The technology of inkmaking mimics the technology of the vegetable sacrifice, with burning and aromatic gums serving as their common denominators.

> The [preparation of the] ink is as follows: In a purified container, burn myrrh, cinquefoil, and wormwood; grind them to a paste and use them.[50]

Within the corpus, the instruction for the preparation of ink is often given a liturgical rubric, *skeuē melanos*,[51] at times in immediate juxtaposition to the rubric for the sacrificial offering.

The ritual of writing is more than a replacement of the archaic temples as major sites of scribal activities and ritual book libraries — although, at times, use is made of the familiar motif of the alleged discovery of a book or spell in a prestigious temple, as in one of the older surviving papyri.[52] It is, rather, a displacement of ritual practice into writing, analogous, in important respects, to the displacement of sacrifice into speech in the emergent Judaisms and Christianities (as discussed above), and it is also a continuation of the impulse towards miniaturization.

We have already noted Lévi-Strauss's assessment of the small scale model as compensating "for the renunciation of sensible dimensions by the acquisition of intelligible dimensions."[53] In a somewhat similar vein, the literary critic and folklorist Susan Stewart, who has written an extended meditation on miniaturization,[54] insists that small does not equal insignificant (in both senses of the term), that:

> A reduction in the physical dimension of an object depicted can, in fact, increase the dimension of significance ... The miniature always tends towards exaggeration — it is a selection of detail that magnifies detail in the same movement by which it reduces detail.[55]

As major theorists of ritual from Freud to Lévi-Strauss have rightly maintained, ritual, with its characteristic strategies for achieving focus and its typical concern for "microadjustment," is often itself a miniaturization and, simultaneously, an exaggeration of everyday actions.[56] Miniaturization, when applied to ritual — as is the case in the Magical Papyri — then becomes a sort of *ritual of ritual*, existing, among other loci, in a space best described as discursive or intellectual.[57]

Notes

1. A.P. Stanley, *Sinai and Palestine in Connection with Their History*², New York 1870, p. 451.
2. Cyril of Jerusalem, *Catecheses mystagogicae*, 2.4; text and translation in F.L. Cross, *St. Cyril of Jerusalem's Lectures on the Christian Sacraments*, Crestwood 1977, pp. 19, 60.
3. Jerome, Epistle 108: *To Eustochium*, in J. Wilkinson, *Jerusalem Pilgrims before the Crusades*, Warminster 1977, p. 49.
4. J.Z. Smith, *To Take Place: Toward Theory in Ritual*, Chicago 1987, pp. 74–95, *et passim*.
5. *Ibid.*, pp. 86–87.
6. *Ibid.*, p. 168, note 66.

7. Wilkinson, *Jerusalem Pilgrims* (above, note 3), p. 83.
8. E.D. Hunt, *Holy Land Pilgrimages in the Later Roman Empire, AD 312–460*, Oxford 1982, p. 130.
9. To the bibliography in Smith, *To Take Place* (above, note 4), pp. 166–167, note 57, add the fundamental study by P. Sheingorn, *The Easter Sepulchre in England*, Kalamazoo 1987, in Medieval Institute Publications: Early Drama, Art and Music Reference Series, 5.
10. G. Dalman, *Das Grab Christi in Deutschland*, Leipzig 1922, in the series, *Studien über christliche Denkmäler*, 14.
11. R. Krautheimer, *Early Christian and Byzantine Architecture*[2], Harmondsworth 1975, pp. 72–74; idem, *Studies in Early Christian, Medieval and Renaissance Art*, New York 1969, p. 141, note 9.
12. Dalman, *Das Grab Christi* (above, note 10), p. 26: "*Hoc altare deo dedicatum est maxime Christo, cujus hic tumulus nostra sepulcra juvat.*"
13. J. Hubert, "Le Saint-Sépulchre de Neuvy et les pèlerinages de Terre Sainte au XIe siècle," *Bulletin Monumental*, XC (1931), pp. 91–100; cf. V.H. Elbern, "Das Relief des Gekreuzigten in der Mellebaudis-Memorie zu Poitiers: Über eine vorkarolingische Nachbildung des Heiligen Grabes zu Jerusalem," *Jahrbuch der Berliner Museen*, III (1961), pp. 141–189, especially p. 177.
14. K. Weitzmann, *Age of Spirituality: Late Antique and Early Christian Art, Third to Seventh Century*, New York 1979, pp. 564–565 and Fig. 76. For the ampullae, see especially D. Barag, "Glass Pilgrim Vessels from Jerusalem," *Journal of Glass Studies*, XIII (1971), pp. 45–64; J. Wilkinson, "The Tomb of Christ: An Outline of Its Structural History," *Levant*, IV (1972), pp. 83–98; A.D. Kartsonis, *Anastasis: The Making of an Image*, Princeton 1986, pp. 20–26 *et passim*. All of these build upon the fundamental work of A. Grabar, *Ampoules de Terre Sainte*, Paris 1968.
15. Sheingorn, *The Easter Sepulchre* (above, note 9), p. 16.
16. K. Lanckoronski-Brzezie, G. Niemann and H. Swoboda, *Der Dom von Aquileia*, Vienna 1906; P.L. Zovatto, *Il Santo Sepulcro di Aquileia e il dramma liturgico medievale*, Udine 1956.
17. C. Lévi-Strauss, *The Savage Mind*, Chicago 1966, pp. 23–24.
18. Sheingorn, *The Easter Sepulchre* (above, note 9), pp. 33–41.
19. Smith, *To Take Place* (above, note 4), p. 87, and see the literature cited there; Sheingorn, *The Easter Sepulchre*, pp. 52–368.
20. Sheingorn, *The Easter Sepulchre*, p. 53.
21. Smith, *To Take Place*, p. 167, n. 59.
22. Cf. Sheingorn, *The Easter Sepulchre*, p. 58.
23. *Ibid.*, pp. 56–61.
24. J.Z. Smith, "The Temple and the Magician" (1976), reprinted in idem, *Map Is Not Territory: Studies in the History of Religions*, Leiden 1978, pp. 172–189.
25. K. Preisendanz, *Papyri Graecae Magicae*, Leipzig–Berlin 1928–1941; K. Preisendanz & A. Henrichs, *Papyri Graecae Magicae*[2], Stuttgart 1973–1974; H.D. Betz (ed.), *The Greek Magical Papyri in Translation*, Chicago 1986–. All citations will be from the Betz translation, with occasional small emendations. Please note that my citations are meant to be exemplary and not exhaustive.

26. IV.900; III.616; III.25, 286; III.286; IV.27; other outside loci include: a bathhouse (II.49); a stadium (II.43); the eastern section of a village (IV.58–59); a bean field (IV.769); "a place where grass grows" (IV.3091); a crossroads (LXX.16).
27. E.g., I.83, 84; II.148; III.193; IV.2188.
28. VIII.59; XII.104; cf. IV.2373–2440, where this is implied.
29. E.g., II.1–182; IV.62; VII.490, 593–619, 628–642, 664–685.
30. I.70; IV.2771; LXI.6; I.56; IV.2469, 2711; IV.171.
31. E.g., I.80–84.
32. I.40–41, 54, 290–292, *et passim.*
33. IV.2189; VII.875(?); II.148.
34. E.g., IV.215; V.395; VIII.58; with frankincense specified in I.63 and IV.908, 1269, 1909; gums in III.23; and spices in III.300 and IV.919.
35. Respectively, IV.2235; IV.2235; III.611; III.614; LXXII.3; and XII.22; an example of libations appears in III.694.
36. IV.26–51, 2189–2192, 2359–2372; XIII.364–382 (+ pigeon).
37. IV.2394–2399.
38. Dung or organs appear, e.g., in I.285 and IV.1309–1315, 3092; a bird with vegetable series in IV.2892.
39. I.285; V.203; III.468; V.198, 371. For plant code names, see XII.401–444.
40. IV.2873–2879; for a most complex example of differing evaluation, in several recensions, see the slander spells involving "hostile" offerings, IV.2571–2707.
41. XIII.91–96, 373–375, 646–651.
42. IV.919.
43. Respectively, I.21–26; III.290–320; V.370–399; VII.866–879; X.1–9; V.159–160, admittedly obscure.
44. IV.3170, editorial conjecture.
45. IV.3125–3171.
46. E.g., V.390–423.
47. E.g., I.293–347; cf. I.74–90.
48. F. Graf, "Prayer in Magic and Religious Ritual," in C.A. Faraone and D. Obbink (eds.), *Magika Hiera*, Oxford 1991, pp. 195–196.
49. Most dramatically, VIII.70–72.
50. II.36; cf. I.244–246.
51. E.g., I.243; IV.3199; VII.998.
52. CXXII.1–4.
53. See above, note 17.
54. S. Stewart, *On Longing: Narrative of the Miniature, the Gigantic, the Souvenir, the Collection*, Baltimore 1984, Chap. 2.
55. Idem, *Nonsense: Aspects of Intertextuality in Folklore and Literature*, Baltimore 1980, pp. 100–101.
56. Cf. Smith, *To Take Place* (above, note 4), pp. 103–112, *et passim.*
57. Part II of this essay has been adapted from my paper, "Trading Places," delivered at the International Conference on Magic, University of Kansas (Lawrence), August 1992.

3

A City of Many Temples: Ḫattuša, Capital of the Hittites

Itamar Singer

In 1144 C.E. the Muslims conquered the city of Edessa, capital of the first crusader state established in the Orient. Joshua Prawer has described the loss of Edessa as "ominous, painful, a psychological shock."[1] Some 2,400 years earlier, a similar disaster took place not far from Edessa. The Hittite king Tudḫaliya IV was utterly defeated by the Assyrians, eventually leading to the fall of his empire.[2] His desperate attempts to regain the favour of the gods are the subject of this presentation.

The German excavations at Boğazköy, ancient Ḫattuša, some 150 kilometres east of Ankara, have been going on for nearly a century. Begun in 1906, the project has been interrupted only during the two world wars, and may well qualify as the longest-running excavation in the Near East. In their systematic methodology, in the prompt and high-quality publications of both the archaeological data and the inscriptions, and, not least, in the constant effort towards the preservation of the site and its finds, the excavations of Ḫattuša may serve as a model for archaeologists and philologists all over the world.[3]

The proto-Hattian city of Ḫattuš was a major political and commercial centre at the beginning of the second millennium B.C.E., and probably even earlier. In the mid-eighteenth century the city was conquered by the troops of the Hittite king Anitta, who utterly destroyed the city and cursed it forever. Nevertheless, Ḫattuša recovered and about a century later became the seat of the Hittite kings, eventually becoming the capital of a vast empire extending from the Aegean to the Armenian mountains and from the Black Sea to the borders of Canaan. For more than four hundred years, with only a short interim in the early thirteenth century, when the capital was moved to Tarḫuntašša in the south, Ḫattuša served as the capital of the Hittite kingdom. Naturally, it became not only a true metropolis competing in size and splendour with Babylon, Aššur and Thebes, but also a pre-eminent religious centre, the main seat of the "thousand gods of Hatti."

The total dominance of Ḫattuša in every aspect of Hittite studies is further intensified by the fact that other sacred centres have not yet conclusively been located. We are still ignorant of the locations of Arinna, the city of the proto-Hattian sun-goddess, and of Nerik and Zippalanda, the homes of two important storm-gods, her sons. However, the abundance of material from Ḫattuša, both archaeological and textual, compensates for this disproportional documentation, unparalleled in neighbouring countries.

One of the most valuable aspects of the evidence is the optimal combination of textual descriptions and archaeological finds. About 30,000 clay tablets, primarily religious texts containing descriptions of celebrations and ceremonies, bring to life the silent vestiges of this once teeming city. With a relatively large proportion of the site already excavated, we have a rare opportunity to actually reconstruct the topography and the everyday life of Ḫattuša: the actions of the royal couple in the palace and elsewhere, the daily rituals performed by the clergy in the numerous temples, as well as the ceremonies celebrated by the entire populace on special occasions, such as the yearly festivals.

The most impressive cult edifice in Ḫattuša was no doubt Temple 1, the Great Temple in the Lower City, which already attracted the attention of Winckler at the beginning of the century. This is a huge sacred complex covering an area of nearly twenty acres, which was surrounded by a temenos wall. Built in the thirteenth century upon a massive artificial terrace, this sacred precinct consisted of the temple proper, a ring of storehouses surrounding it, and an annex building which housed the numerous cult functionaries serving in the temple. It probably also contained the kitchens, breweries, workshops, equipment stores and scribal chambers of the temple.

The storehouses which surround the temple originally had two or even three floors, bringing the total number of rooms to about two hundred. Large storage jars, each with a capacity of some two hundred litres, were still found intact in some of the rooms. They are marked with hieroglyphic signs indicating their content and measure. The upper floors probably contained more perishable receptacles, as shown by the numerous bullae which came from knotted bundles and boxes stacked on wooden shelves. There was also a temple archive of several thousand tablets, including some of the most important state treaties, such as the Hittite–Egyptian peace treaty signed in 1258 B.C.E.

The temple building proper was entered through an elaborate gateway (*ḫilammar*), leading to a central courtyard (*ḫila*), which gave access to the holy of holies (*tunnakeššar*). The most sacred parts of the temple were emphasized by the use of a special building stone — a granite-like dark green gabbro — which contrasts with the white limestone walls. The holy of holies contains two adyta, which may be attributable to the presence of both a god and a goddess at the top of the Hittite pantheon. This assumption is supported by a text describing the building of a temple complex dedicated to the storm-god of Heaven and the sun-goddess of Arinna. The divine images stood on low platforms of stone. No cult statue has survived, but the size of the surviving bases suggests that they must have been life-size. The representation of the Hittite deity could have been anthropomorphic, theriomorphic (for example, representing the storm-god as a bull), or abstract, as it was in the carved stone called *ḫuwaši*, comparable to the biblical *maṣṣebah*.[4]

In the building complex located south of the temple proper, a partly preserved text was found listing 205 members of the cult personnel (DUMU.ḪI.A É.GIŠ.KIN.TI / *bīt kiškatti*, literally: "House of the work performance"): 18 priests (SANGA), 29 priestesses (*katra*), 19 scribes (DUB.SAR), 33 scribes on wood (DUB.SAR.GIŠ), 35 incantation priests (LÚ.ḪAL) and 10 Hurrian singers (NAR *Ḫurri*); further items covering the remaining 61 persons are lost. All these temple servants were probably engaged in the cult of the Great Temple and were entitled to live on its premises. The Hittite cult personnel fell into two main categories: "men of the sacred enclosure" (*ḫaliyatalleš*), who patrolled outside the temple courtyard but were not authorized to enter the temple itself, and "men of the temple" (*karimnaleš*), who served within the temple. This division has been compared with the custody of the Israelite tabernacle, shared by Priests (*kohanim*) and Levites.[5] The clergy was fully responsible for maintaining the safety and secrecy of the temple by day and by night, as shown by the following passage from the Instructions for Cult Officials.[6]

> You who are temple officials, be very careful with respect to the precinct. At nightfall go promptly down (to the town), eat and drink, and if the desire for a woman overcomes anyone, let him sleep with a woman. But as long as [he is in charge] let him promptly come up to spend the night in the temple. Whoever is a temple official — all high priests, minor priests, "anointed," or whoever else is allowed to cross the threshold of the gods — let them not fail to spend the night in the temple. Furthermore, there shall be watchmen employed by night who shall patrol all night through. Outside, the enclosure guards shall watch; inside the temples, the temple officials patrol all night through, and they shall not sleep. Each night one of the high priests shall be in charge of the patrols. ... A guard must not fail to spend the night with his god. If he fails, however, in the event that they do not kill him, they shall humiliate him. Naked — there shall be no garment on his body — he shall bring water three times from Labarna's cistern to the house of his god. Such shall be his humiliation.

A deity would surely be enraged if his house were trespassed by an unauthorized person. A Hittite oracle text from Alalakh records such a case:[7]

> Since it has been established (by oracle) that the god was desecrated by a ritual offence, we asked the temple officials, and Tila said: "People should not look at the Storm-god; but a woman looked in at a window and a child went into the temple." ... If (the cause is) this, ditto (i.e., and nothing else), then let the Ḫurri-bird omen be favourable. Result of oracle favourable.

Although the sacred precinct was closed to ordinary people throughout the year, the deity came out from the temple on special occasions, such as the annual festivals.[8] The cult image, adorned with precious metals and stones, was placed on a ceremonial carriage drawn by two oxen, and was taken outside the city to the open-air sanctuary at Yazılıkaya. This impressive site, some 2 km north-east of Boğazköy, is a natural rock shrine carved with reliefs showing a great assembly of all the gods and goddesses of the kingdom, gathered to honour the storm-god of Hatti and the sun-goddess of Arinna on the occasion of the New Year festival. It is an inspiring reminder that in ancient religions the worship of the gods in nature was just as important as their worship within the cities. Archaeology is often aware of the built temples only, because open-air cults usually leave meagre tangible evidence.

Whereas the home of the two chief gods has safely been identified, both within and outside the city, our knowledge with regard to all the other deities resident in Ḫattuša is quite limited. The texts speak collectively of the "thousand gods of Hatti," which may not be very far from the actual number of recorded deities. Obviously, not all these deities, many of whom were local gods in the provinces, had lodgings in the capital. But the texts explicitly mention at least a few dozen temples located in Ḫattuša itself, including some dedicated to imported deities, such as Hadad of Aleppo and Ištar of Nineveh.[9] Until about a decade ago, the whereabouts of these cult buildings remained a mystery. In 1978, with the completion of the excavations at the royal citadel of Büyükkale and at the Great Temple in the Lower City, the new excavation director, Peter Neve, set out to investigate the large area of the Upper City, which comprises nearly two-thirds of the city's territory.[10] In this area, surrounded by a massive fortification system, four temples (2–5) had already been unearthed at the beginning of the century. The recent excavations have increased their number by at least 26 more, bringing the total count to 31 independent temples within the city. The ongoing excavations will no doubt reveal more cult buildings.

All the temples in the Upper City were built in a relatively short period, within the last decades of the kingdom. This previously suspected hypothesis has been confirmed by the evidence of the recent finds, including a hieroglyphic stone inscription of King Tudḫaliya IV found in secondary usage in a Middle Byzantine chapel. Incidentally, many Hittite stone blocks were reused by the Byzantine builders in the tenth–eleventh centuries C.E., the only period in which this area of the site was reinhabited.

Ḫattuša in the thirteenth century B.C.E.

The ground plan of this temple city is beginning to crystallize with the thorough excavation of the individual buildings and the areas separating them (see figure 1). The Central District, lying north of the Sphinx Gate, consists of a large cluster of some 25 temples. Most of these have a uniform layout: a square ground plan with an inner court, often including a basement floor underneath the adyton (Temples 6–20). Two temples (2 and 3) were decorated with sculptures representing lions and sphinxes integrated into the architecture as orthostats or pillar bases. They are made of the same greenish gabbro that was used in the most sacred parts of Temple 1 and of other temples. The temples yielded many cult objects, comprising the typical inventory used in the Hittite cult: figurines, zoomorphic rhyta, miniature votive vessels, so-called "Syrian bottles," libation arms, relief pottery, ivory carvings, and so on. All the temples yielded inscribed objects — clay tablets, seals and seal impressions. They were usually found on the floor of the underground cellar, which must have served as a small temple archive. The tablets display donation grants, ritual descriptions, oracles and mythological texts.[11]

The richest archives were found in the adjacent temples 15 and 16. They contained, among other texts, several Akkadian fragments of the Gilgameš Epos and a valuable bilingual text composed in Hittite and Hurrian.[12] This text, dated by its script and language to the early fourteenth century B.C.E., contains a most interesting mythological tale with some moralistic maxims. The opening sentence provides the first surprise, with the mention of the well-known Old Syrian city of Ebla:

> If in some town there is an eloquent orator, whose arguments no-one can contradict— Zazalla is such an eloquent orator, and no-one can dispute his arguments at the assembly. And Zazalla began to speak to Meki: "Why do you say such unworthy things, Meki, star of Ebla?"[13]

The protagonists of this intriguing debate are unknown to us. The city of Ebla, famous for its third-millennium archives, was still an important city-kingdom in the early second millennium, until it was conquered by the Hittite king Ḫattušili I (or his successor Muršili I). The mythological Hurrian text probably originated from northern Syria and was later translated into Hittite. The bilingual text, preserved on three complete tablets and over a hundred fragments, provides invaluable new insights for the study of the Hurrian language. The following passage exemplifies the nature of the proverbs, which may certainly be classified with the ancient Near Eastern wisdom literature:

> (There is) a deer grazing on a meadow which (lies) on the bank of a river. It gazes time and again at the meadow which is on the other side of the river, but it did not manage to get to the meadow on the (other) side, and could not reach it.
> But (it is) not a deer, (rather) a man. This man was designated by his master as a commander of border guards and has been appointed as a commander of border guards in a certain district. But he keeps turning his eyes towards another district. Now the gods have given him wisdom, and he did not get to that district and did not reach the other district.[14]

This ancient forerunner of "the grass is always greener on the other side" is concluded, like the other proverbs, with the following phrase: "Let the matter drop! I want to tell you another story. Listen to the message, I want to teach you wisdom."

Near the temples various annex buildings were unearthed, such as residential blocks, workshops and various industrial installations. Each temple apparently was conceived as an independent economic unit, providing its own means for the cult and the maintenance of the personnel. This may explain the discovery of land donation deeds (*Landschenkungsurkunde*) in the temples, which record the granting of fields and other real estate to various cult institutions. The extent of these grants, which entail an exemption from taxes and levies, grew considerably towards the end of the Hittite Empire.

The Central District, with its agglomeration of small and medium-size temples, was flanked on both sides by two large sacred precincts, Temples 5 and 30, symmetrically located near the monumental King's Gate and Lion Gate respectively. The temenos wall of Temple 5 encompasses the temple building itself, a palace-like annex and three small chapels. On the evidence of an inscription of Tudḫaliya, it seems that this complex may have been a private temple district belonging to this king, with chapels dedicated to his ancestors. Temple 30 shows remarkable similarities with Temple 5, but its state of preservation is far less impressive.

After the excavation of large parts of the Upper City, it is now evident that most of its territory was occupied by temples and buildings functionally connected with them. The three monumental gateways — the King's Gate, the Sphinx Gate and the Lion Gate — were symmetrically placed around this purely sacred town, and were probably integrated into a ceremonial road which encircled the Upper Town outside the city wall. Processions started from Temple 5, left the city at the King's Gate, passed by the Sphinx Gate, and continued all the way to the Lion Gate, where they reentered the city. We possess textual descriptions of such ceremonial processions, headed by the royal couple, touring the sacred edifices of Ḫattuša on festive occasions.

The stratigraphy of the Upper City consists of four phases, all dated within the late thirteenth century. After a short first phase (phase 4), in which several scattered rock outcrops were built up as fortresses (Nişantepe, Sarikale, Yenicekale), there followed the main building phase (phase 3), attributed to Tudḫaliya IV (c. 1245–1220 B.C.E.). In this phase the massive fortification system of the Upper City, including the monumental gateways, was erected, and the temple city was laid out according to an overall plan. The architecture, and especially the monumental art, show close affinities with the rock-temple at Yazılıkaya, which also reached its final shape in the days of Tudḫaliya. For example, the deity represented on the so-called King's Gate (a isnomer) is probably Šarruma, the personal god of Tudḫaliya, who is also shown embracing his protégé on a relief from Yazılıkaya.

In its last decades, the city of Ḫattuša suffered two consecutive destructions. The first has been attributed by the excavator to inner struggles between two contenders to the Hittite throne, Tudḫaliya IV and his cousin Kurunta, king of Tarḫuntašša, a kingdom situated in southern Anatolia.[15] The events connected with this struggle over the succession have only recently been disclosed by the discovery of a perfectly preserved bronze tablet bearing the treaty between the rival cousins.[16] Eventually Tudḫaliya gained the upper hand, but not before the capital itself suffered a serious conflagration which destroyed some of the temples and damaged the city wall. After this first destruction, some of the temples were restored (e.g., Temples 2, 3 and 5), while others were deserted (e.g., Temple 30) and replaced by secular residences and workshops. The partially rebuilt city (phase

2), which must be contemporary with the reign of the last Hittite king, Šuppiluliuma II, was again demolished in a conflagration, this time with a more permanent effect. This destruction marks the end of Ḫattuša as the capital of a vast empire. The people responsible for sacking the city cannot be identified with certainty, but it is usually assumed that they were the Kaška, restless mountain tribes who inhabited the Pontic ranges of northern Anatolia. Like many other sites destroyed in the wake of the population movements at the end of the Bronze Age, Ḫattuša, too, was soon resettled by squatters whose material culture is almost undistinguishable from that of the previous inhabitants (phase 1). They may have been the defenceless survivors of this once proud metropolis. *Sic transit gloria mundi!*

It is now time to incorporate the results of the new investigations at Ḫattuša into a larger historical context. Tudḫaliya's age was one of faded Hittite power.[17] Gone were the glorious days of his ancestors, who carved out a vast empire at the expense of Mitanni and Egypt. As a son of King Ḫattušili and Queen Puduḫepa, the architects of the Pax Hethitica, he inherited a declining great power, whose international status was maintained more by skilful negotiations than by the sword. The peace with Egypt concluded by his parents was maintained, and so was the cordial relationship with Babylon. Both contacts were reinforced by royal marriages.[18] However, the rivalry of the empire with the growing power of Assyria became increasingly desperate, reaching its unavoidable climax in a major battle fought east of the Euphrates in 1234 B.C.E.[19] The Hittite monarch, deserted by his allies, barely managed to escape from the battlefield after a painful defeat. The situation in the west was hardly better.[20] An acceptable *modus vivendi* was worked out with the Aḫḫiyawa, the Mycenaean Greeks. The real threat, however, came not from this traditional rival, but rather from the warlike tribal groups of the Sea Peoples inhabiting the long Aegean coasts. These unconventional fighters eventually gave the final blow to the gradually disintegrating empire. Moreover, as if the enemies from east and west were not enough, Hittite resistance was further weakened by a severe famine that ravaged the kingdom for several decades. Grain was bought expensively in Egypt and Canaan, but the heavily laden trade ships were often ravaged or sunk by the swift vessels of the Sea Peoples. The overall situation around the borders was all but calm. At the court, too, an arduous conflict raged over succession rights, splitting the royal family and the nobility. If the excavator is right about the cause of the penultimate conflagration in Ḫattuša, this conflict led to civil war, with detrimental results.[21]

Faced with these tremendous difficulties, Tudḫaliya opted to pin his hopes on the gods. In a religious reform of unprecedented extent, he sent cult officials to all parts of the kingdom to survey the state of the temples and their inventory.[22] Every little village was inspected and meticulous reports were prepared, many of which have come down to us.[23] Temples were renovated; cult images made of stone and wood were replaced by better ones made of gold, silver and iron; additional cult personnel was appointed; and various religious institutions were granted extensive tracts of agricultural land devoted to their support. Not only these divine households, but also sacred cities (Arinna, Nerik, Zippalanda) and whole regions (such as Tarḫuntašša) were exempted from taxes and levies.

The centrepiece of this hectic activity was of course the total rebuilding of the capital, Ḫattuša. As we have seen, the size of the city was more than doubled, with the additional terrain densely filled with dozens of new temples. Perhaps a hidden motive for this tremendous effort on Tudḫaliya's part was his wish to measure up at least to the architectural achievements of his arch-enemy, the Assyrian king Tukulti-Ninurta. The latter had built a new capital a few kilometres north of Aššur, on the other side of the Tigris, and named it Kar-Tukulti-Ninurta. A late Hittite text may refer to the designation of the New City as "Tudḫaliya's Ḫattuša,"[24] possibly echoing the name of the Assyrian capital. Tudḫaliya's effort to match the fame of his rival is clearly reflected in his adoption of the Mesopotamian title *šar kiššati*, "King of the World." How pretentious this title sounded from a king who was utterly defeated by the Assyrians, and whose own son witnessed the fall of the mighty Hittite Empire.

In sharp contrast to the effort invested in this religious renaissance, there is hardly any evidence of serious military preparations. The imposing fortifications of the New City were more suited to impressing the viewer, and perhaps the gods, than to withstanding a determined military attack. When the inevitable assault came at the turn of the century, the thousand-year-old city fell haplessly. And the gods failed to come to its rescue.

Notes

This study was supported by the Israel Science Foundation administered by the Israel Academy of Sciences and Humanities. I wish to thank Dr. Peter Neve for permission to reprint the plan of the Boghazköy excavations, from *Archäologischer Anzeiger* (1991), p. 304. The manuscript was concluded in September 1992.

1. J. Prawer, *The World of the Crusaders*, Jerusalem 1972, p. 34.
2. I. Singer, "The Battle of Niḫriya and the End of the Hittite Empire," *Zeitschrift für Assyriologie*, 75 (1985), pp. 100–123.
3. For the excavations at Boğazköy see K. Bittel, *Hattusha, the Capital of the Hittites*, New York 1970. Preliminary excavation reports are annually published by the present director, Peter Neve, in *Archäologischer Anzeiger* and in other journals. The cuneiform texts are being published by H. Otten in the series *Keilschrifttexte aus Boghazköy*, Berlin.
4. On cult and on Hittite religion in general see O.R. Gurney, *Some Aspects of Hittite Religion*, Oxford 1977.
5. J. Milgrom, "The Shared Custody of the Tabernacle and a Hittite Analogy," *Journal of the American Oriental Society*, 90 (1970), pp. 204–209.
6. For a translation see A. Goetze, "Hittite Instructions," in J.B. Pritchard (ed.), *Ancient Near Eastern Texts Relating to the Old Testament*, Princeton 1969[3], p. 209.
7. O.R. Gurney, "A Hittite Divination Text," in D.J. Wiseman, *The Alalakh Tablets*, London 1953, pp. 116 ff. (*AT* 454).
8. For Hittite festivals see H.G. Güterbock, "Some Aspects of Hittite Festivals," in *Actes de la XVIIe Rencontre Assyriologique Internationale* (Brussels), pp. 175–180; I. Singer, *The Hittite KI.LAM Festival, Part One*, Wiesbaden 1983.
9. See H.G. Güterbock, "The Hittite Temple According to Written Sources," in *Compte rendu de la XXe Rencontre Assyriologique Internationale* (Leiden 1972), 1975, pp. 125–132.
10. For the excavations in the Upper City see especially P. Neve, "Hattuscha, Haupt- und Kultstadt der Hethiter — Ergebnisse der Ausgrabungen in der Oberstadt," *Hethitica*, 8 (1987), pp. 297–318; idem, "Boğazköy-Hattusha — New Results of the Excavations in the Upper City," *Anatolica*, 16 (1990), pp. 7–19.
11. H. Otten, "Die Textfunde der Ausgrabungen in Boğazköy — Oberstadt," X. *Türk Tarih Kongresi'nden ayribasim. Türk Tarih Kurumu Basimevi*, Ankara 1990, pp. 113–100.
12. H. Otten, "Blick in die altorientalische Geisteswelt; Neufund einer hethitischen Tempelbibliothek," *Jahrbuch der Akademie der Wissenschaften in Göttingen*, 1984, pp. 50–60; E. Neu, "Das Hurritische: Eine altorientalische Sprache in neuem Licht," *Akademie der Wissenschaften und der Literatur, Mainz*, Wiesbaden 1988; idem, "Zur Grammatik des Hurritischen auf der Grundlage der hurritisch-hethitischen Bilingue aus der Boğazköy-Grabungskampagne 1983," in V. Haas (ed.), *Hurriter und Hurritisch*, Konstanz 1988, pp. 95–115.
13. Otten, "Tempelbibliothek" (above, note 12), p. 54.
14. *Ibid.*, pp. 56 f.
15. Neve, "New Results" (above, note 10), p. 10.

16. H. Otten, *Die Bronzetafel aus Boğazköy, Ein Staatsvertrag Tutḫalijas IV*, Wiesbaden 1988.
17. On the age of Tudḫaliya (with references) see H. Klengel, "Tutḫalija IV, von Ḫatti: Prolegomena zu einer Biographie," *Altorientalische Forschungen*, 18 (1991), pp. 224–238.
18. On the Babylonian spouse of Tudḫaliya see I. Singer, "The Title 'Great Princess' in the Hittite Empire," *Ugarit-Forschungen*, 23 (1991).
19. See above, note 2.
20. I. Singer, "Western Anatolia in the Thirteenth Century B.C. according to the Hittite Sources," *Anatolian Studies*, 33 (1983), pp. 205–217.
21. For a general overview with previous bibliography see H.A. Hoffner, Jr., "The Last Days of Khattusha," in W.A. Ward & M. Sharp Joukowsky (eds.), *The Crisis Years: The 12th Century B.C.*, Dubuque, Iowa, 1992, pp. 46–52.
22. E. Laroche, "La réforme religieuse du roi Tudhaliya IV et sa signification politique," in F. Dunand & P. Lévêque (eds.), *Les syncrétismes dans les religions de l'antiquité (Colloque de Besançon, 1973)*, Leiden 1975, pp. 87–95.
23. C.W. Carter, *Hittite Cult-Inventories*, Ph.D. Dissertation, University of Chicago, 1962.
24. H.G. Güterbock, "The Hittite Conquest of Cyprus Reconsidered," *Journal of Near Eastern Studies*, 26 (1967), p. 80, n. 12.

4
The Sacred Sea

Abraham Malamat

In a discussion of sacred space, we ought not to overlook bodies of water such as rivers (with their river ordeals), wells and springs (note the theophanies at such localities), lakes and seas. Moreover, when such a discussion focuses on the Levant — and more specifically Syria-Palestine — then the Mediterranean Sea is of immediate concern. We shall thus deal mainly with this sea, over a time span from approximately 1800 B.C.E. to the Byzantine period. Such a *longue durée* of some 2,500 years should enable us to expose elements of the divine nature of the Mediterranean, to the extent that they are to be found — a matter that has scarcely received its due scholarly consideration.[1]

My starting point will be the documents from the ancient city of Mari,[2] situated on the Euphrates, some 25 km to the north of the present-day Iraqi-Syrian border, within Syria. King Yahdun-Lim, the first true ruler of Mari in the Old Babylonian period, who brought prosperity to his kingdom, left one highly intriguing document of great importance to our subject, known as the Foundation Inscription from the temple of the god Shamash.[3] Here Yahdun-Lim vividly describes a bold campaign to the West through Syria, finally reaching the Mediterranean coast, the crowning achievement of his military operations. The relevant passage in this document implies that the Mediterranean Sea was regarded, at least at Mari, as a divine-mythological entity hundreds of years earlier than scholars previously realized. The passage in question reads:

> Since days of old, when god built Mari, no king residing in Mari had reached the sea (*tāmtum*). To the Cedar Mountain and the

> Boxwood (Mountain) ... they had not reached. ... But Yahdun-Lim ... marched to the shore of the sea (*tāmtum*) in irresistible strength. To the Ocean (*ayabba*, "Vast Sea") he offered his great royal sacrifices, and his troops cleansed themselves with water in the Ocean (*ayabba*). To the Cedar and Boxwood Mountain, the great mountains, he penetrated, and boxwood, cedar, cypress (or juniper?) and *elamakkum* trees, these trees he felled. He stripped (the forest) bare (?), established his name, and made known his might. He subjugated that land on the shore of the Ocean (*ayabba*). He made it obedient to his command; he caused it to follow him. He imposed a permanent tax upon them that they should bring their taxes to him regularly.

The king of Mari praises himself for his unprecedented campaign to the Mediterranean shore. The extraordinary encounter with the Mediterranean was accompanied by cultic ceremonies — the offering of sacrifices to the sea, which is most likely a West Semitic or Amorite notion, later adopted by the Mesopotamians. Furthermore, the king's troops bathed in its waters in what was surely a cultic ritual, a sort of baptism. The significance of such an act is probably indicated, in addition, by the use of the Akkadian verb *ramākum*, which refers to cleansing the entire body in water in a ritualistic context.[4] Thus, we may liken the function of the Mediterranean here to that of a *miqweh* in Judaism, a ritual bath for purifying the body; metaphorically, the Mediterranean would be a sort of macro-*miqweh*.

In the first millennium B.C.E., the neo-Assyrian monarchs also recorded their arrival on the Mediterranean coast. They offered sacrifices at the seashore to their gods, but not explicitly to the god of the Sea. Their troops dipped their weapons in the water, symbolically purifying them, with no further ceremony. They thus were following the example of Sargon the Great of Akkad, who, in the twenty-fourth century B.C.E., washed his weapon in the sea.[5] However, it should be noted that he did so in the Lower Sea, that is, the Persian Gulf. Here, too, the dipping of weapons in the sea doubtless indicates the sacred and purifying aspect of such a great body of water, but Yahdun-Lim's inscription differs with regard to the deity involved and to the actual ritual use of the sea's waters.

In dealing with Yahdun-Lim's inscription many years ago, I touched on the illuminating distinction between the two Akkadian terms used here to designate the sea.[6] We see the ordinary word for sea, *tāmtum (tiamtum)*, used twice in a secular, empirical sense. In contrast, the solemn term *ayabba*, recorded three times, has a mythological aura to it. In its Sumerian form, A.AB.BA, it already appears in Ebla[7] and in old Akkadian (spelled AB.A in a lexical text from the second half of the third millennium B.C.E.), in connection with Sargon the Great and the West Semitic king Shamshi-Adad I (early eighteenth century B.C.E., slightly after Yahdun-Lim), who both fought campaigns in the West.[8] In all of these texts, the word A.AB.BA undoubtedly refers to the Mediterranean, while in other texts it designates the Persian Gulf. The word seems to be reminiscent of the Greek concept of *Okeanos*, in both its mythological and its factual, marine sense.[9]

In the El-Amarna letters[10] of the fourteenth century B.C.E., and particularly in the letters of the king of Byblos on the Syrian coast and those of the king of Tyre and the king of Jerusalem, *ayabba* appears several times with reference to the Mediterranean Sea, or perhaps only part of it. It is also used at El-Amarna in a literary-epic composition, where the word escaped scholarly attention until recently (EA 340).[11] There, A.AB.BA (not to be read *tāmtum*, as by the editor) most likely signifies the Mediterranean or Great Sea and not simply any sea. Although the text is very fragmentary, it seems that a royal military campaign, like the expeditions of Yahdun-Lim and of other Mesopotamian rulers, was conducted as far as this sea.

The precise meaning and etymology of the Sumerogram A.AB.BA, rendered *a(y)yabba* in Semitic, is still obscure, despite its relatively frequent use in Sumero-Akkadian literature.[12] A recently published Old Babylonian bilingual hymn from South Babylonia gives us the earliest equation of the two terms. To be sure, the editors of the hymn suggest reading *a-ia-a-ma* instead of *a-ia-a-ba*[13] — thus tempting us to interpret the spelling *ayyama* as Canaanite-Hebrew *yam*, the sea proper — but this assumption is far-fetched.

Several years ago, reference was made to an unpublished document from Mari which is of great significance for the concept of a sacred sea, notably the Mediterranean.[14] Now that this document, a letter from Zimri-Lim's ambassador at Aleppo to the king of Mari, has been published, we may consider more fully its impact on our issue.[15] Adad, the great god of Aleppo, was engaged in a battle with the sea, wielding weapons against the rebellious Mediterranean.

After the sea's defeat, the weapons were presented as a coronation gift to Zimri-Lim, king of Mari and son of Yahdun-Lim, when he made a pilgrimage to Aleppo. It is likely that these weapons were the very same club and spear (*ṣmd* and *ktp* in the Ugaritic myth) that were depicted four or five hundred years later on the stele of "Baal and the thunderbolt" ("Baal au foudre") at Ugarit, depicting the battle of Baal with Yamm, the sea deity.[16]

This leads us straight to Ugarit of the fourteenth and thirteenth centuries B.C.E., perhaps the major source for the divinity of the sea. The Ugaritic texts recount several epic tales of the war between the god of the sea (*Yamm*) and other deities.[17] These myths may have originated centuries earlier, presumably in the Old Babylonian period — that is, in the age of Mari. Yamm, the god of the sea, is most prominent in the Ugaritic pantheon and is equated there, *inter alia*, with the term A.AB.BA. Moreover, the element *yamm*, sea, appears in personal names both at Mari and at Ugarit, as a theophoric name-element. At Ugarit, Yamm is know by the epithets "Prince Yamm" (*zbl ym*) and "Judge Nahar" (*ṯpṭ nhr*), the ruler of the river. Yamm represents the cosmic force of raging waters, a personification most likely derived from the character of the Mediterranean Sea, whose waters threatened the coast and occasionally inundated it.

Many Ugaritic myths, echoed faintly in the poetic parts of the Bible, derive from this conception of the Mediterranean. The classic myth of Ugarit concerns the struggle between Yamm, the sea deity, and Baal, Lord of the Earth and of fertility,[18] which may go back to Old Babylonian times, an assumption now supported by the material from Mari. The Ugaritic text is too fragmentary to provide a continuous narrative, but it may be outlined as follows. The god Yamm, beloved son of El, the head of the Ugaritic pantheon, seeks majestic status. El proclaims that status for him and promotes the construction of Yamm's palace, but Baal, another son of El, is jealous and battles Yamm for hegemony. Eventually it is Baal, with the help of his sister, the goddess Anat, who strikes the fateful blow for power. It is then that Baal rises to kingship and erects his palace, similar to the event in Mari.

On the other hand, the myths of Yamm's contest with the goddess Anat and his struggle against the goddess Aṯatar are poorly preserved. It is significant that Yamm is included in the sacrificial lists of the gods at Ugarit, indicating his integral position in the canonical pantheon of Ugarit. A further list of deities includes ^{d}A.AB.BA (=Yamm), and here it expressly carries the theophoric determinative DINGIR=god. Most significantly, in parallel lists of the gods in the Ugaritic language proper, the counterpart of A.AB.BA is Yamm, the West Semitic god of the sea.[19] In other words, several hundred years after Yahdun-Lim, the god bearing the name of the West Semitic word for sea, *yamm*, was identified in Ugarit with the Sumerogram A.AB.BA — the very form that appears in Yahdun-Lim's inscription.

Close in time to Ugarit are the documents from Emar, which also speak of the god Yamm. The editor of these texts, followed by several scholars, interprets the deity named Ashtar (*ša*) *abi*, mentioned several times, as "Ashtar (Ishtar) of the Sea" (taking the word *abu* as identical with A.AB.BA).[20] However, this interpretation of *abu* has been contested by other scholars, who assume that the word refers to *abū*, "father, ancestor," or that it is equivalent to Hurrian or Akkadian *apu*/*abu* ("pit") and Hebrew *ōb*, "spirit of the dead."[21]

Before we approach the Hebrew Bible and the Egyptian sources, which display the closest affinity in this regard to Ugarit, let us mention in passing the Hittite sources from Anatolia, where, like in Akkadian and in the Bible (which refers to *hayyam haggādōl*), the Mediterranean is frequently called the "Great Sea." In these texts the sea is conceived, at times, even as a deity — for example, in the fourteenth-century B.C.E. treaty lists of Suppiluliuma I — and sacrifices are brought to it.[22]

Three Egyptian tales are also relevant to our subject, two of them dating from the period of the New Kingdom. Here the sea deity bears the Canaanite appellation "Yam," a loan word appearing in Late Egyptian, from the eighteenth dynasty (fifteenth century B.C.E.) on, as an alternative to the indigenous term *w3ḏ-wr* (literally, "the great green"), not only in myths but also in factual texts.[23] In a legend known as the "Tale of Two Brothers,"[24] Yam snatches a lock of hair from the head of his younger brother's wife. This part of the story takes places in the "Valley of the Cedar (or Pine)," apparently in Lebanon, and more specifically in the Beqa valley. Thus, it may be assumed that this Egyptian tale was influenced by Canaanite mythology. The second legend,[25] a small fragment related in the so-called Astarte Papyrus from about 1300 B.C.E., consists of an actual Canaanite myth. Yam, who holds dominion over the earth and its deities, is entrapped by the beauty of Astarte, the Canaanite goddess, as she sits naked on the sea-shore, thus bringing him into conflict with her consort. The myth reflects the violent power of the sea, which threatens mariners and inhabitants of the coast alike. Finally, in the tale of the Swallow and the Sea (Yam),[26] written in Demotic and dating very late, from the Roman period, Yam is portrayed as a robber. Asked by the swallow to guard her young, he eventually carries them away. The swallow, in revenge, empties the sea with her beak and fills it with sand.

Coming now to the Bible, it displays faint echoes of the rebellion of a mythic sea deity and its accompanying monsters against Yahwe, the God of Israel, as noted in particular by the late Professor Cassuto.[27] In fact, one of the central themes in the comparative study of biblical literature and Ugaritic poetry relates to this conflict. Numerous allusions to this theme, including the demonic creatures associated with the sea god Yam, are found in the poetic passages of the Bible. Examples include Psalms 74:13 ("Thou didst divide the sea [*yam*] by thy might; thou didst break the heads of the dragons on the waters"), Job 7:12 ("Am I the sea [*yam*], or a sea monster, that thou settest a guard over me?"); and, in the prophetic literature, passages like Isaiah 51:9-10 ("... was it not thou that didst cut Rahab in pieces, that didst pierce the dragon? Was it not thou that didst dry up the sea [*yam*], the waters of the great deep ...?") and Jeremiah 5:22 ("Do you not fear me? says the Lord .... I placed the sand as the bound for the sea [*yam*], a perpetual barrier which it cannot pass; though the waves toss, they cannot prevail, though they roar they cannot pass over it").[28]

It is possible, and even likely, that at the late stage of the composition of the biblical passages these metaphors of raging waters were already viewed as referring to cosmic forces, but it is logical that they ultimately reflect what was seen as the divine nature of the Mediterranean Sea. In talmudic literature this concept, surprisingly, occurs more overtly than in the Bible. The Sages hinted at it in midrashim like this one: "When the Holy One, blessed be He, created the sea (*yam*), it went on expanding, until the Holy One, blessed be He, rebuked it and caused it to dry up" (BT *Hagiga* 12a). Above all, this theme is to be seen in the talmudic appellation *śar šel yam*, "prince of the sea," so reminiscent of "Prince Yamm" at Ugarit.[29]

Let us finish with two sources by Greek authors of the classical and post-classical period, both alluding to notions and practices originating in the East. First, in a well-known episode related by Herodotus (VII, 34 ff. and 54), the bridges of ships crossing the Hellespont during the Persian-Greek war in 480 B.C.E. were broken and scattered. Xerxes subsequently "punished" the rebellious sea, proclaiming that "no man is to offer thee sacrifice, for thou art a turbid and briny river." When the Persians were finally about to cross the straits, Xerxes brought incense and "at sunrise poured a libation from a golden phial into the sea, praying to the sun that no accident should befall him" in his attempt to subdue Europe — thus echoing the belief that the Mediterranean Sea and the Pontus were a deity, or at least that the Persians conceived of them as having a sacred nature.

Another seldom-noted but intriguing passage, this one from late antiquity, reveals the tenacity of this cultic and sacred tradition. The Byzantine historian Procopius of Caesarea (sixth century C.E.), in his *De bello persico* (II:XI, 1), describes how Chosroes, the Sassanian king, having taken Antioch from Justinian, went down to the Mediterranean shore and "bathed himself alone in the sea water, and after sacrificing to the sun and other such divinities ... he went back." This ritual bathing of royalty in the Mediterranean in the sixth century C.E. closes the circle which opened with King Yahdun-Lim of Mari and his troops around 1800 B.C.E. It was based, as we saw, on early West Semitic — Amorite/Canaanite — concepts of the sacred sea, which find clear expression centuries later at Ugarit and in the Egyptian tales, and occur still later in the biblical and talmudic traditions.

A daring but not unreasonable suggestion has recently been made that the Babylonian epic of Creation, *Enumma-Eliš*, telling of the combat between the god Marduk and the primordial sea (*Tiamat*, equivalent to the Canaanite-Hebrew term *tĕhōm*), has its origin in the West, on the Mediterranean coast, like the Yamm myth of Ugarit.[30] It was then, presumably, transmitted to the Mesopotamians by the Amorites in the Old Babylonian period. This would mean that the myth spread eastward to Babylonia from the West, and not vice versa!

Notes

The abbreviations in the notes follow those used in the *Chicago Assyrian Dictionary*.

1. This study, prepared with the assistance of a grant from the Basic Research Foundation administered by the Israel Academy of Sciences and Humanities, is based on an extensive revision and expansion of material appearing in my chapter "Kingly Deeds and Divine Exploits," in A. Malamat, *Mari and the Early Israelite Experience* (Schweich Lectures, 1984), Oxford 1989.

   On the mythological nature of the sea, see the comprehensive work by O. Kaiser, *Die mythische Bedeutung des Meeres in Ägypten, Ugarit und Israel* (*BZAW*, 78), Berlin 1962. Kaiser's horizon is limited to the three places mentioned in the book's title, thus excluding Mari and the talmudic and Greek sources.
2. On the city of Mari and the documents unearthed there see Malamat, *Mari* (above, note 1).
3. The document was published by G. Dossin, "L'inscription de fondation de Iahdun-Lim, roi de Mari," *Syria*, XXXII (1955), pp. 1–28; and see D. Frayne's newer study, "Iahdun-Lim, Text 2," in *The Royal Inscriptions of Mesopotamia*, IV: *Old Babylonian Period (2003–1595 B.C.)*, Toronto–London 1990, pp. 604–608. For an early interpretation of the passage given below, see A. Malamat, "Campaigns to the Mediterranean by Iahdun-Lim and Other Early Mesopotamian Rulers," in H. Güterbock & T. Jacobsen (eds.), *Studies in Honor of B. Landsberger* (*AS* 16), Chicago 1965, pp. 367ff.
4. The verb *ramākum* means simply "to wash"; its ritualistic sense in certain contexts, however, is indicated by the noun *rimkum*, particularly in the ritual series *bīt rimki*; and cf. *AHw*, II, p. 985: "Bad[ekult], Ganzwaschung."
5. See the text on Sargon the Great in *ANET*[3], p. 467b.
6. See Malamat, "Campaigns" (above, note 3), p. 367.
7. See G. Pettinato, *MEE*, nos. 1343, 016; cf. M. Krebernik, *ZA*, LXXII (1982), p. 43; von Soden, *AHw*, III, p. 1353, s.v. *tiamtu(m)*, *tāmtu(m)*, and see there the unusual form *ab*).
8. Cf. Malamat, "Campaigns" (above, note 3), pp. 367–368.
9. Cf. G.M.A. Hanfmann, in the *Oxford Classical Dictionary*, Oxford 1949 (reprinted 1953), p. 616, s.v. *Oceanus (mythological)*; F. Lasserre, in *Der kleine Pauly*, IV, Munich 1979, pp. 267f., s.v. *Okeanos*, I: Mythologie; M. Eliade (ed.), *The Encyclopedia of Religion*, New York 1987, XI, pp. 53–54, s.v. *Oceans*.
10. See Amarna letters nos. 74, 105, 114 (Byblos); 151 (Tyre); 288 (Jerusalem). For a translation (and most recent edition) of the documents, see W.L. Moran, *Les Lettres d'El-Amarna*, Paris 1987.
11. See now P. Artzi, "A Further Royal Campaign to the Mediterranean Sea?" in *Festschrift A. Malamat* (*EI* 24), 1993, pp. 23–30 (in Hebrew), and see there for the other references in EA.
12. For this term see the dictionaries: *CAD*, A/1, p. 221, s.v. *ajabba*; *AHw*, p. 23, s.v. *a(j)jabba*, and above, note 7; and see the important remark by A. Goetze in *JCS*, IX (1955), p. 16, note 58.

13. Published by B. Alster & U. Yeyes, *ASJ*, XIV (1990), p. 8; and see the comments concerning a.ab.ba by D. Charpin (*NABU*, 1990, no. 122, p. 101), who rejects the reading *a-ia-a-ma*, as well as A.R. George (*ibid.*, 1991, no. 19, p. 16).
14. D. Charpin & J.M. Durand, "'Fils de Sim'al': Les origins tribales des rois de Mari," *RA*, LXXX (1986), p. 174.
15. See J.M. Durand, "La mytholegème du combat entre le dieu de l'orage et la mer en Mésopotamie," *MARI* VII (1993), pp. 41 ff. In the text, which bears the number A.1968, the sea is represented by the word *temtum*. On this document see my paper "A New Prophetic Message from Aleppo and Its Biblical Counterparts," in A.G. Auld (ed.), *Understanding Poets and Prophets: Essays in Honour of G.W. Anderson*, Sheffield 1993, pp. 236–241. For the depictions of the storm-god fighting the sea-god in glyptics, see P. Matthiae, "Some Notes on the Old Syrian Iconography of the God Jam," in D.J.W. Meijer (ed.), *Natural Phenomena*, Amsterdam 1992, pp. 169–192.
16. Cf. now P. Bordreuil, "Recherches Ougaritiques," *Semitica*, XL (1991), pp. 17–27, and the more recent article by P. Bordreuil & D. Pardee in *MARI* VII (1993), pp. 63–70.
17. See Kaiser, *Die mythische Bedeutung* (above, note 1), pp. 40 ff.; S. Loewenstamm, *Comparative Studies in Biblical and Ancient Oriental Literatures* (*AOAT* 204), Neukirchen–Vluyn 1980, pp. 346–361; S.L. Gibson, *Canaanite Myths and Legends*, Edinburgh 1978, pp. 37–45.
18. Cf. Kaiser, *Die mythische Bedeutung* (above, note 1), p. 58; and M. Dietrich et al., *Die keilschriftalphabetischen Texte aus Ugarit*, Neukirchen–Vluyn 1976, I, 39:19, 46:6.
19. See Nougayrol, *Le palais royal d'Ugarit*, IV, Paris 1955/6, pp. 45 (l. 29) and 58. The deity Yamm yielded a theophoric element in the onomasticon of Ugarit, but more surprisingly also at Mari and, later, in biblical Hebrew.
20. See D. Arnaud, *Emar* VI:3, Paris 1986. Nos. 153:2, 274:9, 373:92', etc. And see more recently the remarks of J. Oliva (*NABU*, 1993, no. 94), who, however, casts doubt on this interpretation.
21. Oliva (above, note 20). But for an association of Ashtarte with a river god (^{d}ID) already in Old Akkadian or even in the late Early Dynastic period, and in connection with Mari, see W.G. Lambert, "The Pantheon of Mari," *MARI* 4 (1985), pp. 535–537. It should be borne in mind that the deity Yamm at Ugarit bears the epithet "Judge/Ruler of the River" (see above).
22. Cf., e.g., M. Popko, "Hethische Rituale," *AOF* 14 (1987), p. 262; G. Wilhelm, "Meer: bei den Hethitern" (3: Meer in der Religion), *RLA*, VIII:1, pp. 4–5.
23. Cf. A. Erman & H. Grapow, *Wörterbuch der ägyptischen Sprache*, I, Berlin 1926, p. 78; R. Giveon, *LÄ*, III, Wiesbaden 1980, cols. 242–243, s.v. *Jam* (Meer). R.O. Faulkner, in *A Concise Dictionary of Middle Egyptian*, Oxford 1962, s.v. *w3ḏ-wr*, p. 56, cites one form that should be read *w3ḏ-wr-'im*(!), that is, the unusual idiom "Great Green *Yam*."
24. M. Lichtheim, *Ancient Egyptian Literature*, II, Berkeley, Calif., 1976, pp. 203ff.
25. Cf. Kaiser, *Die mythische Bedeutung* (above, note 1), pp. 81 ff.; R. Stadelmann, *Syrisch-Palästinensische Gottheiten in Ägypten*, Leiden 1967, pp. 125 ff.; and E. Brunner-Traut, *Altägyptische Märchen*, Munich 1989, pp. 107–110 and 301–302.

26. Cf. Kaiser, *Die mythische Bedeutung* (above, note 1), pp. 80 f.; Brunner-Traut, *Altägyptische Märchen* (above, note 25), pp. 161–162, 317 f.
27. See U. Cassuto, *Biblical and Oriental Studies*, II, Jerusalem 1975, pp. 70 ff. On *yam* in the Bible see also R. Ringren, Ø, *ThWAT*, III, Stuttgart 1982, cols. 649 ff.; as well as O. Eissfeldt, "Gott und das Meer in der Bibel," *KS*, III (1966), pp. 256–264. On the dragon monster see M.K. Wakeman, *God's Battle with the Monster*, Leiden 1973. And see most recently T. Ringer, "Fighting the Dragon," *SJOT*, VI (1992), pp. 139 ff.; and J. Day, "Dragon and Sea," *Anchor Bible Dictionary*, II, New York 1992, pp. 228–231.
28. For the Bible in general see F.M. Cross, *Canaanite Myth and Hebrew Epic*, Cambridge, Mass., 1973, pp. 121 ff. On Psalm 74:13 see J.C. Greenfield, in S.E. Balentine & J. Barton (eds.), *Language, Theology and the Bible* (*Essays in Honour of James Barr*), Oxford 1994, pp. 113–119.
29. Cassuto, *Biblical Studies* (above, note 27), p. 71.
30. See T. Jacobsen, "The Battle between Marduk and Tiamat," *JAOS*, LXXXVIII (1968), pp. 104–108.

5

Some Biblical Concepts of Sacred Place

Sara Japhet

i

From the conceptual richness of the Bible with regard to sanctity of place, I should like to sketch a number of lines of general validity. Doing so means that I will have to leave aside certain nuances of biblical thought and their literary expression, but only this will make it possible to highlight the basic notions, within which and by reference to which even the expressions that deviate from them exist.

I should add, by way of preface, that the point of departure for my discussion is anchored in biblical thought itself, as reflected in the biblical text. I am not coming to the world of biblical thought from the outside, with a comparative method that has recourse to models built outside the Bible, which are reinforced, supported, or confirmed by the Bible. My approach is from within, using a cautious examination of the biblical data, in all their variety; starting from the Bible, one can then move on to comparative material and to general theories. Because 'sanctity' is one of the central concepts of biblical thinking, with its own clear linguistic counterpart in the root *qdš*, we shall begin our investigation of the concept, and more particularly of the concept "sacred place," in this context.

This methodological approach means that we can make only little use of various sociological theories, among which particular mention should be made of the school of Mircea Eliade. Eliade considers "sacred space" a key term for understanding "religious experience" and illustrates his view partly with examples from the Bible. However, it is not the details of Eliade's approach —

which are certainly not above criticism[1] — but its starting point and conceptual context which are fundamentally different from my own. Eliade begins with the existential distinction between the "sacred" and the "profane" as alternative modes of being, of humanity's relationship to the world. In essence, this distinction is valid for modern humanity and characterizes the modes of its existence. One concept, "the sacred," is based on the fundamental experience of the existence of the "absolutely other" (to use Rudolf Otto's term; or, in another definition, God), and as such it is identical with the religious attitude towards the world; Eliade defines one who holds that attitude as *homo religiosus*.[2] The second concept, "the profane," is fundamentally and essentially "godless" and characterizes "modern and non-religious man."[3] According to these terms, the Bible, in its very essence and totality, is "sacred;" everything in it, on every subject, belongs to the realm of the "sacred."

However, the Bible itself does not share these assumptions. In general we can say that, in biblical thought, the sacred is much more sharply defined and delimited than it is by the distinction we have just reviewed. While according to the biblical belief the entire universe was created by God, who is present in it, rules it, and directs it in his providence, this presence, control, and providence are not enough, in themselves, to endow the universe with the quality of holiness or even to justify adding the adjective "sacred" to every one of the deity's acts within that universe. In the biblical view, the two realms, the sacred and the profane, co-exist, and it is both possible and necessary to separate them. The "sacred," according to the Bible, is truly what is "absolutely other," not only in terms of the human experience of standing vis-à-vis God, but also in terms of the physical and material aspects of humanity's relationship to holiness and its latent perils.

In any consideration of the biblical conception of holiness, and, more specifically, the biblical conception of the sacred place, we must begin with the term used by the Bible itself: the root *qdš* and its derivatives, referring both to the deity[4] and to the entire spectrum of phenomena and objects that are associated with him: sacred space, sacred time, sacred persons, sacred objects, and so on. At the same time, we must remember that the text may express the concept and experience of holiness in other ways, and not only by using the root *qdš*. A good example is Jacob's dream (Gen. 28:11–22). The root *qdš* is to be found nowhere in the passage, although the description of the dream ("A ladder was set on the ground and its top reached to the sky, and angels of God were going up and down on it. And the Lord was standing beside him and He said: I am the Lord. ..."), Jacob's response, that is, his words and emotions ("'Surely the Lord is present in this place.' ... Shaken, he said, 'How awesome is this place! This is none other than the abode of God, and that is the gateway to heaven'"), his actions ("Jacob took the stone that he had put under his head and set it up as a pillar and poured oil on top of it") and his vow ("If God remains with me ... this stone ... shall be God's abode"), all attest that the place where Jacob lay down is a "sacred place." Moreover, holiness obligates people to observe certain rules of behaviour, prohibitions and obligations of various degrees, and their very observance attests to the fact that the place is "sacred."

In order to examine the biblical concept in its fullness, then, we must go beyond what is designated explicitly as "sacred" and also include what, according to its attributes, meaning, and rules, is considered to be sacred.

ii

Holiness is an attribute of the deity; hence whatever belongs to him or is linked to him is "sacred." The notion of "sacred place," then, depends on three variables: the specific image of the deity, the nature of the link between him and the "place," and the definition of the sacred.[5] For each of these elements we can find various shades and conceptualizations in the Bible. At the most basic level, however, the sanctity of a place is determined exclusively by the existence of a direct and immediate link between that place and God.

Clarifying the nature of this fundamental concept requires that we also consider what it is not, by scrutinizing other factors which determine the ascription of sanctity to places in other cultures. Two of these may be mentioned here. One such factor is the existence of a link between a place and a human being who is considered to be a saint, by virtue of his or her extraordinary deeds or attributes. This is most prominent in connection with the sanctity ascribed to the birthplaces or burial places of "holy men," in accordance with each society's particular definition of the term (ancestors, prophets, apostles, etc.), or to places where relics of those saints are kept. One may put forward the hypothesis that the initial source of that sanctity is the godlike nature of those holy persons, or, alternatively, the fact that the deity is the source of their superhuman power; but on the immediate level of the definition of the place as sacred, its sanctity stems from a direct link with the persons associated with it. By the same token, and subject to the same reservations, a place may be sacred because of events that occurred there. Supernatural events, or saving acts performed on behalf of an individual or community, may mark and define the sanctity of a place.

These categories are not found in the Bible. There is not a single verse in which places associated with righteous persons — the places of their birth, activity, or burial — or places associated with historical portents or events, however wondrous and extraordinary they may have been, are described explicitly or implicitly as sacred places, either by the terms used to refer to them or by the customs said to have been practiced there.

This point requires further clarification, chiefly with regard to burial places, because the tombs of righteous persons have been regarded as sacred in various cultures and periods.

There is no doubt that the Bible gives special attention to burial places. It notes the fact and place of burial of various figures, such as the Patriarchs and Matriarchs, Joseph, Aaron, Joshua, Eleazar, Samuel, the kings of the house of David, Elisha, and others.[6] Some burial sites are marked by a special monument.[7] The lack of a proper burial and a tomb is one of the most severe punishments that the Bible can imagine.[8] In addition, there are echoes in the Bible of the view that the bones of a holy man may be endowed with extraordinary powers, and of the particular reverence accorded his grave.[9] The biblical attitude towards burial sites is clear in the words of Nehemiah — directed, it is true, to the Persian king — "How should I not look bad when the city of the graveyard of my ancestors lies in ruins, and its gates have been consumed by fire" (Neh. 2:3; cf. also v. 5). Yet despite these instances, nowhere does the Bible ever suggest that a tomb is a sacred place, in any respect whatsoever.

We should round off this question with another point. The Bible does recognize the existence of the "cult of the dead,"[10] as well as the concept of the familiar spirit and necromancy,[11] but all of these are presented precisely to be rejected. Even in the few contexts in which they do appear, it is highly doubtful that any sanctity was ascribed to them. They are compatible with the fundamental biblical view that death is the realm of impurity and bones the "ultimate source of impurity."[12]

Is the biblical position, which ascribes absolutely no sanctity to places associated with persons, a naive stance that does not recognize that any other attitude is possible? Or is it an intentional polemic against existing sites and prevailing customs? Though it is difficult to make any unequivocal statement on this matter, we should recall that some scholars have viewed the Bible's care to note that Moses' grave is unknown — "no one knows his burial place to this day" (Deut. 34:6) — and so, too, the indication of the burial place of Deborah, Rebecca's nurse (Gen. 35:8), as evidence of deliberate opposition to the attribution of sanctity to graves.

iii

As I have already noted, the basic biblical idea is that the sacred place is one that has a direct and immediate connection with God. This connection is perceived in two different ways:[13] (1) a sacred place is a place where God dwells; (2) a sacred place is one where God reveals himself to humanity.

From a certain perspective it seems that the first category is broader than the second. It is not determined exclusively by God's association with human beings, nor is it limited by a specific definition of God's abode. Hence, alternative identifications of God's dwelling place can co-exist within it — in heaven, in the temple, and so forth. On the other hand, we can say that for this category, the presence of the deity has a "static" sense.[14] The second category, by contrast, despite the limitation inherent in the fact that it determines sanctity exclusively through God's association with human beings — the sacred place is the site of revelation — does not bind the sanctity of the place to the deity's fixed presence there, and hence is more dynamic. It leaves open a broad field of existential possibilities with regard to God's dwelling place and the modes of his revelation.

The idea that God resides in heaven can be described as a universal biblical view. It seems to be almost self-understood and is expressed in different ways in the different strata of biblical literature. There are explicit statements, of course, such as "Look down from Your holy abode, from heaven;"[15] "hear in Your heavenly abode;"[16] and "The heaven is My throne" (Isa. 66:1). There are also less explicit references, such as Jacob's ladder, or the indication that the ten commandments were spoken "from the very heavens."[17]

Nevertheless, so far as the question of sanctity is concerned, the idea that God dwells in heaven is of secondary importance. It is true that God's dwelling place in the heavens is called his "holy abode," as we have just noted; and in one passage the heavens themselves are called "His sacred heavens" (Ps. 20:7). But the essence of sanctity is the distinction from the profane,[18] and therefore the very existence of the sacred requires the countervailing existence of the profane. Given the existential distance of the heavens from anything else, this condition is not fulfilled there. In this particular context the term "sacred" has already distanced itself from its original meaning and begun to serve in a metaphoric and abstract sense.

Another aspect of God's abode, one that has drawn the greatest attention in biblical studies and inspired the greatest interest among scholars, is the theme of the "the mountain of God" or the "sacred mountain," which scholars view as the biblical equivalent of the pagan cosmogonic mountain of the gods found in various mythologies and especially in Canaan.[19] Even though traces of such an idea, and especially its metaphoric adjuncts, are indeed to be found in the Bible, it should be seen as a fundamentally foreign element rejected by the Bible. We find "the mountain of God" as a metaphor referring to the temple, to Jerusalem, and even to the entire country,[20] but the actual biblical concept is linked to God's revelation and not to his dwelling.[21]

iv

The concept of the "sacred place" as a place where God resides finds its clearest and fullest expression in the idea that God dwells in the sanctuary, in the midst of human beings. The main literary context in which this view is manifested is the Pentateuch, in the passages that deal with the construction of the tabernacle and the statutes associated with it (Ex. 25 ff.). But it also returns in many other loci, such as the construction of Solomon's temple (1 Kings 8:13) and Ezekiel's description of the temple of the future (Ezek. 43:7, 9). It is certainly significant that the alternate view, too, namely, that the sacred place is where God reveals himself, finds ample expression in the same literary context, in the description of God's revelation on Sinai (Ex. 19-24). Thus both views are associated with the founding event in the history of the people of Israel, which determined its character and laid the foundations for its existence.

God's presence in the tabernacle is stated explicitly: "Let them make Me a sanctuary that I may dwell among them" (*ve-'asu li miqdash ve-shakhanti betokham*).[22] We should pay attention to each component of this statement, starting with the last: "among them" — that is, among human beings. This phrase should be interpreted *literally*, actually in their midst. "I will dwell" — God's abode among human beings is an actual domicile. "Sanctuary" — that is, a sacred place; the place in which the deity dwells is one characterized by the fact that it is sacred.

Another facet of the same matter is the idea that the place of God's abode is the site where he is worshipped. As Menahem Haran has demonstrated in a series of articles, according to the precise definitions in the priestly literary stratum in the Pentateuch and in Ezekiel, the tabernacle is God's "house" in the fullest sense of the term. This is determined not by the semantic associations of the root *šḵn*, but by the physical structure of the tabernacle and the ritual practiced in it. The cult practiced there is "the daily satisfaction of the 'needs' of the deity";[23] it is the activities connected with the regular service that make the tabernacle like a residence.

God's dwelling place and the site of his cult are thus two sides of a single coin. As we shall see later, such a linkage exists even when the sanctity of a place is viewed as determined not by God's dwelling in it but by his revelation there. Hence a cult site is sacred, whether or not it explicitly receives this epithet.

v

What are the specific attributes of the sanctity of "God's dwelling?"

(1) First of all, this sanctity is "local," and, moreover, focussed

in a specific point. It is demarcated within and limited to a particular physical and geographical area and does not extend beyond it. Within this precinct, however, it encompasses and defines everything. This domain of sanctity is the tabernacle (or temple) with its courtyards; everything outside that precinct is profane.

(2) That this sanctity is localized can also be seen in its juxtaposition to the profane. According to the portrayal in the second chapter of Numbers, the architectonic structure of the Israelite camp fixed the sanctuary, the tent of meeting, at its centre. The Levites surrounded it, while the twelve tribes encamped in a square surrounding the tent on all four sides.[24] This arrangement prevailed when they made camp and also when they travelled: the tribes of the east and south in the vanguard, followed by the centre — the tent — and last of all the tribes of the west and north.

Another concentric plan is found in the book of Ezekiel, describing the future re-settlement of the land of Israel (Ezek. 48:1-29). The location of the sanctuary at the centre of the tribes of Israel (vv. 8-22) in principle parallels the scheme followed during journeys of the tabernacle in the wilderness.[25]

(3) In addition to being "local," sanctity is described in hierarchical terms, both internally and externally. Internally, there is a clear hierarchy among the parts of the structure: first, the holy of holies, which contains the ark, with its cover above it, where God reveals himself; second, the sanctuary, the space within the tabernacle, where the primary rituals are performed; and finally, the courtyard, where the altar stands and various other rituals are performed. This threefold hierarchy is also reflected in the classification of the ritual servitors: at the top, the high priest, who alone may enter the holy of holies, and even this only once a year; below him, the priests, who perform the various rituals inside and outside the tabernacle; and finally, the Levites, who occupy a third degree of sanctity and mediate between the sacred and the profane.

Further reflections of this hierarchy are to be found in the materials from which the structure and its furnishings are constructed, in the priestly vestments, and in the rules of conduct that apply to each part of the structure and to each class of ritual servitors.[26]

Externally, the three-level hierarchy is manifested in the general concept of the space in which the sanctuary existed, with its threefold division: first, the sacred precinct itself — the tabernacle with its various levels of holiness; second, the profane — the entire Israelite camp; last, the area outside the camp — variously denominated as the domain of the "goat-demons" (*se'irim*, Lev. 17:7), the "wilderness" (*midbar*, Lev. 16:10), or "an inaccessible region" (*erez gezera*, Lev. 16:22). This division represents a parallel, in concentric circles rather than a vertical line, to the biblical conception of the three domains of being: the sacred heavens, the profane natural and human world, and the world of demons, chaos, and the netherworld. The question of whether the three-level hierarchy consciously symbolizes the three realms of the universe needs further study and must be left for another opportunity.

(4) The last aspect of the sanctity of the tabernacle, and perhaps the most interesting, is its mobility, which stands out so conspicuously against the principle of localization. The entire architectonic structure I have just described — the Israelite camp, with the tabernacle at its centre — is a mobile entity that moves from place to place. The sanctity of a place is established only when the tabernacle has been set up there at some point and by virtue of that fact. But the place itself, as a particular geographically defined tract of land, has no intrinsic sanctity.

The account of the Israelites' journeys in the book of Numbers tells us that the decision as to where the camp was set up, and thus where the tabernacle was erected, was a divine act (Num. 9:15–23): "And whenever the cloud lifted from the Tent, the Israelites would set out accordingly, and at the spot where the cloud settled, there the Israelites would make camp. At a command of the Lord the Israelites broke camp, and at a command of the Lord they made camp" (vv. 17–18). Nevertheless, the places where the tabernacle rests have no intrinsic sanctity. As long as the camp, with the tabernacle at its centre, remains in a particular location, the ground occupied by the tabernacle is sacred. But the moment the tabernacle is moved, the spot returns to its previous status, whether profane or "wilderness." Here we witness the interweaving of two attributes with a sharp internal tension between them. On the one hand, sanctity is characterized by rigid, strict ideas as to its material and physical significance and the practical conclusions that stem from it — "the stranger who comes near will be put to death" (Num. 1:51) — and by a pronounced localization of the sacred as the place of God's abode in the midst of the camp, at the centre of the Israelites, in the holy of holies. On the other hand, however, geography is quite meaningless. The natural place, north or south, east or west, in the hills or in the valley, at sea or on land, has no significance whatsoever. Any place can *become* sacred, but no place *is* sacred.

This characterization arouses many questions, such as that of the relationship between the tabernacle and the permanent sanctuaries, first and foremost the one in Jerusalem; it also presses us to inquire into the origin of the priestly notion of the tabernacle. Does this notion also refer to Jerusalem? Does the place where the Temple stands have no intrinsic sanctity? Ezekiel's vision of the future suggests that this is indeed his position: According to his new map, the future sanctuary is not to be built in Jerusalem at all (Ezek. 48). If so, can we truly see the priestly idea of the tabernacle, in line with what has become a commonplace of biblical studies, as a projection of the temple into the wilderness period?[27] Or perhaps as a projection of some other permanent sanctuary to the wilderness period?[28] What is the relationship between this conception and the understanding of the holy mountain? These questions require attention; I hope to return to them in a different context.

vi

In contrast to all the passages I have cited thus far, the Bible offers another formulation of the idea that God resides in his sanctuary. This extremely theological and polemical formulation defines God's residence in his house as the residence there of his "name." The sanctuary (or the city) is "the site that the Lord your God will choose ... to establish His name there."[29] This view, characteristic of the Deuteronomic stratum of the Bible (including the book of Deuteronomy and other literature created by the same school), advances a polemical position against the view I have presented above, in that God dwells in his sanctuary by means of his name, and the place where he dwells is "the site He chose," whereas his true abode is in heaven (1 Kings 8:39, etc.).[30] What is more, this view avoids using the noun *qodesh* (holiness) and the adjective *qadosh* (holy) with reference to the sanctuary.[31] Implicit here is a different concept of the status of Jerusalem, defined here as the "chosen city"; this, too, is a topic for further study.

vii

Against the view that God dwells in the sanctuary, the Bible offers another idea: the sacred place is that where God is revealed. This latter view, too, is expressed in the Bible several times; the most important such passages are included in the narrative complex relating to God's revelation on Mount Sinai. There are three accounts of revelation on Mount Sinai: God's appearance to Moses in the burning bush (Ex. 3:1-22), the revelation to all Israel (Ex. 19-20, 24), and God's appearance to Elijah (1 Kings 19:8-18). In the first story, we are told that Moses, pasturing his flock in the wilderness, comes to a certain area known as the "mountain of God": Moses "drove the flock into the wilderness, and came to Horeb, the mountain of God" (Ex. 3:1). Here the angel of the Lord appears to him "in a blazing fire out of a bush" (v. 2), and when Moses attempts to come closer in order to find out why the bush does not burn up, God responds with a double command: "Do not come closer" and "Remove your sandals from your feet." The reason for these injunctions is that "the place on which you stand is holy ground" (vv. 3–5).

Here, too, we find in essence the idea of concentricity: the sanctity is focussed in the bush itself, in which God reveals himself to Moses in the fire, and which Moses cannot even approach. The area around the bush, whose geographic confines are not stated, is "holy ground," where Moses must adhere to the customs of sanctity and remove his shoes. Everything outside this area is profane and has no function in the story.

If the revelation in the burning bush is a minimalist one, the revelation to the entire people at Sinai is certainly maximalist. Moses is told: "on the third day the Lord will come down, in the sight of all the people, on Mount Sinai" (Ex. 19:11). Hence, more numerous precautions must be observed: "set bounds for the people round about" (v. 12), and again: "set bounds about the mountain and sanctify it" (v. 23). "Moses came down from the mountain to the people and warned the people to stay pure, and they washed their clothes. And he said to the people, 'Be ready for the third day: do not go near a woman'" (vv. 14–15). This revelation is also described in greater detail: "there was thunder, and lightning, and a dense cloud upon the mountain, and a very loud blast of the horn. ... Now

Mount Sinai was all in smoke, for the Lord had come down upon it in fire; the smoke rose like the smoke of a kiln, and the whole mountain trembled violently" (vv. 16–18).

viii

How is sanctity characterized in these stories of revelation?

(1) First of all, God's appearance on the mountain is a one-time event rather than a manifestation of a permanent presence — "the Lord will come down" (Ex. 19:11; and cf. v. 18). God's "descent" onto the mountain endows it with holiness, and this mandates various precautionary rules: the people must be pure, and even then they are not allowed to come near; the priests, too, must purify themselves (v. 22),[32] and only Moses himself (or, according to another version, Moses and Aaron) may ascend the mountain.

The one-time nature of the Sinaitic revelation stands out clearly. It is seen as such not only in the narrative of the story itself, but also from the perspective of the entire history of the people of Israel. This is precisely the reaction of the book of Deuteronomy: "Has anything as grand as this ever happened, or has its like ever been known? Has any people heard the voice of a god speaking out of a fire, as you have, and survived?" (Deut. 4:32–33). But what is the actual meaning of the mountain's sanctity? Does it continue to exist even after the one-time revelation? Does it have any cultic consequences?

(2) In the story of the giving of the ten commandments at Sinai as well as in the other, personal epiphanies to Moses and Elijah, the mountain on which the revelation takes place is called "the mountain of God" (Ex. 3:1; Ex. 24:13; 1 Kings 19:8); another passage refers to it as "the mountain of the Lord" (Num. 10:33). The epithet "the mountain of God," in and of itself, can indicate that the mountain belongs to God or that God resides on it, and as such it may reflect one version of the idea of the cosmogonic mountain of the gods. Nevertheless, these narratives imply a different, explicitly contradictory stance vis-à-vis the mountain. "The mountain of God" is mentioned a number of times as a purely geographical designation, denoting a particular region in the wilderness where Moses pastured the sheep and where he made camp, both before and after the Exodus: "Moses ... came to Horeb, the mountain of God" (Ex. 3:1); "The Lord said to

Aaron, 'Go to meet Moses in the wilderness.' He went and met him at the mountain of God" (Ex. 4:27); "Jethro, Moses' father-in-law, brought Moses' sons and wife to him in the wilderness, where he was encamped at the mountain of God" (Ex. 18:5); "They marched from the mountain of the Lord a distance of three days" (Num. 10:33); "and with the strength from that meal he walked forty days and forty nights as far as the mountain of God at Horeb" (1 Kings 19:8).

The mountain itself seems to have no extraordinary attributes. It is not even described as particularly high; it is simply a patch of ground where bushes grow; *a priori* no particular conduct is required there. Hence, Elijah "went into a cave and ... spent the night" (1 Kings 19:9).

Here we may be encountering a certain tension in the conceptualization of the mountain. If the name truly embodies some special affinity of the mountain to God, or even God's permanent abode there,[33] this significance has totally disappeared from the narrative as we have it. The mountain is designated as God's not because he dwells on it, but because he may reveal himself there (Jud. 5:4–5; Deut. 33:2; Ps. 68:8–9). It is this revelation that makes the mountain sacred; hence it is an *ad hoc* rather than a permanent sanctity.

(3) Both the element of impermanence and the element of sanctity are reflected in the third aspect of the "sacred place" — the fact that it is a cultic site. Already in the account of the burning bush, the "mountain of God" is presented as a ritual site: "That shall be your sign that it was I who sent you ... when you have freed the people from Egypt, you shall worship God at this mountain" (Ex. 3:12). So, too, rituals are conducted there, on the occasion of Jethro's visit: "And Jethro, Moses' father-in-law, brought a burnt offering and sacrifices for God" (Ex. 18:12), and when the covenant was proclaimed: "... he set up an altar at the foot of the mountain ... and they offered burnt offerings and sacrificed bulls as offerings of well-being to the Lord" (Ex. 24:4–5).

Here, too, we may assume that these texts reflect a more ancient situation, when some regular ritual — annual or perhaps seasonal — was observed on the mountain of God. But according to the biblical narrative, this ritual has no sequel. The "mountain of God" never plays any role whatsoever in the history of Israel, except in the historical context of the Exodus.[34]

ix

The view that the sacred place is the place of divine revelation has several additional manifestations in the Bible, in both narrative and legal contexts.

We recall, on the one hand, the story of God's appearance to Joshua, which has lineaments similar to the revelation to Moses (Josh. 5:13–15), and, on the other hand, the story of Jacob's dream (Gen. 28:11-22). The divine revelation to Joshua — "he looked up and saw a man standing before him, drawn sword in hand. ... [The man] replied, 'No, I am captain of the Lord's host. Now I have come!' ... The captain of the Lord's host answered Joshua, 'Remove your sandals from your feet, for the place where you stand is holy'" — incorporates motifs from various sources, and keenly expresses the idea that a place where divine revelation occurs is a "sacred place." But the account omits all identification of the place, and absolutely no ritual activity occurs there. The sanctity of the place is temporary and has no sequel.

In contrast, the story of God's appearance to Jacob founds and perpetuates the sanctity of the place through its geographical identification with an external sign — the stone pillow that becomes a pillar (Gen. 28:18). This detail hints at the source of the story — evidently the *hieros logos* of the Bethel sanctuary.[35] Between these two poles, Genesis contains several accounts that reflect a tradition of divine revelation which includes geographic identification of the spot, but no parallel evidence of any permanent sanctity, such as Mahanaim (Gen. 32:3) and Peniel (Gen. 32:25–31).

In the realm of law, we should mention the statute of the altar (Ex. 20:19–23 [22–26]), which touches on one of the central issues in the Bible's concept of the cult. As is well known, the Bible offers two alternate views as to the place of worship. The more ancient view is that of a multiplicity of cult sites, whereas the later and more problematic prescribes a single place of worship.[36] One of the most important instances of the former view is the altar statute, with its precise definition of location: "in every place where I pronounce my name (*azkir et shemi*) I will come to you and bless you" (Ex. 20:21b [24b]). This is, in fact, an expression of the very essence of God's appearance to humanity, since every revelation begins with the self-identification of the divinity that is being revealed: "I am the Lord" (Ex. 6:2 and elsewhere); "I am the Lord, the God of your father Abraham" (Gen. 28:13); "I am El Shaddai" (Gen. 17:1, 35:11); and so forth. "The place where I pronounce my name" is thus "the place where I reveal myself to you by declaring my identity." It is in such places that worship of God is appropriate.

Even though this statute does not explicitly declare that the altar is sacred, there seems to be no need to do so, in light of the criteria established above. At the same time, the sanctity of the altar is represented, in practical terms, by the regulation that requires that it be built of unhewn stone ("do not build it of hewn stones; for by wielding your tool upon them you have profaned them" — Ex. 20:22 [25]), and the prohibition against ascending it by steps. These restrictions express, in practice, the sanctity with which it is endowed.

x

To sum up: the Bible's heterogeneous concepts of sacred place stem, on the one hand, from the existence of views and traditions originating in different sources, which express the fundamental richness from which the biblical faith took form, and, on the other hand, from the theological evolution that is associated with and responds to historical circumstances. Still, despite this heterogeneity, there remains an unambiguous principle: the source of the sanctity of a place is its immediate link with the deity, conceived in two ways: as the place where God resides, or as the place where he is revealed. These two types of link have something else in common — the quality of impermanence. True, God's dwelling in the sanctuary endows his presence among human beings with a degree of permanence, locality, and stasis; but the tabernacle's wanderings from place to place and erection at various locations deprive the geographical site itself of any intrinsic importance. Even more so, the idea that God dwells in heaven and reveals himself to human beings on earth deprives any particular geographical site of all intrinsic sanctity. Even the revelation itself is temporary and transient, and only the element of worship at the place of revelation endows that sanctity with some aspect of permanence.

The place itself, the tract of land, the geographic district, the natural object, and so forth — all lack any dimension of intrinsic sanctity.

Nevertheless, by virtue of historical and theological circumstances, the central sanctuary in Jerusalem, and the city of Jerusalem, ultimately acquired special status in biblical thought. The principles of mobility and impermanence were replaced by stability and permanence, and the need arose to institutionalize the status of Jerusalem and give it an appropriate theological expression. This need led in two opposing directions: on the one hand, there was an intensification of the sanctity of the city, through the creation of terminological identity between Temple and city ("the place that God will choose") and the extension of the sanctity of the Temple to the city, using metaphors borrowed from different ideological ground (especially the idea of the "sacred mountain"). On the other hand, we also find the opposite trend: the emergence of a universal concept of God's presence ("Holy, holy, holy! The Lord of Hosts! His presence fills all the earth!" — Isa. 6:3), which abolishes the need for an earthly focus of sanctity and for the very existence of sacred places: "The heaven is My throne and the earth is My footstool: Where could you build a house for Me, what place could serve as My abode?" (Isa. 66:1).

At this point we should move to two additional issues, which have to do with the later development of biblical thought: the sanctity of the city of Jerusalem, which became established during the biblical period itself, and the sanctity of the Land of Israel, of which only the first stirrings can be found in the Bible (Isa. 11:9, Zech. 2:16), and whose manifestations date chiefly from later periods. We must defer these issues to another time and place.

Notes

1. See, for example, J. Z. Smith, *To Take Place*, Chicago–London 1987, pp. 1–22; S. Talmon, "The Navel of the Earth and the Comparative Method," in *Festschrift J.C. Rylaarsdam*, Pittsburgh 1977, pp. 243–268.
2. M. Eliade, *The Sacred and the Profane*, New York 1957, p. 15. For a study in the spirit of Eliade, cf. M. Fishbane, "The Sacred Center: The Symbolic Structure of the Bible," in M.A. Fishbane and P.R. Flohr, eds., *Texts and Responses: Festschrift N.N. Glazer*, Leiden 1975, pp. 6–27.
3. Fishbane & Flohr, *Texts* (above, note 2), p. 14.

4. Like "The Holy God" (Isa. 5:16); "For I am God ... the holy one in your midst" (Hos. 11:9); "the Lord, this Holy God" (1 Sam. 6:20); "the Holy One of Israel" (Isa. 10:20), and many more. In general, but not in every detail, the biblical text follows the translation of the Jewish Publication Society; deviations from this translation have not been noted.
5. For distinctions within the concept of sanctity, see J. Licht, *Encyclopaedia Biblica*, VII, Jerusalem 1976, col. 44, s.v. *Qodesh, Qadosh, Qedusha.*
6. Gen. 23:2, 9, 19; 25:9–10; 50:5–13; Num. 20:28; Josh. 24:30, 32, 33; etc.
7. Such as the pillar on Rachel's grave, cf. Gen. 35:19–20.
8. Cf. 1 Kings 21:23–24; 2 Kings 9:30–32; Jer. 22:19; 36:30, etc.
9. Cf. 2 Kings 13:20–21, where a dead man is resurrected by contact with the bones of Elisha, and 2 Kings 23:17–18.
10. E.g., Deut. 26:13–14 — "I have cleared out the consecrated portion from the house ... I have not deposited any of it with the dead;" or Isa. 65:4: "Who sit inside tombs and pass the night in secret places."
11. E.g., Deut. 18:11; 1 Sam. 28:13.
12. See also the rebuke of Ezekiel in 43:7–8.
13. The historical and literary relationship between them has not been fully clarified, but its discussion is beyond the scope of this presentation.
14. See W. Eichrodt, *The Theology of the Old Testament* (English transl. by J.A. Baker), II, London 1967, p. 190.
15. Deut. 26:15. Cf. also Jer. 25:30; 2 Chron. 30:27.
16. 1 Kings 8:39, also vv. 32, 34, 43, 45, 49, and the parallels in 2 Chron. 6:21, 23, 25, 27, 30, 33, 35, 39; Ps. 33:13–14.
17. Cf. Ex. 20:19 (22); Deut. 4:36.
18. Durkheim viewed the distinction between the sacred and the profane as the very essence of religion; see E. Durkheim, *The Elementary Forms of the Religious Life* (English transl. by J.W. Swain), London 1915, 1965, pp. 52–57.
19. See R.J. Clifford, *The Cosmic Mountain in Canaan and the Old Testament*, Cambridge, Mass. 1972, pp. 98–181; S. Talmon, *Har*, *TDOT* III (1978), pp. 440–442.
20. Among the relics, the most conspicuous is Ps. 68:17: "O majestic mountain [literally: mountain of God] Mount Bashan ... the mountain God desired as His dwelling."
21. Cf. below, pp. 272–273.
22. Ex. 25:8. Cf. also Ex. 29:45: "I will abide among the Israelites;" Lev. 26:11–12: "I will establish My abode in your midst ... I will be ever present in your midst;" Ex. 29:46; Num. 5:3; 35:34; Ez. 43:9; and many more.
23. M. Haran, *Temples and Temple-Service in Ancient Israel*, Oxford 1978, p. 218.
24. Cf. Num. 2:2: "The Israelites shall camp each with his standard, under the banners of their ancestral house; they shall camp around the Tent of Meeting at a distance." On the east were the tribes of Judah, Issachar and Zebulun (vv. 3–9); on the south were Reuben, Simeon and Gad (vv. 10–16); on the west — Ephraim, Manasseh and Benjamin (vv. 18–24); and on the north — Dan, Asher and Naftali (vv. 25–31).
25. Smith has dealt extensively with the concepts of Ezekiel, but does not mention this analogy. Cf. idem, *To Take Place* (above, note 1), pp. 47–73.

26. See Haran, *Temples and Temple-Service* (above, note 23), pp. 158–188.
27. See, for example, *ibid.*, pp. 189–194.
28. This is the alternative view of Kaufmann, who regards the legal system of the priestly material as reflecting the ancient system of the high places. See Y. Kaufmann, *The History of the Israelite Religion*, I, Jerusalem 1960, pp. 114ff. (in Hebrew).
29. Deut. 12:5. This is probably the most characteristic Deuteronomic phrase, which appears in variations throughout the book, e.g.: 12:14, 21, 26; 14:23, 25; 15:20; 16:5–6, 7, 11, 15, 16; 17:8, 10; 18:6.
30. For the meaning and use of these terms, see S. Japhet, *The Ideology of the Book of Chronicles and Its Place in Biblical Thought* (English transl. by A. Barber), Frankfurt a/M–Bern–New York 1989, pp. 63–81.
31. It should be noted that the root *qdš* (holy) is not very common in Deuteronomy and appears only 17 times. The most Deuteronomic phrase among them is "holy people" (*'am qadosh*; JPS renders this also as "consecrated people" — 7:6; 14:2, 21; 26:19; 28:9). The only use of *qdš* to refer to God's dwelling is found in 26:15, where it explicitly refers to the heavens: "Look down from Your holy abode, from heaven."
32. The reference to priests here is problematic, because according to the narrative context the priests have not yet been appointed; but this does not concern us here.
33. Noth considers Moses' encounter with God on "the mountain of God" as the primary tradition and its most ancient core. See M. Noth, *A History of Pentateuchal Traditions* (English transl. by B.W. Anderson), Englewood Cliffs, N.J., 1972, pp. 136–141; idem, *Exodus* (OTL), London 1962, pp. 31–33.
34. V. Turner has argued that the location of pilgrimage sanctuaries is "outside," in the periphery, beyond the bounds of the living space of the social unit (in total contradiction to Eliade's theory). Thus, he holds, making a pilgrimage to the sacred place is going out to "a center out there." See his article, "The Center Out There: The Pilgrim's Goal," *History of Religions* 12 [1973], pp. 211–215. The concept of the mountain of God, as reflected in the account of the revelation at Sinai, is in perfect harmony with this model: the sacred place is in the wilderness, outside the settled lands of both Egypt and the Land of Israel. But nowhere in the Bible do we find any continuation of this tradition. This lack of a continuation may reflect sociological and historical realities, or it may be a happenstance of what material was included in the biblical literature. According to the extant texts, however, the sanctity of the mountain remains a one-time event, with no later sequel in the history of Israel. (I wish to thank Professor Erik Cohen for drawing my attention to Turner's works and to his own.)
35. See, for example, H. Gunkel, *The Legends of Genesis* (English transl. of 1901), New York 1964, pp. 30–34.
36. Cf., for example, Kaufmann, *History of the Israelite Religion* (above, note 28), pp. 81–87; Haran, *Temples and Temple-Service* (above, note 23), pp. 26–42.

6

The Temple in the Hellenistic Period and in Judaism

Doron Mendels

Professor Joshua Prawer taught me to be a straightforward historian, whose main concern should be the sources. It is in line with his historical methods that I wish to discuss the Hellenistic temple.

Three principal considerations must be borne in mind in discussing the temple in the Hellenistic period: the temple as a religio-political centre; the temple as an architectonic edifice, and the temple in its historical dimension. The chronological framework is the period from 323 B.C.E. — that is, after the eastern conquests of Alexander the Great — to 70 C.E.

Temples in the Hellenistic monarchies were first and foremost major political centres. Holy spaces were filled with none-too-holy political and economic activities. In this respect, we must distinguish between the traditional temples of the native populations, the new Greek temples of the colonizers and their descendants, and the temples built by the Hellenistic (that is, Greek) monarchs for their native populations. Thus, we speak of the old, native temples of Memphis and Thebes and Heliopolis, Babylon and Uruk, and of course the one in Jerusalem, as against the new Greek temples erected in Alexandria in Egypt, Seleucia on the Tigris and Caesarea Maritima.[1] These different categories are not just a matter of shapes and forms, but in many ways express the nature of Hellenistic society in general.

The native temples all over the ancient Near East were the religio-cultural centres of the native populations, or, to use here a Greek term, the *ethne* (peoples). During the Hellenistic period, they became the unchallenged repositories of the ethnic heritage all over the ancient Near East, and the priesthoods thus became the champions of their "national" identities. The traditional aristocracy was eliminated in many places at the end of the Persian period, and into this vacuum entered the priesthoods. Their power throughout the Hellenistic period derived precisely from this, combined with the economic strength of the temples. During the Hellenistic period, it was the Egyptian priests who pressed the Ptolemies hard on many issues, and the provisions of the famous Rosetta Stone of 196 B.C.E. are a good example of their success. On this occasion, following a period of national unrest in Egypt, the king granted many concessions to the priesthood — that is, to the national cause of the natives.

In many of the central autochtonous temples, a ruler cult of the Hellenistic monarchs was established, as we know from Hellenistic Uruk and Babylon. But this still pertained to the "national" cult, since the Seleucids as well as the Ptolemies were seen by the natives as rulers of the newly created superstructure and hence of the state (if we may use the latter term in this particular context). At any rate, these populations in the Hellenistic Near East were self-contained in the cultural and religious sense, and so were their centres, the temples.[2] This situation filled the holy space of the temples with a great deal of politics of a somewhat different nature than in former times.

Moreover, the various temples, such as Memphis, Thebes and Shechem, were also the main indicators of the differences between the various *ethne* of the Hellenistic Near East. Although sociologists will point to many similarities in the structure of the temples and in their functioning as religious institutions, a Greek traveller in the third and second centuries B.C.E. would nevertheless have recognized how different the peoples were from each other in their religio-political behaviour. The Greeks, notwithstanding their somewhat stereotyped view of the whole of the non-Greek world as barbarian[3] were deeply aware that the barbarians were divided into many *ethne*. The temples were surely associated with these divisions and differences.

The Greek temples, on the other hand, were established all over the ancient Near East by Hellenistic monarchs or their subjects, usually in the Hellenistic Greek cities, and constituted an extension of the state of religious affairs in the Greek homeland.[4] The worship of Greek deities such as Heracles and Zeus served the Greeks living in Seleucia, Tyre, Alexandria and all the other Greek centres as a common denominator, together with their shared history and language. These temples were a major facet of the national Greek identity formed all over the ancient Near East, and constituted a universalizing factor among the different regions. To be sure, this was true only up to a certain limit, because we do find that a sort of awareness of a national or ethnic identity developed within the Greek strata of society, as exemplified by such figures as Theocritus in Egypt, or Dius and Laetus in Phoenicia.[5] But this "national" identity of the Greeks, and the interpretation they gave to their new national frameworks, differed in many respects from that of the natives. In Egypt, for example, both the Greek colonizers and the natives revered the image of their common king, Ptolemy. The former, however, worshipped him as Dionysus, while the latter viewed him as Osiris[6] — a distinction that makes a big difference in terms of cultural, religious and political associations and behaviour. These differences found expression in the temples. But there were also the temples built by the Greek monarchs for the natives. These, such as Edfu and Philae in Ptolemaic Egypt, were built on the lines of the traditional native temples.

This was a clever device of the Ptolemies to placate the native populations, and it is no accident that they built enormous temples rather than other edifices.[7] These temples, incorporating many Hellenistic "improvements" in their architecture, in many respects symbolized the cultural and religious syncretism that developed in the Hellenistic era, a phenomenon we also encounter in the temples of Hellenistic Uruk and Babylon.[8] To be sure, the Hellenistic architecture may have been skin-deep; in order to discover how far-reaching the syncretism it expressed really was, one would have to undertake a comparative study of this particular phenomenon in the different regions of the Middle East, a complicated subject that cannot be tackled in the present framework.[9] What should be stressed, however, is that the Hellenization of holy space, as reflected mainly in architecture, was a sign of the willingness of the priesthoods to accept something of the new culture. The creation of a new Hellenistic deity named Serapis to serve as the state deity in Egypt is an extreme example of this attitude.[10]

Thus, the temple in its different forms and structures became part of the reshaped national identities of natives, Hellenists and Greeks all over the Hellenistic Near East, identities that came to expression in the works of such writers as Hecataeus of Abdera, Manetho, Berossus, Dionysius Scytobrachion, Megasthenes, and later Philo of Byblos.[11] In short, holy space in the ancient Near East, like so many other aspects of life, was affected to varying degrees by changing socio-cultural and political conditions in the period after Alexander the Great.[12]

How, then, was this expressed in literature — that is, in the consciousness of the various strata of society? I have argued elsewhere that a new kind of national identity, or identities, emerged in the Hellenistic monarchies.[13] The peoples of the Hellenistic Near East interpreted their own political experience through recourse to their histories, which they reinterpreted to fit their new conditions. Whereas the Greeks in the West at that time theorized their political experiences, the peoples of the East were still at the stage of reshaping their thoughts within the historical framework of their own traditions. Issues like territory, kingship, and other national symbols were transferred into the remote past and given aetiologies that provided answers to the burning political problems of the present. The same kind of strategy, bringing to expression the reshaped identity of the various strata of society, was brought to bear on the temple, which became part of a historical process indissociable from the emergence of statehood and the monarchy.[14] In this respect, a competition between the different national literatures can be observed.

Above all this, we find the literary elaborations of the utopian temple, which was the most magnificent of all in its architecture, at least in the perception of the writers who conceived it. But the utopian temple, too, did not float in the air; it existed in the midst of a utopian political entity. For example, the utopia of Euhemerus (third century B.C.E.) may be understood as an idealized picture of Ptolemaic Egypt.[15] Not only is the temple central to its constitution, but its priesthood, too, has a major role in this ideal state. The combination, which seems so natural, of holy space and political arena is typical of the Hellenistic age. On the other hand, there were utopias that negated the existence of the temple in their political constitution (*politeia*), such as those of the Stoa and the Hellenistic utopia of Iambulus. Even the classical Greek evocations of utopia, in Plato's *Republic* and the *Birds* of Aristophanes, diminished the status of the temple among the institutions of the *polis*.[16]

After the Roman conquest of the ancient Near East in the first century B.C.E., the political stature of the major temples of the native populations, generally speaking, was "lowered" all over the empire. Although the ruler cult of the emperor was usually incorporated in them, it was no longer associated with local monarchs such as Antiochus of Commagene or Ptolemy of Egypt, but became a universal symbol of governance.[17] Rome tried to eliminate the local, national and political aspects of the temples of the ancient Near East and turn them into mere religious and cultural centres. Where Antiochus IV failed, Rome succeeded. To be sure, this policy ran into difficulties in places like Germany and Judaea, whose peoples sought to accentuate the political and national aspects of the native cults, but the case of the Jews is the only one from that period in the East where matters got out of control. It is perhaps a paradox of history that the vast, multi-ethnic Roman Empire succeeded even more than its predecessors in suppressing the political overtones, or rather the nationalistic aspects, of local native temples — a process which, for obvious reasons, did not occur in the Greek temples of the East during the period of Roman domination there.

The Jewish Temple in the Hellenistic Period

The changing conceptualization of the temple throughout the Hellenistic Near East affected the role played by the Temple in Judaism in the same period. Here, too, we must distinguish between the historical evolution of the Jerusalem Temple and its literary understanding.

The historical evolution of the Temple may be divided into six stages. First, before the Maccabean upheaval (168–160 B.C.E.), the Temple, like many other temples of the ancient Near East, was a local native holy place nostalgically associated with the people's traditional links with the land of Israel. The political aspect was less evident.[18] In the seventies of the second century B.C.E., there was a vigorous attempt by the so-called Hellenists, or Hellenizers, to universalize the Temple.[19] Seeking to take a more extreme version of the path adopted by the Hellenist priests of Uruk and Babylon, they obtained the approval and even help of Antiochus IV Epiphanes (called "Epimanes" by Polybius). The involvement of the high priests and their followers in politics on both the local and the international level politicized the holy space of Jerusalem, a development given an ugly depiction by the opponents of the Hellenistic party in the two books of Maccabees.[20]

This development, in which the Temple became an international issue, led to a reaction by those groups that wished it to remain pure in its status as a place of native religious worship — a holy space without unholy politics. Interestingly, there seems to be a limit to the amount of politics and other activities one holy space can absorb. Later events will show that when other, non-sacred activities became dominant, many people were reluctant to go on seeing the Temple as a holy place: it had no more room for sacredness. The universalization of the Temple and its transformation into a centre for international political games aroused the same kind of opposition by champions of the autochtonous cult that we find elsewhere in the ancient Near East.[21]

The second stage, then, was the Maccabean revolt, which lasted from 168 to 160 B.C.E. The stated goal of the revolt, the purification of the Temple, was actually achieved by 164, but an appetite for more, and developments in the region that favoured the Jews, led to a striving for further action. In the third stage, from about 160 B.C.E. until the fall of the Hasmonean kingdom in 63 B.C.E., the Temple became the national political centre of a newly created state, with an extensive territory, an army and a king.[22] Scholars have made comparisons between this entity and the small temple states of Asia Minor, consisting of a temple surrounded by "chora," but the Jewish Temple in the Hasmonean period was a different story altogether; its political status was unique in the history of the Hellenistic Near East. One of the reasons for this, of course, was the fact that the Hasmoneans took upon themselves the high priesthood alongside the secular rulership.[23] The priests of Egypt may have been proud of the agreements they achieved with the Ptolemies, as exemplified in the Rosetta Stone,[24] but the native high priests of Israel themselves became the nation's political leaders and were acknowledged as such by the very same Ptolemies, by Rome and by other nations.

Not everyone was happy with this situation, in which the Temple became the paramount political symbol of the nation. We hear of criticism of the dual rulership of the Hasmoneans from different quarters. Groups like the Essenes yearned for an alternative temple that would be free of the temporal vicissitudes of the existing one. But these objections did not, as yet, constitute a negation of the institution itself.[25]

After the fall of the Hasmonean state in 63 B.C.E., there were several attempts, notably that of Mattathias Antigonus in 40–37 B.C.E., to re-establish the Temple's political role. Here we reach the fourth stage.[26] When Herod took over as client king of Judaea, he toned down the political stature of the Temple, though he did not eliminate it altogether. Paradoxically, this megalomaniac emphasized the religious and cultural significance of the Temple over its political functions. In this he was true to his Roman masters, who, as we have seen, wanted temples to be places of religion and no more. Three aspects of Herod's policy contributed to this change in the status of the Temple. First, Herod did not assume the high priesthood; this separation of functions meant that the king was no longer the religious leader of the state. Second, he chose high priests from the Jewish Diaspora, thus universalizing the Temple (this time it was a Jewish kind of universalism) and making it more of a religious centre for world Jewry.[27] Third, he replaced the existing structure on the Temple Mount with a magnificent new Temple for the Jewish "natives," but took care to place the Roman eagle on its gate — signifying that the higher, secular political authority was, after all, the Roman oppressor.[28]

In the period before and immediately after Herod's death in 4 B.C.E., the groups that viewed the Temple as a national, political centre came out into the open.[29] We meet them as they remove the notorious eagle, the symbol of the Roman Empire, from the Temple's gate. Nevertheless, these groups remained a minority. During the next few decades, however, reports of clashes with the Roman authorities indicate that the majority of Jews cared about the religious rather than the political aspect of their Temple. Basically, the Temple continued functioning as a non-political religious institution, an impression we also gain from the narrative parts of the New Testament.[30] The delicate balance between these circles — those who viewed the Temple as a holy, non-political place, and those who thought that it was and should be a political space around which a Jewish state should be re-created — was ruptured in the fifties and sixties of the first century C.E. In the sixth and last stage in our survey, it was precisely the latter, political trend that prevailed, leading the Jews to launch their revolt against Rome in 66 C.E. But what happened, in the Empire or in Palestine, to bring about this reversal of minority and majority attitudes?

In the fifties and sixties of the first century C.E., the Temple lost much of its sanctity in the eyes of those Jews who had viewed it principally as a religious site, a trend illustrated by the reaction of Paul in the fifties. Many Jews dissociated themselves from the Temple as a holy space when they realized that the leaders of the nation, the priests, had abused the Temple and turned it into an unholy place. Since holy space is a matter of consciousness rather than of physical reality, this perception significantly weakened the support the Temple had from the majority as a religious institution. Into the vacuum thus created in the Temple as a holy place stepped those Jews who wanted the Temple again to become a supreme political symbol of the Jewish nation, and thus also a major local Israelite centre (the Jews of the Diaspora did not participate in the rebellion). Thus began the chain of events which led to the outbreak of the Great War in 66 C.E., and its extension to Jerusalem in 68–69 C.E.[31]

But this is not the whole story: our conference is about sacred space: shrine, city and land. Recalling Joshua Prawer's great passion for Jerusalem and the land of Israel, which he transmitted to his students in a very subtle and academic manner, I should like to ask: How did these three elements — Jerusalem, Temple and Land — interact in the period under discussion? Jerusalem and its Temple could stand as religious spaces even when the land of Israel was occuppied by an oppressor, such as the Ptolemies, the Seleucids or the Romans. However, the moment the land, or part of it, was declared independent, the Temple automatically regained its political stature. This political conceptualization was the main reason for the fall of Jerusalem. Even when the whole country was again in Roman hands, the Zealots in Jerusalem believed that holding the Temple would nevertheless guarantee their political independence. But, as Josephus wrote, God had abandoned his people — that is, God had abandoned the holy space of Jerusalem. Once God left the Jewish camp — a notion that unfortunately was not clear at the beginning of the war — the Temple was no more than a political space. Without its holiness, which had persisted to a degree even in the worst period of Hellenization, in the seventies of the second century B.C.E., the Temple could not survive.

Despite the unique status of the Jerusalem Temple as the principal national and political symbol of the Jewish state in the Hasmonean period, its literary evocations reflect the same kind of nuances as those we have already seen in the Hellenistic pagan literature.[32] For instance, in the writings of Eupolemus, the son of John (second century B.C.E.), the Temple appears as a major religio-political centre that had already been acknowledged as such in biblical times by Egypt and Phoenicia, the "predecessors" of the great superpowers of the Maccabean period. Although Eupolemus sets the circumstances of the Temple's erection in the traditional biblical framework, he changes them completely in order to give a greater legitimacy to the political stature of the Temple in his own time, and to show that the Temple of Jerusalem received international recognition — a subject I have dealt with extensively elsewhere.[33]

As in the other descriptions we found from the Hellenistic milieu, the architectonic details of the Temple became a major issue. The Jews during the Hasmonean period seem to have vied with their neighbours concerning whose temple was more important and magnificent, and had the older claim to political legitimacy. Thus, detailed descriptions of the Jerusalem Temple appear in the writings of Eupolemus, in the Temple Scroll and in the Letter of Aristeias from the Diaspora of Egypt. The Jews were not influenced by Hellenism in this respect, but no doubt constantly were conscious of and reacted to what was happening around them. Interestingly, we find much less of this after the Roman conquest of Palestine. With the loss of its political significance after 63 B.C.E., and even more so after 37 B.C.E., the literature about the Temple becomes low-keyed. When the Temple is mentioned, as in the synoptic Gospels, the Gospel of John, or the Acts of the Apostles, it is seen merely as a religious place (or one that is supposed to be religious). We receive the same impression from the writings of Josephus.[34]

In times of political independence and their aftermath, the Temple, in terms of its architecture, its historical significance and its association with the land, was seen as a major symbol of Jewish nationalism. The moment its political aspects were suppressed, the literature reflects this situation as well. The religious abuse of the Temple brought about its rejection by people like Paul, perhaps (but not necessarily) in line with the Stoa and the Hellenistic utopias mentioned above. The Temple's political and religious vicissitudes ultimately led to the idea expressed in the Book of Revelation — that in the apocalyptic future no Temple at all would be found in the holy city of Jerusalem.[35]

Notes

1. On these temples see D. Mendels, *The Rise and Fall of Jewish Nationalism: Jewish and Christian Ethnicity in Ancient Palestine*, New York 1992, pp. 107–159.
2. On ethnicity and politics as reflected in the temples and priesthoods, cf. *ibid*, pp. 13–33.
3. With regard to this problem see, for instance, F. Hartog, *The Mirror of Herodotus: The Representation of the Other in the Writing of History*, Berkeley–Los Angeles–Oxford 1988.
4. On Greek temples in the East see, for instance, H. van Steuben, "Seleukidische Kolossaltempel," *Antike Welt*, 12 (1981), pp. 3–12.
5. On Theocritus see F.T. Griffith, *Theocritus at Court*, Leiden 1979; on Dius and Laetus see M. Stern, *Greek and Latin Authors on Jews and Judaism*, Jerusalem 1976, pp. 123–130.
6. See E.E. Rice, *The Grand Procession of Ptolemy Philadelphus*, Oxford 1983.
7. See A.K. Bowman, *Egypt after the Pharaohs*, London 1986, pp. 165–190.
8. See S.B. Downey, *Mesopotamian Religious Architecture*, Princeton 1988.
9. For a general account of Hellenism in the ancient Near East, see A. Kuhrt & S. Sherwin White (eds.), *Hellenism in the East*, Berkeley–Los Angeles–London 1987; and also R. Bichler, *Hellenismus*, Darmstadt 1983.
10. On Serapis see W. Hornbostel, *Sarapis: Studien zur Überlieferungsgeschichte, den Erscheinungsformen und Wandlungen der Gestalt eines Gottes*, Leiden 1973.
11. See Mendels, *Rise and Fall* (above, note 1), pp. 35–54.
12. For a general survey of the Hellenistic era see P. Green, *Alexander to Actium: The Historical Evolution of the Hellenistic Age*, Berkeley–Los Angeles–Oxford 1990.
13. Cf. D. Mendels, *The Land of Israel as a Political Concept in Hasmonean Literature*, Tübingen 1987.
14. Cf. idem, *Rise and Fall* (above, note 1), Chaps. 5 and 10.
15. On Euhemerus see J. Ferguson, *Utopias of the Classical World*, London 1975, pp. 102–110.
16. *Ibid., passim.*
17. On the ruler cult of the Roman emperor see S. Weinstock, *Divus Julius*, Oxford 1971; and S.R.F. Price, *Rituals and Power: The Roman Imperial Cult in Asia Minor*, Cambridge–Sydney 1984.
18. For Ben Sira's description of the Jerusalem Temple see Mendels, *Land of Israel* (above, note 13), pp. 9–17.
19. On this stage see in particular M. Hengel, *Judaism and Hellenism*, London–

Philadelphia 1974, I, pp. 277–283; and Mendels, *Rise and Fall* (above, note 1), *passim*.

20. On these two books see the excellent survey of M. Stern, *Encyclopaedia Biblica*, V (1968), pp. 287–292, s.v. *Maccabim*.
21 *E.g.*, the Oracle of the Potter; cf. S. Burstein, *The Hellenistic Age from the Battle of Ipsos to the Death of Kleopatra VII*, Cambridge 1985, pp. 136–139.
22. For the history of the period see E. Schürer, *The History of the Jewish People in the Age of Jesus Christ*, Edinburgh 1973, I, pp. 125–242.
23. Mendels, *Rise and Fall* (above, note 1), Chap. 5.
24. For this episode see Bowman, *Egypt after the Pharaohs* (above, note 7), pp. 30 ff.
25. *The Rise and Fall*, (above, note 1), Chap. 5.
26. For the history of this stage see Schürer, *The History* (above, note 22), pp. 243–329.
27. Cf. Philo's later observation that Jerusalem and the Temple were the religious centres of the Jewish people throughout the world (*In Flaccum*, 45–46).
28. For more details, see Mendels, *Rise and Fall* (above, note 1), Chap. 10.
29. The leaders of one of these groups were members of the so-called Fourth Philosophy school; cf. M. Hengel, *The Zealots*, Edinburgh 1989; M. Stern, "The Suicide of Eleazar ben Jair and His Men at Masada, and the Fourth Philosophy," in idem, *Studies in Jewish History*, Jerusalem 1991, pp. 313–343.
30. Mendels, *Rise and Fall* (above, note 1), Chap. 10.
31. On the Great War see J.J. Price, *Jerusalem under Siege: The Collapse of the Jewish State 66–70 CE*, Leiden–New York–Köln 1992.
32. For a more detailed discussion see Mendels, *Land of Israel* (above, note 13); and idem, *Rise and Fall* (above, note 1), Chaps. 5 and 10.
33. Idem, *Land of Israel* (above, note 13), pp. 57–88.
34. Idem, *Rise and Fall* (above, note 1), Chap. 10.
35. On this issue in general see D. Flussser, "No Temple in the City," in idem, *Judaism and the Origins of Christianity*, Jerusalem 1988, pp. 454–465.

7

The Divinity as Place and Time and the Holy Place in Jewish Mysticism

Haviva Pedaya

Introduction

Place and time are the two primary forms which fashion our comprehension of reality. One of the main aspects of what Kant described as his "Copernican revolution" lies in the understanding of place and time, not as objective concepts in themselves, but as patterns of *a priori* perception found in the consciousness of the observer. One might say that these forms of *a priori* perception are understood in mystical religious thought not merely as intuitions of time and space, but as mirrors reflecting the objective-ideal perception of reality. Images and stories about divine time and place serve as ideals that guide the act of gazing upon the world — by concretizing the relative nature of the rhythms of time and place in earthly reality; by sharpening consciousness of the distinction between the way things are perceived and their existence in themselves; by emphasizing the dissonance or correspondence between supernal and earthly reality; or by indicating the ladder of ascent between them. From these, we may gain an understanding of the concepts of time and supernal time, and the corresponding concepts of place and supernal place, in Jewish mysticism.

In other words, descriptions of the divine through concepts of time and place in early Jewish esoteric doctrine and in kabbalah may also be understood as providing a model for looking at reality. They provide tools for fashioning time and space in a pictorial and sensual manner that expresses an idea or state. By using this mode of perception, one may "enter into" earthly holy space or time and make manifest their holiness; that is, one may act upon, or be acted upon by, the quality of potential holiness inherent in them.

Thus, the religious consciousness, in its striving toward perfection, ascends by means of constant perfection of structures, feelings and activities associated with time and place and their relation — different as they may be from one another — to divine time and place. It does so by means of isolating — and at times shattering — concepts of time and place in ordinary reality, thus allowing for the direct perception of earthly time and place from the perspective of supernal time and place.

In the following discussion, I shall describe various modes of perceiving the divine as residing within spiritual time and place, or as itself being time and place, and I shall suggest the relationship between these supernal forms of time and place and earthly time and place. This will involve an examination of the mythical, or, alternatively, the mystical consciousness as bearing within itself the memory and longing for time and place; as creating the forms of contemplation of time and place within reality; or as rising from time and place to the crystallization of concepts of supernal time and place — or towards the ideal time and place which are themselves the Divinity. Given the limitations of the present framework, however, the dimension of time will remain more in the background, and will be discussed only insofar as required by the discussion of place.[1]

One might add that it is possible to characterize those concepts of the Divinity which are more closely connected with the concept of place, and those more closely connected with the concept of time. However, it is my opinion that in practice — even if not always manifestly — these two aspects frequently appear together. The characterization of their changing interrelations and the nature of their interaction in relation to actual holy space and time constitute one of the ways of describing different religious types, or different stages in the religious life.

The following discussion will be divided into two main parts. In the first part, a survey of the main developments from early Jewish mysticism until the emergence of the kabbalah, we will follow the transition from the perception of the Divinity as dwelling within space to the description of the Divinity in terms of concepts of time and space. We shall attempt to characterize the primary place or the basic types of place connected with the Divinity in early Jewish mysticism, and to ascertain the differences in this regard among various early kabbalistic circles. In the second part, we shall construct several models of the relations between the supernal divine place and the holy place, and attempt to identify what gives the holy place its power in each approach.

Holy Space in Ancient Jewish Mysticism

Judaism's initial characterizations of holy places are connected to the concept of divine revelation. In the earliest biblical texts,[2] God's revelation consists of his descent from the heavens, accompanied by dramatic changes in the natural order of the heavens and the landscape, generally emphasizing the element of fire.[3] We discern the first hints of a new approach in the classical prophets: God is described as an *anthropos* seated on a throne, revelations of whose presence take place primarily in the sanctuary.[4] In this context, the interest displayed by apocalyptic literature in place is linked to the view that God, in addition to revealing himself from his place in the heavens, dwells in an elaborate celestial framework. The most prevalent image of that place in apocryphal literature is of an actual palatial structure. Deriving from concepts of majesty and monarchy, this image is also bound up with the concept of the sacrificial cult. If the spiritual place is depicted in terms of sanctuary, house, and temple, it follows naturally that there will be an entire complex of related imagery of inner space: rooms, gates, treasury, archives, throne, and altar.

In keeping with this concrete approach, not only is supernal reality conceived as a specific, physical place, but the mystic is likewise described as a pilgrim[5] who physically ascends towards and briefly sojourns in the heavens, although it is quite probable that the pilgrim's ascending body is conceived as astral in character.[6] In the Ethiopic Book of Enoch, for example, the heavens are described as a kingdom containing a myriad dwellings and chambers, where the various elements of nature, the angels, God, and the hypostases of morality and knowledge are to be found in peaceful, harmonious coexistence. The view that the elements of nature dwell in closed rooms is associated with the idea that time's cycles are essentially a process whereby departure from a specific place is ultimately followed by return to the very same place.[7]

Another image used for depicting the heavens is that of the Garden of Eden. In this image, the conceptualization of God as revealing himself from Heaven fuses with that of the Garden of Eden as God's primal shrine of Creation. Descriptions of the heavens frequently include individual motifs taken from the description of the Garden of Eden. Less frequently, the Garden as a whole is depicted as a smaller entity within the larger place — the heavens.

In the portrayal of God's revelation in I Enoch, motifs from the Garden of Eden merge with motifs from the architecture of royal palaces. One such passage describes a structure with thick, protecting walls, at the centre of which stands the throne of God; however, the palace also contains rivers and cherubim, derived directly from the conceptualization of God as dwelling in the Garden of Eden.[8] Even the angels guarding the threshold of the palaces in the Merkavah literature remind us of the manner in which the path to the Garden of Eden is barred by a constantly turning sword.[9] That the holy place is surrounded by both a wall and rivers plainly expresses the merging of the concepts of the structure and of the Garden;[10] the wall surrounding the palace is rooted in Ezekiel's vision of the future Temple in Jerusalem.[11]

In several of the testimonies, we sense that these images refer to different literary strata, possibly reflecting various living traditions, some of which give greater prominence to the Garden of Eden or Paradise,[12] while others favour the Temple. By incorporating the Garden of Eden into the heavenly environment, the site of revelation is identified with the site of creation; by incorporating the Temple or the divine palace, that site is also identified with the site of the cult. It would be worth investigating whether the Garden/Paradise conception was the more ancient, and was subordinated following the destruction of the Temple as the need grew to compensate for the loss of the cult, or whether it emerged later in connection with the rejection of the cultic content. Seen from this perspective, it may be that the Pauline allusion to Paradise in 2 Corinthians 12:2 ff expresses rejection of the second branch of the tradition — that associated with the Temple. Likewise, the incident of the four sages who entered *pardes* (BT *Hagiggah* 14b) may derive from the image of the Garden of Eden.[13] On the other hand, there is an essential phenomenological significance to the merging of these two motifs, which may be described as a merging of structured and unstructured — a key attribute of the redemptive time, as I have noted elsewhere.[14]

The concept of holiness underlying this architectural model is one in which the Holy of Holies appears as a centre, an interior, surrounded by a border — walls, rivers, gates, or the threshold. The dual nature of the holy,[15] simultaneously attractive and repellent, is expressed by these two basic elements of the structure. This dual structure already exists in the descriptions of the tabernacle and the Temple, and even in the preparations for the Sinaitic revelation. The drawing of a border around the mountain at Sinai was intended as protection against penetration, against an act of bursting through to the sacred place, which carried with it a mortal danger, whereas the experience of revelation, of contact with the divine, occurred in the centre. This concept finds later expression in the restriction of the realm of the sanctuary and the Temple to Levites and priests, with a special restriction of the Holy of Holies to the high priest.[16]

Essentially, the distinctions between threshold and centre found in the concrete Temple are maintained in the apocalyptic literature, and especially in the Merkavah or Hekhalot literature, the principal collection of written texts of early Jewish mysticism (dating approximately from the first half of the first millennium C.E.). Both emphasize the danger present specifically at the threshold. Apocalyptic literature speaks of a sense of terror in approaching the sanctuary, while the Merkavah literature usually sets guards at the threshold who impose dangerous trials upon those wishing to enter. However, the divine Temple is much more highly structured, from an architectonic point of view, in the Hekhalot literature than in the apocalyptic literature, and this corresponds to a much more structured process of mystical experience, with more closely fit stages. There are well-coordinated relationships between the mystic's religious-spiritual experience and his point of orientation within the architectonic structure.[17] Paralleling the boundary where nobody except the priests is allowed to enter, the threshold is where mystical initiation takes place, expressing the liminal situation of the mystic, with all its fearful and dangerous aspects. By contrast, the centre is the site of the sacrificial cult and, in parallel, of mystical experiences of the revelation of God. The approach of the Merkavah mystic to the sacred centre, the Holy of Holies — the throne, the altar, or the Chariot — is accompanied by metaphors of religious joy and intense ecstasy, stemming from spiritual proximity to God (again, further study as to whether each of the motifs associated with the centre derives from a different literary stream is a desideratum). To be sure, this joy is combined with great agitation, but actual danger is associated more with the stage of entrance, or the threshold.

In the Hekhalot literature, the site of the divine dwelling is perceived almost exclusively as a palace. A striking characteristic in the schematic development of this understanding of the celestial locale is the expanded discussion of the seven temples or palaces. The construction of architectural models in accordance with the principle of the Seven Heavens reflects a pattern originally associated with Judaism's basic organization of time, as well as with several astronomical conceptions current in antiquity.[18] This view may express a wish to correlate the organizational character of time and that of the sacred place.

At the centre of the palace is the Chariot, identified with the immediate presence of the divine throne; other outstanding motifs from the apocalyptic literature are also present — first and foremost that of the Garden — but they are marginalized. Already in the Book of Ezekiel, the Chariot is depicted as a vehicle used to explain sudden transfers from one place to another in the prophetic vision. While serving as the vehicle for the epiphanic God, the Chariot also conveys the prophet from place to place on the face of the earth.[19] In apocalyptic literature, the Chariot is included among the vehicles conveying the mystic from his earthly dwelling to the heavenly place. The function of the Chariot as a means of conveyance becomes somewhat blurred in Merkavah literature, which focusses more on the specific mystical techniques employed for ascent heavenward.[20] From here on, the image of the Chariot serves as the "static" representation of the immediate environment within which God dwells, and primarily of the Throne of God. The hierarchical distinction between the margins and the centre is emphasized, the Chariot constituting the very heart of the mystical vision.[21]

It is interesting to note that the dominant number in all three of these structured systems is four:[22] the Garden of Eden is surrounded by four rivers, the image of the Chariot consists of four creatures, and the palace apparently has four corners. The fourfold pattern is anchored in cosmological concepts, being associated with both time (the seasons of the year) and place (the four compass points). In Judaism this serves as the basic pattern for House and world; the Sanctuary and the Temple are fashioned after it; and its full development is expressed in kabbalah by means of the four letters of the Ineffable Name.

In Early Kabbalah

One way to characterize the initial phase of the kabbalah during the early twelfth century is to say that the concrete entities formerly seen as dwelling with God inside his heavenly house now became symbolic descriptions that could be broken down into seven distinct categories. These are most striking in *Sefer yeẓirah* and in *Sefer ha-bahir*, and in the early kabbalah. The structure is then completed as a decimal form with the addition of the three highest levels. On the one hand, the region wherein God dwells is not described in terms of an actual structure, so that the concept of the spiritual reality is less concrete. On the other hand, the symbolic place expresses God himself, rather than the region in which he dwells or reveals himself. Thus, one might say that the celestial structure undergoes a process of apotheosis, together with a parallel process of either spiritualization or mythologization.[23] In what follows, we shall concentrate upon the former.

Also prominent in the early kabbalah is an emphasis on the parallelism or coordination between heavenly and earthly reality. A striking change occurs in the relationship between the mystic and the supernal place. No longer does the mystic ascend to an actual heavenly world in order to pay a brief visit there and worship God; the sense of the supernal place as an integral, untouched unit has disappeared. Moreover, the central element of devastation has shifted to the celestial world. The major thrust of the spiritual efforts of the mystic now becomes a theurgic attempt to repair the spiritual world, the Heavenly Jerusalem or the Heavenly Temple. The earthly place, the Land of Israel, has no significance — not even as a reflection of the supernal place — as long as the supernal place remains damaged.[24]

In my study of the twelfth- and thirteenth-century kabbalists of Provence and Gerona, I looked at the positions of these thinkers in the context of the shifting theological attitudes towards the Heavenly Jerusalem apparent in late Jewish apocalyptic writings. My analysis led me to suggest that the renewed prominence of the Heavenly Jerusalem among twelfth-century Provence kabbalists may be related, among other things, to the crusades.[25] My research has derived much impetus from the studies of the late Professor Joshua Prawer, in whose memory the gathering that led to this volume was held.[26]

From the point of view of our subject, the transition from ancient Jewish mysticism to the spiritualistic doctrines of the early Provencal and Gerona kabbalists involves a complex change of attitude. On the one hand, the concept of Divinity as place makes the idea of place more symbolic: the understanding of God is symbolic, and the place is one of its symbols. On the other hand, there is intense pressure to establish a complete parallelism and sense of transparency between above and below. The experiential content of "below" is understood as reflecting the "above," so that the Divinity itself, as place, is understood as destroyed, since the lower Temple is destroyed. The ascent to this destroyed place takes place in the mind, by way of a clearly defined process of meditations (*kavvanot*) connected with the Ineffable Name, which sustains the Temple of the Divinity in the thought of the kabbalist. Thus, instead of the accounts found in the Hekhalot literature of the mystic who ascends to the heights to participate in the celestial ritual of worshipping God through song, one finds a ritual marked by meditative and theurgic characteristics. As we shall see, rather than the Divinity being the place to which men ascend, man becomes the place to which the Divinity is brought down.

As the intensity of the discussions revolving around thedeity as place[27] subsides, early kabbalistic thought begins to focus, in two especially salient ways, upon the concept of the deity as time. First, the process of emanation is regarded in terms of a seven-day week, which, in turn, is taken as an expression of the cyclical nature of time.[28] Second, the concept of cosmic cycles becomes increasingly prominent,[29] with every dimension of the deity being identified with a different cosmic cycle.[30] This is an extreme expression of the manner in which spiritual time shapes the understanding of reality.

The most radical early kabbalistic development of the concept of cosmic cycles — that is, of the conception of the laws of time as a controlling element — may be seen in the school of thought that grew up around *Sefer ha-temunah*, "the Book of the Picture," whose title refers both to the image of the deity and to that of the letters of the Torah.[31] Cosmic cycle doctrines emphasize the dimension of existence in time and the aspiration to return to the primal place at the end of time. In the school of *Sefer ha-temunah*, the role of the deity as the primal place to which all is ingathered is vital. The work is primarily concerned not with the question of where God dwells, nor with the identification of the deity with a city or persona. Rather, it represents a totally different model of the primal place, one that does not refrain from using "negative" symbols of the deity,[32] in which the supernal place or the deity is identified as the Dead Sea,[33] as a tomb,[34] as the place in which the yeast is put,[35] as a land that consumes its inhabitants,[36] or as "upper Egypt."[37] The idea of a return to the source is likewise expressed in numerous images relating to storage and containers. The most striking of these is that of the sheath: "Thus, in re-entering their sheath, their unique sheath, the spirits will return to become a part of God, the most majestic Lord."[38] Other key images of return and cyclicality are those of the quarry[39] and of the Divine Breath, in which existence and its destruction are compared to Divine exhalation and inhalation.[40]

In apocalyptic literature, the deity dwells in a specific place which is both the point of departure and the point of return for the sun and moon. In the kabbalah, by contrast, the Divinity, who is both place and time, departs from itself and returns to itself.[41] At the end of each cycle, the entire cosmos returns to the deity; in other words, from the standpoint of redemption, the concrete place ultimately will cancel itself out.[42]

The concepts of repetition and cyclicality are generally connected in kabbalah with the idea of return, not only to a certain state, but also to a certain place — that place being the Divinity. Both the concept of return and that of cyclicality thus have a special connection with the concept of place. Existence is seen as the departure from a primal point, redemption as the return to that very same point.[43] Moreover, the reference, at times, is expressly to a point as the smallest possible unit of space. The return to the One in Neoplatonism is the arithmetic analogue of the geometric image of the point.

Among these kabbalists, the order of time is perceived not only in the sense of a cosmic week, but also in the sense of a *shemittah* — that is, a cosmic cycle or aeon. As I have already noted, images of cyclicality in time are frequently connected with the idea of a primal place that constitutes the point of departure and the point of ingathering of all being — including the Divinity itself, whose *sefirot* return and are incorporated within one another. The absolute return, the ingathering of the Divinity, is portrayed at the end of the greatest cycle of all — the jubilee.

A further focus of return is that level within the Divinity from which the souls come into being. While the body, according to Genesis, may originate from the dust, the origin of the soul lies in God. According to the kabbalists, the soul does not return to heaven or to a Paradise located in heaven; even if we do encounter these terms, they generally constitute symbols for the Divinity itself. The souls are ingathered into the "bundle of life," which corresponds to the *sefira* of *Tiferet*. The destruction of the cosmos at the end of each cycle of time indicates the absolute identity between the dimensions of time and of space within the existence of the world.

In the foregoing paragraphs, we saw that, in the continuum from the Bible through the apocalyptic literature and the Hekhalot literature, the supernal place is identified with two main types of place: the Garden of Eden and the Temple. After analyzing the characteristics of each architectonic structure in itself, we noted the phenomenological significance in principle of the combination of the two. We demonstrated further that the model of place in Hekhalot literature is deeply influenced by models of time, including Judaism's classic sevenfold model, yielding seven palaces. In the transition to early Kabbalah, we saw how the structure that, so to speak, ensconces the Divinity, or God and his Glory, itself becomes God, perceived primarily as seven places, or seven aeons. The perception of the *sefirot* as seven temples, or, more broadly, as seven different places, and their striking apprehension as an order of aeons, thus has a distinct categorical status, consisting of principled forms of organization of symbol systems. The status of these forms is distinct, or higher, or categorically different from that of all the different symbols that constitute the language in which the *sefirot* are depicted.

I have further attempted to describe how certain aspects of

the Divinity as space — such as the supernal Jerusalem — are perceived in a substantive way as lacking completion, and that such descriptions are opposed to descriptions found in earlier mystical doctrines in which the supernal place always incorporates greater beauty and power than the lower place. This is in keeping with the growing tendency to emphasize the precise analogical relationships between above and below in the early Kabbalah.

I now turn to the second focus of this paper, the typology of the relations between the supernal place and the concrete place. Typological discussions of sacred space attempt to identify the source from which the earthly holy place derives its strength — that is, to identify the various ways in which the spiritual place is presented in the concrete holy place.

The essential factor in all types of relationship between the holy and the heavenly place is presence, providing as it does the sacred dimension. Mircea Eliade has argued that the sacred place is connected with a primal story, so that the process of arriving at the sacred place is tantamount to arriving at that place at which "the hierophany repeats itself." In this way, the place becomes an inexhaustible source of power and sacredness, enabling one, simply by entering it, to have a share in that power, to hold communion with sacredness.[44] Eliade's description to a great extent fits the earlier models from ancient Jewish mysticism, in which the place itself is viewed as sacred, so that entering therein implies an immediate participation in its holiness.

Early Jewish mysticism made no claim of an absolute parallel or of a relationship of doubling or reflection between the earthly place and the supernal place.[45] On the contrary, the supernal place contains much more than the earthly place does; that is what makes it special, and what motivates the mystic to ascend heavenward.[46] Similarly, Merkavah literature makes no claim of an identity between the supernal place and the earthly place, whose role as Temple is augmented on high. Accordingly, the purpose of the spiritual ascent is participation in the indescribable heavenly ritual.[47]

As against this, the kabbalists explained the presence of the divine within the holy place by means of various models of relationship between the supernal place and the earthly place. Relating to Eliade's[48] definition of the religious life as being focussed upon processes connected to a sacred geographical centre, Moshe Idel[49] has proposed a distinction between two types of relation to the sacred centre, that of "man being in the centre" and that of "man being the centre." He associates the former with theosophic kabbalah and the latter with ecstatic kabbalah and hasidism. Indeed, this distinction is an important one for the description of Jewish mysticism. In my opinion, however, examples of the religious impulse of "being the centre" exist in theosophic kabbalah as well, via the spiritualistic analogy of the structure and components of the cult to man's body and thoughts. Man becomes the Temple, his heart is the altar, and his meditative activity the fire. Such motifs already occur in the earliest treatises of theosophic kabbalah[50] and continue as late as its eighteenth-century representatives.[51]

In the kabbalah, a common feature of all the various categories of relationship between the earthly and the supernal place is the claim that it is this relationship which imparts a sacred character to the holy place. The kabbalist or mystic often feels, upon entering the holy place, that he must "activate" or "make present" the holiness inherent therein. Revelation or magical activity, however different they are from a typological point of view and from the point of view of the preparatory processes involved, are both a kind of sacred experience or realization of this holiness — the common denominator is the desire to make the holy present.

In the following paragraphs, I shall outline several models of the relationship between earthly and supernal place in early kabbalistic thought, invoked through the use either of striking metaphors or of conceptual formulations. Note, however, that a given metaphor does not always stand for the same religious model; my present remarks refer to specific kabbalistic movements of which the metaphorical expressions discussed here are characteristic, reflecting the terminology and language of the school in question. Moreover, no particular model may be attributed exclusively to a single school. Various conflicting explanations exist simultaneously, sometimes even in the writings of the same kabbalist. At times, a given model, such as that of the exile of the Shekhinah, may be strengthened and stressed over the course of generations.

(1) *The principle of the mirror, the picture or the reflection:* This principle occurs in the writings of R. Moses Nahmanides (1194–1270), generally in connection with the metaphor of the

"image." It corresponds to another Nahmanidean principle, that of "double things" or "double for counsel" — that is, the substantive parallel between the upper world and the lower world.[52] Nahmanides applied the principle of "imaging" to the realms of sacred text,[53] holy time,[54] and holy place.[55] In line with this principle, to enter a "concrete" holy place — the Tabernacle, the Temple, the Garden of Eden, or even the Land of Israel as a whole — is to enter into a concrete picture of a celestial spiritual place. By studying the concrete pictures, one may come to understand the celestial pictures.[56] Such a relationship is at times linked to a visual mystical experience.

(2) *The principle of the container or vessel:* In this model, also used by Nahmanides and by others, the holy place is the vessel for the spiritual inspiration that descends from the celestial place — a view that has clear points of contact with magic and astrology.[57] There are several different versions of this approach. They generally pose a time factor as well, by which alone the potential holiness in the holy place is activated or completely fulfilled. That is, the esoteric knowledge relates to when it is correct to be or to act in the holy place.

Both of the above principles are related to an ontological conception of the sacred. There is an additional development towards a dualistic approach, according to which there are two types of heavenly place, sacred and profane, the latter containing the stars and the ghosts. According to this view, there are also two types of worship: internal and external — that is, within the Temple and outside its boundaries. A striking example of external worship in Nahmanides' *Commentary* is the ritual of the scapegoat.[58] According to Nahmanides, a place is either sacred or profane. The Holy Land, which serves as a model for a divine territory, attracts holiness and rejects or vomits out the profane.[59] The motif of vomiting is connected to the terrifying dimension embodied in holiness.[60] Nahmanides uses images that refer clearly both to the attraction of holiness and to the rejection — through vomiting — of the profane by the sacred.

(3) *The principle of man:* This view is closely connected with the ancient perception of the Temple as the structure in which the cult is conducted or in which God is revealed. Man, as the smallest unit of place, is analogized to the holiest unit of place — the Temple — or to God in the image of a man, an image occurring,

for example, in the description of the corpus of God (*Shi'ur qoma*) in the Merkavah literature. Alternatively, the organs of the human being may be analogized to an architectonic structure, that of the Temple — that is, each human organ is envisioned as corresponding to an architectonic or cultic element, a motif emphasized in the *Tiqqunei zohar* and *Ra'aya mehemana*.[61] Man is thus perceived as a miniature temple, in whom the sacrificial service or the revelation takes place. The cultic or sacrificial conception takes three main directions: the ethical direction, in which the refinement of the passions and of bad character traits are understood as the destruction of the animal element within man;[62] the direction of mystical union (*devequt*), in which the sacrificial fire is interpreted in terms of the soul approaching God and being caught up within him[63] (in Hebrew, the words for "sacrifice" and "to come close" are derived from the same semantic root: *qrv*); and the theurgic direction, in which man views himself as building the supernal Temple through a process of meditation.[64] The revelatory conception stresses the quest for ecstatic phenomena of vision or speech, in which man is the vessel drawing spirituality towards himself.[65] In many allegorical or symbolic expositions of this model, the human heart is equated, from the cultic perspective, with the altar,[66] while from the revelatory perspective it is seen as a tablet.[67]

These conceptions are not contradictory, and may co-exist within the same framework, usually as two stages within the mystical experience itself, in which the process of purification (the cult) precedes that of revelation, or in which theurgic *devequt* anticipates the inflow of the divine flux.

In ancient Jewish mysticism, as we saw, man vaults up to heaven, God's holy dwelling place, with the goal of attaining an ecstatic experience and revelation. By contrast, in this model — which was expounded, among others, by Abraham Abulafia (1240–1291), the chief representative of the school of ecstatic kabbalah — man turns himself into the holy place, bringing revelation down into himself. This model is also to be found in "theosophic" kabbalah.[68]

(4) *The world as prison:* According to this view, the divine presence is imprisoned, during the exile of the Jewish people, in the profane, unholy place. Thus, paradoxically, the holy is present on the unholy side of the concrete place. What we have here is the well-known gnostic view of the world as one large prison: the spiritual is trapped

within the physical, the soul within the body, and divinity within the world. This motif, which finds its extreme Jewish expression in Lurianic kabbalah as well as in Hasidism, is already to be found in early kabbalistic thought.[69]

(5) *One place at the end of days:* An additional aspect of Abraham Abulafia's approach to place parallels his approach to text.[70] In the same way as he does not seek two levels of meaning in the text, so does he understand the time of redemption as that in which the distinction between corporeal and spiritual will disappear, even within the realm of place. This view is the diametrical opposite of those approaches that posit a basic duality — whether of complementarity or of antagonism — between the earthly and the supernal place. Its proponents regard duality itself as a sign of exilic existence. This idea has its origins in the prediction that the heavenly Jerusalem will descend to earth in the messianic period, or, conversely, the earthly Jerusalem will ascend heavenward.[71] In his *Sefer ha-ot* ("Book of the Sign"), which contains his messianic visions, Abulafia expresses this idea in more spiritual form:

> The coming day is the Day of Judgment / the Day of Remembrance to be called. / The time of reckoning has arrived / and the End has come full. / The heavens shall be earth / and the earth shall be heavenly.[72]

(6) *The principle of the mask or facade:* The extreme expression of this position reappears in the parable of the walls by the Baal Shem Tov (R. Israel b. Eliezer, 1698–1760), which exists in several versions. In an image drawn from the world of Merkavah literature, God is depicted as dwelling within the structure of the Hekhalot: the king is seated in his palace and appears to be surrounded by iron walls and barriers. However, upon approaching the king, the individual becomes aware that the walls do not really exist and are merely a facade concealing the essence of God.[73]

> The parable is of a king who made several barriers before his palace by means of magic so that no one could come to him; and he hid himself there, and made walls and fire and rivers, all by means of illusion, before his sons. But one of them, who was wise, spoke thus: How is it possible that this merciful father

> should not wish to show his face to his beloved children? Surely this is nothing more than sleight of hand, and the father wishes to test whether his son will attempt to come to him, but in fact there is no hiddenness there. And behold, as soon as he risked walking in the river, the illusion disappeared, and he crossed it; and so with all the other barriers, until he came to the palace of the king. But there was also a fool, who saw and turned back because of the walls and the fire; and the object of this homily is clear.[74]

Of course, this approach is not concerned with the conceptualization of place, but with the sense of God's concealment. In this context, place is a metaphor for the disruptive element which, like all vessels, must fall away and disappear. The earthly place is a barrier to the perception of the genuine supernal place that is present. In a number of hasidic works, the experience of concealment is associated with parables of place. Another outstanding example appears in *Yosher divrei emet* by R. Meshullam Feibush of Zbarazh (second half of the eighteenth century):

> And God, may he be blessed, prepared me a true homily concerning this. A person is travelling on the road in a carriage and falls asleep, while the wagoner who is with him ascends a high mountain, and afterwards, when he comes to the [top of the] mountain, the road is flat, because he has already passed the steep incline. Afterwards, should the person who was sleeping wake up and be told that he is on the mountain, he would not believe it, because he does not see any sign, for had he seen the slope upon which they travelled at the beginning and ascended it, he would have known .... But how can he know afterwards? When he descends the mountain on the other side that goes down from the mountain to the valley, he will discern that beforehand he was on the mountain.[75]

The Journey to the Holy Centre, the Impure Centre, or the Lost Focus

Let us look briefly at the relationship between the theoretical conceptualization of the holy place and the concrete steps its proponents may take in reality, by undertaking a journey towards the holy place. That undertaking has two basic forms in Jewish mysticism: (a) a journey by the individual to the Land of Israel in order to live there, to die there, or to visit there as a pilgrim;[76] (b) a journey towards a centre constituted by a figure seen as messianic, or as having a destiny connected with redemption.

As we have seen, the outstanding spokesman within the kabbalah for the conceptualization of the holy place as the "depiction of things" (*ẓiyyurei devarim*), or as a receptacle bearing ontic holiness, was Nahmanides. At the end of his life, acting on this conception, he went to live in the Land of Israel.[77] Indeed, such a view fosters pilgrimage to the holy place. By contrast, exponents of the conceptualization of man himself as the locus of holiness are more likely to forgo the journey to a specific place and concentrate upon altering themselves so as to become more worthy. As we have seen, this view also finds expression in early kabbalah, in the analogization of the Temple as a holy place, and the sacrificial cult practiced therein, to ethical purification and mystical experience. Outstanding representatives of this conception in early kabbalah are R. Ezra and R. Azriel of Gerona. It was discussed widely in the Gerona circle and among those kabbalists who were influenced by it, and by the circle of Nahmanides.[78]

The spiritualization of the holy place and the emphasis upon man as centre are thus represented both in theosophic kabbalah, as we have shown, and in ecstatic kabbalah, as has been noted by Moshe Idel. Nevertheless, R. Abraham Abulafia went to see the Pope — an act belonging to an additional category of events along the axis of space, that of rites and acts of initiation[79] connected with a specific place, and usually associated with messianic aspirations. Abraham Abulafia,[80] R. Solomon Molcho (1500–1532),[81] the Baal Shem Tov,[82] Sabbatai Zevi (1626–1676),[83] and R. Nahman of Braslav (1772–1810)[84] all focus on the attraction of a specific place — whether it be the seat of the Pope or the Land of Israel — connected with the performance of a ritual that is essential to paving the way, within the realm of time, for the advent of the Messiah.

Not only the conceptualization of spiritual place or spiritual time is significant, but also the sense of time[85] and the sense of place. A sense of obstruction on the axis of place may lead to intensive treatment of the supernal place — the heaven above — or to intensive expectations of the end of time, or both. Conversely, a sense of time coming to an end often motivates journeys towards places — either impure places, in order to destroy them, or sacred places, in order to perform rites of initiation in them, and thereby accomplish the End of Days. I am referring here not only to journeys in the external sense, but also to inner journeys. On an ideal pilgrimage, there is a complete correspondence between the pace of progress in time and in place, and the sense of these two dimensions.

The ability to feel place as time, or to feel time as place, is one of the most important characteristics of the religious experience at its peak. The rhythms of the combination of time and space are connected with states of redemption — whether at the End of Days or in the course of religious experience. I have attempted to show that in those states of elevation for which the religious soul yearns, the two dimensions are depicted as two aspects of a single unity — whether time is described as residing within place and striving for place, or place is described as once again becoming "time."

Translated from the Hebrew by Jonathan Chipman.

Notes

1. I have discussed elsewhere the question of mystical approaches to time, in the context of Nahmanides' doctrine of cosmic cycles. See H. Pedaya, "Time, Will and Elevation in Nahmanides' Kabbalah in Light of the Doctrine of *Shemittot*," M.A. Thesis, Hebrew University of Jerusalem, 1980 (in Hebrew, forthcoming).
2. Our discussion here is limited to biblical concepts relevant to the development of Jewish mysticism.
3. Ex 19:16–18; 1 Kgs 19:11–12. Exceptions to this pattern are revelations to an individual in a dream or vision, such as occur in the Book of Genesis or in the revelation to Balaam (Num 23–24).
4. Already in the version of the Sinaitic revelation in Exodus 24 there is an allusion to the vision of God in the form of a man: "and under His feet ..." Moreover, the image of the footstool and "under his feet the like of a paved work of sapphire stone" (v. 10) prefigures the image of the throne (see B. Uffenheimer, *Ancient Prophecy in Israel* [in Hebrew], Jerusalem 1973, pp. 100–101) — that is, an anthropomorphic image of God in the form of a seated human figure. Another allusion to the throne occurs in Ex 17:16 — "The hand upon the throne of the Lord" — although not within the context of theophany. Isaiah's call to prophecy is rooted in a vision: "I saw the Lord sitting upon a throne, high and lifted up" (Isa 6:1); cf. Isa 66:1, 1 Kgs 22:19 and 2 Chr 18:18. The throne is generally located in the Temple (Isa 6:1); on whether this was the earthly or heavenly Temple see V. Aptowitzer, "The Heavenly Temple According to the Aggadah" (in Hebrew), *Tarbiz* II (1931), pp. 137–153, 257–287. In Ezekiel, the Throne revelation is connected with the

vision of the Merkavah, the divine Chariot. True, the Chariot is fundamentally a vehicle of travel, opposed to the image of the stable house. However, in this context, it is used to stress the mobility of God and to provide a framework for his revelation to the prophet living in exile following the destruction of the Temple (cf. Y. Kaufmann, *History of Israelite Religion* [in Hebrew], III, Bk. 2, Jerusalem–Tel Aviv 1967, pp. 543–547). The vision of the Chariot is hierarchical, advancing by degree to the vision of the throne upon which God is seated in the image of a man (Ezek 1:26; cf. Ezek 10:1; 43:7). However, the eschatological reference to the Throne (43:7) takes place within a vision of the Temple. The visions of the Merkavah mystics focus on the image of God upon a throne. See G. Scholem, *Major Trends in Jewish Mysticism*, New York 1961, pp. 43 and 49.

5. I. Chernus, "The Pilgrimage to the Merkavah: An Interpretation of Early Jewish Mysticism," in J. Dan (ed.), *Proceedings of the First International Conference on the History of Jewish Mysticism: Early Jewish Mysticism* (*Jerusalem Studies in Jewish Thought*, VI: 1–2), Jerusalem 1987, pp. 1–35. Applying the concepts of "liminality" and "anti-structure" as developed by Victor Turner, Chernus suggests that the ecstatic "journeys" of the Merkavah mystics, as recorded in the Hekhalot texts, are to be understood as analogues of the phenomenon of pilgrimage.
6. The experiences of the Merkavah mystics are often regarded as happening to the "soul." In my opinion, it is more appropriate to speak here of an astral body, a possibility raised by Moshe Idel in connection with the description of "double-presence" of R. Nehunyah ben Hakanah (M. Idel, "Appendix: On the Artifical Anthropoid" in his *Golem: Jewish Magical and Mystical Traditions*, New York 1990, pp. 285–286). In most of this literature, the language used to describe the general ascent includes concrete descriptions of the entire body, such as the right hand, the left hand, the heart, the experience of falling, shaking and trembling, supplying oneself with seals, etc. On this see H. Pedaya, "Seeing, Falling, Song: The Longing to See God and the Spiritual Element in Early Jewish Mysticism," in M. Benayahu (ed.), *Asufot*, VIII (in Hebrew, forthcoming). Prof. Yehudah Leibes noted in a private conversation that this may be the meaning of the saying of Paul in II Corinthians 12:2ff.: "I knew a man in Christ who fourteen years — whether in the body or out of it, I do not know; God knows — was caught up as far as the third heaven. And I knew that this same man — whether in the body or out of it, I do not know; God knows — was caught up into paradise."
7. "And I saw the chambers of the sun and moon, whence they proceed and whither they come again, and their glorious return," I Enoch 41:5–6; "And thence comes forth hoar-frost, and days, seasons and years pass way," *ibid.*, 77:4–5 (R. Charles, *The Apocrypha and Pseudepigrapha of the Old Testament*, II, Oxford 1966, pp. 212 and 243).
8. I Enoch 14:11–12 (Charles, *Apocrypha*, p. 197).
9. The guards of the door of the sixth temple chamber punish whoever is unworthy by slaughtering him or breaking his head with iron cutters; see J. Dan, "The Entrance to the Sixth Gate" (in Hebrew), in idem, *Proceedings* (above, note 5), pp. 197–220. The Hebrew word *lahat* in Gen. 3:24 may refer to the blade of the sword, but it also connotes fire and may be connected with the motif of throwing into the coals in the Hekhalot literature.

10. The rivers surrounding the Garden of Eden fulfill a function parallel to that of the wall surrounding the Temple: a periphery which protects the inside. The former image draws more upon nature — even domesticated nature — while the second draws more upon the idea of the "house."
11. For an interesting approach to Ezekiel's vision, within the framework of a larger discussion of architectonic structures and how they reflect the understanding of the sacred realm, see J. Z. Smith, *To Take Place*, Chicago–London 1987, pp. 47–50. See also David Flusser's discussion of the influence of Ezekiel 48 on the visions of Jerusalem at the End of Days, in "*Pesher Yeshayahu* and the Idea of the Twelve Apostles in Early Christianity," *Jewish Sources in Early Christianity* (in Hebrew), Tel Aviv 1982–3, p. 289.
12. A striking example appears in another vision, from which it follows that God dwells and reveals himself from above the Tree of Life in the Garden of Eden. On the Garden of Eden as a real place in heaven, see 2 Enoch 8–9 (Charles, *Apocrypha*, p. 434); 2 Corinthians 12:2–4; Apocalypse of Moses 38:4. See also I. Gruenwald, *Apocalyptic and Merkavah Mysticism*, Leiden–Kouln 1980, pp. 49–50.
13. See G. Scholem, *Jewish Gnosticism, Merkabah Mysticism and the Talmudic Tradition*, New York 1965, p. 16; idem, *Major Trends* (above, note 4), p. 51; E.E. Urbach, "The Traditions of an Esoteric Doctrine in the Tannaitic Period," in *Studies in Mysticism and Religion Presented to G.G. Scholem*, Jerusalem 1968, Hebrew Section, p. 13.
14. In my article, "From the Margin to the Center" (forthcoming).
15. R. Otto, *The Idea of the Holy*, New York 1958, pp. 12–30.
16. For a general discussion of the holy as centre in the Jewish view of the altar, the Temple, and the land, see J.Z. Smith, *Map Is Not Territory* (Studies in Judaism in Late Antiquity, 23), Leiden 1978, pp. 112–115; cf. M.A. Fishbane, "The Sacred Center: The Symbolic Structure of the Bible," in M. Fishbane and P. Flohr (eds.), *Texts and Responses*, Leiden 1975, pp. 6–27; H. Pedaya, "From the Margin to the Center" (above, note 14).
17. I have discussed these processes at length in "The Impulse to See God" (above, note 6); and cf. Pedaya, "From the Margin to the Center" (above, note 14).
18. We still need to determine the extent to which the septimal structure is connected with astronomic and astrological views, such as the theories of Ptolemaeus; see J.L.E. Dreyer, *A History of Astronomy from Thales to Kepler*, New York 1953, pp. 149–206; S. Sambursky, *The Laws of Heaven and Earth* (in Hebrew), Jerusalem 1954, pp. 65–71.
19. God's appearance upon the Chariot occurs four times in the Book of Ezekiel (Ezek. 1; 3:23; 8–10; 43–44). These are always connected with movements of God or of the prophet from place to place. See Kaufmann, *History* (above, note 4), pp. 488–490 and the notes there, and pp. 505, 543–547: "Ezekiel is in Exile, upon 'impure land' outside of the lands of prophecy. For this reason, he sees God coming to him from a distance to sanctify him as a prophet, from whence the motif of revelation of God in a chariot" (p. 544). Compare also Kaufmann's discussion of the ark and the cherubim as elements of the Israelite cult, pp. 349–354.
20. For a description of the various images for ascent, see Gruenwald, *Mysticism* (above, note 12), pp. 119–123. We must distinguish between the mystical

techniques and the actual forms of ascent: ascent *per se* is not a mystical technique, but is already part of the experience itself. There are also descriptions of ascent via the Chariot: cf. *Hekhalot rabbati* 22:1–2, in Wertheimer (ed.), *Batei Midrashot*, Jerusalem 1989, p. 100; P. Schaufer, *Hekalot Studien*, Tuubingen 1988, sect. 236.

21. The centrality of the Chariot is also to be seen as a continuation of the idea that revelation occurs in the Holy of Holies, the place of the ark, and of the conception of the cherubim upon the ark as the place where God dwells.
22. On the dominance of the pattern of four in the Merkavah vision of Ezekiel and its cosmic significance, see Kaufmann, *History* (above, note 4), pp. 545–546.
23. In general, one may say that the spiritualistic tendency was primarily represented in early kabbalah by the circle of R. Isaac the Blind (ca. 1160–1235) and the mythical tendency by the circle of the *Zohar* (late thirteenth century). The latter tendency has been given a comprehensive treatment by Yehudah Liebes, "The Messiah of the Zohar" (in Hebrew), in *The Messianic Idea in Israel*, Jerusalem 1982, pp. 87–236 (an abridged English translation appears in his *Studies in the Zohar*, Albany, N.Y., 1993, pp. 1–84). Liebes discusses a mystical experience, one of whose symbolic expressions is the union of the mystic tsaddik with the Shekhinah, the Divine Jerusalem.
24. H. Pedaya, "Land of Spirit and Land of Reality: R. Ezra, R. Azriel and Nahmanides," in M. Halamish & A. Ravitzky (eds.), *The Land of Israel in Medieval Jewish Thought* (in Hebrew), Jerusalem 1991, pp. 233–289, esp. pp. 247–251, and see below, note 67.
25. H. Pedaya, "'Flaw' and 'Correction' in the Concept of the Divinity in the Teachings of R. Isaac the Blind" (in Hebrew), in J. Dan (ed.), *Proceedings of the Second International Congress on the History of Jewish Mysticism: Jewish Mysticism in Europe* (*Jerusalem Studies in Jewish Thought*, VI), Jerusalem 1987, pp. 271–274.
26. J. Prawer, "Jerusalem in the Jewish and Christian Perspectives of the Early Middle Ages," in *Settimani di studi sull' alto medio evo*, Spoleto 1980; idem, "Christianity between Heavenly and Earthly Jerusalem" (in Hebrew), in Y. Aviram (ed.), *Jerusalem through the Ages*, Jerusalem 1969, pp. 179–192; idem, *The Latin Kingdom of Jerusalem*, London 1972.
27. An interesting point of transition occurs in the commentary of R. Judah al-Bargeloni (b. 1043) to *Sefer Yezirah*, constituting a kind of proto-kabbalistic link, in which the Shekhinah is identified as the site of the world: "... the body of the world itself is the Indwelling [Shekhinah] of the Creator of the Universe and His Glory, and the holy sanctuary of above, because He is the place of the world, and the world is not His place..." — ed. Halberstam, Jerusalem 1970 (facsimile of the Berlin edition of 1855), pp. 231–233. Cf. Pedaya, "Flaw and Correction" (above, note 25), pp. 221–227.
28. For example, the *sefirot* are described as "the order of time." See Nahmanides on Gen 1:3: "And know that the days mentioned in the Account of the Creation ... in the inner meaning of the thing [are] the *sefirot* which are emanated from the Almighty, called days, because each [Divine] utterance that brought about a particular being is called a day ..." R. Ezra of Gerona (d. 1245) wrote in his *Perush shir ha-shirim*: "and from there it was separated and it became four streams. It

speaks in a language of that which is present and exists in every time ... Secrets of the acts of Creation: ... one day — everything was still unique, because all this was through the expansion of being" (in *Kitvei ha-Ramban*, II, ed. Chavell, Jerusalem 1964, pp. 498, 505–512).

29. Allusions to the doctrine of cosmic cycles appear in early kabbalah in the circle of R. Isaac the Blind, and it was clearly current among the Gerona kabbalists who were considered his disciples, notably R. Azriel (early thirteenth century) and R. Ezra, as well as in the thought R. Moses Nahmanides — whose intellectual sources were in northern France — and of R. Jacob ben Sheshet (early thirteenth century).
30. This opening is particularly characteristic of the circle of *Sefer ha-temunah*, an anonymous work of unknown provenance, evidently composed no earlier than the fourteenth century, Jerusalem 1984 (facsimile of the Lemberg edition of 1892).
31. The book's title reflects the view that the visual appearance of the letters of the Torah are like a picture which elucidates processes within the Divinity, in the world and in history.
32. See H. Pedaya, "Shabbat, Shabbetai and the Diminution of the Moon: Sabbath, Sign and Image," in idem (ed.), *Myth in Judaism = Eshel Beer Sheva*, III (1966), p. 5, and notes 7 and 8.
33. *Ibid.*, 60a, on the letter *qof*: "For in it are locked all the gates, *shemittot* and jubilees and days, all of them to the highest gate, where there is the power of the Sea of Salt, the supreme jubilee, in which all the palaces are closed, both upper and lower ..." Cf. 25b: "And the final *nun* has not been perceived by any eye, for it is hidden from all; and it is the secret of the Sea of Salt, the long, hidden and final jubilee." For more on the Sea of Salt (i.e., the Dead Sea), see 23b, 54b.
34. *Ibid.*, 60b: "This letter (*resh*) is a hidden secret, the supernal world, to be an inheritance to the souls from the beginning of emanation, where is hidden and buried the light of the first day with his partner, 'for there I buried Leah.'" 61a: "And in the future Rachel will be within, and Leah in her place at the gate, for all will return to its sheath, and the sheath to another sheath, and Rachel will be buried and hidden away alive ..."
35. *Ibid.*, 40a: "And these ways are many and wonderful, which are all covered up, all come from the attribute, its Torah and law in its time, for it is the source of all the yeasts."
36. *Ibid.*, 71b: "And if his perception is not complete — it is better that he distance himself and not draw near to the holy within, and not die, for it is a land that consumes its inhabitants."
37. *Ibid.*, 48a: "And from there these 'names of the children of Israel who go to Egypt,' the supernal Egypt, and there those who are exhausted shall rest, and these are the children of the living God." 31b: "And the exodus of the souls from the supernal Egypt, with severe judgments and fears."
38. *Ibid.*, 41a: "And all the supernal kingdoms were gathered in one case in the name of God, all together..." 58b: "and so the singers, and so in the angel and the star — all will return to its sheath, for it will ascend via its borders." Cf. 67b, 68b.
39. *Ibid.*, 33a: "And the journeys at the end allude to the journeys of the souls and

the holy and perfect spirits, who ascend higher and higher to the quarry of all." 57a–b: "That all will return, all of them to their quarry, lights and souls; therefore all of the exiles, being the supreme part with them, will all return to their quarry from which comes all."

40. *Ibid.*, 44b: "For all will return to the first redeemer, who redeemed all in peace, and he who was sold shall be redeemed, 'in the jubilee they shall all go out,' which are the days of the supreme Messiah, 'when the captivity of Egypt shall return,' and not her nation; and then all shall ascend to the place of its emanation, where is its place, as Solomon wrote in his wisdom seven vanities, corresponding to the *shemittot*, and their abolition in the supernal vanity ... ."
41. In this context, it is interesting that the centrality of the symbolism of the sun and moon for the Divinity stands out most strongly in the early kabbalah, with its clear affinity to ancient Jewish mysticism — for example, in *Sefer ha-bahir*, in the circle of Nahmanides, and in the *Zohar*. Later on this symbolism was pushed aside, though it emerged again in Safed under the influence of the doctine of *shemittot*, in the circle of R. Moses Cordovero. See Pedaya, "Shabbat, Shabbetai" (above, note 32), and the Diminution of the Moon: Sabbath, Sign and Image," in idem (ed.), *Myth in Judaism = Eshel Beer Sheva*, III (1966).
42. Compare E. Gottleib, *Studies in Kabbalistic Literature* (in Hebrew), Tel Aviv 1976, pp. 24–25.
43. Mircea Eliade sees in the very act of defining a holy place a reflection of the longing to return to the holiness once present in that place (*Patterns in Comparative Religion*, London–New York 1958, p. 368). In practice, the principle of return is central to most of the patterns Eliade suggests, in the areas of myth, ritual, place and time.
44. Compare also M. Himmelfarb, "From Prophecy to Apocalypse: The *Book of the Watchers* and Tours of Heaven," in A. Green (ed.), *Jewish Spirituality from the Bible Through the Middle Ages* (World Spirituality, 13), New York 1986, pp. 145–165.
45. The superlative aspect stands out in apocalyptic literature, first and foremost in the description of God (I Enoch 14:3–15: "And it was most high in its great glory and honor and greatness, until one could not describe to you its glory and greatness"), but see, for example, I Enoch 17:5–6 (Charles, *Apocrypha*, p. 199): "And I came to a river of fire in which the fire flows like water and discharges itself into the great sea ... I saw the great rivers and came to the great river and to the great darkness." Or, for example, 18:11 (p. 200): "And I saw a deep abyss, with columns of heavenly fire, and among them I saw columns of fire fall, which were beyond measure like towards the height and towards the depth." Cf. also 24:4. Expressions of magnitude — e.g., glorious, colourful, awesome, uninterrupted, constant, endless, very beautiful, precious, to afar, miracle, great and wondrous miracles, to know all — are used widely throughout this literature. All these indicate that the key to understanding the whole and gaining a proper persective concerning time, nature, life and death, reward and punishment does not lie only in the heavens; however, the celestial scenery is distinguished by rarity, difference, sublime beauty and power, whose like cannot be found in this world.
46. One of the main venues for this "much more" in Hekhalot literature is participation in the heavenly cult. The recitation of song and praise by the

Merkavah mystic is superior to that of the angels who respond to him. In the semantic realm, the divine power is expressed not only by dwelling on the beauty and dimensions of the Divinity, as in the apocalyptic literature, but also by the tireless pursuit of adjectives for glorifying and praising God, His beauty and His properties, which are a main component of the Merkavah hymns. See also R. Elior, "The Concept of God in Hekhalot Mysticism" (in Hebrew), in Dan (ed.), *Proceedings: Early Jewish Mysticism* (above, note 5), pp. 13–64.

47. Eliade, *Patterns* (above, note 43), p. 368.
48. M. Eliade, *Images and Symbols*, New York 1969, p. 55; idem, *The Sacred and the Profane*, New York, 1961, p. 65.
49. See M. Idel, "The Land of Israel in Jewish Mystical Thought" (in Hebrew), in Halamish & Ravitzky, *The Land of Israel* (above, note 24), pp. 207–208, 211.
50. I have discussed the ecstatic aspect and the relationship of theosophic kabbalah to Sufi mysticism in H. Pedaya, "'Possessed by Speech': The Prophetic Ecstatic Model in the Early Kabbalists and Its Relation to Sufic Jewish Mysticism," *Tarbiz*, LXV (in Hebrew, forthcoming); on the theurgic aspect, see Pedaya, "Land of Spirit" (above, note 24), pp. 243–244, 256–257.
51. See R. Hayyim of Volozhin (1749–1821), *Nefesh ha-ḥayyim*, ed. Rubin, Benei Berak 1989, Part I, Chap. 4, pp. 6–10, and see below, note 62. R. Isaiah ha-Levi Horwitz refers to this important theosophic-kabbalistic passage in his *Shenei luḥot ha-berit*; cf. R. Abraham Noah Heller of Zbarazh, *Zerizuta de-Avraham*, New York 1952, p. 2a.
52. "Scripture speaks of the lower realms and alludes to the upper ones" (Nahmanides, commentary on Gen 1:1; ed. Chavell, p. 15). See also E. R. Wolfson, "By Way of Truth: Aspects of Nahmanides' Kabbalistic Hermeneutic," *AJS Review*, XIV (1989), pp. 110–114; and Pedaya, "Land of Spirit" (above, note 24), pp. 270–277.
53. Nahmanides alludes to the understanding of the Torah as "depictions of the things" (*ẓiyyurei devarim*) in the Introduction to his *Commentary* on the Torah, where he notes that all human knowledge is learned from the Torah. The visual appearance, the form of the letters, is thus one of the keys to exegesis. See on this H. Pedaya, "Picture and Image in Nahmanides' Exegesis" (in Hebrew), *Mahanayim* 6 (1994).
54. See A. Funkenstein, "Nahmanides' Symbolic Reading of History," in J. Dan & F. Talmage (eds.), *Studies in Jewish Mysticism*, Cambridge, Mass., 1982, pp. 129–150.
55. In *Sha'ar ha-gemul*, Nahmanides writes that the Garden of Eden, the Land of Israel and Jerusalem are places in which God draws the "supernal world ... in corporeal images," that these are "honorable places set aside for prophecy," and that the people who live there are "learned in the depictions of the things of all the supernal secrets" (*Kitvei ha-Ramban*, II, p. 296). Nahmanides's disciple, R. Joshua ibn Shuaib (late thirteenth century), writes in his *Derashot 'al ha-torah*: "The images of the Tabernacle are like the images of the spiritual beings" (Cracow 1573, p. 30b). See Pedaya, "Land of Spirit" (above, note 24), pp. 278–280; Eliade, *Patterns* (above, note 43), p. 373. Cf. note 53 above.
56. Medieval approaches to study, such as that practiced by the twelfth-century Christian school of the Victorian biblical exegetes, often required the imagination

of specific pictures, in relation to which the text is no more than an illustration and commentary. See B. Smalley, *The Study of the Bible in the Middle Ages*, Oxford 1982, pp. 95–97. In Pedaya, "Picture and Image" (above, note 53) I note the parallels between the hermeneutic approach of Nahmanides and the approach and terminology of Hugo of St. Victor.

57. In the writings of Nahmanides, this approach is represented by the expression "the power of the upper [realms] in the lower [ones]" ("Sermon on Kohelet," *Kitvei ha-Ramban*, ed. Chavell, p. 200; "Sermon for Rosh Hashanah," *ibid.*, p. 250), while Abraham ibn Ezra (1089–1165) speaks of "the power of receiving according to the place" (Commentary on Deut. 31:16). On Nahmanides see Pedaya, "Land of Spirit" (above, note 24), p. 266, note 132; on Ibn Ezra cf. Dov Schwartz, "The Land of Israel in the Fourteenth Century Jewish Neoplatonic School" (in Hebrew), in Halamish & Ravitzky, *The Land of Israel* (above, n. 23), pp. 138–150.
58. See Nahmanides, commentary on Lev 16:8.
59. See *ibid.*, Lev 26:11 (ed. Chavell, p. 184): "But this matter is one of the secrets of the Torah; he said that He would place His indwelling among us, and the soul — from which the indwelling comes — will not abominate us." We may infer that he understood the terms *mishkan* and *nefesh* ("indwelling" and "soul") esoterically, as alluding to two levels within the Divinity. The "indwelling" is the Shekhinah, while the "soul" alludes to a higher dimension — possibly *Binah*. The place of God among human beings can only be maintained as long as the spirit of God does not expel or reject the people. Cf. the "Sermon on Kohelet," (loc. cit., above, note 57): "Scripture says concerning sexual immorality: "and the land is defiled; therefore I do visit the iniquity thereof upon it, and the land itself vomits out its inhabitants" [Lev 18:25]. "[Scripture] was particularly strict concerning the practice of sexual immorality within the Land, as it becomes defiled and vomits out those who practice it"; and cf. Nahmanides' commentary on Lev. 18:25.
60. Aviezer Ravitzky discussed an aspect of this subject in relation to attitutes toward Zionism in his paper presented at the conference on "Sacred Space" on which this volume is based.
61. This conception, already represented in rabbinic midrashim such as *Pirkei de-rabbi Eliezer*, underlies several kabbalistic sayings, though it is not always stated explicitly. See, for example: "Come and see: When the Holy One blessed be He created man in the world, He made him like the model of the supernal honorable ones, and give him strength and force in the middle of his body, where there resides the heart ... And in this manner the Holy One blessed be He created His world ... and the Sanctuary surrounds the Holy of Holies, where there dwells the Shekhinah and the kaporeth and the cherubs and the ark, and that is the heart of all the land and of the world ...," *Zohar* III:161a–b. The *Zohar* is attributed by contemporary scholarship to the Castillian kabbalist Moses de Leon (ca. 1240–1305) or to a circle to which he belonged. See Y. Liebes, "How the *Zohar* was Written" (in Hebrew), in Y. Dan (ed.), *The Age of the Zohar* (Jerusalem Studies in Jewish Thought, 8), Jerusalem 1989, pp. 1–71.
62. See Hayyim of Volozhin, *Nefesh ha-ḥayyim* (above, note 51): "Every sin which a

Jewish person performs brings into his heart a strange fire, Heaven forbid, of anger or other evil lusts, Heaven forbid. Is this not like the matter that was written (Isa 64:10): 'Our holy and beautiful house ... is burned with fire'?" (Chap. 4, p. 8). "... If he sanctifies himself properly in the fulfillment of all the commandments ... then he himself is literally the Temple, and God, may His Name be blessed, is inside him" (p. 9). "... To purify all his limbs from head to feet ... and these are the hoof-marks of the animal soul" (Chap. 20, p. 69). Cf. Nahmanides, commentary on Lev 1:9 (ed. Chavell, p. 12), which gives a spiritualistic-ethical interpretation of the act of sacrifice, without incorporating it into the kabbalistic dimension.

63. On the sacrifice as *devequt*, modelling the return of the soul to God, see the supercommentary of R. Joshua Ibn Shuaib (misattributed in the printed edition to Ibn Sahula) to the *Commentary* of Nahmanides on Leviticus: "... the souls draw close and ascend, as was the manner of their descent at the beginning of their descent into the world, and they ascend to the place of their source, like water which rises to the level from which it has flowed" (*Oẓar mefarshei ha-torah*, Part 2, Jerusalem 1976 [facsimile of Warsaw edition], p. 23). See also E. Gottleib, "Sacrifices in Kabbalah" (in Hebrew), *Studies in Kabbalistic Literature*, Tel Aviv 1976, pp. 561–563; and cf. M. Idel, *Kabbalah: New Perspectives*, New Haven–London 1987, pp. 46–49.

64. See the remarks by R. Ezra of Gerona (d. c. 1245): "Because he knows how to unite the Unique Name, it is as if he builds a palace of above and below," Commentary to Song of Songs, in *Kitvei ha-Ramban*, ed. Chavell, II, p. 521. Cf. Idel, *Kabbalah* (see previous note); Pedaya, "Flaw and Correction" (above, note 25).

65. R.J. Zwi Werblowsky, in *Joseph Karo: Lawyer and Mystic* (Philadelphia 1980), notes that the equation between man's heart and the Temple of God is a typical Sufi idea, and that several of the kabbalists of sixteenth-century Safed were heavily influenced by Sufi ideas, especially via the writings of R. Isaac of Acre (pp. 56–60; p. 58, note 3 and p. 59, note 3). Cf. Pedaya, "Possessed by Speech" (above, note 50), pp. 221 ff.

66. "And the righteous and the pious and the people who seclude themselves and unite the Great Name and stir up the flame *on the pyre burning in their hearts ...*" MS Berlin Or. Qu 833, p. 98c.

67. Cf. *Peraqim be-haẓlaḥah* (anonymous), Davidowitz, pp. 1–2: "... And know that the sanctuary of your heart is the sanctuary of the ark, in which are hidden the tablets of the testimony; so is it hidden in your heart, written upon the tablet of your heart .... And by the word of God, may He be praised, shall He give life to the dead souls .... Likewise in life, when the holy spirit is nullified from this heart, he dies for the present moment, and this is his death." This image is a central one both in Sufi mysticism and in ecstatic kabbalah. Cf. also Abraham Abulafia, *Ve-zot le-Yehudah*, ed. Jellinek, p. 22.

68. Thus, for example, R. Ezra of Gerona expressed his opposition to any initiative by Jews to resettle the Land of Israel with a comment on Song of Songs 2:7: "'I adjure thee' — thus speaks the Shekhinah in the time of Exile, making Israel swear that they will not force the End and that they will not 'arouse love' until the time of grace shall come, and that they will not say, 'by the gazelles and by

the hinds of the fields,' because *the Shekhinah is not in its place.*," Commentary to Song of Songs (above, note 64), p. 514. See Pedaya, "Land of Spirit" (above, note 24), pp. 249–255, especially p. 252. See also Pedaya, "Possessed by Speech" (above, note 50).

69. Moshe Idel has recently dealt with various aspects of this issue. See his recent book, *Hasidism: Between Ecstasy and Magic*, Albany, N.Y., 1995.
70. See the discussion of the hermeneutics of ecstatic kabbalah in Idel, *Kabbalah* (above, note 63), pp. 200-249.
71. This subject has already been widely discussed in the literature. See Aptowitzer, "The Heavenly Temple" (above, note 4); E.E. Urbach, "Earthly Jerusalem and Heavenly Jerusalem According to the Aggadah" (Heb), *Jerusalem through the Generations*, Jerusalem 1969, pp. 156–171.
72. A facsimile of *Sefer ha-ot* is printed in A. Jellinek, *Ginzei hokhmat ha-qabbalah*, Jerusalem 1969, pp. 2–21; the hymn is in section III, pp. 5–6. Also in J. Schirmann, *Hebrew Poetry in Spain and Portugal*, IV (in Hebrew), Tel-Aviv–Jerusalem 1961, p. 455:
היום הבא יום הדין הוא / ויום הזכרון יקרא / ועת המשפט הגיע / וזמן הקץ תם ונשלם /
השמים יהיו ארץ / והארץ תהיה שמימית
73. J.G. Weiss, "The Origins of the Hasidic Path" (in Hebrew), *Zion*, XVI, (1951), pp. 97–99.
74. R. Ephraim of Sudylkow (1740?–1800?), *Degel maḥaneh Efraim*, Jerusalem 1961, pp. 264–265. This version seems closer to the original kernel, and compare also the longer paraphrase on pp. 257–258.
75. Jerusalem 1974, p. 2.
76. E. Reiner, "Aliyah and Pilgrimage to the Land of Israel, 1099–1517," Ph.D. Dissertation, The Hebrew University of Jerusalem, 1988.
77. On the significance of Nahmanides's decision to settle in the Land of Israel see Y. Baer, *A History of the Jews in Christian Spain*, I, Philadelphia 1961, p. 159; G. Scholem, *Origins of the Kabbalah*, Princeton 1983, pp. 383–384; M. Idel, "Some Conceptions of the Land of Israel in Medieval Jewish Thought," in R. Link–Salinger (ed.), *A Straight Path; Studies in Medieval Philosophy and Culture: Essays in Honor of Arthur Hyman*, Washington, D.C., 1988, pp. 131–133; and Pedaya, "Land of Spirit" (above, note 24), pp. 264–289.
78. In this light, it is worthwhile to re-examine the texts brought by Idel in *Kabbalah* (above, note 63), pp. 51–58. Concerning the esoteric conception of the Divinity as a temple that has been destroyed and the corresponding view of man as having the potential to rebuild this temple by his thought, see Pedaya, "Flaw and Correction" (above, note 25), pp. 221–228.
79. See V. Turner, *The Forest of Symbols: Aspects of Ndembu Ritual*, Ithaca, N.Y., 1970.
80. See M. Idel, *Chapters in Prophetic Kabbalah* (in Hebrew), Jerusalem 1990, pp. 51–74.
81. See Solomon Molcho, *Hayyat qaneh*, Amsterdam 1658, p. 3; cf. Idel, *Chapters* (above, note 80), pp. 73–74.
82. See the letter of the Baal Shem Tov to his brother-in-law, R. Gershon Kutover, in *Shivhei ha-Besht*, ed. Mintz, Jerusalem 1969, pp. 167–169; cf. Y. Tishby, "The Messianic Idea and Messianic Tendencies in the Growth of Hasidism" (in

Hebrew), *Zion*, XXXII (1967) pp. 1–45; B. Dinaburg (Dinur), "The Beginnings of Hasidism, Its Societal and Messianic Foundations," in G. Hundert (ed.), *Essential Papers on Hasidism*, New York–London 1991, pp. 86–208.

83. G. Scholem discusses Sabbatai Zevi's wanderings in the Land of Israel and the beginning of the Messianic movements there in *Sabbatai Sevi: The Mystical Messiah, 1626–1676* (English transl. by R.J.Z. Werblowsky, Bollingen Series, 93), Princeton 1973, Chaps. 2–3, pp. 103–325.
84. See A. Green, *Tormented Master: A Life of Rabbi Nahman of Bratslav*, University, Ala., 1979, pp. 63–93.
85. For an approach emphasizing the nature of the experience of time, see Frank Kermode, *The Sense of an Ending; Studies in the Theory of Fiction*, Oxford 1968.

8

Byzantium's Dual Holy Land

Evelyne Patlagean

i

Byzantium and the crusades hold negative positions in each other's histories, as currently reconstructed from Latin sources, and from the account of the First Crusade given by Anna Comnena (died 1153) in her history of the reign of her father Alexios I (1081–1118). Historians usually take for granted that from the beginning of the First Crusade in 1096 to its decisive turning-point in 1204, Byzantium's only interest in that great upsurge of conquering spirit lay in keeping it away from Byzantine territory and utilizing it for self-interested ends, since at that time Byzantium was fighting defensive wars in the East and was soon to undertake its own reconquest of lost territory. Neither the historians of the crusades nor those of the Greek empire seem willing to investigate the true motives of this Byzantine non-involvement or even to attempt to revise their traditional interpretations through a new examination of the twelfth-century Greek sources. In order to do so, one must consider, beyond the established diplomatic and military facts,[1] the values with which the Holy Land of Palestine was apt to be invested in Constantinople. In this essay, dedicated to the memory of Joshua Prawer, that is what I propose to consider.

Early Christianity had produced a definition of the Holy Land which suited the two logically connected principles on which depended its innovative break with the Jewish tradition from which it claimed to be derived. These were the Incarnation, which gave the divine Word the earthly identity that provided its redemptive and messianic legitimacy, and the New Covenant with the "true Israel," concepts which, in Christian eyes, replaced the original Covenant and the original Israel.[2] The Holy Land thence became the place where this dual basis of legitimacy found its literal and symbolic confirmation. From the beginning, the Christianized Roman Empire had both supported the work of reinterpretation and undertaken the building campaign which concurred to insure that Christianity should legitimately supersede a now obsolete Judaism in the very space where the Incarnation had taken place. This dual enterprise focussed especially on Jerusalem, and in particular on the site of Mt. Zion.[3]

Now for the Greek Christians, the Christian Holy Land was not necessarily identical with or exclusive to the real Palestine. For them, it was possible to acknowledge a New Jerusalem, by virtue not of a mere substitution, but of a duplication supported by exegesis and by the tangible evidence of significant relics, in the same way that the New Rome had been recognized since the time of Constantine.[4] The New Jerusalem and the New Rome were both Constantinople, which attracted to itself, and thus combined, the two forms of legitimacy required for recognition as the seat of a Christian empire. The identification of Constantinople as a New Jerusalem may already have been dawning from the time of Constantine; it was reinforced when Justinian rebuilt Sancta Sophia, the Church of the Holy Wisdom, which from that time onwards came to be identified with the destroyed Temple, and it grew stronger still during the wars of the seventh century. By the tenth century it was well established.[5] At the heart of this theological legitimation was the emperor himself, who was seen as a new David and a new Solomon.[6] He was intended to be the human and terrestrial image of the heavenly Christ-emperor (*basileus*), as suggested to start with by the imperial theology of Eusebius of Caesarea,[7] and by Constantine's construction of the Church of the Holy Apostles in Constantinople as his own burial place.[8]

Greek Christianity, of course, was also alive to the concepts of the eschatological and the heavenly Jerusalems. The eschatological Jerusalem appeared in *The Apocalypse of Methodius*, written in the seventh century, apparently under the impact of the Arab conquest, and continuously disseminated from that time onwards. In this work, Jerusalem was the place where the end would happen and where the last emperor, whose identity remained open, would go to lay down his crown.[9] The heavenly Jerusalem was described in a version of *The Life of Basil the New*, whose narrative takes place in the second half of the tenth century.[10] The narrator, troubled by the question of the position of the Jews in the Christian scheme of things, considered the criteria that determined the selection of the elect and the damned. The figures of the Old Testament were among the former, while the Jews who had remained deaf to the Christian message were among the latter, along with the heretics and sinners. The description of the New Jerusalem was clearly inspired by Constantinople,[11] and we shall see later that this was by no means surprising.

These interpretations did not cause Byzantium to forget the real Palestine, but, curiously, from the very first centuries of the Christian empire there was a real difference in this respect between the Latins and the Greeks, if one is to judge by the texts. The Latins described themselves as pilgrims in the full sense of the term — that is, as believers who came in person to walk through and gaze at the places where the founding events of their faith, in both the Old and the New Testaments, actually happened.[12] In the same period, the Greeks left only one guidebook for such pilgrims, ascribed to a certain Epiphanios of the Holy City (*hagiopolitis*) and possibly written in the ninth century.[13] The journey to the holy sites, which they venerated no less than the Latins, was for them rather the occasion for an ascesis, an ascetic apprenticeship. The ancient legend of Pelagia of Antioch, the penitent prostitute who secluded herself in a cell on the Mount of Olives,[14] appears side by side with stories about saints. Simeon of Emesa, the Fool-in-Christ, and his companion, in the seventh century,[15] and the Sicilians Elias the Younger, in the ninth century,[16] Marina the Younger, born in 1062,[17] and Lazarus of Mount Galesios near Ephesus, who died in 1053,[18] are instances of a drive which is easily explained by the antique glory and medieval continuity of the Greek monastic communities in Palestine.[19]

Furthermore, the Greek emperors assumed the responsibility for the reconstruction of the Church of the Holy Sepulchre, whose demolition by the Caliph al-Hakim in 1009 was capped by the earthquake of 1034. Clauses to this effect exist in the agreements concluded by Constantine VIII with the Fatimid Caliph al-Zahir in 1027, and by Michael IV with the caliph's widow in 1036.[20] The Church of the Anastasis was restored by Constantine IX in 1048.[21]

This, briefly, was the Greek tradition with regard to the Holy

Land on the eve of the Comnenes' century and the period of the crusaders. It featured legitimation of Byzantium and its emperor by means of their prototypical identification, a permanent trend in Byzantine political and religious discourse. However, from the last years of the eleventh century until the breakup of 1204, this tradition was challenged within the framework of a vastly expanded international context, which included the crusades with their political repercussions, the debate with Rome over the union of the Churches and the issue of primacy, and finally the Greek response, which was to demand a restoration of imperial authority under the auspices of the ruler of Constantinople, the successor to Constantine.

The existing tradition continued during this period. Greeks reached Palestine as before, with the same motivations. Neophytos the Recluse, for instance, born in Cyprus, related that he left for the country at the age of twenty-four in order to stay there and find a master in ascetic discipline (1158).[22] Greek monasticism in Palestine is attested by several authors, including Neophytos,[23] the Russian *hegumen* (abbot) Daniel, whose pilgrimage took place in 1104–1109,[24] and John Phokas, who set out for the Holy Land in 1177.[25] The journey of the latter was probably more than a simple pilgrimage, as we shall see later; so, too, was that of Constantine Manasses, who took part in an ambassadorial mission to Jerusalem when the emperor Manuel I became a widower in 1160.[26]

On the other hand, prominently, the elaboration of Constantinople as New Jerusalem carried on. It is reflected in accounts by foreign pilgrims. The first we should mention is a Latin one, probably from England, the Mercati Anonymus, whose textual tradition, based on a slightly earlier Greek text, goes back to the beginning of the twelfth century.[27] The relics he venerated in the capital of the empire were visible signs of its identification with the New Jerusalem of Christian revelation: relics of Christ and of his Passion, of the Virgin, of John the Baptist and of the Apostle Paul; Peter is not included. The Old Testament was represented by Moses's rod and the mantle of Elijah; the latter was expected to fight the Antichrist together with Enoch. The testimony of the Mercati Anonymus was confirmed both by Dobrynia Jadrejkovič, the future Anthony, Archbishop of Novgorod, in 1200,[28] and by Robert de Clari in 1204.[29] The identification is thus made materially obvious.

The same process was at work, and to an even greater degree, when Manuel I Comnenus, between 1166 and 1169, ordered the stone on which the dead Christ had been laid to be sent from Ephesus for his own tomb, receiving it at the quayside and personally carrying it from there.[30] This was not merely the transfer of a highly significant relic from Jerusalem to Constantinople; it indicated the Christlike nature of the emperor, earthly image of the heavenly *basileus*. John Phokas's remark that he had seen the same relic in the Church of the Holy Sepulchre in Jerusalem, covered with precious ornaments given by the same emperor,[31] is not necessarily a sign of inconsistency, but rather a reduplication.

Interpretations of Scripture, or at any rate commentaries rife with scriptural quotations, confirmed the official identification of Constantinople with Jerusalem. Thus, when Manuel I Comnenus in 1153 awarded the fiscal revenues from a provincial Jewish community to Sancta Sophia, it served as an occasion for him to recall that the prototype of the Great Church was the Temple of Solomon, and that it stood for the New Zion.[32] After 1204, the biblical analogy was reflected in the account by the official chronicler, Niketas Choniates, of the fall and sack of the sovereign city.[33]

Against this background, the configuration of events in the twelfth century faced Byzantium with the eastward expansion of the West, specially the crusades, and the Roman claim to primacy. Other texts testify that the Greek tradition of the dual Holy Land provided thorough responses to both.

ii

Byzantium promoted the claims of Jerusalem against the Roman primacy. In the debate in 1112 between Greeks and Latins in Constantinople, one of the official Greek theologians, Niketas Seides, put forward the first systematic criticism of Roman primacy, replying to the usual Roman argument that it was based on the fact that Peter had been the first bishop.[34] Actually, he said, the first bishop was none other than Christ himself, who ordained his brother James, and afterwards Peter obtained the see of Antioch. At the same time, Niketas Seides turned this argument of anteriority inside out, representing temporal succession as a kind of ascension. Thus, he claimed, one proceeded from the Law to the Gospels, from the blood sacrifices to the one that was bloodless, from the sacrificial lamb to the ideal one, and from the tent of meeting to the Temple of Solomon, and thence to Sancta Sophia. In accordance with this principle, Constantinople, precisely because it was the last in the line, came to stand for Rome, Jerusalem (which, however, remained important as the site of the Passion), Babylon and Antioch. And the same principle applied, observed Seides, with regard to political power.

One finds echoes of this argument throughout the twelfth century. At the meetings of 1136, the papal envoy himself, Anselm of Havelberg, officially declared that James, the brother of Jesus, had been the first bishop.[35] The Greeks maintained that the Church founded by Christ was one and indivisible, and that if one insisted on introducing a hierarchy into it, the first place went to Jerusalem. In 1156, Giorgios Tornikes, then Metropolitan of Ephesus, wrote a letter to the pope in the name of the emperor.[36] He pointed out that Peter had indeed established the Jerusalem Church first, and then the one in Antioch, but that Christ himself was the apostle and High Priest of the single and indivisible Church, and also its emperor. The use of the term *archiereus* in both its senses — of a Jewish High Priest and of a Christian bishop — and the attribution of the imperial title to Christ, stress the sequence of the Old Jerusalem, the New Jerusalem and Constantinople.

The same ideas are to be found in the dialogue of Manuel I with the cardinals during the years 1170–1175. The text is no doubt not authentic, but it was included in *The Sacred Arsenal* (*Hiera Hoplotheke*), written at Manuel's request by his relative and close friend Andronikos Kamateros, who had a distinguished public career.[37] Manuel argued that if one entertains the idea of the primacy of one Church over another, then one must recognize that Antioch is older than Rome, and Jerusalem still older, having had Christ himself as its first bishop and therefore deserving the title "mother of all the Churches."[38] Giorgios Tornikes's brother Demetrios, a high-ranking state official, wrote a letter to the Pope in the name of the Patriarch in 1193.[39] He explained yet again that in the single, indivisible Church, the sole conceivable primacy, if such exists, is that of Jerusalem, on account of the earthly career of Christ, who was after all the one shepherd of the one Church.

However, the Greeks, facing Rome, went still further. They claimed that the "New Zion," the foundation-stone of this one Church of Christ, was at the same time Constantinople. Here ecclesiology merged with politics. The shift in interpretation can be seen in Giorgios Tornikes's letter, supported by verses from the prophets and the psalms.[40] It is reflected also in texts of an essentially political nature. One example among many was the ceremonial speech addressed to Manuel I by the rhetorician John Diogenes on the feast of the Epiphany. Diogenes draws a parallel between the "old Zion" of the prophet Jeremiah and the "new Zion," "the Zion here," which, unlike the old one, triumphantly gathers in its children from all parts.[41]

iii

This brings us to the emperor, or rather to a succession of emperors, because we are dealing not with a static situation but with a history in which Byzantine policies had constantly to adjust to those of the Latin states and the papacy. The facts are known, but the Byzantine theory of the dual Holy Land was an element which has not sufficiently been taken into account.

A study by Paul Lemerle of the Byzantine reactions to the crusades did not go beyond the first expedition.[42] His negative conclusions concerning the strategic anxieties and cultural incomprehension of the Byzantines were based, essentially, on the work of Anna Comnena. To be sure, the First Crusade represented the forceful entry of an entirely new factor into the Greek political arena, one that affected the very concept of "Holy Land," and our observations will in a sense simply record the response progressively worked out by the Greek imperial authorities on the basis of their own tradition. Moreover, under Alexios I Comnenus the Holy Land was hardly mentioned by a historiography and by a formal rhetoric which both insisted, rather, on the apostolic character of the emperor.[43] All the more attention should be given to one page by John Zonaras, an account of the death of Alexios I (1118), as an exception which proves the rule.[44]

Where Anna Comnena went into great detail about the illness that was carrying away her father,[45] Zonaras, who was a contemporary of Anna's and perhaps close to her, gave a quite different view of his death. The physicians, he said, concealed from the emperor the seriousness of his condition, but some monks had told him that he would not die before he had gone to Jerusalem to worship at the tomb of Christ and given up his crown there. Since he was only too ready to believe them, he never realized he was dying. In this way, Zonaras goes on, Alexios did lay down his crown before reaching Jerusalem, but against his own will; or rather, he migrated to the Jerusalem above.

The monks' prediction clearly refers to *The Apocalypse of Methodius*, which held that the emperor of the Romans would set down his crown on the cross, returning his empire to the Father. The cross, the story continues, would be carried away to heaven with the crown and reappear at the time of Christ's Second Advent, and the emperor would then breathe his last.[46] These events would follow the appearance in the world of the "son of destruction,"[47] or Antichrist, which happens after the arrival of the peoples of the north, who are eaters of human flesh, drinkers of the blood of wild beasts and devourers of unclean animals, snakes and scorpions.[48] The practices described here are obviously to be compared to those imputed to the Franks during the twelfth century by the branch of the anti-Latin polemic derived from the "Pseudo-Photios."[49] Byzantium's initial reply to the new question forcefully posed by the crusades was thus indebted to Greek eschatology. Note that the same circumstances aroused messianic expectations in Jewish communities in the empire, among them that of Thessalonika, as demonstrated by a famous letter from the Geniza.[50] However, Zonaras's narrative leaves no room for the Holy Land on earth between the Jerusalem of the end-time and that of the heavens.

The position of John II Comnenus, son and successor of Alexios I, presents a contrast. The historiographer Niketas Choniates depicted the imperial reconquest whereby John II recaptured Antioch in 1137 along the lines of a Western crusade.[51] He related that John II's longstanding desire had been to rejoin the city of Antiochos to that of Constantine, and after that to offer up magnificent gifts in the Church of the Holy Sepulchre in Jerusalem and drive the barbarians out of the country. In 1142, John launched another Syrian campaign, once more against the prince of Antioch. He died in 1143, the victim of a hunting accident that may have been a murder. According to Choniates, he explained on his deathbed that the real aim of the expedition had been to reach Palestine, the place of Christ's sacrifice, to ascend the mountain of the Lord, to stand in His holy place according to the word of the psalmist (Psalm 23:3–4), and to drive out the enemies who had so often captured the Holy Sepulchre, as the foreign tribes had captured the ark.[52]

The land route from Constantinople to Jerusalem did pass through Antioch, and a new openness towards the West, already perceptible during the reign of John II, could well explain the motivation described by an author as close to the seat of power as Choniates. Following the death of John II, an anonymous orator composed a panegyric to him declaring that those travelling on the roads or in distant places no longer had anything to fear, as John had favoured them by taking pity on the visible Jerusalem below, while he himself had taken the greater, holier road that led to the holy Jerusalem above, where his soul was now enraptured by the contemplation of Jesus.[53] This writer was a contemporary of Zonaras.

John II was succeeded by his son Manuel I Comnenus (1143–1180), whose contributions to the tradition of Constantinople as a New Jerusalem (in connection with the cathedral of Sancta Sophia) and of the emperor as an image of Christ we saw earlier. The real Palestine, however, also played a significant role in his activities, in the context of a general diplomatic situation that need not be described here.[54] We have mentioned Manuel's dispatch of Constantine Manasses as an ambassador to Jerusalem after the emperor became a widower in 1160. In July 1169, a Byzantine fleet set out to assist a new expedition by King Amalric of Jerusalem, against Egypt. Amalric himself visited Constantinople in March 1170. In 1177, Byzantium again was due to send naval assistance to an expedition of the Latin kingdom to Egypt.[55]

These same years saw other imperial gestures that punctuated and commented on the relationships we have just reviewed. Kinnamos apparently dates the arrival in the capital of the stone of Christ's deposition, an episode to which we have already referred, between the years 1166 and 1169. In the year 1169, the Church of the Nativity in Bethlehem was adorned with a mosaic donated by Manuel. The accompanying inscription[56] gives the date in terms which require no elucidation. The mosaic was donated, it says, "under the empire of Manuel, the great emperor, born to the purple (*porphyrogenitus*), the Comnenus, in the days of the great King of Jerusalem, the Lord Amalric, and of the most holy bishop of holy Bethlehem, Radulfus."[57]

In 1177 John Phokas set out for Palestine. He wrote a "description" (*ekphrasis*) of his journey which was no less than a guide to the Holy Land.[58] All we know about the writer is that he had a military career and later became a monk at Patmos,[59] but one is tempted to ascribe to the work, somewhat unusual of its kind for Greek literature, an official character. Referring to the covering of pure gold given to the stone of Christ's deposition by Manuel, he described the latter as "my master and emperor Manuel, *porphyrogenitus* and Comnenus" (col. 944), and gave the same description of him in connection with his reconstruction of the monastery of the Prodrome, destroyed by an earthquake (col. 952). When mentioning the Bethlehem mosaic, he called Manuel "my most gracious (*kosmiotatos*) emperor" (col. 957). He added that the Latin bishop, perhaps in recognition of Manuel's magnanimity (*megalopsychia*, the virtue of a donor), had hung Manuel's portrait in various places, notably in the shrine of the grotto. The display of the imperial image in such a place was obviously of great significance.

Phokas also described the situation and internal arrangement of the "Holy Zion," "facing the Holy City," calling it the "mother of Churches" (col. 941). Moreover, he recorded that in the Church of the Holy Apostles next to the convent of Kalamon, he saw an icon of the "Virgin-Who-Shows-the-Way" (*hodigitria*), identical to the one so greatly venerated in the sanctuary of that name in Constantinople (col. 953). This icon, said to have been painted by the apostle Luke, had presided at the victory of John II Comnenus over the Pechenegs, and had since been not only an object of public veneration, but also an object of particular devotion for the imperial family.[60] Finally, Phokas noted the Greek and Iberian monks whom he met in Palestine. The munificent gestures of Manuel I Comnenus undoubtedly accord with an imperial tradition going back even before the First Crusade. In their context, however, they represent an imperial accent deliberately added to the relations of Byzantium with the Latin Kingdom of Jerusalem.

Isaac II Angelos is the last ruler we shall deal with. Saladin took Jerusalem in 1187. Isaac had appointed to the patriarchal throne of the city a monk from the monastery of Stoudiou, situated in Constantinople and traditionally close to the seat of power. This monk, Dositheos, had told him that he would become emperor.[61] Dositheos now informed him that he would have sole authority (*monarchia*), and that he would liberate Palestine and drive the "Ishmaelites" beyond the Euphrates, applying expressions to him which the prophet Isaiah had used in connection with Jerusalem itself (Isa. 60:13 and 16). The struggle being waged was thus clearly placed in an eschatological context, and Choniates, who reported these statements, did not approve of them.[62] Dositheos enjoyed such favour that in 1189 Isaac appointed him Patriarch of the capital, despite the canonical rule forbidding such transfers. In 1193 Demetrios Tornikes wrote the Pope a letter as from the emperor, calling for union and lamenting the fate of Jerusalem, subtly noting that the Latins on their own were incapable of remedying a situation which their sins had undoubtedly played a part in creating.[63]

The actions of the twelfth century thus at first sight appear to be entirely in conformity with a Greek tradition underlying the Byzantine responses to an international situation whose development does not concern us here. The elements of this tradition were an acceptance of Zion as the "mother of all Churches," of Constantinople as a New Zion, of the emperor as the earthly figure of Christ, who was the heavenly *basileus*, and a tendency for all this at any moment to be transposed into the sphere of eschatology. The circumstances of the period, however, seem to have given rise to a new awareness of the real Palestine in official thinking. Above all, Byzantium demonstrated at that time that the logic of the "true Israel" is endless, and followed this logic to the point of setting itself apart even from the other Christian nations. It maintained this stance after 1204 and after 1261, in the face of Latin and then Turkish threats, and after 1453 transmitted this notion to its Greek and Slav successors. The positions presented here in an essentially political context penetrated deeply into the consciousness of the Orthodox nations, beginning with Byzantium itself but also extending far beyond the spatial and temporal limits of the former empire.

Notes

A French version of this paper appeared in *Annales Histoire, Sciences sociales*, 1994, pp. 459–469.

Abbreviations used in the notes: *AA. SS.* = *Acta Sanctorum; PG* = J.P. Migne, *Patrologia Graeca*, Paris 1857–1886; *PL* = J.P. Migne, *Patrologia Latina*, Paris.

1. It is enough to mention R.J. Lilie, *Byzanz und die Kreuzfahrerstaaten: Studien zur Politik des byzantinischen Reiches gegenüber den Staaten der Kreuzfahrer in Syrien und Palästina bis zum Vierten Kreuzzug (1096–1204)*, Munich 1981; and, despite their early dates, F. Chalandon, *Essai sur le règne d'Alexios Ier Comnène (1081–1118)*, Paris 1900; and idem, *Les Comnène: Etudes sur l'Empire byzantin au XIe au XIIe siècles;* II, 1–2: *Jean II Comnène (1118–1143) et Manuel Ier Comnène (1143–1180)*, Paris 1912 (reprinted 1971).
2. Cf. the classic study of M. Simon, *Verus Israël: Les relations entre Juifs et Chrétiens sous l'Empire romain*, Paris 1964 (1948), with a postscript.
3. Cf. A. Linder, "Ecclesia and Synagoga in the Medieval Myth of Constantine the Great," *Revue belge de philologie et d'histoire*, LIV (1976), pp. 1019–1060; J. Prawer, "Jerusalem in the Christian and Jewish Perspectives of the Early Middle Ages," in *Gli Ebrei nell'alto Medioevo, Settimane di studio*, XXVI (1978), Spoleto 1980, pp. 739–812; P.W.L. Walker, *Holy City, Holy Places? Christian Attitudes to Jerusalem and the Holy Land in the Fourth Century*, Oxford 1990.
4. G. Dagron, *Naissance d'une capitale: Constantinople et ses institutions de 330 à 451*, Paris 1974.
5. Sufficient evidence may be found in A. Pertusi, *Fine di Bisanzio e fine del mondo: Significato e ruolo storico delle profezie sulla caduta di Constantinopoli in Oriente e in Occidente*, Rome 1988, pp. ix–xi (note by E. Morini); G. Dagron, *Constantinople imaginaire: Etudes sur le receuil des 'Patria'*, Paris 1984, p. 303 ff.
6. Cf., for example, H. Buchthal, "The Exaltation of David," *Journal of the Warburg and Courtauld Institutes* XXXVII, (1974), pp. 330–333 (with regard to Constantine VII); concerning Solomon, cf. Dagron, *Constantinople imaginaire* (above, note 5), and my paper, "Une image de Salomon en basileus byzantin," *Revue des études juives*, CXXI (1962), pp. 16–18.
7. Cf. J.M. Sansterre, "Eusèbe de Césarée et la naissance de la théorie 'césaropapiste'," *Byzantion* XLII (1972), pp. 131–195, 532–594. An excellent article despite its title.
8. Dagron, *Naissance d'une capitale* (above, note 4), pp. 401–409.
9. A. Lolos, *Die Apokalypse des Ps. Methodios*, Meisenheim am Glan 1976; idem, *Die dritte und vierte Redaktion des Ps. Methodios*, Meisenheim am Glan 1978, pp. 130–132.
10. Ed. Veselovskij, *Sbornik otdel. russk. jazyka i slovesnosti Imp. Ak. Nauk*, XLVI (1890), *Prilož.*, and LIII (1892), *Prilož.*
11. C. Angelidi, "Remarques sur la description de la Jerusalem céleste," *Jahrbuch der österreichischen Byzantinistic*, XXXII/3 (1892), pp. 207–215.
12. *Itinera Hierosolymitana et descriptiones Terrae Sanctae lingua latina saec. IV–XI exarata*, ed. T. Tobler & A. Molinier, I–II, Geneva 1880.

13. *PG*, CXX, 259–272.
14. Cf. P. Petitmengin (ed.), *Pélagie la pénitente: Métamorphoses d'une légende*, I: *Les textes et leur histoire*, Paris 1981.
15. Leontios de Neapolis, *Vie de Syméon le Fou et Vie de Jean de Chypre*, ed. with commentary by A.J. Festugière with L. Ryden, Paris 1974, pp. 58 ff. (Greek text) and pp. 109 ff. (French translation).
16. *Vita di sant'Elia il Giovane*, ed. G. Rossi Taibbi, Palermo 1962, Chaps. 17–20 (pp. 24 ff.).
17. *Martirio di S. Lucia: Vita di S. Marina*, ed. G. Rossi Taibbi, Chap. 9 (p. 94).
18. *Vie anonyme, AA. SS. Novembris* III (1910), Chaps. 14 ff.
19. With regard to these monasteries, the Byzantine period remains to this day the one most studied. Cf. O.F.A. Meinardus, "Notes on the Laurae and Monasteries of the Wilderness of Judaea," *Liber annuus studii biblici franciscani*, XV (1964–65), pp. 220–250; XVI (1965–66), pp. 328–356; XIX (1969), pp. 305–327; Y. Hirschfeld, *The Judean Desert Monasteries in the Byzantine Period*, New Haven 1992.
20. F. Dölger, *Regesten der Kaiserurkunden des oströmischen Reiches von 565 bis 1453*, Munich 1924–1965, nos. 824 and 843.
21. Cf. H. Vincent OP & F.M. Abel OP, *Jérusalem: Recherches de topographie, d'archéologie et d'histoire*, II: *Jérusalem nouvelle*, Paris 1914, p. 250.
22. Cf. C. Galatariotou, *The Making of a Saint: The Life, Times and Sanctification of Neophytos the Recluse*, Cambridge 1991, p. 14.
23. Cf. the bibliography in Galatariotou, *Making of a Saint* (above, note 22), p. 262. Text published in H. Delehaye, *Analecta Bollandiana*, XXVI (1907), pp. 162–175, with a commentary.
24. French translation by B. de Kitrowo, *Itinéraires russes en Orient*, I, Geneva 1889, pp. 33–35 (description of St. Sabas and St. Euthymios).
25. John Phokas, *Ekphrasis*, *PG*, CXXXIII, 928–962.
26. Ed. K. Horna, "Das Hodoiporikon des Konstantin Manasses," *Byzantinische Zeitschrift* XIII (1904), pp. 313–355.
27. The work was discovered and published by S.G. Mercati, "Santuari e reliquie costantinopolitane secondo il cod. Ottob. lat. 169 prima della conquista latina (1204)," *Rendiconti della pontif. Accademia romana di archeologia*, XII (1936), pp. 133–156, based on an English manuscript from the twelfth to thirteenth centuries. On the basis of another English manuscript, Bodl. Digbeianus lat. 112, from the beginning of the twelfth century, K.N. Ciggaar published an older version ("Une description de Constantinople traduite par un pèlerin anglais," *Revue des études byzantines* XXXIV [1976], pp. 211–267), which she dates to 1089–1096, and which would be a translation of a Greek text of 1063–1081.
28. Kitrowo, *Itinéraires* (above, note 24), pp. 85–111.
29. Robert de Clari, *La conquête de Constantinople*, LXXXII, ed. P. Lauer, Paris 1924, pp. 81–82. In the "Holy Chapel" of the palace of Boukoleon, de Clari claimed to have seen relics of the Passion, the Virgin's garment and the head of John the Baptist.
30. Joannis Cinnami, *Epitome rerum*, VI, 8, ed. A. Meineke, Bonn 1836, pp. 277–278; Nicetas Choniates, *Historia*, ed. J.A. Van Dieten, Berlin 1975, pp. 222, 227 ff.
31. John Phokas, *Ekphrasis* (above, note 25), 944.

32. Text quoted (and translated) by Dagron, *Constantinople imaginaire* (above, note 5), p. 300.
33. Choniates, *Historia* (above, note 30), e.g., p. 577.
34. The text was analyzed in J. Spiteris, *La critica bizantina del primato romano nel secolo XII*, Rome 1979, pp. 70 ff., and published by R. Gahbauer, *Gegen den Primat des Papstes: Studien zu Niketas Seides: Edition, Einführung, Kommentar*, Munich 1975.
35. Anselm of Havelberg, *Dialogi*, III, *PL*, CLXXXVIII, 1222. On the author and on the work, written by order of the Pope, probably in 1149, cf. G. Salet's introduction to his edition, Anselme de Havelberg, *Dialogues*, Book I (*Sources chrétiennes*, 118), Paris 1966.
36. J. Darrouzès, *Georges et Dèmètrios Tornikès, Lettres et Discours*, Paris 1970, No. 30 (pp. 324–335).
37. The text is analyzed in Spiteris, *Critica bizantina del primato romano* (above, note 34), pp. 323–324.
38. The expression, and hence the idea, are already to be found in the letter of the Synod of Constantinople to Pope Damasus and the Western bishops in the year 382. Cf. Theodoret, *Kirchengeschichte*, ed. L. Parmentier, revised by F. Scheidweiler, Berlin 1954, p. 294/4 (V,9). On the date, cf. H.G. Beck, *Kirche und theologische Literatur im byzantinischen Reich*, Munich 1959, p. 53.
39. Darrouzès, *Georges et Dèmètrios Tornikès* (above, note 36), No. 34 (pp. 346–353).
40. Georges Tornikès, in *ibid.*, pp. 328/8 ff.
41. W. Regel (ed.), *Fontes rerum byzantinarum: Rhetorum saeculi XII Orationes politicae*, II, Petrograd 1917, p. 305.
42. P. Lemerle, "Byzance et la Croisade," in *X congresso internazionale scienze storiche, Relazioni*, III: *Storia del Medioevo*, Florence 1955, pp. 595–620.
43. E.g., Anna Comnena, *Alexiade*, ed. B. Leib, Paris 1937–1945, XIV, 8 (vol. 3, p. 181).
44. John Zonaras, *Epitomae Historiarum*, XVIII, 28, ed. Th. Büttner-Wobst, Bonn 1897, III, p. 760.
45. Anna Comnena, *Alexiade* (above, note 43), XV, XI, pp. 14–19 (p. 237 ff.).
46. *Apokalypse des Ps. Methodios* (above, note 9), XIV, 2–4, 6.
47. *Ibid.*, XIV, 1.
48. *Ibid.*, XIII, 20.
49. Cf. J. Darrouzès, "Le Mémoire de Constantin Stilbès contre les Latins," *Revue des études byzantines*, XXI (1963), pp. 50–100.
50. Text edited by A. Neubauer, *Jewish Quarterly Review*, IX (1897), pp. 26–29; cf. J. Starr, *Jews in the Byzantine Empire 641–1204*, Athens 1939, No. 153, pp. 203–208.
51. Choniates, *Historia* (above, note 30), p. 39/34–36.
52. *Ibid.*, p. 42/20–31.
53. Regel, *Fontes rerum byzantinarum* (above, note 41), pp. 338–339.
54. Cf. J. Prawer, *Histoire du royaume latin de Jérusalem* (French transl. by G. Nahon), Paris 1969, I, pp. 427 ff.
55. *Ibid.*, pp. 547 ff.
56. Bishop Radulfus, chancellor of King Amalric, was first mentioned in 1156 and died in 1174. Cf. *Dictionaire d'histoire et de géographie ecclésiastiques*, VIII (1935), col. 1250, s.v. *Bethlehem (évêché de)*, by G. Leveng.

58. John Phokas, *Ekphrasis* (above, note 25).
59. H. Hunger, *Die hochsprachliche profane Literatur der Byzantiner*, Munich 1978, I, p. 517.
60. Choniates, *Historia* (above, note 30), pp. 15/88 and 19/90. Cf. R. Janin, *La géographie ecclésiastique de l'Empire byzantin*, Part I: *Le siège de Constantinople et le patriarcat oecuménique*, III: *Les églises et les monastères*, Paris 1969.
61. Choniates, *Historia* (above, note 30), pp. 404 ff.
62. *Ibid.*, p. 432/69–77.
63. Darrouzès, *Georges et Dèmètrios Tornikès* (above, note 36), No. 33, p. 341.

9

Intellectual Activities in a Holy City: Jerusalem in the Twelfth Century

Benjamin Z. Kedar

The relationship between sacredness and space depends to a considerable extent on the physical dimensions of the space in question. When that space is relatively small — a tomb, a temple — sacredness tends to pervade all of it. The space in its entirety is set apart from ordinary life: all activity within its boundaries may be limited to dealings with the sacred (with specific kinds of dealings often confined to distinct sub-areas), and all behaviour on the premises may be expected to conform to definite prescription.

How different the situation when the sacred space encompasses an entire city or country! Within the boundaries of so extensive a space, sanctity must necessarily coexist with ordinary life. To a pilgrim formerly habituated to small sacred spaces, the coexistence of sacred and profane may come as a shock; the profane activities within the hallowed space may appear to him bewildering, repugnant, scandalous. On the other hand, profane life in a holy city may become colored by sanctity; as Emile Durkheim put it, the sacred is contagious, remarkably apt at invading the profane.[1] Yet the various spheres of activity may differ according to their "sacralizability," or susceptibility to the pressures of the sacred.

I would like here to raise questions that concern a single sphere of life within a holy city — namely, that of intellectual activity and creativity. To what extent does such activity refer to, revolve around, the city's sacred space? To what extent can that space coexist with intellectual activities of a profane nature? Is it possible to generalize about the kinds of intellectual activity typically generated, stimulated, or hampered within a sacred space? What can be said about the mental make-up of creative persons who choose to settle down in a holy city — or who pass their entire lives there?

Twelfth-century Jerusalem is a convenient starting point for such an inquiry. It was not merely a holy city, but one that contained Christendom's most sacred place, whose endangered sanctity triggered an unprecedented outburst of holy warfare, the First Crusade of 1096-1099; and it was the capital of a kingdom — the Frankish Kingdom of Jerusalem — that came into being expressly in order to safeguard that sanctity. And twelfth-century Jerusalem constitutes an appropriate starting point also because it lay at the centre of the scholarly interests of Joshua Prawer, to whose memory this volume is dedicated.

The crusader conquest of Jerusalem entailed a radical reorganization of the city's sacred space. With its Muslim and Jewish inhabitants slaughtered or enslaved, Jerusalem, for the first time since the Byzantine period, became an exclusively Christian city. The Dome of the Rock and the Mosque of al-Aqṣa fell into Christian hands. The crusaders could have destroyed these Muslim shrines on the erstwhile Jewish Temple Mount, and turned the area back into the heap of ruins that it had been in pre-Islamic times — an act that would have commemorated not only the destruction of the Jewish Temple, as it did in the days of the Christian Byzantine Empire, but also Christianity's recent victory over Islam. However, the crusaders did not choose this option; instead — like the contemporaneous Christian conquerors in Sicily and Spain — they christianized the Muslim shrines, turning the Dome of the Rock into the Lord's Temple and the Mosque of al-Aqṣa into the Temple of Solomon. The immediate consequence, one that had no parallel in Sicily or Spain, was that Frankish Jerusalem's sacred space became bifocal: the new focus on the Temple Mount arose alongside and to a certain extent in competition with the old focus, the Church of the Holy Sepulchre.[2] This totally unprecedented situation posed problems for consciousness and liturgy alike. We see the end result in the seal of one of the Frankish kings of Jerusalem: it shows the Tower of David at the centre and, in a remarkable equilibrium, the Church of the Holy Sepulchre to its right and the Lord's Temple (that is, the christianized Dome of the Rock) to its left. The two shrines are depicted as if they were of equal size, with the cross atop the Lord's Temple somewhat higher than the open dome of the Sepulchre.

How was this equilibrium attained? The Franks occasionally denied the Muslim origin of their Lord's Temple altogether and attributed its construction to some Christian emperor of antiquity. This willful obliteration of the Muslim past succeeded only partially: there is evidence that some Franks were aware of the shrine's Muslim origin or of its paramount importance for Saladin and his men.[3] Nevertheless, it was now endowed with Christian content, and several biblical events that in pre-crusade times had been commemorated in the Church of the Holy Sepulchre were now attributed to the Lord's Temple.[4] The programme of processions that the Frankish clergy established in Jerusalem allocated a prominent place to the Lord's Temple, and the coronation processions of the Frankish kings passed through it as well.[5] Two priors of the Lord's Temple, Achard and Geoffroi, composed lengthy poems on the edifice's history, entirely disregarding its Muslim past. (It is symptomatic of the lack of interest in intellectual activities in twelfth-century Jerusalem that Geoffroi's poem has not yet been published in its entirety.)[6]

The Church of the Holy Sepulchre, too, posed challenges to its new Frankish occupants. First, there was the problem of liturgy. The Franks had to make their choice among the usages of the various regions of Europe from which they had come; they had to decide to what extent local, Jerusalemite elements were to be incorporated; and they had to strike a balance between the traditional Christian quest for celestial Jerusalem and the novel praise of the terrestrial city they had conquered and settled. The solutions at which the Frankish clerics arrived, as well as their meaning and impact, call for detailed study. As of now, we know, for instance, that the roster of saints commemorated in the liturgy of the Church of the Holy Sepulchre included seven Jerusalemite saints of the early Christian centuries, fourteen French saints (most of whose cults radiated from locations in central France), and one southern Italian saint.[7] We also learn from extant liturgical books of the Church of the Holy Sepulchre that the liturgical programme underwent significant modifications around the middle of the twelfth century. Evidently, the Sepulchre's canons devoted considerable thought and energy to moulding the celebration of Christendom's primordial events at the very locations where they are presumed to have occurred.[8] In addition, they produced texts for strictly contemporary occasions, like the prayer to be recited at Jerusalem's gate that appears in a missal now preserved in the Bibliothèque Nationale.[9]

Some of these clerics appear also to have pondered the nature of the basic message emanating from their sanctuary. During the first forty years or so they habitually referred to it, in conformity with traditional Western usage, as the Church of the Holy Sepulchre; in later years it came to be denoted more and more frequently as the Church of the Holy Resurrection, a term obviously derived from the sanctuary's Greek name, *Anastasis* (resurrection).[10] The term adopted by the Franks reveals not only the impact of Oriental influence but also a conscious preference for a designation that evokes triumph over that which habitually connotes death. Unfortunately, we do not know how the Frankish clerics justified and interpreted the introduction of the new term. While the patriarchs of Jerusalem, in the second half of the twelfth century, regularly styled themselves patriarchs of the Church of the Holy Resurrection, the popes continued to refer to them as to the patriarchs of Jerusalem[11] — which suggests that the new term signaled an amplification of the sanctuary's stature to which the papacy did not subscribe.

Beyond the establishment of the regular liturgical programme, the canons of the Church of the Holy Sepulchre also had to evolve a Latin liturgy for the Descent of the Holy Fire, an event that recurred on Holy Saturday and was considered a miracle.[12] Before the Frankish conquest, the Descent was celebrated by Jerusalem's Oriental Christians. Now it required a Latin garb — and vindication in the face of skeptics, as disclosed by a remark in the *Ritual of the Holy Sepulchre*.[13] The canons also had to elaborate a liturgical programme for the yearly commemoration of the crusader conquest of Jerusalem — a programme that called, among other things, for a procession from the Church of the Holy Sepulchre to the spot at which the city wall was breached in 1099 by Godfrey of Bouillon's men. A fragment of a sermon composed for that occasion has survived. Here, too, the programme underwent modifications during the eighty-eight years of Frankish rule over Jerusalem, and it is possible to distinguish two, or even three, stages in its evolution.[14]

The True Cross was yet another major focus of liturgy and

consciousness. Considered a fragment of the cross on which Jesus was crucified, the True Cross was the kingdom's most precious relic, its care entrusted to the canons of the Church of the Holy Sepulchre. In 1120, one of them, Ansellus, sent his own substantial account of the relic's history, together with a fragment of the Cross, to Notre Dame of Paris, his church of origin.[15] Additional fragments, often encased in precious receptacles and accompanied by letters of authentication, were sent to other churches in the West. The True Cross itself was much more than a precious relic, an object of minutely regulated rites: it was considered a concrete sign that the spirit of God was hovering over the Franks. That is why it was habitually carried into a battle or siege, either by the patriarch or by a subordinate[16] — a symbol of holy warfare waged in defence of the holy places. The entries made by an anonymous cleric in the rudimentary annals of the Frankish Kingdom kept in the Sepulchre reveal that, for him, the presence of the True Cross on the battlefield was crucial for Christian victory: In 1177, the Franks routed Saladin at Montgisard "with the presence of the vivifying cross"; in 1179 they were defeated, "and we think" — so writes our anonymous cleric — "that this happened because they left at Tiberias the Holy Cross that the king had ordered to carry in aid of the entire army; and since they confided in their own strength more than in the Holy Cross, it did not turn out well for them."[17] There is ample evidence that our cleric was not alone in his belief. Indeed, even Saladin's secretary 'Imād al-Dīn observed that the capture of the Cross by the Muslims at the Battle of Ḥaṭṭīn in 1187 broke the Franks' spirit: "Its capture was for them more important than the loss of the king and was the gravest blow that they sustained in that battle. The Cross was a prize without equal, for it was the supreme object of their faith. ... So when the Great Cross was taken, great was the calamity that befell them, and the strength drained from their loins."[18]

The evidence for the preoccupation of Jerusalem's Frankish clergy with sacred places and objects is thus considerable. Yet it was the one and only preoccupation for which this clergy stood out, the one and only area in which it exhibited creativity. This is a remarkable exclusivity, for at that very time clerics in the Catholic West were creatively engaged in philosophy and theology, in the application of dialectics to Roman and canon law, in the translation and absorption of Arabic and Greek scientific treatises — in short, in the various facets of the so-called Renaissance of the Twelfth Century. Nothing of this kind took place in Frankish Jerusalem (though a few Arabic texts were translated into Latin elsewhere in the Frankish Levant).

Why this striking disparity in intellectual interests and activities? One may argue that a peripheral town like Jerusalem should be compared not with centres of the Twelfth-Century Renaissance in northern and central France or northern Italy, but with towns in other European peripheries.[19] Yet Frankish Jerusalem was never just a peripheral town; it attracted settlers — and clerics — from various parts of Catholic Europe, including such major centres of the Twelfth-Century Renaissance as Paris and Chartres. Moreover, there was a constant stream of pilgrims from Europe, and these included such towering figures of twelfth-century culture as Otto of Freising and Joachim of Fiore.[20] Besides, the considerable creative activity of Jerusalem's clerics stood out against that of Europe's peripheral towns — even though it was marked, as we have seen, by a narrowness of focus.

I assume that this exclusivity stemmed from the particular inclinations of the European clerics who chose to go East and settle in Jerusalem, and who should not be considered a cross-section of the European clergy of the day. Only a specific segment, or — to use the term Louis Hartz introduced in his study of new, immigrant societies[21] — a specific "fragment" of Europe's clergy chose to live in Jerusalem. Members of this fragment did not stand out for their intellectual eminence. Guibert of Nogent, one of the most learned men of his time, alludes disparagingly to the dearth of learning among the clerics who participated in the First Crusade and in the conquest of Jerusalem[22] — that is, among the men who formed the nucleus of the Frankish Kingdom's clergy. These men were notable, rather, for their urge to live in the Holy Land, in the Holy City, at the Holy Places. Not satisfied with symbolic renderings, replicas, miniatures, even relics, theirs was a tactile religiosity that yearned for the genuine object itself. We know that such clerics were sometimes rebuked for their wish to live at the Holy Places by churchmen whose conception of the sacred was spiritual rather than place-bound. We may consequently assume that the one-sidedness of the Frankish clergy was the result of a process of self-selection, and that this trait was perpetuated by the attraction such one-sidedness exerted on like-minded newcomers, and its repulsion for broader-minded ones.

It should be added that we now know, too, of Frankish immigrants who were impelled by an intense though less rigidly place-bound religiosity. These were men who preferred caves on the slopes of Mount Tabor or of the Black Mountain near Antioch, or cells along the shores of Lake Tiberias or the River Jordan, to Jerusalem's major sanctuaries. Theirs was a quest for the eremitical life in (or near) the Holy Land, at locations marked for their remoteness from the bustle and temptations of ordinary life and evocative of biblical events only in a general sense. In a way, these hermits combined the sensual urge for life in a historically delimited sacred space with a determination to construct, by their own spiritual exertions, a space pervaded by sanctity. Only recently have late adaptations of the biographies of some twenty of these hermits come to light, and further information on the phenomenon can be gleaned from contemporary sources.[23] Our knowledge of these hermits should make us wary of chroniclers' and historians' generalizations about the presumably low-keyed tenor of religious life in the Frankish Kingdom.

Arnold Toynbee once pointed out that some former capital cities — like Benaras, Yathrīb and Rome — became holy cities after having lost their original political roles.[24] In twelfth-century Jerusalem, the nexus was inverse and possibly unique: because of the city's holiness, the crusaders made it their capital, the preferred residence of their rulers. In other words, Frankish Jerusalem was both a holy city and the capital of a kingdom. To what extent did the latter aspect shape intellectual activity within the city?

As is well known, many rulers of contemporaneous Europe patronized intellectually creative men. In Jerusalem, such patronage appears to have been rare. Foucher of Chartres, chaplain to Frankish Jerusalem's first king, wrote a chronicle of the First Crusade and of the early history of the Frankish Kingdom (the work made its way to France, where Guibert of Nogent remarked condescendingly on its style and content).[25] Baldwin III, Frankish Jerusalem's fourth king, ordered the compilation of a chronicle that virtually amounted to an abridged version of Foucher's; as far as we know, it was never brought to completion.[26] Only Jerusalem's fifth king, Amalric — who ruled between 1163 and 1174, invaded Egypt on four different occasions, and in his charters styled himself as "King in the Holy City of Jerusalem"[27] — is known for his considerably wider interests.

William of Tyre, the great chronicler of the Frankish Kingdom, knew King Amalric well and left behind a detailed description of him that highlights the king's disharmonious physique and complex, intense personality. William suggests that Amalric's modest Latin was more than offset by his keen intellect and retentive memory. He stresses the king's outstanding knowledge of customary law, his interest in history, and his indifference to mimicry and games of hazard. Above all, William emphasizes Amalric's curiosity, which led him to read, to indulge in conversations about distant countries and their customs, and, constantly, to ask questions.

William repeats just one of those questions. It is a telling one that scandalized William, a question suggestive not only of Amalric's interests but probably also of some of the intellectual influences with which he had come into contact. The king demanded nothing less than rational, non-scriptural evidence for the future resurrection! William's account leaves no doubt that Amalric had in mind the resurrection of the flesh, the *carnis resurrectionem* of the Credo.[28] Now, bodily resurrection, and the possibility of proving it by rational evidence, had been at issue in the realm of Islam at least since Avicenna wrote his *Letter on the Future Life* at the beginning of the eleventh century. The question was also being debated among Oriental Christians and Jews (a few years after Amalric's death, Maimonides, then living in Cairo, wrote his *Treatise on the Resurrection* in response to accusations that he had denied the future resurrection of the body). It is plausible that Amalric, who — as William attests — "loved to converse with men familiar with far countries and foreign customs," was prompted to ask his "novel and unusual question" after having heard of the discussions that were taking place among infidels and schismatics.

Amalric ordered William to write two chronicles, one describing the history of the Frankish Kingdom and the other recounting the deeds of the rulers of the Orient, from Muḥammad onward, on the basis of Arabic written sources.[29] The second assignment was truly extraordinary: no other twelfth-century Christian ruler, whether living on the borders of Islam or not, ever contemplated a history of the Saracens.[30] But Amalric evidently was curious about his enemies' past.

There was also an Oriental Christian physician-astrologer at Amalric's court, Abū Sulaymān Dāwūd, probably the author of an astrologically tainted *Book of Fates* that was composed in Amalric's honour.[31] Amalric appears also to have patronized a French vernacular poet, Guiot of Provins; and a short Latin poem that made its way into the *Carmina Burana* may have been written under Amalric's aegis.[32]

What does all this add up to? Quantitatively not much, especially when compared with cultural activities sponsored by such European contemporaries as Henry II of England or William I of Sicily.[33] But when variety and originality of outlook rather than volume of literary output are considered, this "King in the Holy City of Jerusalem" acquires considerable stature.

Amalric, however, was an extraordinary figure whose example does not appear to have been followed by his successors, and it is hardly accidental that the most original of the works he ordered, the *History of the Oriental Rulers*, did not survive. The cleric to whom he entrusted the writing of his two historical works, William of Tyre, was also an exceptional man: though born in Jerusalem, he spent some twenty years studying in France and Italy, because it was impossible to pursue higher learning in Jerusalem's cathedral school, or indeed anywhere in the Frankish Levant.[34] Incidentally, it appears that he wrote much of his extant chronicle in Tyre, not Jerusalem.

We have seen that the typical interest of twelfth-century Jerusalem's Frankish clerics revolved around the holy places. To what extent did such exclusivity also characterize men of letters active in other periods of Jerusalem's long and tortuous history? A longitudinal intellectual history of Jerusalem has yet to be written, and it might well show that other periods witnessed a wider spectrum of intellectual activity than did the Frankish one. Nevertheless, I am willing to risk the generalization that this holy town rarely if ever witnessed the thriving of religiously and morally neutral branches of knowledge before the belated onset of modernity a little more than a hundred years ago, and certainly never gained prominence in them.

Does there exist, in general, a *Wahlverwandtschaft*, an elective affinity, between sacred space and sacredness-centred, sacredness-related, rather pedestrian intellectual concerns? It is a tempting idea, one that appears to be supported by data on Mecca and Rome (in its phase as a holy city), though not Benaras;[35] but only a systematic comparative history of holy cities could enlighten us as to the validity of such a nexus and its determinants, variations, and limits.[36]

In the meantime, all we have are hunches, many of them quite unacademic. But I submit that it would not be prudent to dismiss them out of hand on this account. On the contrary, I believe that we are all indebted to Teddy Kollek — former mayor of this all-too-often sanctified, embarrassingly beautiful, and, as it would appear, interminably tragic city — for having reiterated the belief of many an artist, poet and ordinary Jerusalemite that there is sacredness in Jerusalem's air, and that it is somehow shared by all its inhabitants[37] (I know that Joshua Prawer harboured similar thoughts). On the other hand, let us not overromanticize matters. Whatever it might be that we are groping to comprehend, it is not an unequivocal blessing (even if, as Mr. Kollek apparently believes, it makes Jerusalem's street-sweepers abstain from strikes). As we see around us all too clearly, sanctity has its price, or its prices. Intellectual one-sidedness or mediocrity may well be one of them.

Notes

1. E. Durkheim, *Les Formes élémentaires de la vie religieuse*, Paris 1925², pp. 458–459.
2. See N. Kenaan-Kedar, "Symbolic Meaning in Crusader Architecture: The Twelfth-Century Dome of the Holy Sepulcher Church in Jerusalem," *Cahiers archéologiques*, XXXIV (1986), pp. 113–115.
3. See the texts on the shrine's construction assembled by P. Lehmann, "Die mittellateinischen Dichtungen der Prioren des Tempels von Jerusalem Acardus und Gaufridus," in *Corona Quernea: Festgabe Karl Stecker, Monumenta Germaniae Historica: Schriften*, VI, Leipzig 1941, pp. 302–303. During Saladin's siege of Jerusalem the Franks threatened to destroy the Dome and uproot the Rock, thereby disclosing their awareness of the shrine's sanctity for the Muslims: 'Imād al-Dīn in Abū Shāma, in *Recueil des Historiens des Croisades: Historiens Orientaux*, IV, Paris 1898, p. 328.
4. On this transition of traditions, see H. Busse, "Vom Felsendom zum Templum Domini," in W. Fischer & J. Schneider (eds.), *Das Heilige Land im Mittelalter: Begegnungsraum zwischen Orient und Okzident*, Neustadt an der Aisch 1982, pp. 19–31; S. Schein, "Between Mount Moriah and the Holy Sepulchre: The Changing

Traditions of the Temple Mount in the Central Middle Ages," *Traditio*, 40 (1984), pp. 175–195.

5. See A. Schönfelder, "Die Prozessionen der Lateiner in Jerusalem zur Zeit der Kreuzzüge," *Historisches Jahrbuch*, XXXII (1932), pp. 584–586, 590, 594–596; for the coronation procession, see *Livre de Jean d'Ibelin*, VII, ed. A.A. Beugnot, in *Recueil des Historiens des Croisades: Lois*, I, Paris 1841, p. 31. For an overview, see J. Prawer, *The Latin Kingdom of Jerusalem: European Colonialism in the Middle Ages*, London 1972, pp. 100–101, 176–178.
6. Achard's work was edited by Lehmann, "Dichtungen" (above, note 3), pp. 307–330. For excerpts from Geoffroi's work see E.G. Ledos, "Un nouveau manuscrit du poème d'Achard d'Arrouaise sur le Templum Domini," *Bibliothèque de l'Ecole des Chartes*, LXXVII (1916), pp. 64–73.
7. P. Kallenberg, *Fontes Liturgiae Carmelitanae*, Rome 1962, pp. 88, 95–100.
8. For the evolution of Christian ritual in fourth-century Jerusalem, see the stimulating discussion by J.Z. Smith, *To Take Place: Toward Theory in Ritual*, Chicago–London 1987, pp. 86–95. Yet that earlier creation of ritual was not complicated by the presence of Christian-held edifices on the Temple Mount.
9. BN lat. 12056, fol. 301v: "*Oratio ante portam Ierusalem*. Omnipotens sempiterne deus edificator et custos civitatis superne, custodi die noctuque locum istum cum habitatoribus eius. et intercedente beata Maria cum omnibus sanctis sit domicilium incolumitatis et pacis."
10. For the depiction of the Anastasis on the mosaic decorating the Frankish-built part of the church as well as on the seals of the Frankish patriarchs, see A. Borg, "The Lost Apse Mosaic of the Holy Sepulchre, Jerusalem," in A. Borg & A. Martindale (eds.), *The Vanishing Past: Studies of Medieval Art, Liturgy and Metrology Presented to Christopher Hohler*, Oxford 1981, pp. 7–12; Kenaan-Kedar, "Symbolic Meaning" (above, note 2), p. 114.
11. See for example G. Bresc-Bautier (ed.), *Le Cartulaire du chapitre du Saint-Sépulcre de Jérusalem*, Paris 1984, docs. 142–151, pp. 275–301.
12. For a discussion of this miracle, see B. McGinn, "*Iter Sancti Sepulchri* — On the Piety of the First Crusaders," in B.K. Lackner & R.P. Philp (eds.), *Essays on Medieval Civilization*, Austin 1978, pp. 33–38, and, in general, E.W. Hopkins, "The Cult of Fire in Christianity," in J.D.C. Pavry (ed.), *Oriental Studies in Honour of Cursetji Erachji Pavry*, London 1933, pp. 142–150.
13. "Ad incredulorum hesitationem refutandam et fidem confirmandam." C. Kohler, "Un rituel et un bréviaire du Saint-Sépulcre de Jérusalem (XIIe–XIIIe siècle)," *Revue de l'Orient latin*, VIII (1900–1901), p. 421. And see the recapitulation by Prawer, *Latin Kingdom* (above, note 5), pp. 178–179 (but it appears that the Greeks continued to participate in the celebration and to do so prominently, since the *Ritual of the Holy Sepulchre* reports that the prayers were said "in Greek and in Latin": Kohler, "Rituel," p. 420).
14. The most detailed study, based on new evidence from British Library Addit. 8927, fols. 134r–135r, is by my colleague A. Linder, "The Liturgy of the Liberation of Jerusalem," *Mediaeval Studies*, LII (1990), pp. 110–131; on the stages in the office's formation see pp. 112 and 123. For the sermon see C. Kohler, "Un sermon

commémoratif de la prise de Jérusalem par les Croisés attribué à Foucher de Chartres," *Revue de l'Orient latin*, VIII (1900–1901), pp. 158–164.

15. See G. Bautier, "L'Envoi de la relique de la Vraie Croix à Notre-Dame de Paris en 1120," *Bibliothèque de l'Ecole des Chartes*, CXXIX (1971), pp. 387–397.
16. On the twenty-one instances between 1101 and 1187 in which the Cross is known to have been taken into a battle or siege, see B.Z. Kedar, "The Patriarch Eraclius," in B.Z. Kedar, H.E. Mayer & R.C. Smail (eds.), *Outremer: Studies in the History of the Crusading Kingdom of Jerusalem presented to Joshua Prawer*, Jerusalem 1982, pp. 181–182.
17. Kohler, "Rituel" (above, note 13), pp. 395, 401.
18. ʿImād al-Dīn al-Iṣfahānī, *Conquête de la Syrie et de la Palestine par Ṣalāḥ al-Dīn*, ed. C. de Landberg, Leiden 1888, p. 28; English translation in F. Gabrieli, *Arab Historians of the Crusades* (transl. by E.J. Costello), Berkeley–Los Angeles 1969, p. 137. See also E. Sivan, "Islam and the Crusaders: Antagonism, Polemics, Dialogue," in *Religionsgespräche im Mittelalter*, ed. B. Niewöhner, Wolfenbütteler Mittelalter-Studien, Wolfenbüttel 1992, p. 212.
19. For an argument along these lines, see J.S.C. Riley-Smith's remarks in the 1984 symposium "The Crusading Kingdom of Jerusalem — The First European Colonial Society?" in B.Z. Kedar (ed.), *The Horns of Ḥaṭṭīn*, Jerusalem–London 1992, pp. 353–354.
20. For unequivocal proof of Joachim's pilgrimage to Jerusalem, see G. Buonaiuti (ed.), *Tractatus super Quattuor Evangelia di Gioacchino da Fiore*, Fonti per la Storia d'Italia LXVII, Rome 1930, p. xxii.
21. L. Hartz et al., *The Founding of New Societies: Studies in the History of the United States, Latin America, South Africa, and Australia*, New York 1964, esp. Chap. 1.
22. Guibert of Nogent, *Historia quae dicitur Gesta Dei per Francos*, in *Recueil des Historiens des Croisades: Historiens Occidentaux*, IV, Paris 1879, pp. 232–233.
23. See B.Z. Kedar, "Gerard of Nazareth, A Neglected Twelfth-Century Writer in the Latin Levant: A Contribution to the Intellectual and Monastic History of the Crusader States," *Dumbarton Oaks Papers*, XXXVII (1983), pp. 55–77; reprinted in idem, *The Franks in the Levant: 11th to 14th Centuries*, Aldershot 1993, Article IV. For more material and discussion see A. Jotischky, *The Perfection of Solitude: Hermits and Monks in the Crusader States*, University Park, Penn., 1995.
24. A Toynbee, *Cities on the Move*, London 1970, pp. 166–168 (Chap. 8 of the book is entitled "Holy Cities").
25. Guibert of Nogent, *Gesta* (above, note 22), pp. 250–252, 257.
26. *Historia Nicaena vel Antiochena necnon Jerosolymitana*, in *Recueil des Historiens des Croisades: Historiens Occidentaux*, V/1, Paris 1895, pp. 139–185. A detailed comparison of this chronicle with its *Vorlagen* will appear in my *Intellectual Activities on a Sacred Periphery: A Cultural History of the Frankish Kingdom of Jerusalem* (forthcoming).
27. Bresc-Bautier, *Cartulaire* (above, note 11), docs. 135, 156, pp. 262, 306.
28. *Willelmi Tyrensis archiepiscopi Chronicon*, 19, 2–3, ed. R.B.C. Huygens, Corpus Christianorum. Continuatio Mediaevalis, LXIII–LXIIIA, Turnhout 1986, pp. 864–868.

29. *Willelmi Tyrensis Chronicon* (above, note 28), 1, prol. and 19, 21, pp. 99–100, 892.
30. For a similar conclusion, see H. Möhring, "Zu der Geschichte der orientalischen Herrscher des Wilhelm von Tyrus: Die Frage der Quellenabhängigkeiten," *Mittellateinisches Jahrbuch*, XIX (1984), p. 183.
31. Abū Sulaymān's career will be discussed in detail in my *Intellectual Activities on a Sacred Periphery* (above, note 26). In the meantime, see E. Kohlberg & B.Z. Kedar, "A Melkite Physician in Frankish Jerusalem and Ayyubid Damascus: Muwaffaq al-Dīn Ya'qūb b. Siqlāb," *Asian and African Studies*, XXII (1988), pp. 114–115; reprinted in Kedar, *Franks* (above, note 23), Article XII.
32. *Les Oeuvres de Guiot de Provins, poète lyrique et satirique*, ed. J. Orr, Manchester 1915, p. 20, lines 346–348; A. Baudler, *Guiot von Provins, seine Gönner, die "Suite de la Bible" und seine lyrischen Dichtungen*, Halle 1902, p. 28; *Carmina Burana*, ed. A. Hilka & O. Schumann, I/1, Heidelberg 1930, No. 51a, p. 104.
33. A detailed comparison of intellectual activities at the courts of Amalric and his contemporaries will appear in Chap. 3 of my book on the culture of the Frankish Kingdom (see above, note 26).
34. On William's elementary and advanced education, see H.E. Mayer, "Guillaume de Tyr à l'école," *Mémoires de l'Académie des sciences, arts et belles-lettres de Dijon*, CXXVII (1985–86), pp. 257–265, reprinted in idem, *Kings and Lords in the Latin Kingdom of Jerusalem*, Aldershot 1994, Article V; R.B.C. Huygens, "Guillaume de Tyr étudiant: un chapître (XIX, 12) de son 'Histoire retrouvé'," *Latomus*, XXI (1962), pp. 811–829.
35. See D.L. Eck, *Banāras: City of Light*, Princeton 1982, pp. 43, 59, 85; R. Salomon, "The Ukti-vyakti-prakaraṇa as a Manual of Spoken Sanskrit," *Indo-Iranian Journal*, XXIV (1982), pp. 13–25. I would like to thank my colleague David Shulman for enlightening me on these issues.
36. Such a history remains a desideratum. Hopefully it will not neglect the works of such holy-city-dwelling poets as Kabir of Banāras (d. 1518) or Amichai of present-day Jerusalem.
37. T. Kollek, remarks at the opening session of the Jerusalem conference on Sacred Space, on which this volume is based.

10

The Harem: a Major Source of Islam's Military Might

David Ayalon

The harem, into which no virile males except the patron of the house were allowed to enter, was clearly a sacred space. In this review, I shall attempt to demonstrate the tremendous impact, extending far beyond its recognized boundaries, which that institution had on the Muslim socio-military system.

Preface

During over half a century of acquaintance, as students, colleagues and friends, I never missed an opportunity to remind Joshua Prawer that my Mamluks drove his crusaders into the sea — out of the Holy Land, out of the Holy City, out of the area of the Holy Temple, out of the Holy Sepulchre — out of all that immense sacred space. In speaking of Mamluks, of course, I refer to the Ayyubid army as well, whose core and backbone consisted of Mamluks, the latter, in turn, having emerged from the Mamluk element of a Mamluk dynasty, the Zangids of Mosul and Syria. Prawer absorbed all that boasting of mine with a magnanimous crusader chivalry, mingled with no small amount of amusement. The Mamluks and I are utterly lacking in that knightly trait, a lack accentuated by the attitude of another longtime friend and colleague, Uriel Heyd. Though he had more than once been an eyewitness to that teasing, he never took advantage of it to remind me of how his Ottomans wiped my Mamluks out of existence and swallowed their great empire for breakfast — a mere continental breakfast that only served to whet their appetite for more.

In retrospect I regret that Heyd did not make that reminder to me, for I could have made a simple rejoinder. The fight between the Ottomans and the Mamluks was an internal Muslim affair, or, even more precisely, an internal family affair. Two Mamluk systems collided, and the one which had better adapted itself to the requirements of the contemporary art of war gained the upper hand.

The Military Struggle between Islam and European Christianity

Going back to the crusades, they ended, as we all know, in total failure, with far-reaching consequences. But if we stop at that, we miss the critical factor in the struggle between Islam and Christianity, and especially between Islam and Christian Europe. The dismal end of the crusades should be viewed merely as a setback, albeit a very severe one, in the steadily growing preponderance of the West, to which neither Islam nor any other non-Christian European civilization could present a really durable response. It should be pointed out immediately, in this context, that Islam from the outset was in a much better military position vis-à-vis Christian Europe than the other non-Christian civilizations.

To cut a long story short, in the struggle between the two great monotheistic civilizations for world domination, there were two main arenas: the land and the sea. The Muslims ultimately lost out in both, and have made no real comeback up to the present day. But the two defeats did not occur simultaneously: that on the sea, which occurred in the course of the eleventh century, preceded the final defeat on land by several hundred years. Two factors make that maritime defeat extraordinary: (a) in that century, the main Muslim naval power was that of the Fatimids, who were more navy-minded than most other Muslim rulers before or since; (b) nevertheless, the victory of Christian Europe was not accompanied by any major sea battle. The Muslims were gradually swept aside.

The defeat was final, in the sense that Islam ceased to be a world naval power. It is indicative of the process that the Byzantine navy, for centuries the major adversary of Islam at sea but later debilitated by both the Muslim and the Italian navies, was replaced by a formidable Christian West-European naval power. Nothing parallel happened on the Muslim side following the decline of the Fatimid navy.

The practical elimination of Muslim sea power as a factor to be reckoned with in the Mediterranean had two important consequences:

(a) In the short term, it enabled the crusaders to hold on to their conquests for two centuries. Despite their sometimes painful nuisance value, the Muslim navies could not seriously interfere with the lifeline connecting the crusader states with mainland Europe by sea. The end of the crusaders' occupation of the Syro-Palestinian coast only accentuated the naval weakness of the Muslims, who systematically destroyed the fortifications and ports along the coast, especially in the Palestinian part. The scale of that destruction, unprecedented in recorded human history, serves as decisive proof that they did not believe they would regain naval supremacy in the foreseeable future.

(b) In the long term, with the rise of the Italian navies and those of the European lands lying to the west and north of Italy, the Muslims lost any prospect of dominating the lands beyond the sea or the international maritime routes leading to them. They had no chance of capturing the new international routes leading to the Western Hemisphere, or of keeping their hold on the old ones leading to India and beyond, if and when a West-European adversary appeared on the scene. And, indeed, a relatively small Portuguese naval force, thousands of kilometres away from its home base, almost overnight permanently wrested from them the control of routes which they had commanded without contest for 900 years. India and China, notwithstanding their size and grandeur, had presented no challenge to the Muslims in the first place and later constituted no factor in the Muslim–European naval struggle that took place east of Suez. The Ottomans, who temporarily regained Muslim supremacy in the waters of the Eastern Mediterranean, could only look helplessly upon the whole global transformation. They were locked up inside the Mediterranean Sea (or part of it), the Black Sea, the Red Sea and the Persian Gulf, and they could do very little beyond these waters.

Thus, in the eleventh century or thereabout, one can already discern the embryonic shape of the modern world.

On land, the defeat of Islam was postponed for centuries and was much more gradual, owing mainly to the Mamluk military institution. Without it, not only would defeat have come earlier, but the very geographical boundaries of Islam would have been essentially different and very probably much narrower. Here I can give only a brief explanation for this assertion.

After the decline of Arab and Khurasani military power, it was replaced by that of the Mamluks, which lasted many centuries and which, when it had outlived its usefulness, had nothing to replace it in terms of world power. Most of the major Muslim states or empires had Mamluk armies of one sort or another which formed the core and backbone of their military might, and the stronger the Mamluk army they managed to build, the greater were their chances of military success, including territorial expansion. It was the Mamluk armies of the Samanids (261–389/874–999) who advanced deeply into the lands of the Turks and annexed sizeable parts of them. It was the Mamluk armies of the Ghaznawids (351–582/962–1186) who took the lion's share in the conquest and Islamization of vast areas of India, thus laying the foundation for present-day Pakistan and Bangladesh and for the presence of yet another hundred million Muslims outside of these two states in the Indian subcontinent. It was the Mamluk nucleus of the army of the Great Seljuk Alp Arslan which, in the battle of Manzikert against the Byzantines in 1071, turned the almost certain defeat of a disintegrating Muslim army into a resounding victory, opening the way for the conquest of Anatolia and, ultimately, for the rise of the Ottoman Empire. The mainstay of that empire's military and even, to no small extent, its administrative might was the body of slave recruits which grew out of the Mamluk system and could not otherwise have come into being. There is no need to speculate about how the realm of the Ottomans might have developed had its rulers adopted a non-Mamluk system, because one thing is certain: an immense military vacuum would have been created, inviting an ever more powerful Europe to fill it.

To come back to the Egyptian and Syro-Palestinian front: the main credit for driving the crusaders out of Syria and Palestine, and, just as importantly, repulsing their attempts to conquer Egypt, goes to the Mamluk armies of the Ayyubids and the Mamluks, without which nothing could have shaken the Frankish hold on this vital area. (Note, moreover, that in order to control Egypt the Franks had no need to occupy the whole of it; a number of strongholds, especially on the coast, would have sufficed.) Furthermore, it was the Mamluks who, from 1260 (the battle of 'Ayn Jālūt) on, formed a bulwark against the onslaught of the Mongols, until the latter adopted Islam and their empire disintegrated.

But with all due respect to the great achievements of the Mamluks in that crucial period, there does seem to have existed, even then, a weapon which might have succeeded in breaking their power, or at least in weakening it considerably, had it been thoroughly and systematically used. That weapon was the blockade, a notion that existed already in the crusader period, but gathered great momentum after its end. Egypt and Syria, of course, were more than self-sufficient in terms of food supply; but preventing the importation of wood and metals would have caused very great damage to their war machine, and beyond it as well. Moreover, the supply of Mamluks, who were brought over mainly by sea and to no small extent in Frankish ships, would have been reduced very considerably. Since the Franks had full command of the sea, they could also have prevented the importation of Mamluks in Muslim ships. The alternative land route was very unsatisfactory. It was much longer and more exhausting; it was exposed to attacks by nomads; and, above all, the Mamluks were a most precious item. Any Muslim ruler could lay his hand on the Mamluk slave boys crossing his territory, and quite often there was more than one such ruler along the road. The situation would have become even worse when a hostile Muslim ruler stood in the way. Using the land route would very likely have resulted in the arrival of a greatly reduced number of Mamluks, of inferior quality. However, a real blockade never materialized.

The Harem and the Military Might of Islam

Now, how does all this bring the harem into the picture? In medieval Islam there were three uniquely powerful bodies, all of them belonging to the Muslim slave system, which should not be judged by modern European standards, and which, from the time of the early 'Abbāsids had an overwhelming impact on the courts of the Muslim rulers. These three inseparable bodies were the women, the eunuchs and the Mamluks (it is true that not all the women were included in the slave category, but that is of marginal importance). The Great Triangle, as I call it, had a strength and durability unprecedented in the history of Islam. Obviously, the connecting link between the women and the Mamluks was the eunuchs, for they were the irreplaceable trainers, guardians and supervisors of the young Mamluk novices.

The eunuchs formed part of Muslim society from its very beginning. They were institutionalized by Caliph Mu'āwiya (661–680), the founder of the Umayyad dynasty, and they were already a decisive factor in the 'Abbāsid court when the Mamluks were made the major power of the 'Abbasid empire by Caliph al-Mu'taṣim (833-842). During the third/ninth century, the permanence of the close connection between the Mamluks and the eunuchs who supervised them in their youth became evident. The young Mamluk boys were recruited around the age of puberty and stayed in the military schools or training places for several years, a period characterized by intense and growing sexual desires. It was the eunuchs who shielded these unmarried boys, secluded from the outside world, far away from their families and natural environment, and destined to be a one-generation nobility, from the lust of Mamluk and other adults and from one another as well. The fresh novices had to be protected from the older ones, and not only sexually. The way stronger, older boys treat weaker and younger newcomers in a boarding school is well known, and there was never a boarding school so tightly closed to what lay beyond its walls as the Mamluk school.

Most of the eunuchs also had the great advantage of not having families of their own, so that they could dedicate all their time, energy and attention to their protégés, who, in turn, had left their relatives far behind in their countries of origin. The eunuchs often developed fatherly as well as motherly feelings towards them. At the same time, because of their strictness and cruelty, they could inculcate discipline into these youngsters; in addition to their unique trustworthiness (they were often put in charge of treasuries, properties and monetary affairs), the eunuchs were also jailers, punishers and torturers *par excellence*. The connections between the eunuchs and the Mamluks often did not stop at the apprenticeship period, but continued beyond it. It was easy for a Mamluk graduate to obey a eunuch as a commander, because he had obeyed eunuchs throughout his years of apprenticeship. Add to this the eunuch's eagerness to prove himself more manly than the unemasculated male, and it becomes easy to understand the immense role played by so many eunuchs as commanders in various Muslim armies. The famous eunuch Mu'nis al-Muẓaffar al-Mu'taḍidī (846–933) was, according to one version, the first general in Islam to receive the title of *amīr al-umarā'* (commander in chief). Incidentally, whereas virile blacks were barred from joining the high court and military society, the door to that society was generally open to black eunuchs.

Thus, there was a whole set of reasons for preferring the eunuch as guardian of the Mamluk in his apprenticeship period; but it should be emphasized that the first reason, namely, the protection of the novice from pederasty, was sufficient in itself. The absence of such protection would have put an end to the Mamluk system as a respectable military machine, particularly in the context of the prevailing conceptions in a civilization where homosexuality was so widespread. The passive partner in such an intercourse, especially if he was of tender age, was deemed worthless as a soldier. He was a woman, and the earlier in life he began with that practice, which too often turns into a lifelong habit, the more womanly he became, according to those conceptions.

As we have said, Caliph al-Mu'taṣim established the Mamluk military system as the mainstay of Islam's military might during the thirties of the ninth century. At that time, the eunuchs had already accumulated exceptionally strong power and influence in Muslim society, and particularly in its upper echelons. Since they educated the children of the great and of others, what could have been more obvious and natural, when the Mamluk army came into being on a grand scale, than to make them, in due course, the guardians and supervisors of the Mamluk novices? Under the watchful eyes of the eunuchs, who must have been with the novices around the clock, non-eunuchs could be allowed in, at limited times, for specific purposes such as teaching religious and related subjects or various branches of the art of war.

Let us now look at the same phenomenon from a different angle. Let us suppose, for argument's sake alone, that there had been no polygamy, no concubinage and no seclusion of women in Islam, and, consequently, no eunuchs. Then, towards the middle of the ninth century, a great Muslim ruler would come to the conclusion that the only way to retain and increase the offensive and defensive might of Islam would be to adopt the Mamluk system. Would it have been possible *then* to start bringing over eunuchs for that purpose? This seems extremely unlikely, and that alone would have prevented the emergence of a Mamluk military society worthy of its name. It was only at the specific tender age of puberty that the Mamluk could be shaped as a devoted Muslim, a superb soldier and a loyal servant of his patron. For the purpose of protecting these vulnerable boys, concentrated as they were in one place in a distant and utterly foreign country, with nobody of their own adult kith and kin to look to for help or advice, the eunuchs were irreplaceable; and it should be borne in mind that many of the boys were very good-looking according to the prevailing standards of the times.*

It is worth noting in this context that there does not seem to have been any separation between the eunuchs serving in the harem and those in the military schools. They formed one body, and there was a single pool for service in both places. Of course, it may well have been difficult to serve in both at the same time, but the door seems to have remained open for the trainer eunuchs to serve in the harem and *vice versa*. This made the connections between the three elements of the triangle particularly strong.

One might contend, again for argument's sake, that a strong, dynamic and durable army, as good as that of the Mamluks for both offensive and defensive purposes, could have been built on entirely different principles, though I cannot imagine what they might have been. But whether or not such an alternative set of principles could have existed under the prevailing conditions, we may certainly state that Islamic society would have had to undergo a most fundamental transformation in order for a different army to emerge on their

* Today's heated controversy about the enlistment of homosexuals in the armed forces invites an explanatory remark. Recruits to present-day armies, at least the overwhelming majority of them, are not exposed to the same conditions as the Mamluk novices. They start their military service at an older age, and most of them leave the army after a few years. I have discussed this subject at considerable length in my book on the eunuchs (see the attached bibliographical note). Of course, my opinion is that of an outsider, and scholars who have studied the subject of homosexuality more systematically might reach different conclusions. However, for the Muslim rulers in the periods under discussion, the problems and arguments prevalent today in this regard were simply non-existent, and they would in any case have been irrelevant, given the unwavering policy of putting the Mamluk tyros under the guardianship of the eunuchs.

basis. That transformation would have had to take place, first and foremost, within the society's institutionalized slave component. Here, however, we must bear in mind a basic truth: Already during the reign of the early 'Abbāsids, a free person of a purely free descent would have felt completely out of place among the inhabitants of the caliph's court, and especially within his immediate entourage.

Thus, so much goes back to the woman! *Cherchez la femme!* Without the woman, with her particular status in Islam, there would have been no eunuchs, and it is difficult to see how a real Mamluk military system could have emerged without them. In this way, the subdued and secluded woman indirectly made a major contribution to Islam's military might, even before one takes into account her influence and impact behind the scenes, which was considerable indeed. In the Great Triangle, women were far from being the least important angle.

Conclusion

In the protracted armed struggle between Islam and Christianity, Islam began losing out, in global terms, to Christianity — and particularly to Western Christianity — centuries before the major landmarks usually cited in the emergence of the modern world (counted in reverse): the French Revolution, the Industrial Revolution, the Reformation, the Renaissance, the invention of the printing press, and even the introduction of firearms, which took place in parts of Europe and the Mediterranean area in the early fourteenth century. But for the Mamluks, that defeat would have been far more comprehensive and decisive from the very outset. This means that even the processes leading up to those landmarks (processes which are extremely difficult and often impossible to reconstruct) were sufficient to tip the scales against Islam. The study of the military and socio-military history of Islam should be carried out in confrontation with that harsh reality.

From a contemporary vantage point, we may remark that at least from the advent of Islam onwards, world history has been dominated by the monotheistic peoples or civilizations. They form the dynamic, aggressive and expansionist powers that overwhelm the non-monotheistic civilizations. Within the monotheistic camp,

Islam, on balance, has been the loser militarily for almost a thousand years. When the Mamluk institution withered, there was nothing in Islam to replace it. The only alternative was to copy the European military machine, some elements of which had already been adopted. The first to carry this out fully was the ruler of Egypt, Muhammad 'Alī (1220–1264/1805–1848), who very quickly reaped rewards: first, the conquest of most of the Arabian Peninsula; then that of the Sudan; and finally the occupation of Syria and beyond, posing a threat to the very existence of the Ottoman Empire. In the long recorded history of Egypt, no ruler had ever accomplished such a large-scale expansion. But if these new methods were decisively successful against Muslim adversaries who had not yet fully discarded the old Muslim military machine, they proved to be quite insufficient against a European adversary.

Even today, despite the fact that all the Muslim armies follow European models and have no real historical connection with their own military past, the gap between them and the major Western-European armies is not narrowing. In order to adopt the European military model, and for other reasons as well, the Muslim countries had to accept a revolutionary socio-cultural change. That revolution, however, does not seem to have been comprehensive enough, and this is another reality which the student of history will have to confront.

Bibliographical Note

This brief review is based on several studies of mine on the Mamluks and on the eunuchs, including the following published works:

L'Esclavage du Mamelouk, Jerusalem 1951.

"The Mamluks and Naval Power: A Phase of the Struggle between Islam and Christian Europe," *Proceedings of the Israel Academy of Sciences and Humanities*, I (1967), pp. 1–12.

"The Muslim City and Mamluk Military Aristocracy," *Proceedings of the Israel Academy of Sciences and Humanities*, II (1968), pp. 311–319.

"The Impact of Firearms on the Muslim World," *Princeton Near East Papers*, no. 20, Princeton 1975, pp. 32–43.

"The Importance of the Mamluk Institution," *Der Islam*, LIII (1976), pp. 196–225.

"Ayyubids, Kurds and Turks," *Der Islam*, LIV (1977), pp. 1–32.

"Ibn Khaldūn's View of the Mamluk Phenomenon," *Jerusalem Studies in Arabic and Islam*, II (1980), pp. 321–349.

"Egypt as a Dominant Factor in Syria and Palestine during the Islamic Period," in *Egypt and Palestine: A Millenium of Association (868–1948)*, Jerusalem 1984, pp. 17–47.

The Encyclopedia of Islam, new edition, VI, s.v. *Mamluk*, pp. 314a–321a.

Gunpowder and Firearms in the Mamluk Kingdom — A Challenge to a Medieval Society, London, 1956 (reprinted 1978).

"The Eunuchs in the Mamluk Sultanate," *Studies in Memory of Gaston Wiet*, Jerusalem 1977, pp. 267–295.

"On the Eunuchs in Islam," *Jerusalem Studies in Arabic and Islam*, I (1979), pp. 67–124.

"On the Term *khādim* in the Sense of 'Eunuch' in the Early Muslim Sources," *Arabica*, XXXII (Paris 1985), pp. 289–308.

In my forthcoming book, *Eunuchs, Caliphs and Sultans — A Study in Power Relationships* (Jerusalem, in press), I deal extensively with some of the subjects discussed in the present review.

11

Holy Body, Holy Society: Conflicting Medieval Structural Conceptions

Kenneth R. Stow

That Europeans in medieval times used or exploited sacred theologies on the way to self-definition is well known. Jews said they inhabited a *qehillah qedoshah* (a holy community); Christians, a *communis patria* (a common fatherland) — a term that originally referred exclusively to the Church — for which they were prepared to die. None other than the famous English jurist Bracton (d. 1268) referred to royal possessions and prerogatives as *res quasi sacrae*, because they were part and parcel of the *corpus mysticum*, the civic embodiment of the *Corpus Christi*, which had come to symbolize, if not sacralize, the undying body of the sovereign republic, wholly or in part.[1]

It is less well known that Christian ideologies of state, which were far removed from those of the Jews, were instrumental in shaping the Jewish fate. In France, the Jews were said to have offended the *corpus reipublicae mysticum*, in England, the *communis utilitas*. The latter they offended through their lending, which, according to Edward I himself, was causing havoc, creating disorder, and fomenting dissension in the real-estate market.[2] Lending was no less a problem in France. Officially, it was forbidden from about 1223; in practice, even royalty was ambivalent, but its persistence weighed heavily on the royal conscience. The presence of the Jews, it was felt, harmed the integrity of the crown and, indeed, of the republic. A radical solution would have to be adopted.[3] In 1290 and 1306, the Jews were expelled, respectively, from England and France. In Spain, too, the Jews were accused of harming the republic; their offence, according to the 1492 decree of expulsion, was aiding the return of Marranos to the Jewish fold.[4] Wherever the integrity and sanctity of the state were said to be threatened, Jewish existence was in danger.

The same opinion was expressed by less noble exponents of the body politic. Rindfleisch, who wandered through Germany in 1298 preaching the destruction of the Jews, extolled the inviolability of the Christian town.[5] His point of reference was no doubt the *Corpus Christi*. The Jew, said Rindfleisch, must be destroyed, for he was threatening the honour of the Christian polity, symbolized by Christ himself, the Eucharist, borne with increasing frequency in processions, where it demarcated the community both ritualistically and politically.[6] Had Jews been numerous in the thirteenth century in northern Italy, where, according to Marvin Becker, "the polis was spoken of reverently as 'the mystical body of Christ',"[7] they might have been viewed and treated in the same way. There may well be a correspondence between the growing presence of Jews in the region after this time and the increased study of Roman law, which, on a practical level, envisioned the Jews as *cives*, and on a theoretical level inspired the commune to see itself as a *civitas*, an entity sacred unto itself, but now more metaphorically than actually a part of Christ's mystical body.[8]

In fifteenth-century Germany, Roman law, though studied in the schools, had yet to make itself felt in practice. Both there and in imperial Trent in the Italian far north, the Jews continued to be regarded as a civic threat. They were said to have murdered Christian boys and ritually consumed their blood. The Franciscans — some of whom were at least partially responsible for the blood libel in Trent in 1475 — shared this view. Blood imagery pervaded their attacks on Jewish money-lending as well. Money, they said, was the life-blood of society, and the Jews were draining it for their own benefit; they were a gangrenous limb in the civic body which ought to be amputated and discarded.[9] This way of thinking is well illustrated in a six-part *praedella* by Paolo Uccello in Urbino, portraying a Jew who connives to secure a host, which he then defiles by means of usurious perversion and exploitation, seducing a Christian woman into forfeiting her salvation. The painting was commissioned by members of the local Confraternity of the Holy Sacrament.[10]

Images ascribing sanctity to the body politic thus existed on many levels, to the Jew's disadvantage. One of these was that of the sacredness of the corporeal body itself. The individual Christian was regarded as sacred in his own person, either as a member of the civic *Corpus Christi* or through ingesting Christ himself. His or her body was as spiritual as it was corporeal. The familial framework preferred by the Church, accordingly, was a spiritual one, composed of the entire body of the faithful, with the clergy at its head; or, in a more restricted sense, composed of small bands like the retinue of St. Catherine of Siena, popularly known as the "joyous brigade." The Gospels declared that a follower of Christ was to desert father and mother, and the crusaders, consequently, abandoned their biological families and responsibilities. At stake, said Pope Urban II at Clermont, was eternal reward. Innocent III permitted crusaders to absolve themselves unilaterally from paying their wives the conjugal debt, although this raised some doubts among the canonists. The crusade itself, in the eyes of its monk-chroniclers, had the character of a mobile monastery; women were best left at home.[11] This ideal of abstinence applied to non-crusaders as well. A pious person was meant to prefer mystical union with the body of Christ to carnal union even with his or her spouse. Union with the latter, moreover, according to preachers such as Bernardino da Siena, was to be preceded by prayer and fasting to diminish the sinful effects of sexuality (not to mention the relish with which the disobedient majority normally indulged itself).[12] Human corporeality, personal and familial, was ideally to be spiritualized and subordinated to the needs of the greater mystical body of the Church.

That spiritual-Christly body was to be safeguarded at all times, and also protected from dangers lurking outside. Thus, Gregory the Great warned against Jews owning Christian slaves, for such ownership was tantamount to "giving the boot" to the members of Christ.[13] "Do you not know," St. Paul had said (I Cor. 6:15), "that your bodies are limbs and organs of Christ?" From the throne to the most humble homestead, even that of the slave, medieval Christian society was permeated with a sense of belonging to a mythical, mystical body, and it was devoted to keeping that body's oneness intact,[14] for this was the proper service of Christ. And so, very often, the borders between Christ the Lord, Christ as manifest in the individual believer, and Christ the image of the body politic were blurred. Was not the Eucharist, in the high Middle Ages, called the *corpus verum* — originally (in about the ninth century) called the *corpus mysticum* by writers such as Rabanus Maurus? And was this not the very term ultimately used for the corporate entity of the body politic or the state?[15]

Christ was society; society was Christ, as the *Corpus Christi* processions remind us once more. The mystical or civic body of Christ might thus be seen as Christ's very person. And would that body not stand out in even greater relief if the Christly person were to be contrasted with the physiognomy of the Jew? Fifteenth-century paintings of the Last Supper hanging in the Unterdenlinden Museum at Colmar portray Christ as a pure Alsatian, but the Apostles are drawn with bulbous Jewish noses. The Jew's bodily image does not dissolve even after he has professed belief. Christ's divinity, however, transfigures him, distinguishing him from the unalterably human Jew. These pictures are filled with ambiguities; but then, ambiguity pervades the whole Christian record on the Jews, beginning with Chapter 11 of Paul's Epistle to the Romans. They refer no less to man's overall social condition, to the demarcation of the saved from the unsaved,whoever they may be. Christ's body and its human members needed extraordinary protection. The unholy, in this case the Jewish contaminant, the leaven mentioned by Paul in his Epistle to the Galatians, must be kept away from it. Perhaps, as in the case of the son of Hagar, there was no choice, as Paul also said in Galatians; but to cast that harmful element out (Gal. 4:21-5:10), an image evoked once again by the fourteenth-century Avignonese jurist Oldradus da Ponte at just the moment when Pope John XXII had temporarily expelled the Jews from his French domains.

The constant use of such bodily imagery could not fail to affect the social and structural perceptions of the Jews themselves. An intrinsic hostility does not necessarily mean an absence of interaction or borrowings. Medieval Jews, too, acculturated. Some knew the intricacies of canon law, others the latest developments in theological controversy.[16] Even innovations in ritual might be adopted, as was the torchlight procession by the Jews of the Renaissance. At funerals, especially of more prominent figures, such processions emphasized Jewish communal identity, just as Italian Christian confraternal processions served the end of self-assertion.[17] This new custom, however, failed to gain universal approval among the Jews, as the Christian essence was sensed even in the superficial facade. As for the Christian body — which, as Paul had said, was not "for lust (but ... for) the Lord" (1 Cor. 6:13) — and the spiritual or biological Christian family, imitative of Christ, the whole concept was alien. There could be no importation at all.

The Jewish concept of the body was inherently corporeal, its sanctity a question of what that body — as a willful physical entity — did. God had not been made man; neither the individual nor society was obligated to personify his spiritual body or to see itself as a member of or a participant (through the sacrament) in his real one. In Judaism, the *corpus mysticum* and the *corpus verum* did not and could not exist. Jews, no matter how devoted to piety and spirituality, had no reason for renouncing their corporeal selves. As married persons, they entered the "Gate of Holiness" not through abstinence or even continence, but, as R. Abraham b. David of Posquières (Rabad) expressed it in the late twelfth century, through the mutuality achieved in uniting with one's spouse.[18]

In Judaism, participation in marriage, reproduction and sexuality was a way of doing God's will. The Kabbalists taught that human sexual union, imitative of God's union with the Shekhinah, would be rewarded with a male child.[19] Sexuality did not symbolize — as it did for Christians — a state of alienation, of divorce from the spirit of God within the human breast in its pristine, pre-Fall state.[20] Lust, said Isaiah di Trani, was a reason for possibly using a contraceptive device.[21] It was a desire to be contained, said R. Abraham b. David, lest man reduce himself to the level of the beasts, but certainly not what Raymond of Penaforte called a "deadly sin."[22] Discussing sexuality within the context of apparently Christian notions of good and evil, R. Abraham held firmly to the distinctly Jewish notion that marital sexuality is obligatory, not a concession.[23] He would have agreed with Jacob Anatoli in censuring "Christians, who set apart some of their children to be barren until death, as though God hated the human race."[24]

The biological, indeed, the nuclear family remained at the centre of Jewish life. There was no such thing as the shame described by Augustine as "wash[ing] over the household, that mainstay of the classic city and world."[25] The Jewish family, it appears, upheld the ancient Mediterranean pattern depicted in the fifth-century drama of St. Thecla. It is the family that maintains society, says Thamris, Thecla's disillusioned fiancé, challenging her choice of celibacy:

"Marriage is the beginning, root, and fountainhead of our nature; cities, villages, and cultivation have sprung up because of it."[26] On this biological family Chrysostom, Eusebius, and other Church fathers turned their backs; the Jews, on the other hand, clung both to the physical reality and to the ideal image.

In the ninth century, Shefatiah of Oria discovered his daughter Cassia's puberty and quickly betrothed her to his nephew. The time had come, he said, for Cassia "to make love."[27] This he announced to his brother, calling down the street to the house where the latter dwelled — the same kind of Italian urban house still found in Oria's Rione Giudea: narrow-fronted, fit for a nuclear family alone. In Cassia's marital bed there was no shame. Physical intercourse did not condemn her to mortality, untouched by the spirit of God. Nor could anything have been more foreign to her than Eusebius's notion "that there are two ways of life, one above human nature, which is the celibate case, the other of human nature, so to speak, including marriage."[28] Rather, both Cassia and her father would have agreed with Jacob Anatoli, who, discussing the abstinence of Jewish couples from intercourse during the menstrual period and their subsequent reunion, described it as a blessing, benefitting health, and "producing intense pleasure, and release, and great joy, and producing increased love between husband and wife, virtually achieving each month the delight of a new bridegroom with his bride."[29]

It is thus hardly surprising that Christian moralists condemned Jewish sexual behavior, real or imagined. William of Tournay accused Jews of taking second wives while their first ones were pregnant in order to attain sexual release, while Guibert de Nogent associated them with lewd perversity.[30] The Jewish sexual and familial ideal constituted a loud and repeated proclamation that man's destiny was not to become a member of a spiritualized Christ. Jewish and Christian bodies represented totally conflicting ideals.

The same may not so readily be said of the ideals of government. Here, the Jews were influenced by contemporary political theory. However, this was a limited process. As elsewhere, the Christian content of institutions had to be voided before even the facade could be assimilated. And once again, competing concepts of holiness played a major role: the holiness of the Jewish community and its model of self-government were defined by boundaries, precincts, and the persons living and acting therein, not by the concept of a Holy Body.

In order to establish political entities where none had previously existed, the Jewish sages of the Middle Ages — I refer specifically to Northern Europe from the tenth to the thirteenth centuries — manipulated concepts of holiness, as did contemporary Christians, to suit their needs. Like Christians, they had to cope with the almost complete absence of a tradition of political organization and service.[31] But in order to achieve their ends, the Jews did not, as has been suggested, build on long-quiescent a priori ideas of a *Kenesset Yisrael*, a corporate and enduring Assembly.[32] Their thinking, rather, was pragmatic. Jews were dependent on those around them. To the extent that they enjoyed self-rule, it was a grant and a privilege, something whose implementation they themselves were not free to decide upon. Jewish political institutions in the Middle Ages thus had to take shape according to circumstances.

Most definitely, the medieval European Jewish community was not a corporation — certainly not in the early centuries of its existence. The corporation in its true form, like that of the University of Paris, emerged in the thirteenth century.[33] The Jewish communities which came into being in the Rhineland at about the time of Rabbenu Gershom in the early eleventh century thus had no contemporary corporate model to imitate. The Emperor Justinian had rescinded the Jews'corporate communal rights in the early sixth century,[34] and this was not cancelled out by the privilege granted Jews by royal and other charters to live according to "their own law." Indeed, when that privilege began specifically to be bestowed upon the Jews as a group, it reflected their becoming not a "corporation among the corporations," but rather a constitutionally isolated entity — "the Jews" — in an increasingly alien Christian world. Notwithstanding H.H. Ben-Sasson's argument to the contrary, it cannot be said that "Jewish autonomy fell within the framework of the corporations which were permitted to stand between the individual and the sovereign in the Middle Ages."[35]

The foundation upon which the local medieval Jewish polity was erected was that of the halakhah (Jewish law), and so — in the minds of its members — was divinely ordained. Accordingly, that polity was named the *qehillah qedoshah*, the Holy Community.[36] Its holiness derived from and was constantly reaffirmed by its fulfillment of the dictates of the halakhah: a holiness of place achieved by repetitive devotional activity.[37] What signalled the community's borders — there were no geographical ones in the normal sense — were halachically created jurisdictional lines. The community, said the sages of Ashkenaz (Germany), was an autonomous court of law.[38] Such a definition — advantageous to scholars, who were the only people conversant enough with halakhah to serve as communal leaders — failed to provide any idea of how the community maintained its continuity when the court was not in session.

The element of continuity was provided through the introduction of the *herem*. Above and beyond its reference to the excommunication of individuals, the *herem* signified a communal oath.[39] Joseph Bonfils, a contemporary of Rabbenu Gershom, recorded that members of a community had been called upon to "enter" into a *herem* — each to swear an oath — to ensure the return of lost objects.[40] It would seem that the original meaning of the term in the Book of Joshua (6:17) — a text which R. Judah ben Meir in the eleventh century pointedly cited in discussing how individuals were bound by communal decisions — was now revived.[41] The *herem* was a sanctified district within which certain actions were, or were not (on pain of excommunication) allowed to take place (interestingly, the *haram* of the tribes of pre-Muslim Arabia and in later Islamic thought was used in the same sense).[42] Citing earlier sages in an effort to expand the concept of the community as a court, the twelfth-century leader of French Jewry, R. Jacob Tam, declared: "In a place where there is a tradition of a scholar's presence, it is almost certain that there existed a *herem bet din* [a jurisdictional venue], so that one may hold court there [even today]."[43] Other *haramot* were formulated to regulate rentals, business partnerships, and rights of residence.

Through the *herem*, the Jewish community came to occupy a *Jewish* holy space, into which the members of a community were bound by oath to "enter" and in which they were expected to behave accordingly. In the words of R. Meir of Rothenburg in the late thirteenth century: "The *Qadmonim* [the early sages] were in the habit of establishing a *herem* ... by which [they] might obligate communal members [to obey] without [the need to go to] court."[44] That is, the community had certain powers vested wholly in itself. The *herem*, which created and delimited a holy community, had brought the Jews to the verge of a concept of sovereignty. However, the distance between this Jewish spatial concept and the Christian concept of the civic reconstitution of a Holy Body was enormous.

The *haramot* were an original Jewish institution, rooted in talmudic texts and traditional practices. The precursor of one *herem*, that of interrupting prayers to demand that justice be done, may have existed in ancient Palestine. More broadly, the Talmud (*Gittin* 7b–8b) gives local communities the right to fix wages, set prices, and even levy fines.[45] Yet to seek no further explanation of the *herem* as it functioned in medieval Europe would be mistaken. Powers similar to those conferred by the *herem* were simultaneously being exercised among Christians through the device of the feudal, signorial *bannum*, initially a judicial right of the Frankish kings that was appropriated by lay lords for themselves with the demise of the Carolingian Empire. Eventually these lords fused the *bannum* with the pre-existing signorial right "to issue orders and punish those who disobeyed" and expanded it to include the right to make monetary exactions, demand rents and services, and acquire monopolies over mills, presses and the like.[46] The similarity between these Jewish and Christian devices suggests that, to some degree and in a disguised form, a process of emulation and adaptation was taking place.

Emulation also extended to modes of application. To be sure, a *bannum* was established unilaterally by a feudal lord, the *herem* most often by communal legislation. But the Jewish sages would no doubt have liked to play the feudal lord, as attested by the forceful terminology of "establishing," or even "decreeing," used by Rabbi Meir. The eventual compromise of bringing members of the community to adhere to the *herem* by means of an oath reflected neither democratic impulses nor long-defunct German tribal usage.[47] Rather, the sages modified their aspiration to leadership, expressed in their wish to run the community like a court, in a manner comparable with Christian communal practices as they developed in the eleventh century — that is, in the period when the *haramot* were coming into existence. These practices emphasized widespread communal participation. Thus, Bishop Ratherius of Verona, toward the end of the tenth century, wrote of "the civic assembly attended by the entire citizenry." Similarly, the people of Le Mans, in the year 1070, created "an association which they called a commune, joining themselves together by oaths, and forcing the ... magnates of the countryside to swear allegiance to their commune."[48] The communes even began to call the countryside and the small villages they controlled the *banlieu*, the area where their communal *bannum* was valid. In establishing spheres of jurisdiction through *haramot*, the Jewish communities of Northern Europe[49] behaved much like the Christian communes.

Yet if the Jews consciously emulated Christian practice, their records almost universally kept this a well-guarded secret. It seems likely that, to the extent they were familiar with it, Jews were repelled by the overt cult of corporeal sacredness that increasingly characterized the Christian communal image. As a result, the Jews refused to make this image the subject of open debate, or, for that matter, to let emulation go too far. Confining themselves instead within their own oath- and boundary-fixed definitions of holiness and holy community, their concepts of government continued to revolve around persons rather than institutions. As we have seen, Rabbenu Tam justified the continuity of a court on the basis of the presumed presence at that venue of an *individual* scholar in the past; R. Asher (ca. 1310) said that the greatest scholar of the age had the status of a High Court. By contrast, a number of decades later, Accursius wrote: "Just as the [present] people of Bologna is the same that was a hundred years ago, even though all be dead now who then were quick, so must also the tribunal be the same if three or two judges have died and been replaced by substitutes." What did not change, commented Baldus, was the "form," that is, the ongoing institution. There was continuity, he added, *quia populus non moritur*, because the people does not die[50] — the same *populus* which, elsewhere, Baldus defined as *hominum collectio in unum corpus mysticum*, a collection of men in one mystical body.[51]

The Jews' persistent linkage of government to specific persons in specific areas, rather than to undying, mystical, bodily "forms," stunted their political discourse and development. In particular, it had an adverse effect upon the theoretical justifications they gave for developments such as majority rule, which attained its full expression only within the formal corporate framework that medieval Christian political units eventually acquired — although here pragmatic considerations also came into play. Perhaps drawing on talmudic precedent, Jews generally claimed that majorities had the power to bind. "If the ... majority of the upright [leaders] have consented [to enforce an ordinance]," said Meir of Rothenburg, "the minority cannot void [it] by saying, 'Let us go to court to settle the matter'."[52] However, this was not (as would have been maintained in Christian and especially in monastic circles) because the majority represented the *maior et sanior pars* of the body.[53] A majority, Meir explained, was like a High Court; its decisions cannot be impeached.[54] This explanation is surprising. Meir of Rothenburg himself understood legislative mechanisms quite well. If he, and so many others, including his distinguished contemporary in Barcelona, Solomon ibn Adret,[55] chose to justify the binding power of majorities by invoking the hallowed paradigm of a court, this may largely have been because they realized that contemporary Jewish communal life was too unstable — as demonstrated by R. Meir's imprisonment by the Hapsburg emperor — to allow a more complex political theory to become deeply rooted. Moreover, Meir, as we shall see, was equally concerned that the rabbinic authority in the courts be protected against encroachments by the Jewish laity.

The Jews' lack of theoretical sophistication was mirrored in the absence of any uniform pattern of political behaviour. In 1264, Solomon ibn Adret, reflecting on the situation in Catalonia and Aragon, wrote that there were "places where affairs are entirely run by the advice of the elders and the councillors; others where the *majority* (of such councillors and elders) can do nothing without consulting *all* the people and obtaining their consent; and still others where *individuals* are given the authority to do as they see fit in all general affairs."[56] Majority rule was the norm, said his contemporary, Asher ben Yehiel, a former student of R. Meir and now Chief Rabbi of Castile: "For when will the entire *qahal* (the governing council) agree on one opinion?" The impression, even with regard to R. Asher's implied utopian preference for government by consensus, is that practice was determined wholly by circumstance. Representative theory does not seem to have existed.[57]

By contrast, from about the year 1100, Christians were busily elaborating theories of representation and consent. In particular, theorists were examining[58] Roman law, with its corporate ideas for an explanation of how, when, and why town councils should be formed. Elected representatives were accorded "full power" (*plena potestas*) to bind their constituents, which they did in communal councils. "The entire citizenry," wrote John of Viterbo in the early thirteenth century, should elect representatives to decide a course of action; "The [Roman Law] principle to be followed is that all should approve matters of common concern" (*quod omnes tangit ab omnibus approbetur*).[59] The meaning of the verb *approbare* derived from the original context of this phrase in Roman law, where it referred to the duty of consulting all court-appointed guardians in matters affecting an individual ward; the sense was not so much "to approve" as to have the right and obligation to vote on and ratify the issues at hand. Ratification was thus more than a matter of a simple majority. When Christian scholars asked whether *nova jura* — new constitutions, taxes, and ordinances — required unanimous conciliar or perhaps even popular approbation, they quite likely meant a decision by the majority (directly or representationally) of *all* those affected, whose opinion was individually to be sought. Such a vote afforded due process to all;[60] it was an act of ratification in which the civic council embodied the totality of the corporate commune.

Among Jews, there was little movement on these issues after the eleventh-century assertion of Joseph Bonfils that individuals could not exempt themselves from a *herem*. To do so, said Bonfils, was like violating a decree of the court; and, moreover, he cited scriptural and talmudic texts that implied the duty of submission. But Bonfils also confused the issue by arguing that a scholarly minority could force the hand of a majority of the humble. Nor was any use made later on, as it might have been, of certain vague phrases he employed, such as "all as one" (*kulam ke-'ehad*) or "in a single voice" (*be-haskamah* [lit. agreement] *'ahat*),[61] in order to allow Jews to adapt concepts of ratification derived from Roman law to their own version of majority and representative rule.

Attempts to amalgamate theories of ratification and representation into Jewish political life seem to have been made only by Rabbenu Tam and, possibly, Meir of Rothenburg. Discussing the talmudic passage authorizing communities to punish those who violated their rules (*le-hasi'a al qizotam*), Jacob Tam wrote, "The conventions (*qizot*) are made with the knowledge and approval of *all* the councillors of the city (*mi-da'at kol tovei ha-'ir*)."[62] New enactments were made — as the Christians were saying — by polling the entire governing body. The issue, however, is not how decisions were to be made — that is, by majority vote or by consensus — as this text is sometimes understood to imply, but, rather, the principle underlying the legitimacy of those decisions. Indeed, Jacob Tam could well have been the author of the following saying, apocryphally attributed to his grandfather, R. Shelomo Yizhaqi (Rashi): "One is not exempt from public decrees if they are justly enacted; [namely] decrees to which all the *qahal* (the governing council) has consented (*hiskim*)," or as Jacob Tam said in his own name, "if all expressed their readiness to accept the decrees" (*im kulam ne'otu yahad*).[63] The paraphrase of the principle of ratification in Roman law is more than obvious. Only by virtue of *approbare* or *haskamah*, the community acting in concert through conciliar due process, does an ordinance become universally binding and just.

Rabbenu Tam's theorizing, however, was subsequently either misunderstood or deliberately ignored. Like Asher b. Yehiel, nearly all the Jewish scholars of the period[64] discussed issues like majority rule in wholly pragmatic terms. So, too, did Meir of Rothenburg. But Meir personally was far more sophisticated. "The majority or that segment of the city's people (*benei ha-'ir*) who have gathered together and elected a leader without the knowledge and approval of all (*mi-da'at kulam*)," Meir said, "... do not have the authority to make *new* ordinances without the knowledge and approval of all." This is Jacob Tam's version of representative theory, in his own words. Indeed, Meir appears at least once directly to have evoked the principle of *quod omnes tangit*: "Everyone should state his opinion, for the sake of heaven and good government (lit., correction of the city); then they should follow the majority." A majority, that is, was valid only within the framework of a properly representative assembly. On another occasion, Meir was even more pointed: "[Only] seven councillors (*tovim*) who have been chosen by *all* the townsmen ... are authorized to punish those who violated their rules."[65] Yet, in his very next breath, Meir sharply qualified this statement. The seven properly elected *tovim*, he said, have executive power, "except where there is a great man (*gavra rabba*)." From a bold statement of conciliar due process, Meir retreated once more into the concept of the community as a court. The great man, the *gadol*, was a High Court judge or tantamount to the High Court itself; his opinion superseded and indeed could not be bound by any conciliar body.

Only Rabbenu Tam did not flinch. Rather than anticipating, as did Meir of Rothenburg, a rupture between great rabbinic leaders and town councils, Jacob Tam saw the two working hand in hand. The *haver ha-'ir* (the city's important sage), he said, was to propose ordinances; the councils, by conciliar due process (*mi da'at kulam*), were to ratify them.[66] What Jacob Tam really intended, then, was conciliar government by dictate. He would magisterially decree, and the *tovim*, the *qahal*, would approve, a posture that was thoroughly consistent with everything we know about Rabbenu Tam's imperious personal style.[67] No wonder he found ideas of representation and consent so attractive. The closest parallel to Jacob Tam, in fact, would be none other than Edward I of England, summoning the Parliament in 1295 — including the knights and squires — with the dictum *quod omnes tanget*.[68] The whole realm, thought Edward, should ratify the statutes dictated by him from above.

Edward's act set a precedent. Quite the opposite, however, happened in the case of Rabbenu Tam. The combination of Jewish communal instability, vulnerability, and rabbinic-lay tension, coupled with a theory like that of the *herem*, made this outcome inevitable. The sacred precinct, the Holy Community, defined by the *herem*, like all other Jewish sacred areas, depended for its continuity, if not its very existence, on constant acts of participatory rededication. It was safer to take refuge, as did Meir of Rothenburg, in the more acceptable and venerable concept of the community as a court. Theories of representation, inseparable from corporate images derived from Roman law, and made the more attractive through their compatibility with the idea of consent to union in Christ, ultimately were foreign. Jews could accept them, even figuratively, only on a temporary basis, under the guidance of a leader as forceful as Rabbenu Tam. And Jacob Tam was one of a kind.

Wholly different concepts of holiness and sacred space thus distinguished medieval Christians and Jews, in both their public and their private lives. The Jews created holiness through individual acts; and only through the repetition of these acts, which they considered divinely ordained, could the holiness of either family or community be sustained. Christian holiness, on the other hand, was immanent, and participation in it demanded the amalgamation of the individual within the body of the whole, the re-created sacred body of Christ. However much Jews participated in medieval Christian society, then, and however much Christians co-operated, fraternized, and even studied with Jews — all of which they did — the two were living in distinct worlds, which, despite their separation, inevitably conflicted. The denizens of the one could never make more than a temporary truce with those of the other. The optimal solution, it was felt, was to draw a firm line of separation, which all too often meant expulsion or assault.

The sixteenth century found another alternative. As Elizabeth Crouzet-Pavan has suggested, "By creating the ghetto, by locking up those considered in the collective concept as a stain on society, the political powers of Venice took charge of achieving the mythical (mystical) Christian city." On a lesser level, adds Edward Muir: "Since Jews could not be expected to respond as Christians [to relics, images, shrines, etc.], the authorities had to face the reality that their cities were never fully united. In Venice and other cities [like Rome], where ghettos were established, residential segregation created zones free from Catholic notions of sacred spaces, and the movement of non-Christian residents about the rest of the city was carefully restricted."[69] Yet the Jews of Rome were just as anxious about Christian trespassing. The walls of the ghetto, paradoxically, had made the Roman holy community into a physically holy precinct, comparable to the ritual walls Nehemiah had once erected about Jerusalem.[70] The ghetto was the Jews' true *miqdash me'at*, their sanctuary on a small scale. As Rabbi Pompeo del Borgo put it in 1589, it was *nostro ghet*, our "bill of divorce" (*get* in Hebrew), a usage which became so widespread that *get*, written in Hebrew letters, came to be the usual formula for referring to the ghetto in Jewish documents of every sort.[71] The passage of a Christian through the ghetto in certain circumstances — as happened on 9 September 1621, just six days before the Jewish New Year and at the height of the Jewish penitential season — could result in provocation, a brawl, and the Christian's death.[72]

Such phenomena, of course, require further study and investigation. Even at this stage, however, we may conclude that the examination of conflicting sacred structures and conceptions has shed new light on at least one small aspect of the difficult Jewish-Christian past and has conferred greater clarity on at least some of the mystery in which so large a part of that past has perpetually been enshrouded.

Notes

1. See especially E.H. Kantorowicz, *The King's Two Bodies*, Princeton 1957, *passim*, especially pp. 195 and 210; and, more recently, M. Rubin, *Corpus Christi: The Eucharist in Late Medieval Culture*, Cambridge 1991, pp. 259–263.
2. On Edward's attitude to money-lending, see J.A. Watt's recent study, "The Jews, the Law, and the Church: The Concept of Jewish Serfdom in Thirteenth-Century England," in *The Church and Sovereignty: Essays in Honor of Michael Wilks, Studies in Church History: Subsidia*, IX (1991), pp. 156–161; see also K.R. Stow, "Papal and Royal Attitudes toward Jewish Lending in the Thirteenth Century," *AJS Review*, VI (1981), pp. 161–184; and R.C. Stacey, "1240–1260: A Watershed in Anglo-Jewish Relations," *Historical Research*, LXI (1988), pp. 144–146.
3. See W.C. Jordan, *The French Monarchy and the Jews from Philip Augustus to the Last Capetians*, Princeton 1989, pp. 198–199.
4. Y.F. Baer, *Die Juden im christlichen Spanien*, Berlin 1936, pp. 404–408.
5. Lotter, "Die Judenverfolgung des 'Koenig Rintfleisch' in Franken um 1298," *Zeitschrift für historische Forschung*, XV (1988), pp. 413.
6. Rubin, *Corpus* (above, note 1), pp. 266–267.
7. M. Becker, *Florence in Transition: The Decline of the Commune*, Baltimore 1967, I, p. 11.
8. *Ibid.*, I, pp. 11–12. The semi-sacred, semi-secular character of Roman law made it especially suitable to serve as an instrument of transition in late medieval society, which was finding it increasingly difficult to justify the Jewish presence theologically, but which, in places like Italy, had begun to justify that presence on secular grounds. Roman law played the same role in the Jewish re-admission to Germany from the sixteenth century on, and, consequently, despite its many restrictions on Jews, it formed the backbone of eighteenth-century treatises concerning the potential integration of Jews into German society, such as C.W. Dohm's *Concerning the Amelioration of the Civil Status of the Jews* (English transl. by H. Lederer, Cincinnati 1957).
9. K.R. Stow, *Alienated Minority: The Jews of Medieval Latin Europe*, Cambridge, Mass., 1992, p. 212.
10. *Ibid.*, p. 213; and Rubin, *Corpus* (above, note 1), p. 287.
11. Marriage, says J.F. Noonan, ("Power to Choose," *Viator*, IV [1973], p. 429), was to be "'a seedbed of charity' [Augustine] for the heavenly city"; and, hence, absolutely under Church control, achieved through promoting the consent of the individual and so, theoretically, superseding family control. On the "spiritual family," see R. Brentano, *Rome before Avignon*, New York 1974, pp. 171—210; D. Herlihy, *Medieval Households*, Cambridge, Mass., 1985, p. 122, and also p. 114 on the "natural family"; and, on the emergence of priestly celibacy, J. Brundage, *Law, Sex, and Christian Society in Medieval Europe*, Chicago–London 1987, p. 174. On the crusades, see *Roberti Monachi Historia Hierosolimitana, Recueil des Historiens des Croisades, Historiens Occidentaux*, Paris 1844–1895, III, p. 728; and J. Riley-Smith, *The First Crusade and the Idea of Crusading*, Philadelphia 1986, pp. 22 and 151. Riley-Smith points out that Urban II originally required husbands, as pilgrims, to seek their wives' agreement to their departure; but they were exempted from this

requirement by Innocent III in his encyclical, *Ex multa*, discussed by J.Brundage in *The Crusades, Holy War, and Canon Law*, Aldershot, U.K., 1991, essay XV. This notion of abandonment of the married state for the sake of union with a holy cause reflected the ideal rather than the reality, as emerges from a comparison of the statements of Fulcher of Chartres on the pain of leaving wives (Riley-Smith, *First Crusade*, p. 162) with the assertions of Robert the Monk that "the most beautiful wives became as loathsome as something putrid," or, in Riley-Smith's paraphrase, that "they [the crusaders] sought voluntary exile for the love of God" (*ibid.*, pp. 150–151).

Although I argue below that the Jewish family ideal was contrary to the Christian one, it would be interesting to know whether the Jewish ordinance forbidding a husband to leave his wife for more than twelve or eighteen months without her permission, formalized in the twelfth century, was at all influenced by the Christian debate over the necessity for a crusader to obtain his wife's agreement to forgo the "conjugal debt." The Jewish travellers, of course, were not pilgrims; it was only for commercial or educational reasons, the ordinance stipulates, that such extended journeys might take place. The *'onah* (frequency of sexual intercourse) owed the Jewish wife also differs from the "conjugal debt," in that it is owed only to the wife, and it is for sexual satisfaction per se, not simply for the purpose of avoiding fornication. Moreover, and most importantly, the law stresses the need for companionship as the major reason for not permitting a husband's departure. See L. Finkelstein, *Jewish Self-Government in the Middle Ages*, Westport, Conn., 1924 (reprinted 1972), pp. 168–169.

12. Bernardino da Siena, *Le Prediche Volgari*, ed. C. Cannarozzi, Florence 1958, sermons 19–21. On the ecclesiastical control of marriage by means of priests and the Church see also C. Klapisch-Zuber, *Women, Family, and Ritual in Renaissance Italy*, Chicago 1985, pp. 209–212.
13. *Monumenta Germaniae Historica*, ed. G. H. Pertz et al., 1826, IX, p. 213; II, p. 200, cited in E. Synan, *The Popes and the Jews in the Middle Ages*, New York 1965, p. 177.
14. J. Bossy, *Christianity in the West 1400–1700*, Oxford 1985, pp. 3–13, 19–26. A sign of how deeply individuals throughout Christian society, and not only its theoreticians, sought to identify with Christ's spiritual essence (irrespective of no-doubt widespread deviant practice, especially in the marriage-bed or in other beds) may lie, paradoxically, in the inversion this essence underwent in popular thinking in the late medieval and early modern periods. As the nuclear family, based on emotional affection, became the dominant model of the family, especially in cities, the mystical Christ was progressively humanized, becoming a flesh-and-blood model for biological families — as indeed were the other New Testament characters forming the Holy Family. Was the autonomous nuclear family legitimizing itself by claiming to imitate the supposed biological family of Christ? This might provide a partial explanation of the clerical encouragement of, for example, the cult of St. Joseph, one of whose early advocates was none other than Bernardino of Siena; cf. D. Herlihy, *Medieval Households*, Cambridge 1985, pp. 116–117, 122–123; and idem, "The Making of the Medieval Family: Symmetry, Structure, and Sentiment," *Journal of Family History*, VIII (1983), pp. 116–130. One

of the manifestations of this cult was the clerical glorification of the marriage rite of the Virgin and St. Joseph, in which the participation of the Church became ever more prominent (iconographically) and essential (from the legal point of view); see Klapisch-Zuber, *Women* (above, note 12), pp. 178–212. By controlling the cult of the Holy Family, the clergy, it would appear, was seeking to reinstate itself as the arbiter of the biological family, a position it had previously achieved by advocating the ideal of the spiritual family. See also Becker, *Florence*, I (above, note 7), pp. 40–41, 192, 226–227.

15. Kantorowicz, *The King's Two Bodies* (above, note 1), p. 195.
16. On Jews and canon law, see K.R. Stow, *The 1007 Anonymous and Papal Sovereignty: Jewish Perceptions of the Papacy and Papal Policy in the Middle Ages*, Cincinnati 1984, pp. 35–36, 41–44. Jewish familiarity with Christian theological arguments may be seen in J. Cohen, "Rationales for Conjugal Sex in RaAvaD's *Ba'alei HaNefesh*," *Jewish History*, VI, 1/2 (1992).
17. See E. Horowitz, "Confraternal Processions and Social Tensions in the Jewish Communities of the Veneto," in S.N. Eisenstadt (ed.), *Jewish Societies in Transformation in the Sixteenth and Seventeenth Centuries*, in press.
18. Abraham ben David of Posquières, *Sefer Ba'alei ha-Nefesh*, ed. J.Kafah, Jerusalem 1964, "Gate of Holiness."
19. Moses ben Nahman (pseudo), "Iggeret ha-Qodesh," *Kitvei ha-Ramban*, ed. C. Chavel, Jerusalem 1963, II, pp. 316–37.
20. P. Brown, *The Body and Society: Men, Women, and Sexual Renunciation in Early Christianity*, New York 1988, p. 94.
21. Isaiah di Trani, *Tosfot ha-RiD*, Jerusalem 1931, on *Yebamot* 12b.
22. J. Delumeau, *Sin and Fear: The Emergence of a Western Guilt Culture 13th–18th Centuries* (English transl. by E. Nicholson), New York 1990, p. 215.
23. J. Cohen, "Rationales" (above, note 16).
24. M. Saperstein, "Christians and Christianity in the Sermons of Jacob Anatoli," *Jewish History*, VI (1992).
25. Brown, *The Body* (above, note 20), p. 426.
26. *Ibid.*, p. 5.
27. B. Klar, *The Scroll of Ahimaaz* (in Hebrew), Jerusalem 1974.
28. Brown, *The Body* (above, note 20), p. 205.
29. Saperstein, "Anatoli" (above, note 24), p. 12, n. 24
30. On William of Tournay, see A. D'Alvray & M. Tausche, "Marriage Sermons in *Ad Status* Collections of the Central Middle Ages," *Archives d'Histoire Doctrinale et Litteraire du Moyen Age*, XLVII (1980), p. 100; on Guibert de Nogent, see J.F. Benton, *Self and Society in Medieval France*, New York 1970, pp. 134–137, 209–211.
31. See R. Benson, *The Bishop Elect*, Princeton 1968.
32. Y.F. Baer, "Ha-yesodot ve-ha-hathalot shel 'irgun ha-qehillah ha-yehudit biymei ha-beinayim," *Studies in the History of the Jewish People*, Jerusalem 1985, II, pp. 60–100, esp. pp. 70–72.
33. G. Post, *Studies in Medieval Legal Thought: Public Law and the State 1100–1322*, Princeton 1964, pp. 27–60.
34. K.R. Stow, "The Jewish Family in the Rhineland: Form and Function," *American*

Historical Review, XCII (1987), pp. 1085–1110; A. Linder, *The Jews in Roman Imperial Legislation*, Detroit 1987, pp. 107–110.

35. H.H. Ben-Sasson, *A History of the Jewish People*, Cambridge, Mass., 1976, p. 502.
36. Baer, "Ha-yesodot" (above, note 32), pp. 67–69.
37. J.Z. Smith, *To Take Place*, Chicago 1987, pp. 108–117.
38. S. Morell, "The Constitutional Limits of Communal Government in Rabbinic Law," *Jewish Social Studies*, XXXIII (1971), pp. 87–119. On the community as a judicial venue, see also Joseph Tov Elem, as cited and discussed in H. Soloveitchik, *The Use of Responsa as an Historical Source: A Methodological Introduction*, Jerusalem 1990, pp. 67–69.
39. See S.W. Baron, *The Jewish Community*, New York 1948, III, p. 179. Baron suggests that *herem* is generally used in the sense of *taqqanah* (ordinance). In fact, when speaking of the excommunication of individuals, the preferred if not the exclusive usage in many texts seems to be the Hebrew *niddui* or *gezerah* (of *shamta*). *Herem* standing alone is best translated as an abbreviation for the much longer: "there is a jurisdictional district where the following regulation is in force." See M. Breuer, *The Rabbinate in Ashkenaz during the Middle Ages* (in Hebrew), Jerusalem 1976, nos. 76 and 77; and Soloveitchik, *Responsa* (above, note 38), p. 69.
40. Finkelstein, *Jewish Self-Government* (above, note 11), p. 149: "The legislative power of the community was based on nothing more than a vow undertaken by each member to do or refrain from doing certain things." That vow is what Bonfils meant by "entering a *herem*." See also I. Agus, *The Heroic Age of Franco-German Jewry*, New York 1969, p. 173.
41. I. Agus, *Urban Civilization in Pre-Crusade Europe*, New York 1965, p. 449; Soloveitchik, *Responsa* (above, note 38), p. 88.
42. A. Hourani, *A History of the Arab Peoples*, Cambridge, Mass., 1991, p. 11.
43. Finkelstein, *Jewish Self-Government* (above, note 11), p. 193.
44. Breuer, *Rabbinate* (above, note 39), no. 22.
45. Morell, "Limits" (above, note 38), p. 88; and A. Grossman, "The Attitude of the Early Scholars of Ashkenaz towards the Authority of the 'Kahal'," (in Hebrew) *Annual of the Institute for Research in Jewish Law*, II (1975), p. 178.
46. F. Ganshof, "Medieval Agrarian Society in Its Prime," *Cambridge Economic History*, Cambridge 1941, I, p. 333; and J. Le Goff, *Medieval Civilization, 400–1500* (English transl. by J. Barrow), Oxford 1988, p. 93.
47. See K.R. Stow, "The Medieval Jewish Community Was Not a Corporation," in Y. Gafni & G. Motzkin (eds.), *Priesthood and Kingship* (in Hebrew), Jerusalem 1986, p. 144.
48. E. Ennen, *Die europäische Stadt des Mittelalters*, Göttingen 1972, pp.105–138; G. Fasoli, *Scritti di Storia Medievale*, ed. F. Bocchi et al., Bologna 1974, pp.194–198; G. Tabacco, "Lo sviluppo del banno signorile e delle comunità rurali," in G. Rossetti (ed.), *Forme di potere e struttura sociale in Italia nel medioevo*, Bologna 1977, pp. 175–196, 200–202, 208–209; and see I. Agus, "Democracy in the Communities of the Early Middle Ages," *Jewish Quarterly Review*, XLIII (1952), pp. 165 ff.
49. It would appear that contemporary Islamic Jewries understood *herem* only in the sense of excommunication. See M.R. Cohen, *Jewish Self-Government in Medieval*

Egypt, Princeton 1980, pp. 41, 125, 206, 216 and 230; and S. Assaf, *Ha-'onshin 'aharei hatimat ha-talmud*, Jerusalem 1942, pp. 49–51.

50. Kantorowicz, *King's Two Bodies* (above, note 1), p. 295.
51. *Ibid.*, p. 304.
52. Finkelstein, *Jewish Self-Government* (above, note 11), pp. 33 and 121.
53. G. Post, "A Romano-Canonical Maxim, 'quod omnes tanget,' in Bracton," *Traditio*, IV (1946), p. 205.
54. See Rashi on BT *Bava batra* 8b, and the commentary of Mordecai, *ad loc.*; Morell, "Limits" (above, note 38), p. 89.
55. Baron, *Jewish Community* (above, note 39), I, p. 211.
56. H. Beinart, "Hispanic Jewish Society," in H.H. Ben-Sasson (ed.), *Jewish Society through the Ages*, New York 1971, p. 227; and S. Schwarzfuchs, *Kahal: La communauté juive de l'Europe médiévale*, Paris 1986, p. 52.
57. Morell, "Limits" (above, note 38) p. 92, citing R. Asher. One must ask whether Jews in fact discussed the question of consensus versus majority rule; cf. Baer, "Ha-Yesodot" (above, note 32), p. 98. Soloveitchik is not fully convinced; see his *Responsa* (above, note 38), pp. 67 and 102, and especially p. 76. As I point out below, some Jews, particularly R. Meir and Jacob Tam, used expressions such as "the opinion of all" to express their views on representation.
58. P. Riesenberg, *The Medieval Town*, Princeton 1958, pp. 49–50; E. Sestan, "La città comunale italiana dei secoli XI-XIII nelle sue note caratteristiche rispetto al movimento comunale europeo," in Rossetti (ed.), *Forme di potere* (above, note 48), pp. 194–195.
59. Riesenberg, *Medieval Town* (above, note 58), p. 125.
60. Post, "Maxim" (above, note 53), pp. 200–204, 221–251; J. Mundy, *Europe in the High Middle Ages*, New York 1973, pp. 435 and 439; M. Wilks, *Sovereignty in the Later Middle Ages*, Cambridge 1963, p. 107.
61. Agus *Urban Civilization* (above, note 41), p. 466; and Soloveitchik, *Responsa* (above, note 38), pp. 67–68.
62. Morell, "Limits" (above, note 38), p. 90; Breuer, *Rabbinate* (above, note 39), no. 21.
63. Grossman, "The Attitude" (above, note 45), p. 190; and Yehiel Kaplan, "Decision-Making in the Jewish Communities According to Rabbenu Tam — Theory and Practice," *Zion*, LX (1995), p. 282, although Kaplan's analysis is at variance with that in this essay.
64. Ben-Sasson, *History* (above, note 35), pp. 502–503.
65. Breuer, *Rabbinate* (above, note 39), nos. 77 and 88.
66. See Baer, "Yesodot" (above, note 32), p. 98; and BT *Baba batra* 9a.
67. E.E. Urbach, *Ba'alei ha-Tosafot*, Jerusalem 1955, pp. 65–69.
68. See the text in W. Stubbs, *Select Charters Illustrative of English Constitutional History*, Oxford 1900, p. 485.
69. Elizabeth Crouzet-Pavan, "Venice between Jerusalem, Byzantium, and Divine Retribution: The Origins of the Ghetto," *Mediterranean Historical Review*, VI (1991), p. 164; and E. Muir, "The Virgin on the Street Corner: The Place of the Sacred in Italian Cities," in S. Ozment (ed.), *Religion and Culture in the Renaissance and Reformation*, Kirksville, Mo., 1989, p. 28.

70. K.R. Stow, "Sanctity and the Construction of Space: The Roman Ghetto as Sacred Space," in M. Mor (ed.), *Jewish Assimilation, Acculturation, and Accommodation*, Lanham, Md., 1992, pp. 54–76.
71. Idem, "The Consciousness of Closure: Roman Jewry and Its *Ghet*," in D. Ruderman (ed.), *Essential Papers on Jewish Culture in Renaissance and Baroque Italy*, New York 1992, pp. 386–400.
72. S. Feci, "La Morte del molinaro: un processo 'contra ebreos' nella Roma barocca," *Jewish History*, VII (1993).

12

Cities as Cultic Centres in Germany and Italy During the Early and High Middle Ages

Alfred Haverkamp

A glance at a map showing the Western Church around the year 1000[1] will suffice to suggest how foolish I have been in attempting to address the topic at hand. It would seem to be a hopeless task, in the space at my disposal, to make more than a few remarks that might point the way beyond the present state of research, even if I confine myself to the subject of the cathedral cities of Germany[*] and Italy.

Limiting myself to the special category of "cities as cultic centres," and starting with the period before eastward colonization began in the mid-twelfth century, about thirty-five cities within the future German lands must still be considered. Among these were settlements which, before the thirteenth century, showed very limited signs of urban development in economic and social terms, or none at all. Examples include Havelberg, Brandenburg, and Oldenburg east of the Elbe — places where, until the mid-twelfth century, bishops did not actually reside except for short periods of time — and also Zeitz, Meissen, Eichstaett, Minden, and Verden. Within the area of established settlement west of the Elbe and Saale rivers, the number of cathedral cities remained constant, with a few exceptions, including the foundation of the city of Bamberg

* Throughout this essay, the term "Germany" refers to the regions of the medieval empire, including the French-speaking areas. Maps 1–5 appear on pp. 187–191, after the Notes.

in the early eleventh century. The generally long distance between the "functioning" cathedral cities stands out even more clearly if we draw a circle with a radius of 100 km around each of the archiepiscopal sees.[2]

These circles also illustrate the enormous difference that existed between the density of the cathedral cities in the German territories and that in northern or even central and southern Italy. After the Arabs were driven out of Sicily, and after the bishoprics were reorganized in the second half of the eleventh century, following the end of Byzantine rule, the number of cathedral cities in Italy, Sicily, and Sardinia was probably close to 350, around the same number that has been estimated for the earlier Middle Ages.[3] Northern Italy, including Venetia, Istria and those regions in Central Italy which in the twelfth century belonged to the *regnum Italiae*, together accounted for about 130 — four times as many cathedral cities as could be found in the much more extensive German lands.[4]

In contrast to Germany, where the term *civitas* was also used for castles until the twelfth century, in Italy only the *sedes cathedrales* counted as *civitates* — even if they had long since lost their urban character, as in the case of Luni, a settlement dating far back into antiquity. In the *regnum Teutonicum* of the high Middle Ages, the cathedral cities also provided the framework for urban life. Here they acted as "mother cities" to the urbanization process, which only developed from the eleventh century onwards. Those cities that had roots in antiquity had a marked lead, both in cultic terms and in terms of the urbanization process, over the many other places that had only been incorporated into the *orbis christianus* since the early Middle Ages. Not until their elevation to the rank of cathedral cities did the latter receive any of the basic urban amenities, or begin to develop them significantly.[5]

The process of colonization, both within the territory and eastwards, which intensified during the eleventh and twelfth centuries, undermined the urban monopoly of the relatively few cathedral cities. As a consequence of their considerable cultural lag behind the Mediterranean world, this trend was much more strongly felt in the regions beyond the Rhine and Danube rivers than in some regions of northern and central Italy, where *borghi*-settlements, like Borgo San Donnino, emerged at about the same time.[6] Within the German regions, many settlements that had grown up next to abbeys — "monastic" cities like Fulda, Hersfeld, Höxter, Essen, Echternach, Wissembourg and St. Mihiel — proved successful in this competition for urban status.[7] The same was true of places whose urbanization was supported by a dual administrative and cultic function, based on the presence both of a castle or palace and an eminent collegiate church. Examples are Aachen, Goslar, Frankfurt, and also Xanten (*ad sanctos*), with its collegiate church.[8]

In the *regnum Italiae*, the beginnings of urban development were also to be found in the vicinity of abbeys, collegiate churches, palaces or castles, in places like Bobbio, Casale S. Evasio, Monza and Chieri. During the high Middle Ages, however, these settlements were unable, or only temporarily able, to emerge from the shadow of the more powerful *civitates*.[9] This contrast was not only the result of the preservation by the larger cities of northern and central Italy of their domination over the surrounding countryside; it was also supported by differing contemporary evaluations of a settlement's urban status. Only north of the Alps could early medieval abbeys have been considered "ecclesiastical cities, phenotypically equivalent to episcopal sees." This idea is expressed, for example, in an inscription found on the western face of the abbey church at Corvey, which was situated in a spot surrounded by walls: "Civitatem istam tu circumda, Domine, et angeli tui custodient muros eius" — "Surround, O Lord, this city, and may your angels guard its walls."[10] And only north of the Alps could a palatine and canonical city like Aachen be honoured as *caput civitatum*, as it was in a charter given by Frederick I in 1166, shortly after the canonization of Charlemagne, who was buried in Aachen. The same charter celebrates this cultic place as a "sacra et libera civitas" and characterizes it as "a new image of the heavenly Jerusalem."[11]

During the high medieval period of increased urbanization, the number of cities that grew up around cultic centres in the northern part of Central Europe increased enormously, though they varied considerably in their cultic facilities and functions. A rough idea of the extent of urbanization may be gained from Map 2, provided by Heinz Stoob. It shows that around the year 1250 there were about 1,500 cities in the area stretching from Calais and Lyons in the West to Elbing and Ofen in the East. According to the same defining criteria, only 200 settlements had qualified as cities a century before, and half of them lay west of the Geneva–Verdun–Utrecht line.[12]

In the remainder of this discussion, I shall concentrate on the ecclesiastical province of Trier. With its bishoprics of Trier, Metz, Toul, and Verdun, it linked the linguistic and cultural regions of *Romania* and *Germania*.[13] Map 1 shows cultic facilities, including chapters and monasteries, around the year 1000, before the great phase of expansion began. The circles drawn around them using a radius of 50 km demonstrate that the *sedes cathedrales*, all rooted in antiquity, lay relatively close together. They clearly constituted the outstanding cultic centres. With few exceptions, each *civitas* practically monopolized a surrounding area with a radius of 40 km. The exceptions were monasteries like Echternach, Mettlach, Gorze and St. Mihiel, all founded in early Carolingian times.

The findings show no substantial changes until the first decades of the twelfth century. The Benedictine priories that emerged from the eleventh century onward in the bishoprics of Metz and Toul, and occasionally also in the lesser Verdun diocese, have not been recorded on this map, but they do not alter the general picture, especially since many of the priories depended on the urban monasteries. Toul, in particular — a cathedral city much smaller than Trier and Metz — was substantially supported in its functioning as a centre by the many priories of the neighbouring monasteries of St. Evre and St. Mansuy.[14] As in earlier times, the urban monasteries and collegiate churches, with those of the surrounding areas, served as dynamic centres for the development of the social fabric and topography of the *civitas*. With their large estates, which in some cases, like that of St. Maximin in the suburb of Trier, exceeded those of the bishops, and with the urban or suburban markets and fairs associated with them, monasteries and collegiate churches ranked next to the cathedral churches as decisive economic and social factors in the centrality of a *civitas*.

Functionally, these factors worked in concert with the customary processions by the people of the diocese to the cathedral church, and with the pilgrimages of manor subjects to the central church of their *familia*, for both of which we have sporadic evidence.[15] The devotional pledges of various kinds made by individuals or groups to the saints of a cathedral, abbey, or chapter church also fit into this context. They could even take the form of regular payments of taxes to a particular shrine.[16]

These findings prove that the cathedral cities of the Trier

province, functioning as "cultic centres," dominated their respective surroundings to a radius of about 40 km and together constituted an "urban landscape." The intensification of urban influence was decisively favoured by the relatively short distances between the ancient cathedral cities. The situation in Trier is comparable, particularly on the basis of their common tradition, with the nearest part of Italian *Romania* — Upper Italy. A brief glance at Map 3, featuring the Benedictine monasteries and nunneries in the western and central part of Upper Italy, will suffice here.[17] It shows that Trier and Metz, in their functioning as cultic centres, most closely resembled the archiepiscopal metropolis of Milan and the old Lombard capital of Pavia. However, it also shows three nunneries and as many houses for men outside of the *civitas* of Milan, in its extensive bishopric. In Turin, this proportion was reversed: while there were two convents and one monastery within the city, most of the cultic institution of that large and mountainous diocese were situated outside the cathedral city.

These differences between Lombardy and Piedmont to some extent corresponded to those between the urban landscapes constituted by the four cathedral cities of the Trier province and the situation in its eastern regions in the middle Rhine area and beyond. It is an interesting fact, incidentally, that the diocese of Trier did not expand eastward until the early medieval period. The eastern part did not yet have an urban centre, and the cultic institutions were scattered. The first beginnings of a concentration were visible only in Koblenz and Boppard, that is, in places that aquired a modest urban status only in the twelfth century. Whereas the basic structure changed little around the city of Trier in the next hundred years, and the episcopal see remained unchallenged in its dominant position (only the Cistercian monastery of Himmerod gained any importance in the region),[18] the scattered urbanization around a multitude of smaller centres in the eastern part of the diocese was reflected in an increase in the number of monasteries and collegiate churches.

These outlines emerge even more sharply in the next phase, between 1215 and 1300 (Maps 4 and 5). Evidence is provided, perhaps rather more adequately, by the establishment of the so-called mendicant orders, whose pastoral activities were centred in the towns. With Franciscan, Dominican, Augustine and Carmelite houses,[19] the archiepiscopal metropolis of Trier had all the facilities of an outstanding urban ecclesiastical centre. In this respect, Metz had somewhat less, and Verdun and Toul less still. Owing to the support of the counts of Luxemburg, there were Franciscan and Dominican houses in the main city of Luxemburg, and by the end of the thirteenth century there was a Carmelite house in Arlon, which also belonged to the bishopric of Trier. In the eastern regions of the bishopric, in the middle Rhine area and beyond, the Franciscans and Dominicans settled shortly afterwards in Koblenz, the Franciscans in Andernach, Oberwesel, and Wetzlar, and the Carmelites in Boppard.

Although it cannot be proved by means of maps, further research in our project seems to indicate that the situation in the eastern part of the Trier diocese was representative, by and large, of those regions in Germany where no cathedral cities with ancient roots had existed. This would apply to all of the area east of the Rhine and north of the Danube rivers. The regions on the left bank of the Rhine and north of the Trier province, as well as those south of the Danube, also seem to have been less dominated by the their cathedral cities, although this assertion must be made rather more cautiously.[20] In the province of Trier, I would also suggest, the basic pattern of ancient cultic and cultural functions had survived far more completely than in all the other German lands down to the high Middle Ages. On this basis, the region merits comparison not only with southern Gaul, but also with the Italian *Romania*.

As far as northern and central Italy are concerned, given the unchallenged predominance of the cathedral city as a *civitas*, it is evident that the existence of a *sedes cathedralis* was the necessary qualification for city status. Further differences in rank between individual *civitates* depended on the presence of additional religious institutions. This criterion, for which we have evidence from the early medieval *laudes urbium* concerning Milan and Verona,[21] also applied in Germany. Thus, when the bishop of Basle in the early twelfth century gave an account of how he had founded the monastery of St. Alban close to his city, he criticized his predecessors for having been content with a single community of canons — that is, the cathedral chapter. To him, such a *civitas* seemed more like a *vicus quilibet pauper* — like "some poor village" — whereas other cathedral cities in the Besançon province featured three and more monastic communities.[22]

A still more sophisticated view was expressed in 1091 by the dean of the Toul chapter, who founded a house of regular canons, with a *xenodochium pauperum* — a hospital for the poor — attached to it, in the vicinity of his small cathedral city. It was salutary, he explained, and in accordance with the faith that the three high forms of the Christian life should be represented in a *civitas*: canons, who had personal property; monks living according to the Benedictine rule; and regular canons who lived a *vita apostolica* on the model of the apostles and the early Church. Thus, any person eager to be converted to God could find in this one city, in these different communities, the form of life that suited him best. In the opinion of the dean, a city — or urban life —was characterized by its provision of a variety of religious lifestyles, or, in other words, by the wide range of shares it offered in the "salvation market." This included care for the poor and sick, as the *xenodochium pauperum* attached to the monastery indicates.[23]

Participation in charitable activities of this kind is known to have increased greatly from the twelfth century onwards, both in connection with urban monasteries and collegiate churches and through lay brotherhoods and special hospital orders. In this way, the increasing organization of the growing population into brotherhoods expressed itself in new cultic-religious institutions and orientations. This in turn favoured fraternization within the urban community, strengthening social life in a *universitas civitatis* which was often threatened by external as well as internal factors.[24]

These complex relationships of interdependence were by no means undone by the strife and the sometimes violent clashes between urban communities and ecclesiastical institutions spurred, from the late twelfth century onwards, by the demands of the latter for judicial and especially financial privileges. This *discordia generalis* was really a continuation of the old "investiture conflict" at the level of the community, turning as it did on the claim of the clerics — that is, ultimately, of the papally directed *ecclesia universalis* — to superiority over the laymen, a claim put forward more radically since the days of the reformed papacy.[25] That struggle ended, in most of the southern regions of Italy, in favour of the Norman-Staufen monarchy, and, in imperial Italy, as well as in Strasbourg and Metz, in favour of the city communes — which usually, at least to some degree, dominated the surrounding regions.

These city communes regarded their cathedral churches as central shrines of their *civitates* and bishoprics, and the limits of the diocese thus became a concern of urban territorial policy. The saints of the cathedral churches came to be considered patron saints of the cities, effectively intervening in their temporal affairs, and could even legally represent them. Some of the better-known examples are San Ambrogio in the case of Milan, San Marco in Venice, San Giovanni Battista in Florence (in this case the saint not of the cathedral but of the baptistry), Santa Maria in Siena and Pisa, San Sassiano in Imola, and San Petronio in Bologna.[26] It would be worth devoting more than one paper to a study of these patron saints and their role in political life as well as in defence and war; in areas, that is, where the cultic and economic community of the *civitas* was also tried and tested as a warrior community. More attention might also be given to the standard-bearing chariot, the *Carroccio*, and to the bells which it sometimes carried.[27] Bells, primarily a means of communication for religious purposes, soon became the outstanding means of communication for the municipalities. There is some support for the hypothesis that urban communal life could not have developed without control over the bells.[28] The *Carrocci* vanished after the victory of the *Signori* over the city communes. *Ex negativo*, this is further evidence of the strong connection that existed between specific forms of religiosity and a civic community which was by no means purely "political."

German communities, too, had standard-bearing chariots in the twelfth and thirteenth centuries, bearing symbols of themselves and images of their city saints.[29] Significantly, once again, this applied only to cathedral cities: Liège, Cologne, Mainz, Worms, Strasbourg, and Metz; and moreover — apart from Liège, which was the second successor to the Roman *civitas* of Tongres — only to cities of ancient Roman origin. In the case of Liège, Metz, Mainz, and Strasbourg, the city saints were the patron saints of the cathedral, which again shows parallels with the Italian *civitates*.

These and other similarities between German and Italian cathedral cities had common roots in Christian antiquity. In the early period of Christianity, churches and religious communities were founded next to the tombs of saints, which were often situated outside the city walls.[30] These provided the essential cultic basis for the medieval towns and in the long run determined their topography, even if the cathedral churches were sometimes not incorporated within the confines of the city walls until the ninth or tenth centuries, as happened in some Italian *civitates*. Here lay the lasting advantage of the ancient cathedral cities over the younger *civitates*, which did not have autochtonous saints and "cultic centres." These younger cities were forced to search for prominent saints to adopt. Venice, for example, was successful in obtaining relics of St. Mark in the early ninth century.

The advantage of having an autochtonous saint was reinforced by the position it accorded a city within the Christian history of human salvation, as well as within the ecclesiastical organization. It provided the basis for an affinity with those pre-eminently sacred cities, Jerusalem and Rome — the latter closer and in many respects more central to the Western Church. The adaptation of the Roman liturgy, partly derived from the ritual of Jerusalem, contributed to this phenomenon. This affinity was reinforced, especially during the high Middle Ages, by readily believed legends linking the first bishops with the apostles and thus with the ancient Church founded by Christ.[31]

The German cathedral cities beyond the Roman *limes* lacked such a founding role in the history of salvation. It was therefore all the more important for their bishops, who doubtless acted with the broad and active support of the *populus*, to come closer to the *sanctae civitates*, and most of all to their archetypes, Jerusalem and Rome. They buttressed this connection by acquiring relics, holding processions and erecting shrines. Recent findings show that, from the tenth century onwards, the cultic and hence also the topographical character of many cathedral cities was modelled on these archetypes. Examples include Liège, Utrecht, Paderborn, Hildesheim, Minden, Halberstadt, Regensburg, Bamberg, Constance, and Eichstaett, the palatine and canonical cities of Aachen and Xanten, and the "monastic" cities of Seligenstadt, Fulda, and Hersfeld.[32]

In contrast to earlier studies and even to views backed by the authority of Max Weber, our findings show clearly that it was above all the cathedral cities, with their religious and cultic facilities, that gained confirmation and legitimation with the establishment of their city communes. It is for this reason that each of what appear to be the earliest municipal seals in Europe — those of Cologne, Mainz and Trier — represents its particular city as a *civitas sancta*.[33]

The illustration with which I conclude shows the seal of *sancta*

Treviris. Dating from the first half of the twelfth century,[34] it is still frequently used by the city of Trier today. Thousands of years are reflected in its symbolic images, as well as fundamental models of thought and behaviour whose influence has been decisive both within and beyond Italy and Germany. Suffusing those images and models is Jerusalem in its Christian guise — underpinned, in turn, by Jewish Jerusalem.

The Great Seal of the City of Trier, later lead copy
(made to appear positive by turning over the negative)

Notes

I wish to thank my assistants Dr. Gerold Bönnen and Dr. Frank Hirschmann for their valuable aid (see below, note 13) and my doctoral student Christoph Cluse for the English translation.

1. J. Martin (ed.), *Atlas zur Kirchengeschichte: Die christlichen Kirchen in Geschichte und Gegenwart*, Freiburg 1987, map no. 32 (in which Oldenburg is wrongly located), with commentary and bibliography on p. 27*, and maps nos. 22–33, with pp. 21–22*. The map can be no more than a rough guide, especially with regard to Italy (see *ibid.*, note 3).
2. Within the areas to the west of the Rhine in what was to become the *regnum teutonicum*, the cities of Mainz, Worms and Speyer lay closer together. The cathedral cities of the province of Trier — Trier, Metz, Toul, and Verdun — were also relatively close to one another. In these *civitates*, the continuity between antiquity and the early Middle Ages was much more emphatic than in the other subsequently German regions. The cathedral cities east of the Rhine — i.e., beyond the *limes Romanus* — generally had smaller distances between them than those south of the Main. However, the rather undeveloped urban character of most of these episcopal sees, which in the north were not founded until Ottonian times, has to be taken into account.
3. For the dynamics of development in the south, see Vera von Falkenstein, "Die Städte im byzantinischen Italien," *Mélanges de l'Ecole française de Rome, Moyen Age*, 101 (1989), pp. 401–464, which also provides further bibliographical references.
4. Cf. A. Haverkamp, "Die Städte im Herrschafts- und Sozialgefüge Reichsitaliens," in F. Vittinghoff (ed.), *Stadt und Herrschaft: Römische Kaiserzeit und Hohes Mittelalter*, Munich 1982, pp. 149–235, especially p. 153.
5. Cf. B. Schwineköper, *Königtum und Städte bis zum Ende des Investiturstreits: Die Politik der Ottonen und Salier gegenüber den werdenden Städten im östlichen Sachsen und in Nordthüringen*, Sigmaringen 1977, which provides further references.
6. Haverkamp, "Städte" (above, note 4), pp. 224, 232 f., etc.; C. Wickham, *Il problema dell'incastellamento nell'Italia centrale: l'esempio di San Vincenzo al Volturno*, Florence 1985; A.A. Settia, *Castelli e villaggi nell'Italia padana: Popolamento, potere e sicurezza fra IX e XIII secolo*, Naples 1984; idem, *Chiese, strade e fortezze nell'Italia medievale*, Rome 1991.
7. See the entry by E. Ennen, "Abteistadt," *Lexikon des Mittelalters*, I, Munich–Zurich 1977, cols. 64–65 (though I am not entirely in agreement with the definition given there); and, for a monographic study, J.L. Charles, *La ville de St. Trond au moyen âge: Des origines à la fin du XIVe siècle*, Paris 1965. Cf. H. Trauffler, "Abteistädte im südlotharingischen Raum," in *Les petites villes en Lotharingie / Die Kleinen Städte in Lotharingien (Actes de 6es Journées lotharingiennes, 25–27 Octobre 1990)*, Luxemburg 1992, pp. 381–402.
8. Cf. G. Methuen (ed.), *Stift und Stadt am Niederrhein*, Kleve 1984; P. Moraw, "Über Typologie, Chronologie und Geographie der Stiftskirche im deutschen Mittelalter," *Untersuchungen zu Kloster und Stift*, Göttingen 1980, 9–37; and J.-L. Fray, "Saint-Dié et le haut Val de Meurthe du XIe au milieu du XIVe siècle:

développement urbain et centralité géographique dans un milieu du moyenne montagne au Moyen Age," in *Les petites villes* (above, note 7), pp. 359–380.

9. Sometimes the smaller urban centres benefitted from the imperial government, which enabled them to achieve a stronger position. This was the case with Bobbio, to give but one example; see P. Racine, "Le relazioni tra Piacenza e Bobbio nei secoli XII e XIII," *Archivio storico per le province parmensi*, 28 (1976), pp. 185–196. More generally, see also A. Haverkamp, *Herrschaftsformen der Frühstaufer in Reichsitalien*, I–II, Stuttgart 1970–1971; and idem, "Der Konstanzer Friede zwischen Kaiser und Lombardenbund (1183)," in H. Maurer (ed.), *Kommunale Bündnisse Oberitaliens und Oberdeutschlands im Vergleich*, Sigmaringen 1987, pp. 11–44.
10. A.A. Häussling, *Mönchskonvent und Eucharistiefeier*, Münster 1973, pp. 161, 303. Cf. A. Haverkamp, "'Heilige Städte' im hohen Mittelalter," in F. Graus (ed.), *Mentalitäten im Mittelalter: Methodische und inhaltliche Probleme*, Sigmaringen 1987, pp. 119–156, 154 (with further references); C. Frugoni, *A Distant City: Images of Urban Experience in the Medieval World*, Princeton 1983, p. 23.
11. H. Appelt (ed.), *Die Urkunden Friedrichs I*, II (MGH DD, X.ii), Hanover 1979, pp. 430–434, no. 502, including references to the earlier edition by E. Meuthen (1972) and to other literature. Cf. Haverkamp, "'Heilige Städte'" (above, note 10), pp. 143 ff.
12. H. Stoob, "Die hochmittelalterliche Städtebildung im Okzident," in idem (ed.), *Die Stadt: Gestalt und Wandel bis zum industriellen Zeitalter*, Cologne–Vienna 1985^{2}, pp. 125–150, especially pp. 141 and 142 (map).
13. The findings represented here cartographically stem from a research project on Trier carried out under my supervision. One of the sections for which I am responsible within the Trier *Sonderforschungsbereich* (235), "Zwischen Maas und Rhein: Beziehungen, Begegnungen und Konflikte in einem europäischen Kernraum von der Spätantike bis zum 19. Jahrhundert," is "Die Städte des Maas-Mosel-Saar-Raumes im Herrschafts- und Sozialgefüge während des hohen und späten Mittelalters im Vergleich." Its major contributors include my research students Gerold Bönnen and Frank Hirschmann, who have published doctoral dissertations on Toul and Verdun, respectively, in the high and late Middle Ages (G. Bönnen, *Die Bischofsstadt Toul und ihr Umland während des hohen und späten Mittelalters*, Trier 1995; F.G. Hirschmann, *Verdun im hohen Mittelalter: Eine lothringische Kathedralstadt und ihr Umland im Spiegel der geistlichen Institutionen*, Trier 1996). The maps included here differ in many respects from that published previously in A. Haverkamp, "Die Städte Trier, Metz, Toul und Verdun: Religiöse Gemeinschaften und Zentralitätsgefüge einer Städtelandschaft zur Zeit der Salier," in S. Weinfurter (ed.), *Die Salier und das Reich*, Sigmaringen 1991, III, pp. 165–90, 180.
14. These relationships are discussed in the dissertations of G. Bönnen and F. Hirschmann (see preceding note). For a preliminary sketch concerning the priories, see Haverkamp, "Städte" (above, note 13), pp. 186 ff.
15. Haverkamp, "'Heilige Städte'" (above, note 10), p. 139; idem, "Städte" (above, note 13), pp. 184 ff.; and the study by M. Matheus "Adlige als Zinser von Heiligen: Studien zu Zinsverhältnissen geistlicher Institutionen im hohen Mittelalter," *Habilitationsschrift*, University of Trier, 1989.

16. For important new insights and conclusions, see M. Matheus, "Adlige" (see previous note), as well as the doctoral dissertation of my research student Margit Müller, *Am Schnittpunkt von Stadt und Land: die Benediktinerabtei St. Arnulf zu Metz im hohen und späten Mittelalter*, Trier 1993.
17. The map is based on the material provided by Alessandra Veronese, "Monasteri femminili in Italia settentrionale nell'alto medioevo confronto con i monasteri maschili attraverso un tentativo di analisi 'statistica'," *Benedictina*, 34 (1987), pp. 355–416 (including the maps, which, however, are problematic). Unlike the maps of the German territories, this one does not feature the collegiate churches.
18. In the diocese of Trier, only the Cistercian monastery of Orval was added, in the Romance-speaking part of the bishopric, around the years 1221–1232. See G. Despy, "Les origines de l'abbaye d'Orval," *Revue d'histoire ecclésiastique*, 64 (1969), pp. 756–807; P.-Ch. Grégoire, *Orval au fil des siècles*, I: *Des origines au 14e siècle*, Orval 1982; and *Aurea vallis: Mélanges historiques réunis à l'occasion du neuvième centenaire de l'abbaye d'Orval*, Liège 1975. The close contacts between the Cistercian monasteries and the towns are highlighted in the doctoral dissertation of my student Wolfgang Bender, *Zisterzienser und Städte: Studien zu den Beziehungen zwischen den Zisterzienserklöstern und den großen urbanen Zentren des mittleren Moselraumes*, Trier 1993.
19. See H.-J. Schmidt, *Bettelorden in Trier: Wirksamkeit und Umfeld im hohen und späten Mittelalter*, Trier 1986. As in similar cases, the map does not include the Friars of the Sack, whose Trier foundation can be traced back at least as far as 1262 (Schmidt, pp. 33 ff., must be corrected accordingly), because they had ceased to exist by 1300.
20. The project mentioned in note 13 has now also surveyed cultic facilities in the regions outside the ecclesiastical province of Trier. For Lower Saxony and Hesse, see Gudrun Nischke (ed.), *Geschichtlicher Handatlas von Niedersachsen*, Institut für Historische Landesforschung der Universität Göttingen, Neumünster 1989, map no. 32 ("Kirchliche Gliederung um 1500 — Stifte und Klöster vor der Reformation"); F. Uhlhorn (ed.), *Geschichtlicher Atlas von Hessen*, I: *Atlas*; II: *Text— und Erläuterungsband*, Marburg 1960–1984, map no. 12 ("Kirchliche Einteilung: Stifte und Klöster bis in das 16. Jahrhundert," by F. Uhlhorn); W. Alter (ed.), *Pfalzatlas*, Speyer 1964.
21. See, among others, J.-Ch. Picard, "Conscience urbaine et culte des saints: De Milan sous Liutprand à Vérone sous Pepin Ier d'Italie," *Hagiographie, cultures et sociétés, IVe–XIIe siècles*, Paris 1981, 455–67; E. Occhipinti, "Immagini di città: Le *laudes civitatum* e la rappresentazione dei centri urbani nell'Italia settentrionale," *Società e storia*, 14 (1991), pp. 23–52. This article includes the later Middle Ages. Cf. also Frugoni, *A Distant City* (above, note 10).
22. Haverkamp, "'Heilige Städte'" (above, note 10), p. 137, note 53.
23. Dom A. Calmet, *Histoire de Lorraine*, III, Nancy 1748 (reprinted Paris 1973), preuves, cols. 18–20. Cf. G. Bönnen, F.G. Hirschmann & A. Haverkamp, "Religiöse Frauengemeinschaften im räumlichen Gefüge der Trierer Kirchenprovinz während des hohen Mittelalters," in Georg Jenal (ed.), *Herrschaft, Kirche, Kultur:*

Beiträge zur Geschichte des Mittelalters — Festschrift für Friedrich Prinz zu seinem 65. Geburtstag, Stuttgart 1993, pp. 369–415.

24. A. Haverkamp, "Leben in Gemeinschaften: alte und neue Formen im 12. Jahrhundert," in G. Wieland (ed.), *Aufbruch–Wandel–Erneuerung: Beiträge zur "Renaissance" des 12. Jahrhunderts. 9. Blaubeurer Symposion vom 9. bis 11. Oktober 1992*, Stuttgart–Bad Cannstadt 1995, pp. 11–44.
25. See R. Zerfass, *Der Streit um die Laienpredigt*, Freiburg–Basle–Vienna 1974; G. Tellenbach has suggested that the stronger emphasis placed on the distinction between laity and clergy was one of the major themes of the church reform; see idem, "Die westliche Kirche vom 10. bis zum frühen 12. Jahrhundert," in B. Moeller (ed.), *Die Kirche in ihrer Geschichte: Ein Handbuch*, II, fasc. F1, Göttingen 1988, p. 263, note 23: "Die entschiedenere Wertung des Abstandes von Klerus und Laien kann man geradezu für eines der Hauptthemen der 'Kirchenreform' halten." For the urban aspect, see E. Voltmer, *Reichsstadt und Herrschaft: Zur Geschichte der Stadt Speyer im hohen und späten Mittelalter*, Trier 1981.
26. H.C. Peyer, *Stadt und Stadtpatron im mittelalterlichen Italien*, Zurich 1955; A.M. Orselli, "Il santo patrono cittadino fra Tardo Antico e Alto Medioevo," *Atti del Convegno tenuto a Roma dal Consiglio Nazionale delle Ricerche* (1979), II, Rome 1981, pp. 771–784; eadem, "Vita religiose nella città medievale italiana tra dimensione ecclesiastica e 'cristianesimo civico'," *Annali dell'Istituto storico italo-germanico in Trento* , 7 (1981), pp. 361–398.
27. Cf. Hannelore Zug-Tucci, "Il carroccio nella vita communale italiana," *Quellen und Forschungen aus italienischen Archiven und Bibliotheken*, 65 (1985), pp. 1–104; E. Voltmer, *Il carroccio*, Torino 1994; idem, "Nel segno delle Croce: Il carroccio come simbolo del potere, 'Militia Christi' e Crociata nei secoli XI-XIII," *Atti della undecima Settimana internazionale di studio (Mendola, 28 agosto—1 settembre 1989)*, Milan 1992, pp.193–207; idem, "Leben im Schutz der Heiligen: Die mittelalterliche Stadt als Kult- und Kampfgemeinschaft," in C. Meier (ed.), *Die okzidentale Stadt nach Max Weber: Zum Problem der Zugehörigkeit in Antike und Mittelalter*, Munich 1994, pp. 213–242; cf. A. Haverkamp, "Glocke und Gemeinde im Mittelalter," in *Wirtschaft & Wissenschaft*, 4/95, pp. 21–29; idem, "... An die große Glocke hängen: Über Öffentlichkeit im Mittelalter," in *Jahrbuch des Historischen Kollegs 1995*, pp. 71–112.
28. The smaller Jewish communities employed a *shammash* who acted as *shulklaper*, often called *campanarius* or *campanator* (bell-ringer) in sources of German provenance; see A. Maimon, (ed.), *Germania Judaica*, III: *1350–1519*, 2 vols., Tübingen 1987–1995.
29. Voltmer, *Il carroccio* (above, note 27); idem, "Standart, Carroccio, Fahnenwagen: Zur Funktion der Feld- und Herrschaftszeichen mittelalterlicher Städte am Beispiel der Schlacht von Worringen 1288," *Blätter für deutsche Landesgeschichte*, 124 (1988), pp. 187–209; see also Voltmer's other studies (above, note 27).
30. P. Brown, *The Cult of the Saints: Its Rise and Function in Latin Christianity*, Chicago 1981; A.M. Orselli, *L'immaginario religioso della città altomedievale*, Ravenna 1985; J.-Ch. Picard, *Le souvenir des évêques: Sépultures, listes épiscopales et culte des évêques en Italie du Nord des origines au Xe siècle*, Rome 1988; F. Prinz, *Frühes Mönchtum*

im Frankenreich: Kultur und Gesellschaft in Gallien, den Rheinlanden und Bayern am Beispiel der monastischen Entwicklung (4.–8. Jahrhundert) (with attached map), Munich 1965, Darmstadt 1988[2] (including more recent findings). See also the contributions by F. Prinz, M. Heinzelmann and R. Kaiser in F. Prinz (ed.), *Herrschaft und Kirche: Beiträge zur Entstehung und Wirkungsweise episkopaler und monastischer Organisationsformen*, Stuttgart 1988; and F. Prinz, "Der Heilige und seine Welt: Überlegungen zum gesellschaftlichen und kulturgeschichtlichen Aussagewert von Viten und Wundererzählungen," in A. Haverkamp & A. Heit (eds.), *Mönchtum Kultur und Gesellschaft: Beiträge zum Mittelalter*, Munich 1989, pp. 251–268. And see above, notes 10 and 21.

31. Haverkamp, "'Heilige Städte'" (above, note 10), pp. 128 ff.
32. *Ibid.*, p. 131; see also M.L. Gatti Perer (ed.), *"La dimora di Dio con gli uomini" (Ap 21.3): Immagini della Gerusalemme celeste dal III al XIV secolo*, Milan 1983; and, more generally, H. Kugler's literary-historical study, *Die Vorstellung der Stadt in der Literatur des deutschen Mittelalters*, Munich 1986. Cf. M. Matheus, "Zur Romimitation in der Aurea Moguntia," in W. Dotzauer, W. Kleiber, M. Matheus & K.H. Spieß (ed.), *Landesgeschichte und Reichsgeschichte — Festschrift für Alois Gerlich zum 70. Geburtstag*, Stuttgart 1995, pp. 35–49.
33. T. Diederich, *Rheinische Städtesiegel*, Neuss 1984, pp. 261 ff. (Cologne), 287 ff. (Mainz), and 333 ff. (Trier), with bibliographical references; for a different evaluation, see M. Groten, "Studien zur Frühgeschichte deutscher Stadtsiegel: Trier, Köln, Mainz, Aachen, Soest," *Archiv für Diplomatik*, 31 (1985), pp. 443–478; and see also H. Stehkämper, "Die Stadt Köln in der Salierzeit," in Weinfurter, *Die Salier* (above, note 13), III, pp. 75–152, 137 f.
34. The picture is reproduced from Diederich, *Rheinische Städtesiegel* (above, note 33), pl. 90, based on a later lead impression that preserves many of the minute details.
35. J. Prawer, "Jerusalem in the Christian and Jewish Perspectives of the Early Middle Ages," in *Gli Ebrei nell'alto medioevo*, Spoleto 1980, II, pp. 739–795 (followed by a discussion on pp. 797–812); and see also several of the contributions in S. Boesch Gajano & L.Scaraffia (eds.), *Luoghi sacri e spazi della santità*, Torino 1990.

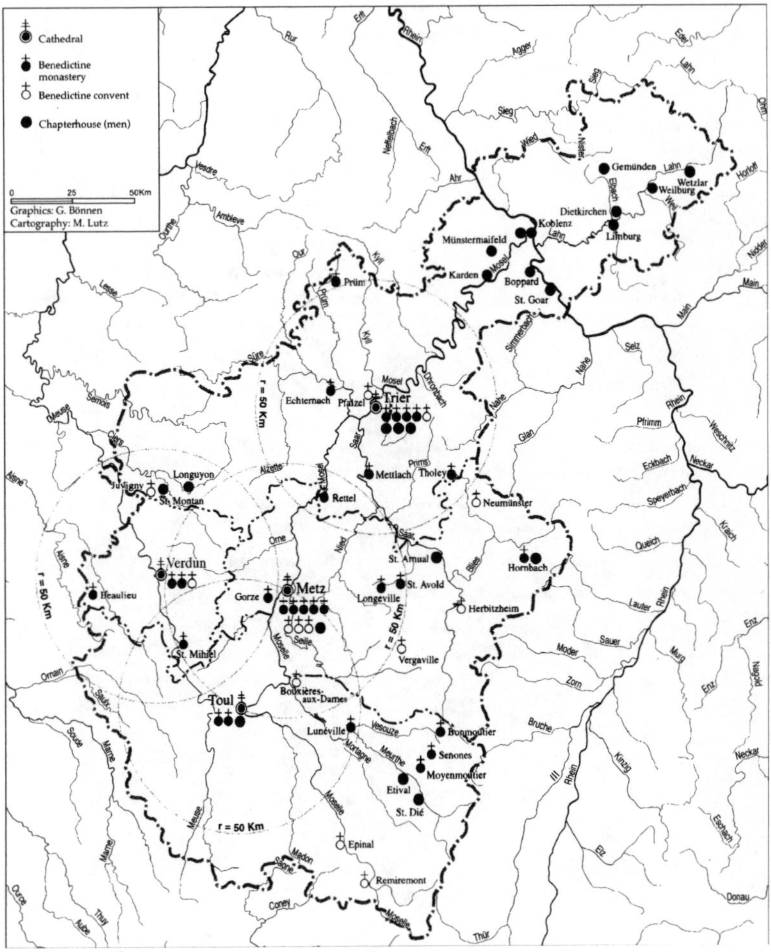

Map 1: Abbeys and chapterhouses in the Archbishopric of Trier around 1000

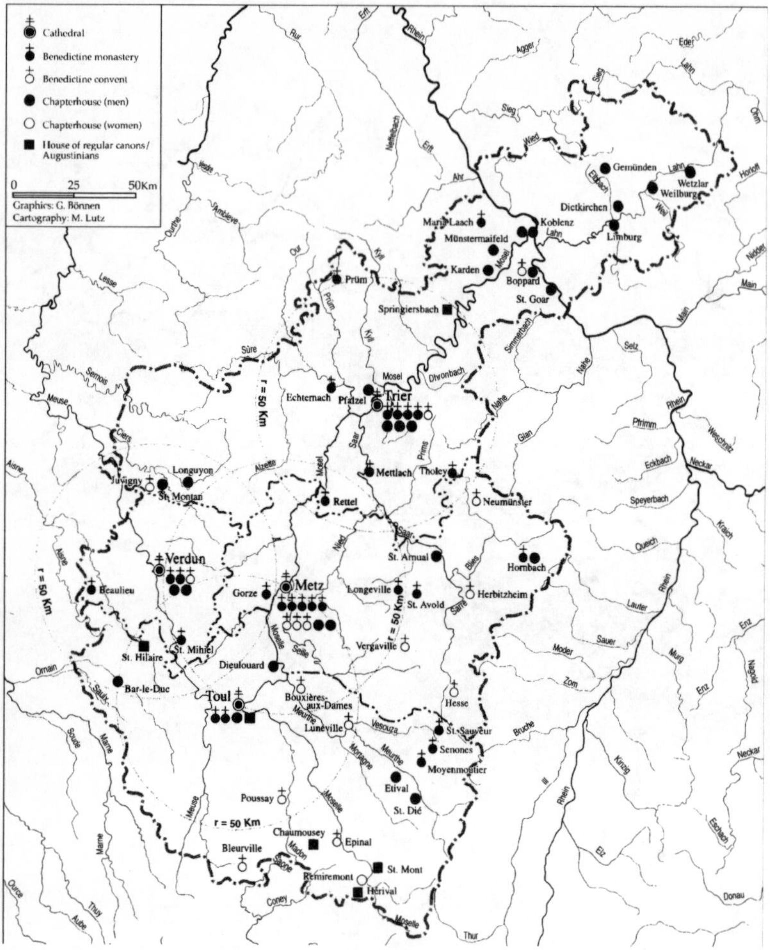

Map 2: Abbeys and chapterhouses in the Archbishopric of Trier around 1120

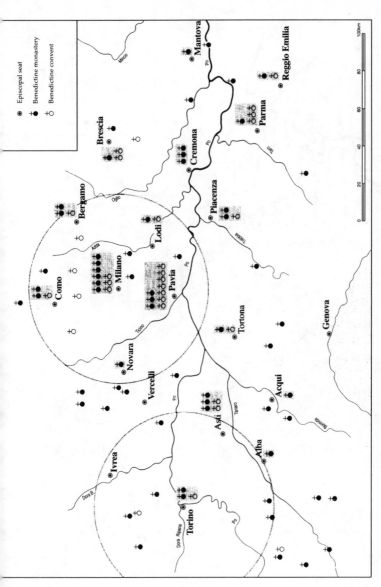

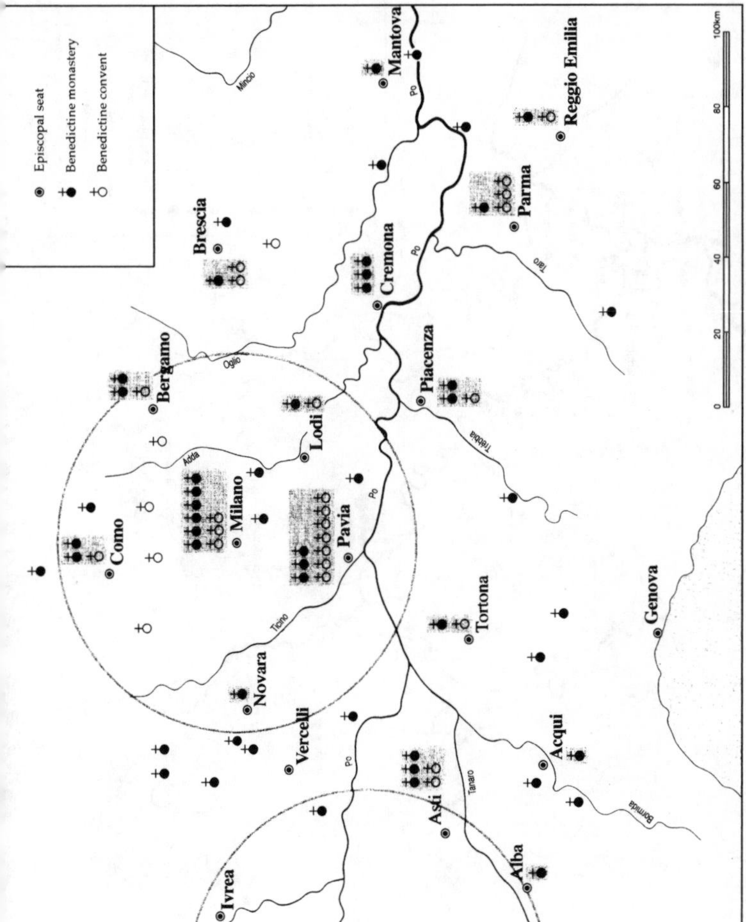

Map 3: Benedictine monasteries and convents in the western and central part of Upper Italy up to 1024

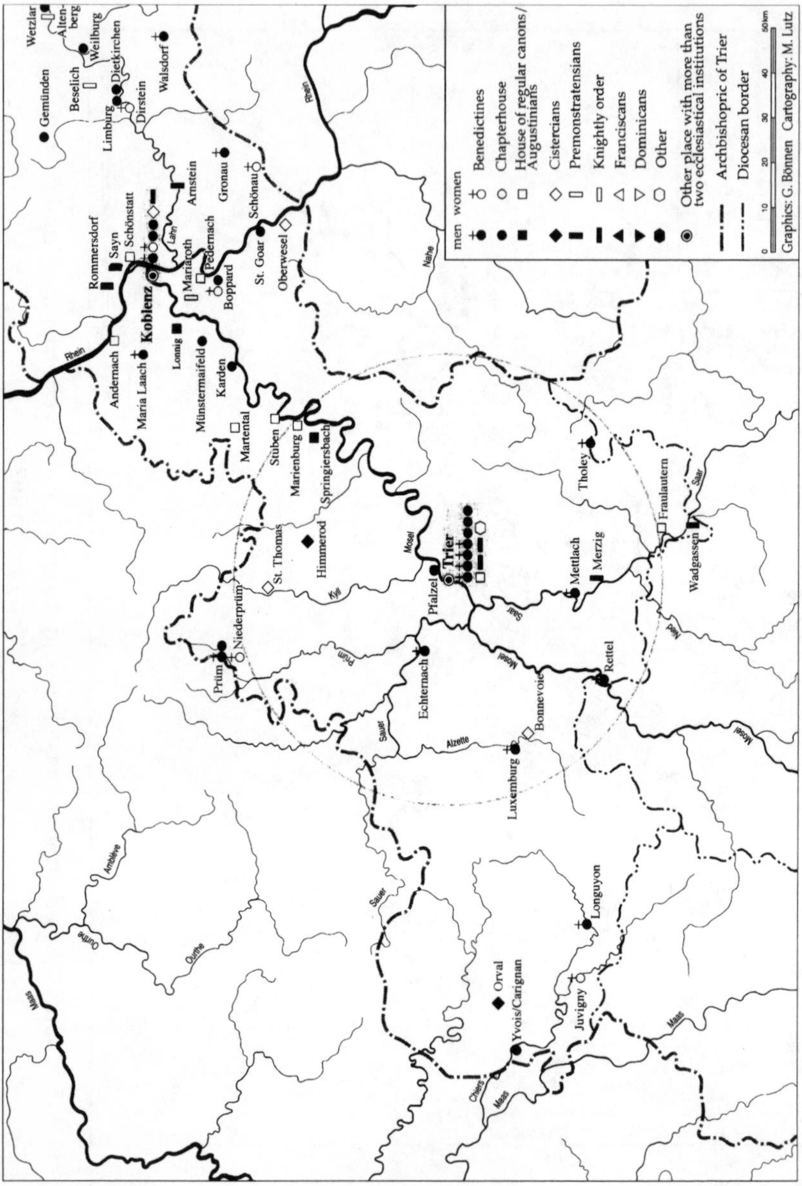

men women
Benedictines
Chapterhouse
House of regular canons/ Augustinians
Cistercians
Premonstratensians
Knightly order
Franciscans
Dominicans
Other
Other place with more than two ecclesiastical institutions
Archbishopric of Trier
Diocesan border
0 10 20 30 40 50km
Graphics: G. Bönnen Cartography: M. Lutz
Wetzlar
Alten-berg
Gemünden
Weilburg
Beselich
Dietkirchen
Limburg
Dirstein
Walsdorf
Rommersdorf
Sayn
Schönstatt
Arnstein
Gronau
Schönau
Koblenz
Mariaroth
Pedernach
Boppard
St. Goar
Oberwesel
Andernach
Maria Laach
Lonnig
Münstermaifeld
Karden
Martental
Stuben
Marienburg
Springiersbach
St. Thomas
Himmerod
Trier
Pfalzel
Niederprüm
Prüm
Echternach
Tholey
Fraulautern
Metlach
Merzig
Wadgassen
Rettel
Bonnevoie
Luxemburg
Longuyon
Orval
Yvois/Carignan
Juvigny
Rhein
Lahn
Nahe
Mosel
Kyll
Prüm
Saar
Nied
Sauer
Alzette
Amblève
Ourthe
Maas
Chiers

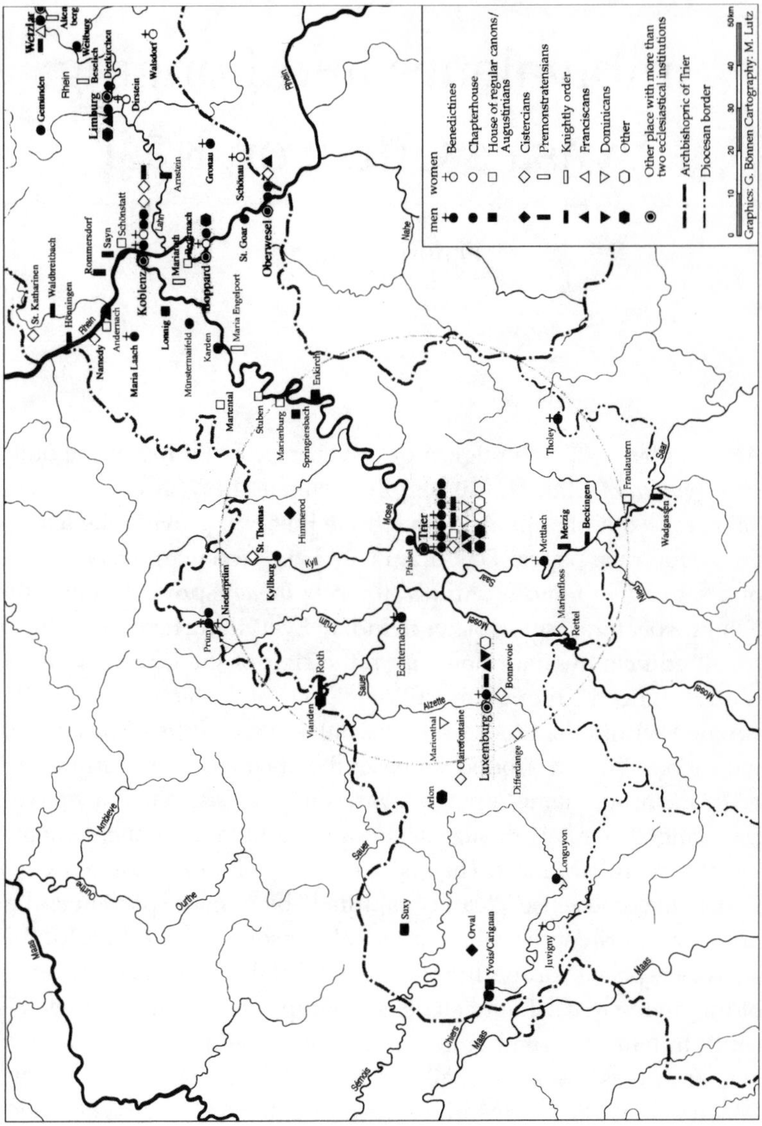

Map 5: Abbeys and chapterhouses in the Saar-Mosel region around 1300

13

Ambivalence and Longing: Vyāsa's Curse on Kāśī

David Shulman

i

At first glance, as the pilgrim or traveller passes through the outer gate (*gopuram*), the Hindu temple seems a study in concreteness. Take, for example, the Andhra temple that will provide the textual focus for this paper, Dakṣārāma in East Godavari District, one of a set of five famous shrines (the *pañcārāma*) spread through the Telugu-speaking region of South India.[1] Everything here — the black basalt edifice; the enormous *liṅga*, the sign of the god Śiva, in the central shine; the miniature replica in stone of the temple as a whole, situated within the inner wall (*prākāra*); the sacred tree (*sthalavṛkṣa*), with icons littered around its base; the stagnant tank outside that bears the proud name Saptagodāvara, and that is said to link up with the Ganges — all of this speaks of a reality that is stable, tangible, visible, intended to last. The god who dwells in this massive edifice is also, in some sense, clearly "captured" by it, made present and at home in a form accessible to physical, sensory contact. Indeed, this sensory aspect is, properly, the other side of the concrete localization of the divine in earth and stone. The temple, especially in its classic south Indian form, embodies an ideology of sensual and emotional exuberance as the major path (*sādhana*), to experiencing ultimacy.[2] Listen to how the fourteenth-century Telugu poet Śrīnātha describes Dakṣārāma in his *Bhīmakhaṇḍamu*, the collection of local traditions he composed on this site:

> Each day in Dakṣārāma
> the gentle breeze from the south,

rinsed in *tilaka* honey and areca-perfume,
blows banyan shoots at the perfect breasts
  of women who watch the growing paddy,
rides the waves of the Saptagodāvara
  with glee,
then penetrates the high windows
  in golden palaces built for women
  who are truly divine,
while serpent-maidens worship in the bowers below.[3]

This verse, merely one in a long passage extolling the physical beauties of this site and, especially, of its various categories of women, characteristically eroticizes the landscape enfolding the no less sensually engaging shrine. At the same time, we should note that a certain tension nearly always attaches to this highly sensual mode of contact; the south Indian devotional context also absorbed notions of yogic "innerness," at odds with sensory and emotional experience, as part of the process of worship (*pūjā*) both inside the temple and in other arenas.[4] The two vectors meet in varying combinations, and produce different forms of balance: the *Bhīmakhaṇḍamu*, like much medieval Telugu devotion (*bhakti*), clearly leans in the direction exemplified in the above verse.

Śrīnātha is, perhaps, an extreme case: the senses are always powerfully present to his mind, whether he is envisioning a mythic or cultic reality or a moment of courtly romance. But the experience of tangibility, with its sensual concomitants, is a natural part of *any* Hindu pilgrimage. It may, then, come as something of a surprise to find the *purāṇa* or *māhātmya* texts, which celebrate local shrines, announcing that such a shrine is actually a simulacrum of another, hidden realm; or that what we see there is only a small part of a much wider reality — for example, of the macrocosmic body of the supreme deity, Puruṣa;[5] or that the "real" city of Kāśī (Benares) was hidden by the gods, whereas the actual city on the Ganges that can be visited today is a secondary, inferior creation (from which even Śiva, the major deity of Kāśī, is absent).[6] Add to statements of this sort the familiar motif of the shrine that must either be buried or destroyed, usually by the very gods who are worshipped there, and the sense of durability and certainty about these temples begins to erode. We begin to intuit an intriguing ambivalence that requires explication. Just what does it to mean to locate the divinity in stone, to seek him in such solid forms? How, in the last analysis, is this theme of localization to be understood?

This paper explores the dimension of ambivalence embedded in the conceptualization of the south Indian sacred site. We will deal primarily with one well-known story — not about any southern temple, but about Kāśī, most sacred of all Hindu places of pilgrimage — as this story is told from the localized, highly specific perspective of Dakṣārāma, the Andhra shrine mentioned above. Dakṣārāma has its own vision of Kāśī, one that resonates strongly with its vision of itself. Before attempting to draw out the essential elements of this conception, let me offer a simple typology of ways in which the south Indian shrine presents itself, in cult and text.

First, the temple is the home of a great lord who controls its immediate vicinity — a king, indeed usually the greatest of earthly rulers, commanding respect and offerings from his subjects. The temple is this king's palace; and the daily rituals are modelled on those performed upon, and for, any royal figure. The god is dressed, paraded, fanned, fed, put to sleep, awakened — all in the fashion suited to any local lord. In this vision of the temple god, power is central; the shrine is the nexus of redistribution of power, honours, and wealth, in ways that have been lucidly analyzed by Appadurai and Breckenridge in a well-known paper.[7] To say this is not to deny that power, as constituted in a south Indian Hindu context, includes expressive and aesthetic components central to its operation; nor should we assume that power means the same thing here as it does in other cultures or cultural modes. We will return to this point later.

Second, the temple is a point of connection with other, hidden worlds. It is almost always situated atop a cosmic mountain (invisible to the mortal eye), and thereby linked to the heavenly spheres and the *muktipada*, the zone of release.[8] A great tree within the temple precincts invariably replicates this linkage and also extends it downwards into the underworlds of snakes, demons, and the fertile dead (Pātāla). A body of water — river, lake, or tank, like the Saptagodāvara mentioned above — also embodies this form of connection, usually by identification with the subterranean (or, alternatively, the celestial) Ganga. These three elements — mountain/rock, tree, and river — also constitute a kind of idealized landscape, ordered, controlled, and, above all, properly situated within the wider Hindu cosmology.[9] In this sense, the marked space is indexical, part of and pointing to the more encompassing cosmic realities. But at the same time, the temple can also serve as a miniaturized model capable of being used to manipulate parts of those realities, condensing within itself the same lines of force and internal relations characteristic of the cosmos as a whole.[10] Here we may have to ask ourselves about the precise ontic status of such a model, even as we explore its roles and functions vis-à-vis the pilgrim/visitor.

Third, largely as a function of the previous set of images,the temple serves as, and is fundamentally perceived to be, a point of transition and transformation — *tīrtha*, a place of crossing. In this sense, any pilgrimage is inherently processual — not the fixed and stable assimilation of a defined and predictable set of experiences and concepts, but a far more open-ended and finally unknowable form of movement between worlds, outside and in. Movement of this sort, based on connectedness with some overriding reality of presence, may entail powerful sensations of anxiety, loss, and destruction; indeed, such sensations, perhaps contrary to our expectations and to the idealized depictions characteristic of the early chapters of the south Indian *māhātmya* texts, often turn out to be primary in some sense to the pilgrimage and to its refractions in *purāṇic* narrative. Even the aesthetic and sensual (or, indeed, openly sexual) components mentioned above may contain, require, or evoke these expressions of difficulty and painful confrontation; indeed, as we shall see, certain *purāṇic* stories explicitly thematize and problematize this side of the process. Pilgrimage can be seen as akin to sacrifice, with all the potential negativity and violence proper to the sacrificial arena; moreover, as with sacrifice, the transformation that is sought is never certain or without danger.[11] Even the best of pilgrims — the paradigmatic sages, such as Vyāsa, the hero of our story — can all too easily go wrong.

Note that of these three closely linked perceptual stances, only the first is entirely "grounded" in the physical reality of the locale; the vision of the temple as royal palace, replete with the accoutrements of power, expresses what we might call a "right-hand" mode, to adopt a common south Indian metaphor for the socio-cultural order. This is the mode proper to agricultural castes, with their rootedness in the soil and their characteristic acceptance of violence in the service of power relations.[12] The second and third conceptualizations allow for the symbolic manipulation of concrete realities, and for the ultimate transformation of the latter — although here, too, the sheer physical grounding of the sacred zone, in all its particularity, clearly matters enormously. It is not by any means a question of freely playing with symbolic and expressive materials, but rather of coming to grips with dimensions of a highly specific and located reality that includes obstacles, blockages, residues of doubt and ambiguity. There is, in fact, a certain boldness about the way the tradition focuses on these issues, even developing for them dramatic narrative forms.

ii

Śrīnātha's *Bhīmakhaṇḍamu* or *Bhīmeśvarapurāṇamu*, which we have already quoted, is a *kāvya*-style *sthalapurāṇa* — literally, the "ancient traditions about a place" — fixing the mythic traditions of Dakṣārāma in literary form. As such, it reveals classic features of the puranic genre: the dialogic frame, agglutinative and encyclopaedic tendencies, self-conscious presentation of normative Brahminical ideology (the *pañcalakṣaṇa* system), a rationalizing and stabilizing drive addressed to local materials no less than to borrowings from the Sanskrit *mahāpurāṇas*, attempts at systematization and comprehensive linkages (e.g., of the five *ārāma* shrines, here brought into relation to a single myth of origin).[13] These are framed within a *kāvya* moulding of elevated poetry, with its standard descriptive and lyrical features. Indeed, this *kāvya*-ization of *purāṇa* goes still further, restructuring the listener's experience of the stories in the direction of the passionate perfection of form and feeling for which Telugu *kāvya* consistently strives. The ideological frame of the *purāṇas* survives, but loses in emphasis to the sensual and experiential immediacy of the poetry. As we shall see, this transformation has consequences for the unfolding of the narrative itself, and of its meanings.

We should also note, by way of introduction, that the creation of Telugu *purāṇas* in the early fifteenth century is part of a wider process of Brahminization in Andhra, especially in the coastal delta zone. This is a formative period of institution-building, which includes the rise of so-called "sectarian" movements such as Telugu Vaiṣṇavism, seen emblematically in Potana's *Bhāgavatamu* (supposedly contemporaneous with Śrīnātha's *oeuvre*).[14] The Dakṣārāma *purāṇa* belongs, however, to a different level of tradition, one that is highly Sanskritized and elitist, with strong classical resonances and ambitions. The text, like so many other local *purāṇas*, presents itself as derived from the Sanskrit *Skandapurāṇa* (see 1.119); but there is good reason to suppose that Śrīnātha's Telugu version of the Dakṣārāma myths was primary — a first crystallization of these materials in literary form — while the existing Sanskrit *māhātmya* now sold at the temple is a much later, secondary recast. As to the stories themselves, there is, of course, no doubt that Śrīnātha derived much of the narrative from classical texts such as the *Kāśīkhaṇḍa* (in the case of the myth with which we are here concerned); as always, we should be curious about the peculiar uses to which he puts these sources and about the new expressive and semantic contents engendered by the Telugu poet.

The base-text is *Kāśīkhaṇḍa* 96.82–204 — a very striking conclusion to the compilation of myths about Kāśī. Śrīnātha gives a version of this story in his own Telugu *Kāśīkhaṇḍamu*; but we will first examine the version offered in the second chapter of the *Bhīmakhaṇḍamu*, as narrated by the Sūta-reciter to the sages in the Naimiṣa forest. These sages have heard about Vyāsa's curse and consequent exile, and they want to learn the precise details; it is, after all, very strange that the great sage Vyāsa himself should have been forced to leave the sacred city. The Sūta begins by showing us Vyāsa as he sits, despondent, on the banks of the Ganges outside Vārāṇasī, after the events connected with the curse. He is reviewing in his mind all the great *tīrthas* of the world, in order to choose one for his new home. He remembers something the goddess Pārvatī herself told him: that Kāśī is preeminent among *tīrthas*, but Dakṣavāṭī (= Dakṣārāma) is even better than Kāśī; it offers both earthly joys (*bhoga*) and release (*mokṣa*). One can live there, or die there — either choice is a good one (2.19). Still, the sage is filled with grief at separation from Kāśī. It is sunset, and the *cakravākī* bird mourns the inevitable separation from her mate during the night, just as Vyāsa is in mourning at the loss of his beloved city (2.31). This theme gathers intensity and power, reinforced by lingering descriptions of the city at sunset, at night, at dawn, as the *kāvya* format demands.

As the moon, grown old, began to sink
after covering the world with its dense rays,
Kālabhairava, the city's guardian, resumed his rounds.
Cakora birds, drunk on moonbeams,
went wild with love
in the palaces of the gods.
Pried loose by the flooding brilliance, flowers fell
from the *sindhuvāra* trees
in the Garden of Joy,
and ascetics held their breath
through the stillness of the night

while Vyāsa, dazzled by the moonlight,
closed his eyes in grief. (2.46)

Soon the sun rises: it is time for Vyāsa to move on. He heads south, toward Dakṣārāma, stopping at various shrines on the way — Kuntīmādhava, Puri, Śrīkūrmam, Siṃhācalam — all described, rather poignantly, as providing partial forms of much-needed "cooling" for the fiery suffering of separation from Kāśī, as a loving wife would fan her over-heated husband (2.51). We will pass over the lengthy descriptions of these shrines, noting only how deftly the poet uses this opportunity to establish and regulate the linkages between scattered elements of a wider sacred geography.

Finally, as Vyāsa approaches Dakṣārāma, he encounters another famous sage — Agastya, who, together with his wife Lopāmudrā, is on a pilgrimage to these same Andhra temples (especially Pīṭhāpuram). Agastya's appearance here is probably far from accidental: in the *Kāśīkhaṇḍa*, Agastya is also sent away from Kāśī, to bring the Vindhya Mountains back down to size. Śrīnātha's Telugu version of this episode includes some of his most moving verses, describing Agastya's heart-breaking farewell to his beloved city.[15] So Agastya knows all too well how Vyāsa must be feeling; when the two sages embrace, Agastya notices that his friend's face reveals some despondency (*vaiklavyamu*), some inner pain. Has some friction arisen between Vyāsa and one of the gods of Kāśī? Did the goddess Annapūrṇā, "Rich with Food," fail to feed him at midday? (As we shall see, this conjecture on the part of Agastya is perfectly on target.) Not even an idiot would dream of leaving Kāśī for some other place — so how could Vyāsa have done just this? Agastya even indulges his nostalgia for Kāśī in several emotional verses:

> At midnight, with great joy,
> standing on the spreading sands
> of the heavenly river
> in the blazing moonlight,
> I would sing to Śambhu, the lord of Kāśī,
> crowned by the crescent moon,
> to Śiva, with his black neck —
>
> and as I sang, my whole body
> came alive. (2.91)

Nostalgic poems of the type, dripping with sentiment, are something of a new departure in the Telugu literature of pilgrimage, where one shrine sometimes views another from a great distance. It is appropriate at this point to note that Dakṣārāma calls itself the "Southern Kāśī" (*dakṣiṇavārāṇaśi*, 2.20) — so, by incorporating verses in this new style, a somewhat unusual, even slightly ironic claim is being made. The irony will now deepen and become more suggestive, as Vyāsa proceeds to explain to Agastya the circumstances of his exile from Kāśī.

After all, he has been called on to give reason for his presence in the Telugu country; and he does so at length, by narrating the history of his curse. The story thus comes to us in the first person — an intimate confession. I will attempt, in the following summary, to preserve something of this pathos-laden tone:

> I arrived in the sacred city together with my famous pupils — Jaimini, Paila, Sumantu and others — after a long pilgrimage through the world. Who knows under what omen we entered Kāśī? For seven days we were hungry there, in Śiva's own house. Though we asked for alms, not one housewife would give us even a spoonful of food. Although the city was flourishing because of Śiva's compassion and King Divodāsa's prowess, we were famished.
>
> Vaiśampāyana was twisting and turning in agony; Sumantu shriveled up; Paila and Jaimini were overcome by misery, Devala

by sorrow; Dālbhya, writhing with cramps, scanned the horizon, hoping for help. On the eighth day, tired, sick, dried-up, our heads aching, we again took up our begging bowls. But again, at every door we were denied: "No, there is nothing here; go away!" Exhausted, famished, sick at heart, I experienced the darkness of anger; my eyes went black; and, as my disciples looked on, I smashed the begging-bowls to pieces against the rocks.

What can I say? My intelligence was in ruins. A certain meanness (*naicyamu*) that I had never known appeared in my mind. Why didn't I think about Viśvanātha [= Śiva at Kāśī}, or Gangā, or Duṇḍhivināyaka, or Kālabhairava? I stretched out my hand to pour Ganges water to accompany this curse: "May there be no learning, no wealth, and no devotion for three generations among those who live in Kāśī."[16] Still, I was shaking, and my hand did not pour the water. Just then a grey-haired woman, fifty years old, with sagging breasts like aged *cakravāka* birds, her body trembling, spoke to me: "Come here, hold back this curse."

I did not know who she was, or from what caste; but the heart knows the true power of that which stands before it (*hṛdayamba nerucun ĕduru prābhavambun erparimpa*, 2.112). I approached her, who is the very meaning of the Upaniṣads and the Vedānta, the consort of Viśvanātha living in Kāśī. She said to me, "Just because you received no alms, you are so overwrought? Śiva has been testing the purity of your mind. There is no lack of food in Kāśī. Don't you know that Viśālākṣī [the goddess in Kāśī] offers ambrosia with a golden ladle each day at noon? You are weeping because for seven days, some obstruction has been at work; your steadiness has disintegrated to the point where you were trying to cause harm to Kāśī, who is Śiva's own wife. It seems that the popular saying is true: *bubhukṣitaḥ kiṃ na karoti pāpam*, 'what evil would a hungry man not do?' You should not be angry at Kāśī. Do you know how angry Śiva will be because of this? But you are a Brahmin, and I should not accuse you. Come and eat."

After so many days, these words were like a flood of ambrosia to my ears. I asked her if I should come alone, or bring my pupils with me. "Is only my life a life?" She sent me to perform the afternoon rituals and return with my disciples, while she prepared the feast.

When we arrived — my 300 disciples and I — she led us into a huge hall hung with thousands of silk cloths, with moonstones on the walls and threshold designs on the floor. She seated us, beginning with the eldest, and spread the banana leaves before us — long, green leaves, not brittle or broken. "Eat this divine food slowly, and may Viśvanātha be pleased," she said. But we were wondering: there were no smoke, no smells, no sign of cooking, no pots and pans; was this all an illusion? Was she, too, illusory? Today, too, we would be disappointed. If you looked at her, she was all innocence, cooling beauty, discrimination; but if you looked down at the banana leaves, your heart sank — there was no rice or vegetables. Still, her servants had sprinkled water over the leaves, and she had invoked Śiva and begged us to eat....

Now, suddenly, there was plenty: an array of delicious curries and rice. Whatever delicacy we thought of, in whatever quantity, immediately appeared on the banana leaves. She — Annapūrṇā herself — kept moving through the rows together with the wishing-cow, the philosopher's stone, and the gods' wishing-tree. We ate to satiety, with deep delight, to the limits of our fantasy. When we had finished, from inside the house appeared the divine couple, Viśvanātha and Pārvatī themselves, wearing golden sandals, holding hands. Looking at the goddess, we saw compassion; looking at the god — anger. Happiness and fear filled our hearts .

I knew: since I had been angry at Kāśī, who is Śiva's wife, *he* was angry at me; but for the same reason — because Kāśī is Pārvatī's rival and co-wife — *she* was pleased with me. First the god spoke to me in fury: "You evil-minded pseudo-sage! Bastard who recites all the Vedic texts in vain! You false scholar, who prides himself on composing the *Mahābhārata*! Who are you to curse my wife, the city of Kāśī, the main path to salvation (*kaivalyakalyāṇagaṇṭ hāpatha*) — and for no reason?! In egoism and arrogance, you entered this city; now leave it at once. If you won't go, I will rub your face against a rock — and even that would be too good for you." I was already on my way, unable to hear these dreadful words, when the goddess spoke

> to me: "Don't worry, my son. Even at a distance of 10,000 miles, I won't forget you. Go to Dakṣavāṭi (= Dakṣārāma) and stay there: Bhīmanāyaka [Śiva at Dakṣārāma] is an honest god. Good things may happen to you there." So, a little relieved at this promise, but grieving at heart because of Śiva's calamitous attack, I left with my disciples, hoping to see Bhīmeśvara. My fault was tiny as a mustard seed, but it was seen as a huge mountain. I am wandering around with no support, in pain. The gods, of course, are compassionate — but Kālabhairava has a harsh mind; Duṇḍhivināyaka is very jealous; in short, Kāśī is no place for people like us to live."

This is Vyāsa's confession, addressed to Agastya, accompanied by flowing tears.

iii

Notice the ending — the ironic reiteration of the gods' supposedly merciful nature, followed by the practical conclusion drawn from the bitter tale. Kāśī is not for Vyāsa or anyone like him. The corresponding implication — that Dakṣārāma, by way of contrast, *is* the perfect place — forms the gist of Agastya's response in the following chapter. It is easy enough to imagine the direction this paean of praise will take; we have already sampled some of Śrīnātha's sensual vision of this shrine, and can thus afford to pass over its re-articulation in Agastya's speech. We will return to the issue of Dakṣārāma's place in the scheme of sacred things; for now, our problem is to understand the import of Vyāsa's experience and its place in the traditions relating to these two sacred sites.

First, let us note, briefly, the way Śrīnātha has handled his sources. As already stated, the story he tells is essentially modelled after the Sanskrit *Kāśīkhaṇḍa* (96.86–204), which today forms part of the printed versions of the *Skandapurāṇa*. This version of the story has its own peculiarities and is marked by a tone very different from Śrīnātha's. A certain mordant playfulness characterizes the telling: Vyāsa is being tested and toyed with by an unpredictable, even somewhat malicious god. This god, Śiva, has just proved his superiority over Viṣṇu, whom Vyāsa had originally claimed to be the supreme deity; the price of this earlier claim, uttered by the sage in Kāśī, was the paralysis of Vyāsa's left arm.[17] Now that Vyāsa has been healed and "converted," as it were, to the worship of Śiva/Viśvanātha, and to various elaborate ascetic practices directed toward this god in Kāśī, it is time to test him: Śiva therefore orders the goddess to see to it that Vyāsa receives no alms. Notice that here the motivation behind the whole episode is clearly stated at the outset, in contrast to the way Śrīnātha unfolds the story in *Bhīmakhaṇḍamu*, where Vyāsa's confusion and bewildered frustration are passed on to the listener or reader before any explanation is offered.

After two days of going hungry for lack of alms, Vyāsa sends his disciples to see if there is a general famine in Kāśī. They return with a clear answer: there is no dearth of food in the city, which, indeed, is richer and happier than the heaven of the gods. Great heaps of wealth and grain grace the houses of Kāśī, whose inhabitants are living incarnations of Viśvanātha and his consort Bhavānī. This tantalizing description enrages Vyāsa; blinded by anger and hunger, he curses the city in the same words recorded by Śrīnātha (with one difference: instead of *bhakti*, devotion, it is *mukti*, release, that will be absent from Kāśī for three generations). Unlike the Telugu version summarized above, the Sanskrit text allows the curse to be uttered and rendered complete, in all its powerful intentionality.

Now the sage sets out again to seek alms, and again meets with no success. In disgust, he throws away his begging bowl and heads back to the ashram. It is nearly sunset; on his way home, a common woman (*prākṛtastrī*) stops him and asks him to be her guest, and the guest of her householder-husband. Vyāsa is overjoyed: this gracious woman could almost be a goddess, perhaps the protectress of Kāśī, the very embodiment of compassion. Yet he agrees to be fed only on one condition — notice the stubborn, demanding quality that still adheres to the famished sage — namely, that she feed all 10,000 of his disciples as well, and before the sun sets. She smiles and accepts this contract. And, indeed, the huge contingent is satisfied by her delectable feast. When it is over, Vyāsa volunteers a statement of thanks and general wisdom: *this* (generous feeding) is the real *dharma*; there is no other. She agrees, but, disingenuously, asks further: what other common forms of *dharma* exist? Vyāsa immediately falls into the trap by listing four critical traits: pacific speech, tolerance for another person's excess (*parotkarṣasahiṣṇutā*), deliberate and prudent action, and concern for the welfare of one's own home (or sacrificial fire, *dhiṣṇya*). At this, the woman's husband suddenly responds in caustic and sardonic tones: "Which of these qualities exist in you, wise man that you are? We can see your calmness and self-control — in the curse you gave to Kāśī. You are, of course, compassionate, steady, in control of anger and desire, a man of pacific speech, tolerant of others' excesses, an exemplar of deliberate action, and concerned with the welfare of your own hearth. Just tell me one thing: when someone curses because his own wishes are frustrated, what happens to him?" Vyāsa, perhaps still not quite realizing the nature of his situation, replies: "Such a curse rebounds against the person who uttered it."

The full revelation can now take place, along the lines Vyāsa has unwittingly set out for himself. Viśvanātha, the householder, tells the sage: "One who cannot see the splendour of my city is truly cursed. You can no longer dwell in this city, which knows no curse (*śāpavarjita*); it is not a proper home for people like you." Trembling, Vyāsa falls at the feet of the goddess and begs for mercy. She grants his request that he be allowed back into the city twice each month, on the *aṣṭamī* and *bhūta* days. Since then, Vyāsa remains on the east bank of the Ganges, across from the city, whose spires and temples he can still see from afar. (This ending explains the existence of Vyāsakāśī, a suburb of Benares on the other side of the river.)

Śrīnātha, as noted earlier, retells this version of the story in his own *Kāśīkhaṇḍamu* (7.129–199). He follows the Sanskrit fairly closely in terms of narrative line, although,once again, the lyrical *kāvya* tone, with its persistent humourous asides and mellifluous interchanges, carries a different burden than the rather ruthless *purāṇic* original.[18] In the *Kāśīkhaṇḍamu*, too, Śrīnātha softens the actual moment of the curse: Vyāsa is only contemplating uttering the fateful words when the goddess intervenes. For the Telugu poet, this curse is simply too powerful and terrible an eventuality; he even ends his narration by making Śiva warn Vyāsa: "Don't ever curse another *tīrtha* or *tithi* (ritual date)!" (7.199). This is an important issue, which helps to clarify the difference between the Sanskrit parent-text and its Telugu descendants (or, perhaps, between the milieux of Sanskritized Benares and the Brahminical temples of medieval deltaic Andhra). The essential point is that the Sanskrit *purāṇa* from Benares itself does not hesitate to allow the curse to exist freely in the world. Moreover, the strategic placement of this story at the end of the *Kāśīkhaṇḍa* — or so close to the end that it may well be considered a kind of culminating closure to the whole anthology — suggests that this theme of cursing and consequent exile holds a special significance.

It is, in fact, a much older theme in the literature on Kāśī. Already the Vulgate of the *Harivaṃśa* tells a story of the "emptying out" of Vārāṇasī in the time of the famous king Divodāsa: This king had agreed to rule the earth only on condition that the gods remove themselves to heaven. But Śiva needed a home for his new bride, Pārvatī, who was unhappy living in her parents' home (especially since her mother was openly critical of the new son-in-law, with his outlandish habits). So Śiva decided to settle in Kāśī — if he could succeed in ousting the king. Nikumbha (= Vināyaka) was asked to settle this matter. He appeared to a barber in a dream and instructed him to build a shrine holding his (Nikumbha's) image. When the shrine was established, many people came to worship there and received great gifts from the god — progeny, wealth, long life. Only Suyaśā, Divodāsa's queen, was denied her request from Nikumbha; she could not conceive a son. In anger at this state of affairs, the king wrecked the god's shrine, and, as a result, Nikumbha cursed the city to be emptied of its inhabitants. The citizens of Benares fled in all directions. Śiva then came to stay there with his wife, and, although she did not like the city and ultimately decided to return home, he refused to leave it — hence its name, Avimuktā, the "undeserted." Śiva dwelled there for the first three cosmic ages. However, in our time, the evil Kaliyuga, *that* city has disappeared, while the city of men has once more come into existence.[19]

Benares, then, is, almost by definition, a city of exile, exiled from itself — undeserted, perhaps, by its primary deity, but truly deserted by everyone else because of a curse proceeding from the gods' nefarious scheming. Underlying this story is the bitter rivalry between man and god for the good things of this world, which, apparently, cannot be shared or harmoniously distributed or recycled. A sacred site is a prime example of these contested goods; hence Benares becomes a war zone where the power relations between the two contestants seek resolution. This is by no means an exotic notion, nor is it lacking in the current traditions of other shrines, which often describe the relations between worshipper and deity as an extended tug-of-war. One implication is, clearly, that the shrine's sacred character actually precedes the arrival of its deities; as Diana Eck cogently states, "Kashi is not such a great *tīrtha* because all the gods are there; all the gods are there because it is such a great *tīrtha*."[20] But this existential primacy of place, which is deeply rooted in the conceptual structure informing many, if not indeed most, *tīrthas* throughout the sub-continent,[21] is also made by this story to incorporate a dimension of hiding, exile, and destruction. For our purposes, this is the crucial point. The existing city, as we know it, is at best an *ersatz* for the one in which Śiva could openly, visibly, be at home. To live there, or perform a pilgrimage there, is thus to feel this gap, this persisting absence; while even memory, preserved in the *purānic* traditions, attests to a structure of relations in which a curse leads to flight, and no one, except the lonely deity, can truly be at home.

In a certain sense, then, the high-flown epithet needs to be reversed. Kāśī-Avimuktā, the "undeserted," might more properly be named "the abandoned," if we look at it from a human perspective. Moreover, this reversal is surely paradigmatic: Kāśī is the holiest of sacred places, its fate a prototype for that of others. A sacred site is thus, by definition, *the place you are exiled from*. If we take this story seriously, there is no reason to believe that one can simply go on living normally at some sacred centre, or even visit it in a straightforward, balanced, untroubled mode. It is far more likely that the meeting with this place and its divine presences will lead to testing, frustration, some form of curse and loss. In this respect, though otherwise divergent in structure and detail, Vyāsa's story repeats the earlier tradition about Divodāsa. Both stories lead inexorably toward exile as the final result of coming to Benares; but in Vyāsa's case, the violent impulse to curse comes from the human side alone. This makes a difference if we wish to understand the kind of process that is being described. It is time we addressed this theme of cursing more directly as a component — perhaps even a necessary component — in the experience of pilgrimage.

iv

What, after all, does it mean? Why should the major teller of tales in this tradition, the original *paurāṇika* himself, be made to curse the most sacred of Hindu cities? If we return to the Dakṣārāma text, our point of departure, a simple — actually far too simple — answer suggests itself. Dakṣārāma, the "southern Kāśī," surpasses its prototype, the "northern Kāśī," since, unlike the latter, it has not been cursed. Moreover, exile from Kāśī leads the unhappy sage directly to Dakṣārāma, where he can come, temporarily, to rest. And yet what looks like, indeed may properly be said to be, a tale of one-upmanship by one shrine bound in relations of rivalry and imitation with another is also considerably more than this. Underlying the surface narrative, with its vision of testing that approaches, and then crosses, the threshold of aggression, is a certain mode of conceptualizing both the constitution of the sacred *tīrtha* and the essential nature of pilgrimage to it.

The curse is clearly a central component to this vision. What has elicited this dramatic verbal act? Whatever else is going on,we need have no difficulty in believing that Vyāsa's proleptic utterance is actually grounded in some perception of reality. Kāśī, like other sacred cities in India (and elsewhere), can certainly inspire distaste and disappointment as well as more positive emotions. The living reality contrasts miserably enough with the ideal; Kāśī may, indeed, be viewed as a city of ignoramuses and beggars. In this respect, our story falls in line with a universal theme in the literatures of pilgrimage and utopia. The curse would thus express a relatively "realistic" standpoint, ironically conjoined to the heavily idealistic depictions that are normative for the *māhātmya* type.

And yet this is a very limited reading, which the Sanskrit version of our story explicitly warns us against. Śiva himself tells Vyāsa that the person who cannot see the beauties of Kāśī is truly cursed — as if it were the inner experience that the pilgrim brings with him to the holy site that really matters, not any impoverished external confirmation or refutation. And Vyāsa acknowledges, implicitly, the truth of this perception when he admits that the curse of the frustrated pilgrim, engrossed in his own needs, inevitably rebounds against him. Both these statements make a serious ontic claim, which at once removes our story from the category of, let us say, Petrarch's aversion to Avignon. Something deeper is at stake than the trivial realization of a gap between the alleged "real" and the preferred "ideal." Indeed, neither of these categories, or pseudo-categories, will take us very far.

It would surely be more to the point to recognize that the curse represents, in this context, a crucial moment of transformation. It is the curse, born of rage and despair, that produces the reversal and revelation — that brings food to the hungry sage and his disciples, and yet ultimately brings about their banishment from the holy city. Up to this point, there is an impasse: no alms, no food, no understanding. Vyāsa's response may be exaggerated, may even constitute a kind of failure (although it is hard not to empathize with the sage who has gone hungry for seven days, in a city replete with food); nevertheless, it is this response that precipitates movement and resolution. Think of the process as a whole: hunger leads to anger, which ultimately gives birth to the curse; this prompts the intervention by the disguised goddess, who, however, is still regarded with doubt and suspicion by the sage and his pupils; out of this background of scepticism and wonder, sensual satisfaction eventually emerges, followed by the final revelation and a counter-curse uttered by the god against his devotee. The end is exile, a punishment which may nevertheless turn into a form of blessing. It is a strangely zig-zagging series of events, very characteristic of Śaiva epiphanies in general.[22] For our purposes, we need to recognize that this course of development is neither exotic nor inexplicable, but rather expresses almost a standard progression.

Nor is Vyāsa's curse the only one of its kind. One thinks of Yudhiṣṭhira's cursing of *dharma* at the very end of his tortured career, when he, too, is being tested (by finding his brothers and wife in hell).[23] There, too, the curse is what turns matters around and produces resolution. There is something in this "negative" discharge in potent language that can transform both the world and human consciousness of the world. In some sense, Vyāsa would never really "see" Kāśī, or experience its richness, or discover the presence of its gods, were it not for the despair seeking expression in the curse. The latter does, of course, exact a price — but even here, the price may well be part of the shrine's inner structure.

One way to analyze this structure is to take as central the *process* embodied in this and similar stories (rather than, let us say, the fixed points of reference that the *māhātmya* texts so readily produce: the stable cosmology, the shopping lists of standardized rewards and expiations available at the shrine, the dependable iconology). In the end, pilgrimage is always processual, involving dynamic movement, and we should not be surprised to find this inherent dynamism apparent in localized ritual and myth. If we return to the three major roles or "visions" of the temple with which we began, we find each of them affected by the story we have told. The sacred site is, first, a focus of power relations, and Kāśī"s power is amply demonstrated here, by the miraculous feeding that the goddess Annapūrṇā brings about. And yet, as we have noted, this miracle issues out of the curse. In this sense, we might say that the power at work in the *tīrtha* must be consonant with the "negativity" active in the curse, and in the experience that produces it; or, to state the issue more strongly, that this form of power entails the ability both to elicit and, perhaps, to sustain such a curse. The somewhat tortuous, indirect process of testing the pilgrim, under conditions of rivalry between him and the deity, literally "takes place" within a paradoxical domain of ambivalence that effectively constitutes the true structure of potential energies at work in the shrine. To enter the sacred space is thus to enter this domain, where movement is possible, and where anxiety and anger are at least as prevalent and powerful as any beatific inner states. In short, "power" here, as in any classical Hindu context, is not constituted by the mere, massive exercise of force, but seems rather to flow out of instability and imbalance, the corrosion of certainty, a vital doubt that generates a test. It is wholly appropriate to such a vision of power that ontological uncertainty, coupled with amazement, emerges at the critical moment: Is this old woman real, or an illusion? Is she human or divine? Will anything substantial, and edible, appear on these leaves?

Lest we be tempted to imagine that this peculiar understanding of power is limited to our story, or to Kāśī, let us turn for a moment to the origin myth about Dakṣārāma, which has given us Śrīnātha's version of the Vyāsa story. The huge *liṅga* at Dakṣārāma is one of five fragments broken off from an even greater *liṅga*, which belonged to the Tripura demons. The latter had worshipped Śiva after being deprived of their share of ambrosial *amṛta* after churning the ocean of milk; so the great *liṅga*, and the rewards of devotion to it, were partial compensations for the original experience of ultimate loss (of the food of immortality). Still, this was a demons' *liṅga*, and the demons, however devoted, remained a target for the gods. Śiva himself went to war against them and burned their three cities; in the end, only the *liṅga* — the broken "sign" left over from the previous state of loving connection — survived this fiery destruction. So here, too, the very constitution of the deity's presence reflects a process of ambiguous externalization — from loss and failure, through momentary compensation and consequent destruction, to fragmentary re-articulation by localization in the Andhra shrine; and from a demonic, disordered "otherness" to an accessibility that still bears the signs of its traumatic origins. Śrīnātha tells this story in the fourth canto of his *purāṇa,* immediately after Agastya's high-flown praise for Dakṣārāma; and this progression, too, is meaningful, a repetition of the earlier pattern which takes us from the idealizing depictions of the introduction to Vyāsa's conflictual pilgrimage to Kāśī. Ambivalence, negation, or destruction help form the consciousness that itself forms any living shrine.

And this consciousness always informs the second level of self-presentation mentioned at the start. If power is partly generated out of the situation of trial and curse, the situation of the *tīrtha* within the cosmos may well reflect a similar perceptual stance. The shrine that connects the pilgrim with unseen worlds is a moving image, an instrument linked to a dynamic, always somewhat elusive or fragmented presence. Were the divine presence whole, perfected, and stable, a story like ours could never happen; nor would it be told at the penultimate moment in the fundamental *purāṇic* text on Kāśī. The very indexicality of which we have spoken in this context embodies an element of self-transcendence, as if the shrine were always pointing beyond itself to a less limited and localized reality. Moreover, its true position is relational, linked to the inner experience that features in Vyāsa's curse and the god's counter-curse. One brings something to the shrine, and loses something there — before losing *it*, the shrine, as well. And while there, at the central moment of the pilgrimage, one perhaps tends to wonder just what is true, and what illusion: the *tīrtha* straddles, or, better, articulates this boundary in awareness. Ultimately, the reality of the shrine becomes fully present only after the fact, elsewhere, in exile — this is Vyāsa staring, grief-stricken, from across the river, at the distant spires of his now-beloved Kāśī. From this perspective, we could even say, again, that it is this very longing and loneliness that actually constitute the shrine, or its experience, together with the linguistic externalization of the pilgrim-storyteller's ambivalence.

Finally, it should be clear that what matters most in the process described by our story is what happens on the third level, i.e., the transformation in being. We can recapitulate the stages of this transformation, taking Vyāsa's story as prototype. First there is hunger, a yearning that meets with frustration; then doubt and anger, as the mind questions what the eyes perceive; but confirmation of the real, and satisfaction, ultimately consummate the earlier residues of anxious and painful emotion, which survive in the end-stage of loss and leaving. This — the culmination in separation, and renewed longing — is the sign that the transformation is real, and complete; the pilgrim has met the god, been fed, and forced to leave. He is no longer the person he was before: the truth of Kāśī, of Śiva's presence, of endless plenty, in short, of some divine reality — this truth is now a stable, and somewhat poignant, part of his awareness. Far from obscuring or diminishing it, exile consistently reinforces it. By the same token, the separation sets in motion the next pilgrimage, which may re-enact the cycle.

The shrine is located, fixed in place, yet in constant motion. Without the reality of localization, which motivates any shrine's persistent claims of superiority and the enduring intoxication with a felt, empowered divinity, nothing else would be possible: this place, every place, is truly the centre of the world, the site of linkage and transition to ultimacy. But localization is not the end but rather the beginning of a process available to any pilgrim, a process that entails transformation of a peculiar and sometimes painful sort. We began with images of tangibility and sensual immediacy, which surely pervade the experience of visiting a shrine, but which also exist on other levels, or in conjunction with other, more hidden sensations, such as anxious doubt. In any Hindu context, movement along the *axis mundi* is also an internal process within consciousness; and it is this process that is, perhaps, in the end most real, tangible, and concrete. Let us risk another definition: the *tīrtha* is a form of labile consciousness enlivened by moving images generated by a stable, rooted, and sensually perceptible reality. The *Kāśīkhaṇḍamu* thus sees Kāśī as a crystallized node within the subtle physiology of yogic being, which comprises the world; while a southern shrine like Dakṣārāma delights in paradoxical images of the god who comes to worship the god, that is, himself, at his sacred home — first bathing in the Saptagodāvara tank, then, his body smeared with ash, climbing the steps to the main edifice, where he will find the radiant image of himself, and achieve release — as if even *he*, the final object of pilgrimage,had also to undergo the whole convoluted process we have been describing, as a subject.[24] By the same token, iconoclastic voices within the southern tradition, in a striking amalgam of continuity and defiance, can make claims like the following:

> To the utterly at-one with Śiva
>
> there's no dawn,
> no new moon,
> no noonday,
> nor equinoxes,
> nor sunsets,
> nor full moons;
>
> his front yard
> is the true Benares,
>
> O Rāmanātha.[25]

Notes

1. On Dakṣārāma and the other *ārāmas*, see M. Krishna Kumari, *Pancaramas in Medieval Andhradesa*, Delhi 1989; also C. Talbot, "Temples, Donors, and Gifts: Patterns of Patronage in Thirteenth-Century South India," *Journal of Asian Studies*, L (1991), pp. 308–340 (especially pp. 316–317). The term *ārāma* carries Buddhist associations, and it has been argued that these five shrines are converted *caityas*; Buddhist icons are still visible today on the grounds of Dakṣārāma.
2. See F. Hardy, *Viraha-bhakti: The Early History of Kṛṣna Devotion in South India*, Delhi, 1983; also D. Shulman, "The Yogi's Human Self: Tāyumāṉavar in the Tamil Mystical Tradition," *Religion* XXI (1990), pp. 51–72.
3. Śrīnātha, *Bhīmakhaṇḍamu*, ed. Ra. Veṅkata Subbayya, Madras 1901, 1. 97.
4. See Shulman, "The Yogi's Human Self" (above, note 2).
5. Umāpaticivācāriyar *Koyiṟpurāṇam*, Madras 1867, 3.69, 70–71; Śrīnātha, *Kāśīkhaṇḍamu*, Madras 1969, 2. 119–133.
6. See below, section iii; also D. Shulman, *Tamil Temple Myths*, Princeton 1980, p. 78, and sources cited there.
7. A. Appadurai and C. Appadurai Breckenridge, "The South Indian Temple: Authority, Honour, and Redistribution," *Contributions to Indian Sociology*, X (1976), pp. 187–211.
8. See, e.g., Ñāṇakkūttar, *Viruttācalapurāṇam*, Madras 1876, 6. 1–24; Shulman, *Tamil Temple Myths* (above, note 6), pp. 40–55.

9. Cf. J. Przyluski, *La Grande Déesse: Introduction a l'étude comparative des religions*, Paris 1950, pp. 60, 64–65.
10. See D. Handelman, *Models and Mirrors: Toward an Anthropology of Public Events*, Cambridge 1990, pp. 22–48. We may recall the miniature model of the Bhīmeśvara temple situated within the inner courtyard at Dakṣārāma — one model representing and condensing another. As Don Handelman remarks (private communication, March 1992), this type of miniaturization, probably based on a principle of synecdochal relations (part reproducing whole), might well apply down to the molecular level, if we were but capable of perceiving these proliferating models of models. Note that modelling also implies both the process of coming into being, without completion, and a dimension of absence — since the model remains a model.
11. I have argued at some length that the myth of divine marriage — always the central narrative of any Tamil *purāṇa* — can be understood in terms of a sacrificial process. For a more recent formulation of this problem, see my "Outcaste, Guardian, and Trickster: Notes on the Myth of Kāttavarāyan̲," in A. Hiltebeitel (ed.), *Criminal Gods and Demon Devotees*, Albany, N.Y., 1989, pp. 34–67.
12. See Velcheru Narayana Rao, "Epics and Ideologies: Six Telugu Folk Epics," in S.H. Blackburn and A.K. Ramanujan (eds.), *Another Harmony: New Essays on the Folklore of India*, Berkeley, Calif., 1986, pp. 131–166; D. Shulman, "Die Dynamik der Sektenbildung im mittelalterlichen Südindien," in S.N. Eisenstadt (ed.), *Kulturen der Achsenzeit II*, Frankfurt 1991, pp. 102–128.
13. See D. Shulman, "Remaking a Purāṇa: The Rescue of Gajendra in Potana's Telugu *Mahābhāgavatamu*," in W. Doniger (ed.), *Purāṇa Perennis*, Albany, N.Y., 1993.
14. On institutional development in fifteenth-century Andhra, see *ibid*. and see Talbot, "Temples, Donors, and Gifts" (above, note 1).
15. *Kāśīkhaṇḍamu* 2.134–158. Agastya leaves, staggering under the burden of sorrow, "like someone in love, confused, almost delirious, exhausted, with faltering steps, as if poison were rising to his head, or as if drunk, his eyes half-closed in grief, sighing and suspiring and sobbing...." (2.134). He bids a slow farewell to each of the major deities, to the ascetics and pilgrims, the gardens and temples and academies; hallucinating in his despair, he begs the ducks on the Ganges, the banana groves, the goddess Viśālākṣī herself to come with him into exile from Kāśī, that veritable "ocean of happiness" (*saukhyajalarāśī kāśī bāsi*, 2.140). In *Bhīmakhaṇḍamu* 3.4, Śrīnātha can thus describe Agastya as "having suffered the same calamity" (of separation from Kāśī — *samānavyasanuṇḍu*) as Vyāsa.
16. The curse is, of course, in Sanskrit: *mā bhūt traipuruṣī vidyā mā bhūt traipuruṣaṃ dhanam/ mā bhūt traipuruṣī bhaktiḥ kāśyāṃ nivasatām sadā* (2.108). Cf. *Kāśīkhaṇḍa* of the *Skandapurāṇa*, Gurumandal Series No. 20, Calcutta 1961, 96.125 (with *muktiḥ* instead of *bhaktiḥ*).
17. See *Kāśīkhaṇḍa* 95; and cf. Civañāṉacuvāmi, *Kāñcippurāṇam*, Kāñcipuram 1964, *cārntācayap paṭalam*.
18. We might also notice the humane, "domestic" tone of the description, as, for example, when Vyāsa seeks alms in vain: "One lotus-eyed lady said, 'We are still cooking'; another said, 'Come back later'; 'There is a ritual going on here today,' said a third; still another refused even to open the door" (7.137). "No

one would give him food, as though each woman had taken a vow not to feed" (*ŏṭṭuvĕṭṭinayaṭlu*, 136). Touches such as these flesh out the narrative skeleton the poet inherits from his Sanskrit source, which now acquires a vivid immediacy and warmth. This transition from Sanskrit *purāṇa* to Telugu *kāvya* requires a detailed study.

19. *Harivaṃśa*, BORI edition, Appendix 7, pp. 28–34 [= Vulgate, Varanasi 1964, 1.29–29–68]. Cf. *Brahmāṇḍapurāṇa*, Delhi 1973, 2.3.67.28–64; *Vāyupurāṇa*, Ānandāśrama Sanskrit Series no. 49, Poona 1905, 2.30.25–55. Hans Bakker informs me that a version of this story is found in the oldest surviving manuscripts of the *Skandapurāṇa*, now being studied and prepared for publication in Groningen.
20. D. Eck, *Banaras, City of Light*, Princeton 1982, p. 157.
21. See the discussion in my *Tamil Temple Myths*, pp. 40–89.
22. See D. Shulman, *The Hungry God: Hindu Tales of Filicide and Devotion*, Chicago 1993.
23. *Mahābhārata*, ed. P.P.S. Sastri, Madras 1933, 18.3.49–50; and see the discussion in my paper, "The Yakṣa's Curse," in G. Hasan-Rokem and D. Shulman (eds.), *Untying the Knot: Riddles and Other Enigmatic Modes*, New York, in press.
24. *Bhīmakhaṇḍamu* 1.113.
25. Devaradāsimayya 98, in A.K. Ramanujan, *Speaking of Śiva*, Harmondsworth 1973, p. 98.

14

Geotyping Sacred Space: the Case of Mount Hiko in Japan

Allan G. Grapard

Shugendō, an institutional and ritual system elaborated in Japan over a period of several centuries, evolved as a vehicle to achieve Buddhahood by means of various austerities and ascetic practices that were performed in mountains, with the assistance of complex rituals related mainly to Esoteric Buddhism and sometimes to Taoism, and through diverse cults rendered to combined native and foreign deities.[1] These cults were given in what is often referred to as [Shinto] shrines and [Buddhist] temples, even though those shrines and temples formed, for much of their history, associated cultic centres known as "shrine-temple multiplexes" (*jisha* or, less commonly, *shaji*).[2] Popularly known as *yamabushi*, the practitioners of Shugendō were ubiquitous in Japanese society for nearly a thousand years. They disappeared almost completely at the end of the nineteenth century, when the Japanese government abolished their institutions and forced them to return to lay life or become Shinto priests.[3] Prior to being submitted to the political and social erasures characteristic of the forms assumed by modernity in Japan, however, the *yamabushi* had produced a striking culture. Though it may have been dismissed or regarded as subsidiary by a number of scholars, it is an essential aspect of Japanese history.

The world of Shugendō was constituted, in part, on the basis of pan-Asian ritual practices issuing from Indian cults, Chinese Taoist practices, Korean mountain cults and Japanese naturalism. These were gradually combined with the high theological and ritual traditions of Esoteric Buddhism to produce a system that was profoundly distinct from other mountain cults in Asia. Shugendō was also grounded in a number of institutions sponsored (or controlled, as was often enough the case) by emperors, aristocrats, warriors, and commoners, and it had an apparently unlimited ability to assimilate, retain, create, or transform an immense variety of practices that ranged from sophisticated "technologies of the self" to the most peculiar therapeutic devices.[4] The world of Shugendō was not only one of the cornerstones of Japanese culture at large; it also produced many of the elements that were central to the constitution of the philosophy and practice of space that characterize that culture, and it was instrumental in the formation of the concept of Japan as a territorial entity.

A significant aspect is missing in all the studies that have heretofore appeared on the topic of Shugendō, however, and it can be characterized in two words: spatial knowledge. That is, even though Shugendō occupied the majority of Japan's mountainous areas, and even though its practitioners stressed spatial aspects in their soteriology, cosmography, and rituals, virtually no scholar has attempted to reconstruct the spatial dimensions of their meticulously elaborated world. In the following pages I will attempt to enhance our knowledge of Shugendō by positing "space," and the *yamabushi*'s understanding and construction of it, as its central problem. As a consequence of this approach, my study will be limited to a given region, and Shugendō will be treated, not as a single phenomenon that remained the same throughout Japan's history, but as something that evolved distinctive features explainable only in relation to a particular locale's geographical and social configurations.

The term "Mount Hiko" is almost a misnomer, for Mount Hiko's constitution as a Shugendō cultic centre involved at least three radically different cultic sites in Japan's southernmost Kyushu Island, and because Hiko Shugendō, as it is sometimes called, evolved peregrinatory practices that took its practitioners along two mountain ranges that extend north from Mount Hiko to Mount Fukuchi (south of Kokura), and northwest to Mount Hōman (next to Dazaifu), each separated from Mount Hiko by about fifty kilometres. Mount Hiko was also deeply related to the Usa Hachiman cult, whose main shrine is located twenty miles to the east, and to the Kunisaki Peninsula cult, which it influenced over the centuries (see map). Furthermore, the institutions of Mount Hiko went on to garner domains in northern Kyushu and to organize numerous

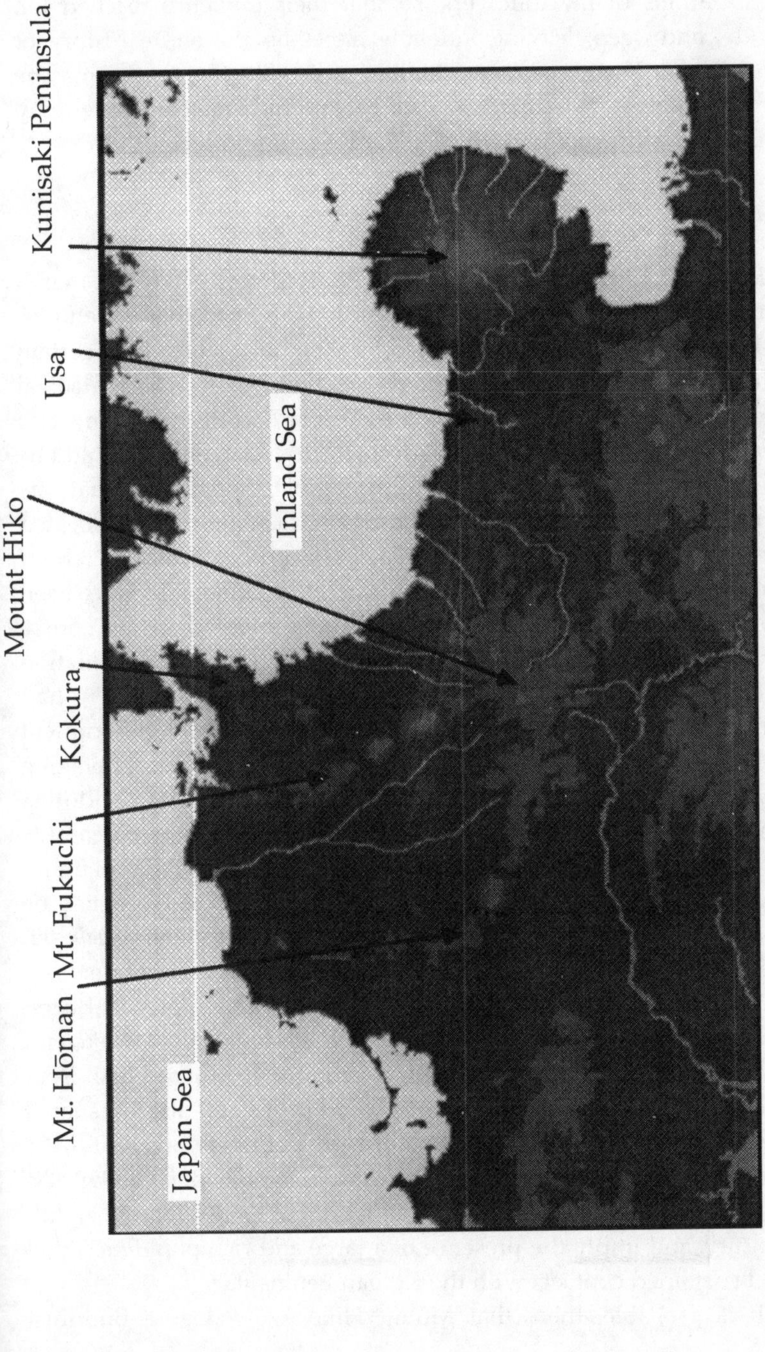

The Region of Mount Hiko

associations of lay followers, so that their influence reached far, wide, and deep, leaving indelible traces on the entire history of that island. The terms "Mount Hiko" and "Hiko Shugendō" may be understood, then, to refer to a vast geographical area and to lengthy historical processes, as well as to varied communities.

History of the Cult on Mount Hiko

Eleventh-century authors believed that Mount Hiko became a Buddhist site of cult in the sixth century C.E., and that its temples were "restored" at the beginning of the eighth century by a certain Hōren.[5] Several reliable documents mention Hōren, whose medical skills earned him recognition by the court in 702. The title/name *Usa no kimi* was granted by imperial decree to his relatives in 721, and he became the abbot of a major Buddhist temple, the Mirokuji, that was erected in 725 on the grounds of the Usa Hachiman Shrine, located near the eastern base of Mount Hiko. Legend has it that he rebuilt the Ryōzanji, Mount Hiko's Buddhist temple. Hōren may have been called upon by the court to heal wounds incurred in the course of local conflicts, or he may have ministered to a local population afflicted by epidemics, at a time when the central government had called for the presence of medical specialists in local government offices, but failed to fulfill that promise. Famines, too, were ravaging the north of Kyushu at the time, and the effort to construct Buddhist temples in the region was geared at rendering assistance to peasants overburdened with taxes and corvées. Hōren became a central figure in the evolution of Hiko Shugendō, and his medical fame may be seen as a building block in the therapeutic activities of the *yamabushi*, who were later to recognize him as one of their founding fathers.

The second largest concentration of Buddhist temples in Buzen Province at the time, after the Usa district, is found in the Miyako and Tagawa districts situated at the western foot of Mount Hiko. Roof tiles found at those sites, made in nine ovens recently excavated by archaeologists in the region, display definite Korean stylistic features. These finds indicate that Buddhism was developing at a fast pace in the northeastern coastal region of Kyushu in the eighth century, and imply the presence of a large and rich population that had sustained contacts with the Korean Peninsula.

It is probable, then, that Mount Hiko evolved as a Buddhist

site of cult during the eighth century. We do not know whether it had previously been the object of indigenous cults. There is no evidence that mountains were the venues of austere ascents or of seclusion on the part of anyone before Buddhist monks in the seventh century, a fact which suggests that mountain asceticism was a Buddhist project informed by continental thought and practices. It did, however, tend to focus on mountains said to have been the objects of pre-Buddhist cults. Some of the ancient inhabitants of Japan may have considered certain mountains themselves to be the "body" of a *kami*, a possibility suggested by the unearthing on several summits of plates for offerings and other cultic implements placed in the proximity of stone groupings.[6] The presence of Buddhist figures and the subsequent creation of Shugendō institutions on those mountains changed their character in a radical fashion. They imposed new "readings" on natural objects, usually by sculpting megaliths and trees representing Buddhist divinities, or as a result of their peregrinatory practices or of their establishment of permanent or semi-permanent sites of seclusion. Their activities may have erased many memories and traces of pre-existing cults.

Like the other Shugendō sites of cult, Mount Hiko is a prime example of a phenomenon that evolved slowly over the entire Heian period (794–1185). In tracing its origins as a site of cult, however, we are frustrated by the paucity of historical records.[7] Even though it may have functioned as such from early times on, its first known appearance in historical documents is in *Engi-shiki* (Procedures of the Engi Era), completed in 927, in which the following is noted: "Tagawa District: Karakuni-Okinaga-ohime-ouma-no-mikoto Shrine; Oshihone-no-mikoto Shrine; Toyohime-no-mikoto Shrine."[8] This compendious statement is instructive, albeit in a cryptic manner, because it does not mention Mount Hiko by name and passes over Buddhism in complete silence, even though Buddhist institutions were dominating the area at the time. The first shrine mentioned in it was originally located on Mount Kawara (north of Mount Hiko), and is suggestively mentioned in the thirteenth-century narrative *Hikosan-ruki*, which says that the three *kami* of Mount Hiko first attempted to take residence on Mount Kawara, but were prevented from doing so by local *kami*, against which they retaliated by cutting down all the mountain's trees (probably to build temples on Mount Hiko, to which they then proceeded).[9] The deity of Mount Kawara must have been of foreign origin, since its name is preceded by "Karakuni," a term which refers to Korea. *Buzen no kuni Fudoki*, part of a compilation ordered in 713 and again in 935, reports that a Korean deity came of itself to Mount Kawara and that its name was Kawaru, a term meaning "iron village" in Korean language — and the area was a site of iron mines. However, we must also note the inclusion of the word *Okinaga* in the name of the deity, because the personal name of Jingū Kōgō, worshipped as the mother of Hachiman in Usa at the foot of Mount Hiko, was *Okinaga* Tarashi Hime-no-mikoto. The second *kami* mentioned in the Procedures of the Engi Era is Oshihone-no-mikoto, an offspring of Amaterasu-ō-mikami, the ancestral *kami* of the imperial lineage. The third *kami* is Toyohime-no-mikoto, another important deity of northern Kyushu who has a prominent place in mythological records. Mount Hiko was thus regarded as the home of three *kami*, each residing on one of the three rounded peaks that form the summit of the mountain. Documents posterior to the Procedures of the Engi Era, however, identify the two last *kami* of Mount Hiko as Izanagi and Izanami, the mythical procreators of the Japanese archipelago. It is not clear when or why the *kami* mentioned in the Procedures were removed from their dominant position; *Hikosan ruki*, dated 1213, simply states that upon bequeathing the mountain to the newly arrived Buddhist deities, they moved to another residence on Mount Hiko. These three *kami* are now enshrined in a small sanctuary near the summit.

The assumption that Buddhism had been present on Mount Hiko at least since the eighth century was reinforced when an inscribed urn dated 1516 was recently excavated from the summit of the northern peak, for it contained a Korean bronze statue of the Buddha dating back to the period of unification of the kingdom of Silla in the eighth century. That statue has been identified as representing a *nyorai* (Skt.: *tathāgata*). The inscription on the urn, signed by a certain Keishun of Echigo Province who resided at the Tsuzō-bō hall of Mount Hiko, states that the statue miraculously "surfaced" on the mountain. There is a possibility, however, that the statue was not "found" on Mount Hiko but was brought there from Echigo Province by Keishun. The neighbouring Kunisaki Peninsula's temples were also given an antique Korean statue from the same region at about the same time. Unless future archaeological finds prove otherwise, all we can say at present is that it is not known when Buddhism settled on Mount Hiko. We do know, however, that its original cult was dedicated to Maitreya (J.: Miroku), the Buddha of the Future, a typical eighth-century phenomenon: the name of the temple created by Hōren in 725 was Mirokuji, "Maitreya Temple."

Given the extent of the Buddhist presence in north Kyushu at least since the seventh century, it is surprising that Mount Hiko's Buddhist institution does not appear in historical records before the eleventh century, at which time it is presented as a large-sized establishment. Chūyūki, the journal of the Minister of the Right Fujiwara no Munetada (covering the years 1087–1138), and *Honchōseiki*, a historical record dating from the end of the twelfth century, mention a gathering in 1094 in Dazaifu, the capital of Kyushu, of the religious communities of Mount Hiko, of the Anrakuji multiplex of Dazaifu, and of the Usa Hachiman shrine-temple multiplex. The ensuing violent protest, which impelled the vice-governor, Fujiwara no Nagafusa, to resign his position abruptly and flee to Kyoto, was sparked by the granting of the abbacy of the Daisenji, a Buddhist temple located on Mount Hōman next to Dazaifu, to a certain Raijō. The latter was assistant abbot of the Iwashimizu Hachiman shrine-temple multiplex in Kyoto, an institution that had gradually come to symbolize the political and economic control of the centre over the periphery during the tenth century. At the time, however, the System of Codes through which the country was supposed to be governed had fallen apart, and the country's political and economic power was divided among various competing social and institutional blocks. The shrine-temple multiplexes were major forces that began to flex their political and even military muscle in order to defend their economic provileges, though not in any unified or concerted manner. They were unable (or unwilling) to avoid intense competition with each other and impinged on one another's territorial domains, leading to gruesome armed encounters which the imperial court bemoaned and criticized but could not bring to a halt. Unable to muster the military, political, and economic authority it needed to exercise control over the multiplexes and over other conditions in the country, the imperium saw its political and economic powers disappear.

The oldest extant narratives concerning Mount Hiko date back to the medieval period (from 1185 to 1600) and disagree on the origins of the site of cult. One record dating from the thirteenth century states that the first ascent of the mountain was accomplished by a hunter named Fujiwara Tsuneo, though the single line stating that claim appears in a most abrupt manner in the midst of a story and thus invites one to see it as a later addition. A record of the sixteenth century — this time giving a wealth of details about the hunter — claims that Mount Hiko's Buddhist establishment was created in the sixth century by a Chinese monk, and that it therefore was the oldest monastery in Japan. Both records, however, agree that Hōren played an important, if not central, role in the foundation of the mountain as a Buddhist site of cult, indicating the influence Usa may have had in the formation of Mount Hiko or of its medieval narratives. Nothing concerning what happened between the early eighth century and the late eleventh century transpires in any of the documents at our disposal. Nonetheless, by the eleventh century Mount Hiko had at least one community called *shuto,* a term commonly used at the time in mountainous and urban sites of cult to refer to Buddhist figures, sometimes ordained but more often lay, who played a central role in the formation of the political power of multiplexes. This is further evidence of the large-scale evolution of Mount Hiko's Buddhist establishment during the first half of the Heian period.

In the eleventh century, the middle of the Heian period, pilgrimages organized by members of the imperial house and of the Fujiwara house in the central part of Japan reached a climax. Their goals were mountains in which Shugendō was evolving within the doctrinal and ritual parameters provided by the Tendai and Shingon schools of Esoteric Buddhism. The region of Kumano at the southern tip of the Kii Peninsula was by far the most popular destination. Retired Emperor Shirakawa's first visit there occurred in 1090, four years before Mount Hiko's name was to surface in official documents. His spiritual mentor was a certain Zōyo, who was subsequently appointed abbot (*kengyō*) of Kumano and of the Shōgo-in temple in Kyoto, an institution established for protecting the body of the emperor as symbol of the state. In 1160 Emperor Go-Shirakawa, who had a particular predilection for Kumano, invoked the Kumano deities in Kyoto and built the Ima-Kumano Shrine to establish them as protective deities (*chinju*) of the Shōgo-in. In 1181, the emperor granted that shrine some economic support from twenty-eight domains scattered all over Japan. First among these was Mount Hiko.

It is on that occasion that Mount Hiko was established as a tax-free place, contained within a perimeter defined by boundaries beyond which government officials were not allowed to make enquiries concerning taxation or to investigate criminal matters. Prior to 1181, Mount Hiko had been regarded as the place where the Buddha of the Future would inaugurate a new cosmic age. Urns containing scriptures related to a hope for rebirth in a better world, excavated in 1951, were interred near Mount Hiko's summits in 1113 and 1145. By the end of the twelfth century, however, it had apparently become the site of beliefs and practices related to the widespread notion of the decadence of the Buddha's teachings and of the universe at large (*mappō*), a belief reinforced by the tumultuous conditions of the time.

The historical consequences of the grant of Mount Hiko as a domain of the Shōgo-in multiplex were of a ritual/practical, institutional, political, and economic character. First, Mount Hiko came to symbolize a particular relationship to the imperium, a feature that had been absent from its foundation. Second, its economic fate became thoroughly related to the welfare of the imperial system, at a time when that system was threatened by administrative incompetence and by the growing power of the warrior class. And, third, Mount Hiko came to be influenced by Kumano Shugendō and to be dominated by Kyoto temples. The subsequent history of Mount Hiko is linked to its efforts to liberate itself from that position.

The Heian period ended in 1185 in a final maritime battle at Dan-no-ura, on the shores bordering Mount Hiko's foot, and Japan came to be governed by the Kamakura military dictator (*shōgun*) Minamoto Yoritomo. The Minamoto house, however, had been created by political *fiat* when descendants of Emperor Seiwa — the grandson of Fujiwara no Yoshifusa, who had created the Iwashimizu Hachiman multiplex in 859 — were granted that name on the condition that they not lay claim to the throne. They never forgot their origins in Emperor Seiwa and therefore carried out a cult to Hachiman. This explains why the Minamoto house was interested in the Usa region and why it threw its support behind Mount Hiko, which was closely related to the Usa Hachiman multiplex. In 1185, Minamoto Yoritomo set up land stewards (*jitō*) and protectors (*shugo*) in each province of the country. Ōtomo Yoshinao became the first protector of Buzen Province, and in 1197, on Mount Hiko, he dedicated a statue of

Amida, referring to it as *gongen mi-shōtai* ("body" of the avatar). The oldest extant narrative concerning the mountain, *Hikosan ruki*, was compiled shortly thereafter. It is a political document in that it emphasizes Mount Hiko's independence from Ima-Kumano and the Shōgo-in while simultaneously attempting to maintain the advantages of being an Ima-Kumano subtemple — that is, to keep its tax-free status and the interdiction of political control on the part of the government. It is said in *Hikosan ruki* that the Ryōzan-ji, Mount Hiko's main temple, had more than 200 meditation halls inhabited by 110 resident monks and 205 *sendatsu* (a term referring to the upper echelons of *yamabushi* as distinct from the scholarly religious community).

In 1333, Utsunomiya Nobukatsu, the steward of the Shiroi district of Buzen Province, appointed Imperial Prince Annin as abbot of Mount Hiko, and the position of abbot was thereafter inherited by that prince's descendants. Mount Hiko thus became a *monzeki*, a vast institution ruled hereditarily by princes of imperial birth. Prince Annin, because he was married, could not reside in the Ryōzanji itself, which was off-limits to women, and he established his offices in Kurokawa, south of the mountain.

The Muromachi period (1336–1573) saw the apex of Mount Hiko's power and influence. That is why its doctrines and practices became the object of a thorough systematization by Akyū-bō Sokuden, originally a member of Mount Futara's Shugendō community at Nikkō, who had become a disciple of Shōun, a high-ranking *yamabushi* of the Kezō-in on Mount Hiko. Akyū-bō Sokuden's documents, which went on to form the bulk of theoretical and practical treatises of Shugendō in Japan thereafter, are of the greatest interest. Although Sokuden composed his *Hiko-san shugen himitsu inshin kuketsu-shū* in 1509, while in residence on Mount Hiko, he also travelled widely. In 1525, for example, he visited the Natadera in Kaga, where he instructed local anchorites and entrusted them, after much begging on their part, with Hiko secret techniques. These secret transmissions form what is widely regarded as a central document of Shugendō, the *Sampō sōshō hōsoku mikki*. That document circulated among quite a few centres of cult, and seems to have formed a bridge not only between cultic sites located far from each other, but also between the *yamabushi* and their lay followers. In 1527 Sokuden wrote *Hashira-moto [Chūgen] hitei-ki*, which also found its way to the Yoshino-Kumano sites of Shugendō, and in 1558 he wrote the important *Hiko-san buchū kanjō mitsuzō*.

Part of the difficulty involved in writing about Mount Hiko lies in the fact that Shugendō was essentially a set of practices and ideas jealously kept secret and transmitted orally. Indeed, it is almost impossible to find a body of coherent doctrines before Akyū-bō Sokuden's writings from the sixteenth century. His works, however, enable us better to understand how the space of Mount Hiko was constructed and experienced.[10]

Mount Hiko as Geotype and Chronotype

There were forty-nine caves located on or near Mount Hiko, connected by paths which the *yamabushi* opened and maintained, and used either for temporary seclusion or for permanent residence. At some point during the Heian period, they became associated with the forty-nine chambers of the Inner Palace of the bodhisattva Maitreya, who resided in the *Tusita* Heavens while awaiting the time at which he would become the next Buddha and initiate a new cosmic era. The earliest written trace of this phenomenon is found in *Hikosan ruki* (1213), in which it is said that the following event occurred during the first part of the seventh century:

> At that point, without a thought for the merits it might earn in converting past, present, and future generations, the Triple Avatar decided to protect the Buddha's teachings and acted as a general, ordering about the myriad Diamond Youths. Discovering that the sacred mountain contained mineral posts, the Triple Avatar had the Diamond Youths mine them, and had them stored on the southern side of the Southern Peak, stipulating that they should be used to erect the Great Lecture Hall in which Maitreya would give his sermon upon becoming the next Buddha.[11] Ideal stone material was found on the two other peaks as well. The architectural style and the materials used for that hall are radically different from those seen in the common world, so unique in fact, that it would be difficult to find anything alike in the sixty or more provinces of this country. These mineral posts are Maitreya's metamorphic body, whose function it is to protect the Buddha's teachings.[12]

The constitution of Mount Hiko as the site of residence of the Buddha of the Future before his apotheosis was structurally related to the discovery of a chronotype Japan had not known before the introduction of Buddhism: the notion of cosmic renewal and of political and economic utopia.[13] It was not before the eleventh century, however, that political figures understood the notion and associated themselves with that cult, although Japan did not form the kind of radical political cults found in China in relation to the Buddha of the Future.

Hikosan ruki states that the deities of Mount Hiko manifested themselves as swords (comets), which, originating in India, travelled eastward through the atmosphere and plunged deep into the mountain's rocky recesses, where they were transformed into crystal. This seismic event caused the appearance of a spring in a cave that was named *Tamaya*, "crystal cave," as described in *Hikosan ruki*:

> Though it was called Wisdom Cave after the discovery of the sword, it was renamed Crystal Cave after the appearance of the eight-faceted crystal. One drop from the dragon source whence the crystal issued can heal a myriad ills, stop aging, and enhance the beauty of women; that is why monks and laymen come from the four oceans and perform their devotions to it, and why men and women from the eight directions pay reverence to it. The sacred water neither increases nor decreases: rain does not add to it, nor does heat evaporate any of it. This excellent dragon water of no increase/no decrease is a marvellous medicine endowed with supernatural potency, and is not dry even at this very moment.[14]

That cave may have been the site of Mount Hiko's oldest temple: ideally located on the side of a well-protected valley through which fairly large streams run, and at the foot of a large vertical cliff, it opens onto a flat area where temples were built over time. It was, in any case, the most important of all the caves used by the *yamabushi* for their austerities, and the first of the forty-nine "cave-chambers" of the Buddha of the Future. It is still an important site of cult today.

The sacred zone of Mount Hiko, granted by Emperor Go-Shirakawa in 1181, was designated as *kekkai*, literally, "bounded realm," a term perhaps better translated as "perimeter." This term referred to three related practices which had their origin in India, where it signified the construction of an area in which deities were invoked. By extension, it went on to refer to the establishment of a consecrated zone for the construction of temples. In Japan, the term referred to these two phenomena, but also, from the ninth century, to entire geographical areas that were set aside as the exclusive property of (Shinto-) Buddhist institutions. This was the case of Mount Hiko in 1181. A *kekkai* area typically faces east or north; the zone of Mount Hiko, however, was a rectangular area that faced none of the four directions directly. A possible reason for this apparent lack of concern for orientation becomes clear when the hydrology of the region is taken into consideration, for the zone was oriented in such a manner that it would include the sources of the main rivers of northern Kyushu. The early Heian period's *yamabushi* may have been engaged in the management of water shrines, known as *mikumari jinja,* through which they maintained water purity and controlled the irrigation of the areas lower down. Indeed, one of the amulets one can purchase from Mount Hiko's shrine today is a bunch of clay bells known as *gara,* which for centuries rice farmers bought and interred by the water gates of their paddies.

Altitude and Altered States of Mind

Mount Hiko's boundaries were formed not only by that perimeter, defined by imperial law in the twelfth century and retraced time and again by peregrinations over the landscape. There was another, vertical type of overlay, consisting in the visualization of Mount Hiko as the geotypical form of a Tendai Buddhist doctrine known as "the four lands boundaries" (*shido kekkai*). The mountain, from bottom to top, was viewed as consisting of four superimposed layers in which life was subjected to growing constraints on behaviour.

Included in the list of the scriptures brought back from China by Kūkai (774–835), of which only a manuscript version copied by Saichō (767–822) remains, is *Jōjū myōhō renge-kyō ō yuga kanchi giki,* purported to have been translated by Amoghavajra (705–774). This text is a manual of instructions for the performance of rituals of visualization linked to the Lotus Sutra, the main scripture of the Tendai school of Buddhism and, subsequently, of Kyushu

Shugendō.[15] It was the object of various interpretations on the part of a number of Tendai scholarly monks during the Heian period, but what appears to have become its dominant interpretation was authored by Jichin (Jien, ?–1255).[16] Jichin's interpretation probably served as the doctrinal and ritual basis for the particular form of sacralization of Mount Hiko's space, since he was then the abbot of the Enryakuji on Mount Hiei and had been promoted to high positions in the nascent Shugendō system of Kumano. Furthermore, Jichin granted title to the domains of the Kunisaki Peninsula to Imperial Prince Asabito in 1213 — which suggests that he knew of the sites of cult in northern Kyushu.[17] *Hikosan ruki*, where we hear for the first time of the four superimposed zones of Mount Hiko, was compiled just five months later. The land grant of Mount Hiko and the establishment of its perimeter in 1181, the granting of title to the Kunisaki domains in 1213, the compilation of *Hikosan ruki* during the same year, and Jichin's composition of the document on the four lands may thus be viewed as a single series of related events.

Jichin's document bears the title *Hokke becchō-shi* (Private interpretation of the lotus ritual) and consists of several parts, the first of which concerns the processes that are to be followed in the "visualization of the space of awakening," *dōjō-kan*. The term *dōjō* is Japanese for the Sanskrit term *bodhi-maṇḍa*, which originally designated the tree under which the Buddha achieved awakening, and was later used to refer to any natural or constructed area set aside for religious practice. It was eventually understood to indicate the mental space in which that practice took place, in which case it was interpreted along the lines of the concept of "suchness" (*shinnyo*; Skt., *tathatā*), which Buddhist philosophers used to express the ultimate character of the Buddha's awakening. Jichin begins his discussion of the space of awakening by stipulating the following: "Next, the practitioner produces a visualization of the *bodhi-maṇḍa* in terms of the essentiality of suchness." He continues: "Should anyone recite the following verses and meditate on their unsurpassed meaning, he will be able to identify his mind with the essence of truth:

> Empty [space] is the place of religious practice.
> Awakening is marked with emptiness.
> Furthermore, the unequalled awakened one
> [is called] thus-come [*tathāgata*] because of suchness [*tathatā*].

Jichin then interprets these four verses in a set of four paragraphs, associating each with one of the "Four Lands" expounded by Chih-i, the founder of T'ien-t'ai Buddhism in China, in his Commentary on the *Vimalakīrti-nirdeśa Sūtra.*[18] The following translation is somewhat tentative, since the text is obscure and may be corrupt in places.

> [The verse] "Empty [space] is the place of religious practice [*dōjō*]" refers to the Land of Co-habitation. Conceive of the [Lotus Sutra's] space assembly as the Land of Expedient Means [Skt.: *upaya*; J.: *hoben*]. When outside of the Land of Co-habitation, provisional distinctions arise. Even though the practitioner is absorbed within emptiness, he nonetheless resides in the site of religious practice. The "divided body" [of the Buddha] under the tree should also be visualized. Although the term "empty space" is used, the ritual of visualization of the place of religious practice is performed completely, and that space is therefore considered as "co-habitation." And although the place of religious practice is identified with the Land of Co-habitation, the practitioner nonetheless proceeds toward the realm of awareness.
>
> [The verse] "Awakening is marked with emptiness" refers to the Land of Expedient Means. [We perceive] emptiness as the aspect of true reality. It is the true Land of Expedient Means. On the basis of that awareness the five disciples cut off their illusions and the Buddha enabled them to be reborn in this land. They were self-enlightened Buddhas of the four fruits.
>
> [The verse] "Furthermore, the unequalled awakened one" refers to the Land of True Retribution. In respect to the awakening of practitioners, a negative term [un-] must be used. Mahāvairocana, the enlightened one of the Thirty-seven deities of the Realm of Diamond emanating from himself, enjoys the self-directed bliss of the *dharma* without interruption. According to this interpretation, a negative term is used. Although the term is negative, it still refers to a modality of absolute being that is the basis of the Land of True Retribution. For further details see below.
>
> [The verse] [the Buddha is called] "thus-come [*tathāgata*] because of suchness [*tathatā*]" refers to the Land of Quiescent Radiance. "Thus-come because of suchness" means that because

> he has realized emptiness, he is [entitled to be] called Buddha. [The term] Buddha [refers to] the Lord of the Teachings, the Great Master Śākyamuni the *tathāgata*. Consider the Buddha of the three bodies (which are actually one) as the main object of worship [in this ritual]. Visualize those four lands as constituting the place of religious practice [*dōjō*]. And consider the secret *mudrā* ["seal," i.e., ritual hand formations] and *vidyā* [spell] of the three bodies, and the threefold *siddhi* [perfection], as the fundamental *mudrā*. Recite the verses of scripture indicated in this ritual, practice the attainment of Mahāvairocana's body in the Diamond Realm by means of the five-fold meditation, and engage in the visualization of the internal fire ritual [*goma*] of the five rings. This is indeed the attainment of Buddhahood in this very body. It is the supreme awakening gained in this very existence. How excellent! How auspicious! Trust these words! Engage in devotion! Do not doubt this!

Jichin's definition of the term *dōjō* is thus presented as consisting of a visualization of the four "lands" discussed by Chih-i. Their names were applied to four horizontal layers encompassing the height of Mount Hiko, which were then subjected to separate regulations whose effect was to determine different types of religious experience (see diagram). As a result, Mount Hiko became a new geotype, that is, a model for a new space of representation and for a new conceptualisation of the space of practice. It was visualized and experienced as though it were a *dōjō*, which means that it was lived, not only as a miniature version or "natural model" of the Buddhist cosmographic and cosmological views implied in the doctrine established by Chih-i, but as the very space of awakening itself.

At the same time, however, the four lands or zones of Mount Hiko were Buddhist metaphors that functioned to reinforce an older social prescription, in that they re-presented the embodiment of a mental map of social hierarchy, itself grounded in a long-established opposition between purity and pollution. In that oppositional schema, pollution was at the bottom and purity at the top, and purity came to be associated with the highest domains of mystical experience, accompanied by restraints on behaviour, while pollution was associated with the realms that were conceived as

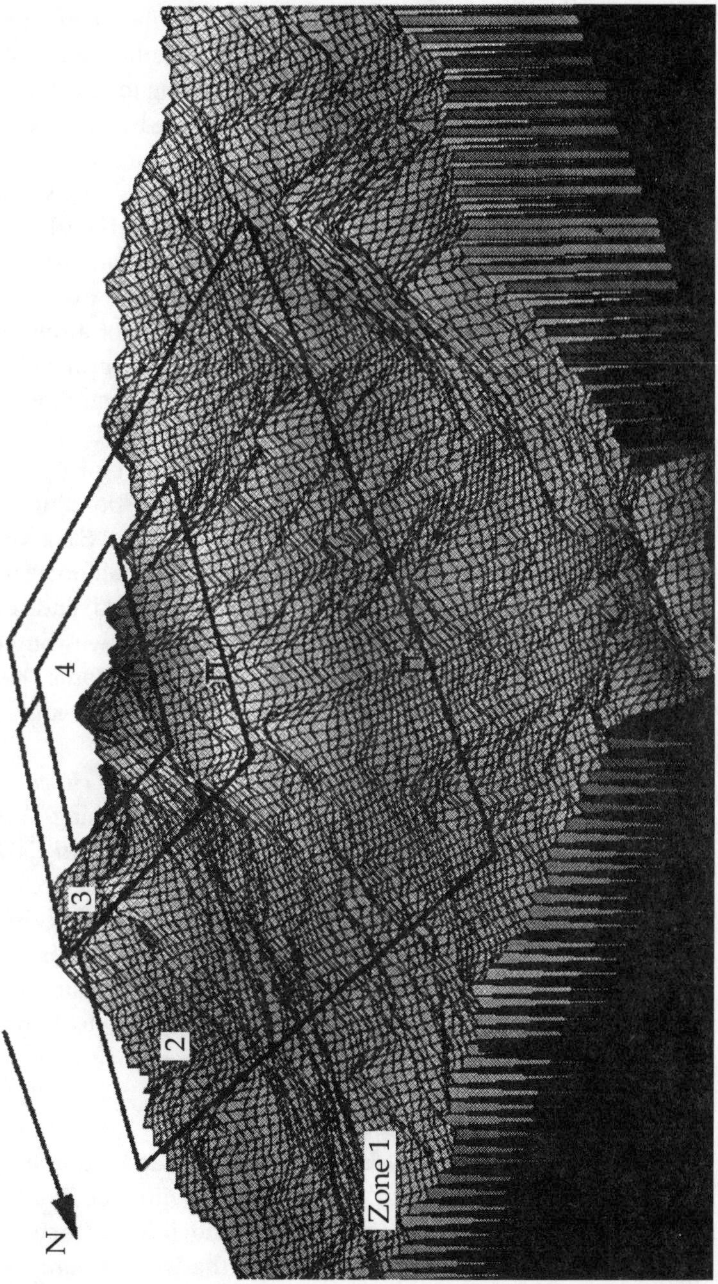

The Four Zones of Mount Hiko

"external" (*gedō*). Mount Hiko was also the site of manifestation of *kami* to which cults were given in various shrines; consequently, "indigenous" views concerning purity and pollution were also in effect. Thus, various notions and practices relating to blood, disease, and biological functions were combined with the Buddhist order of things.[19] The boundaries of the four lands were marked by some of the forty-nine caves noted above, as well as by various shrines, inscribed stones and the like, and were further marked by shrine gates (*torii*) at various elevations that were reached, not just through the physical effort of ascent, but through meditative exercises, the completion of specific visions, and the observance of a number of indigenous purificatory practices. Life was strictly controlled in each of the four zones and was subjected to taboos and restraints which remained in effect until the 1850s:

(1) *Bonshō dōgodo*, literally, "Land of Co-habitation for Anchorites and Common People": In this lowest zone, corresponding to the hamlets of Kita-Sakamoto, Karagatani, and Minami-Sakamoto, it was prohibited to cultivate the five grains and to kill any form of life. The cultivation of tea and vegetables was allowed, and several houses specialized in midwifing, since giving birth was outlawed in the upper zones. *Hikosan ruki* states that the inhabitants "had no fields and survived on a diet of dew and herbs." Rice cultivation became legal for the first time in 1858.

(2) *Hōben jōdo*, "Pure Land of Expedient Means," or *Hōben uyodo*, "Land of Expedient Means Characterized by Remaining Worldly Attachments": This zone extended from the bronze *torii* (500 m.) to the stone *torii* (700 m.). The bronze *torii* is today located lower down than it was in the past. It was moved at the end of the Edo period, when the *yamabushi* village grew in size, probably as a result of the Tokugawa shogunate's policy of lifting travel restrictions to encourage trade. The *yamabushi* were then allowed to transform their temple-like residences (*bō*) into inns where they lodged and educated travellers and pilgrims. In this zone, too, grain cultivation was forbidden. So was giving birth.

(3) *Jippō gondo* or *jippō mushōgedo*, literally, "Land Adorned with True Retribution," also called "Land Adorned with True Retribution and Devoid of any Obstacle": This zone extended from the stone *torii* located in front of the main sanctuary to the wooden *torii* located in front of the Gyōja Hall of the Upper Sanctuary. Since it consists

mainly of steep rocky escarpments that are difficult to reach, there are no halls of residence. It is in this zone that most of the caves in which the *yamabushi* used to practice are found. In the *hōben jōdo* zone, where there were many residential halls, foodstuffs were transported along paths by bulls; in this zone, however, no horses or bulls were allowed. All possible precautions were taken against pollution, particularly concerning death. Preservation efforts have continued to this day to keep the flora and fauna intact.

(4) *Jōjakkōdo*, literally, "Land of Permanent and Quiescent Radiance": The uppermost zone of the mountain extended from the wooden *torii* to the three summits of Mount Hiko, which the *yamabushi* regarded as the actual embodiment of combined *kami* and buddhas/bodhisattvas, the "Avatars of the three sites." The release of excrements, urine, saliva, phlegm, or mucous from the nose was utterly prohibited in this zone. This was regarded as an ideal space, to be left untouched, where the pure land of the buddhas and the world of humans merged.

A chronotype was also associated with this geotype. It suggested that time passed at a different speed at different altitudes, and it was more fundamentally related to desire than any other chronotype, since at one end it focussed on the hope to become a Buddha, and, at the other end, it focussed on production and reproduction. The lowest zone entailed the smallest number of taboos and restraints on the body. It was also a zone of restricted economic production and exchanges (related to the seasonal cycle of production), but all forms of transportation were allowed. Time was conceived differently in the second zone, since neither birth nor death were allowed to pollute space or enter its representation in terms of the span of human life. The third zone, marked though it was by the regular sounds of drums and bells calling on the anchorites to perform all sorts of meditations and rites, was dotted with all the caves, in which the conception of time was marked by the dominant expectation for ultimate apotheosis, or of the possibility of disengaging oneself from transmigration. In the uppermost zone, the body's natural functions were as though non-existent, and time ceased to carry special significance. Furthermore, the dominant chronotype that sustained the four-land theory included a series of four moments — birth, maturity, old age, and death — which were discussed extensively in various Buddhist doctrinal tracts.

Looking at the phenomenon from another perspective, the fundamental opposition between purity and pollution encoded an opposition between culture and nature, and this was inscribed in the materials used in the gates, which were graded according to the amount of human work they necessitated: bronze for the lowest *torii*, stone for the middle *torii*, and wood for the upper *torii*. This distinction was explicitly stated in documents of the early pre-modern period, and its import resides in the quasi-immanentist character of its origins: at Mount Hiko, naturalness or wilderness was the mark of transcendence. The *yamabushi* gained access to both naturalness and transcendence through the royal avenue of visions and restraints on behaviour. As we shall see, what looks like a code restraining the body was regarded as a liberating style of life, a set of technologies of the self that yielded a key to freedom from time through the agency of a thorough immersion in space and time, and through spatial movements conceived as equivalent to the appropriation of the truth of metaphysical principles.

Mandalization

The most complex geotypical construction of Mount Hiko consisted in practices and hermeneutic codes I have termed "mandalization" in another publication.[20] It entailed rituals that were performed during ascetic peregrinations over several mountain ranges at three different times of the year.

Esoteric Buddhism proposed that Buddhahood could be realized in this physical body and during one's lifetime. The validity of this statement rested on two conditions. First, a new conceptualisation of the body had to be produced and accepted. Secondly, specific practices of a ritual character, aimed at transmuting the body-mind of a practitioner into that of the Buddha, had to be applied. These conditions were satisfied by the postulation of the Triple Mystery of body, speech and mind, while the transmutation was made possible by three related notions. First, the physical world was regarded as the actual substance of the Buddha in its diversified body of essence; second, that substance and all natural sounds were regarded as the actual sermon of the Buddha uttered in its body of essence; and, third, the mind of awakening of the Buddha in its body of essence was held to pervade the substance of the physical world and its sounds. In this representational schema, human beings were considered to be a part of the Buddha, but to have somehow become separated from it, to have become deaf to it, and to have become unaware of it. In order to change that situation, three types of ritual practice were devised to bridge the gap between relative and absolute substance, between relative and absolute speech, and between relative and absolute consciousness. The first type entailed physical exercises, yogic practices, and a regimen including dietary practices and the like. The second type entailed chanting and meditating on sounds. The third type entailed a series of meditations, contemplations, and visions aiming at the transformation of consciousness. Graphic supports, called *maṇḍala*, were devised to bolster these practices.

In Japanese Esoteric Buddhism, two main mandalas were used: the womb mandala, symbolically representing the world of the Buddha as an object of knowledge, and the diamond mandala, symbolically representing the nature of that which does the knowing. These mandalas were ritually prepared in either painted or written form, and were used to guide practitioners in their performance of the various practices related to the Triple Mystery, at the end of which the distinctions between the two mandalas, between the Buddha and the practitioners, and between known and knowing, vanished. The *yamabushi*, however, pushed that reasoning to its logical conclusion: since mandalas were representations of the actual structure of the Buddha's body, speech, and mind, and since the world was semiotically treated as the actual substance, speech, and mind of the Buddha, then the world itself could be viewed as the original mandala. This was achieved through the creation of taxonomic tables in which systematic correlations between substances, colours, shapes, sounds, and qualities were established. The *yamabushi* then devised peregrination courses through the mountainous massifs that they considered to be natural mandalas, which they followed while performing the same rituals one would perform in front of painted mandalas in temples. They held various geographical accidents such as massive boulders, waterfalls, peaks, and gorges to be the natural sites of residence of the buddhas and bodhisattvas represented in the painted mandalas, and symbolizing various aspects of the Buddha. The ritual practices in which they engaged enabled them to reach both mystical identification with those deities and thorough identification of the elements forming their bodies with the elementary substance of the Buddha.

Mount Hiko's *yamabushi* produced a three-dimensional miniature model of their mountain in 1616, a wooden sculpture that is remarkably accurate despite some vertical exaggeration. A possible explanation for its construction is that the *yamabushi*, over time, constructed different experiences of space and encoded vast regions with complex signs. They then produced a physical model of the mountain in order to present these experiences to themselves and to others in a direct, graphic manner. Mount Hiko, however, was not the object of a single interpretation or modality of experience; it was like a palimpsest, overlaid at various points in history with successive codifications of experience. Further analyses of these various processes and practices may enable us to understand better how the Hiko *yamabushi* used the mountain to constitute their reality and thereby enhance or radically change the conditions of their existence.

During the medieval period, the *yamabushi* of Mount Hiko developed three mandalized courses which they followed during the spring, summer, and fall seasons. The spring course, called "forward" (*jun*), took the ascetics from Mount Hiko to Mount Hōman (next to Dazaifu), and back to Mount Hiko.[20] This course was a projection of the womb mandala (*taizōkai mandara*). It was stipulated that it followed the logical formula of reaching an effect on the basis of following the nature of its cause, and it was to be performed in terms of an emphasis on the achievement of the mind of awakening; that is, it focussed on the personal liberation of the practitioner. The fall course, called "reverse" (*gyaku*), took the *yamabushi* from Mount Hiko to Mount Fukuchi (south of Kokura), and back to Mount Hiko. This course was a projection of the diamond mandala (*kongōkai mandara*). It followed the logical formula of returning to a cause on the basis of an understanding of the nature of its effect, and it emphasized a turning away from the personal pursuit of awakening for oneself, encouraging conversion of the people met in the villages along the course. Both spring and summer courses passed through forty-eight "stations," some of whose locations are still unknown, while the last was always the object of secret, oral transmission. The summer course was called "neither forward nor reverse" (*jungyaku funi*) and took the *yamabushi* around various peaks in the immediate vicinity of Mount Hiko. That course was also called "flower offering" (*hananoku*) and was based on the *Susiddhikara sūtra*; it was characterized as being neither cause nor effect, and emphasized a lack of distinction between oneself and others. Finally, it was regarded as the site where the differences between the diamond and womb mandalas were abolished. As such, it symbolized the space of awakening, here qualified as the disappearance of oppositions between subject and object in the field of knowledge.

The Body as Ritual Space

The texts by the *yamabushi* that speak of the body always use spatial metaphors. First of all, the body in ritual was always "oriented." The body was primarily conceived in terms of its extension in space, but it needed proper positioning in order to be ritually employed and to reach the stated goals of its ordered movements through space. Furthermore, the body was encoded, in the sense that each of its parts was associated with an element, a shape, a colour, a sound, and a quality, so that the body itself came to be treated as though it were a mandala. This is clearly stated, for example, in passages from Akyū-bō Sokuden's sixteenth-century treatment of the ritual practice known as *toko-gatame*:

> Concerning *toko-gatame* while coursing through the mountains. The term *toko* [literally, "seat"] refers to the mandalas associated with the diamond and womb courses. It is the *dōjō* ["site of practice"] of the Land of Co-habitation. The term *katame* [literally, "solidification"] refers to the [diamond-like] solidity of the five elements [forming] the Body of Essence [of the Buddha]. These [terms signify that] one's body is that of the Buddha. That is, our Revered Patriarch, the *tathāgata* Mahāvairocana, is endowed with the inner realization of the realm of essence, which is permanent and pervades the triple world. His essential corporality knows neither beginning nor end, is perfect, and is endowed with a myriad qualities; it consists of the five elements of earth, water, fire, wind, and ether. Each of those is symbolically manifest in the following shapes: square

[cube], circle [sphere], triangle [pyramid], crescent [half-moon], and tear-drop. These shapes symbolize the following aspects: firmness, humidity, dissipation [like smoke], movement, and absence of obstacle. Furthermore, they are symbolized by five colours: yellow, white, red, black, and blue, and by five "seed letters" [J.: *shuji*; Skt.: *bīja*], namely, *a-bi-ra-un-ken* [*a-vi-ra-hum-kham*]. These five elements pervade the ten realms of both sentient and non-sentient beings. That is why they are called "elemental" [literally, "expansive"]. These five elements are the basis on which the bodies of buddhas and those of common beings are constituted. [...] That is why Shugendō holds the view that our physical body is the Buddha. [...] Recite the following meditation verse:

> This very body is *a-bi-ra-un-ken*
> Waist and legs, navel, heart, neck, and summit of the cranium.
> Below the waist, [*a*] refers to original non-production/
> Yellow colour, square shape, the ground of the Buddha's heart-mind.
> In the wheel of the navel, [*bi*] refers to the sermon beyond language/
> White, circular shape, the water of great compassion.
> Above the heart, [*ra*] refers to the absence of pollution/
> Red, triangular shape, the fire of great wisdom.
> Below the chin, [*un*] refers to separation from cause and effect relations/
> Black, crescent shape, the power of great wind.
> Above the forehead, [*ken*] refers to absolute spatial emptiness/
> Blue, tear-drop shape, the wheel [cylinder] of the great sky [ether].[21]

This ritual aimed at visualizing the human body as though it were a *stūpa* [J.: *sotoba*], conceived not only as the original site of religious practice, but as the true body of the Buddha; it was usually performed on the first day of coursing through the mountain mandala and was followed by a rite called *toko-sadame* ("firming the body position"), defined in the same text as follows:

— First, locate the *toko-gatame* (first, diamond; second, womb).
— Next, form the *ōkyogō* seal [*mudrā*]; [recite the corresponding spell] *vīdya*.
— Next, form the *ryūkyogō* seal; [recite the corresponding spell] *vīdya*.
— Next, [the practitioner should] lie [on the ground] on the right side, and bend the right arm to form the wheel of wind. [He should] extend the left arm, place it on the hip, and remain firm [*sadame*] in that position (*toko*). This configuration is called *ōban* [horizontal *vam* spell]. In the case of the *toko-gatame* ritual, the configuration is called *juban* [vertical *vam* spell].

belly — west

south — feet  head — north

back — east

This particular positioning of the body is related to a symbolic death viewed as liberation from transmigration, since the text goes on explicitly to associate it with the bodily position of the Buddha at the time of his entrance into *mahā-parinīrvāṇa*. In other words, the body was treated as though it were both iconic (in the semiotic sense) and iconographic.

The Mountain as a Social Space

Just as *Hikosan ruki* was composed after the establishment of the Kamakura shogunate, a second narrative, *Chinzei Hikosan engi*, was composed in 1572 at the end of the Muromachi shogunate.[22] In the sixteenth century, Kyushu was divided into three power bases: the Ryūzō-ji house, the Ōtomo house, and the Shimazu house. The first two groups both made military attempts to take control of the mountain and its resources — the Ryūzō-ji house by burning its temples in 1568, and the Ōtomo house by sending 4,000 soldiers to attack it in 1581 — in both cases because they wanted to place their own people as abbots. As a result, many valuable documents and records were lost forever, but *Chinzei Hikosan engi* survived. That text indicates the nature of the socio-political, economic, and ideological changes of the time: its first pages are devoted to a "Shinto" discourse on the mountain, to mythology, and to chthonogony, an emphasis typical of the times — and it also passes in silence over the recent destruction of the mountain's institutions.[23]

Apparently as a result of the fights for influence and succession that dominated those turbulent times, a woman was named abbess of the mountain between 1587 and 1601, but she was removed from her position by the warrior Mori Hisahachirō, against whom the temple then complained directly to Fushimi Castle, the shogunal office of Toyotomi Hideyoshi in Kyoto. The case was brought to trial, and there was a verdict to the effect that Mount Hiko was to return all its domains to the shogunate. As a result, Mount Hiko lost its traditional, land-based economic power, and had to turn to its lay followers for economic support, thus initiating the lay patron sponsorship of Mount Hiko, an important social and economic phenomenon during the Edo period (1600–1868). This event was a major turning point in the history of the mountain, and the verdict issued by Fushimi was to become a central issue in the conflicts that subsequently took place between Mount Hiko and the Shōgo-in multiplex of Kyoto.

The warrior Hosokawa Tadaoki (1563–1645) took control of the province in 1600 and granted his support to Mount Hiko, rebuilding what had been destroyed in 1568 and restoring the entire institution. However, Tadaoki also wished to control Mount Hiko. He had his son (adopted, but born from the aristocratic Hino family) adopted by the abbess, and that son became the next abbot, under the name Chūyū. Upon his nomination to abbacy, Chūyū went to Edo and met with Tokugawa Ieyasu and Ietada. From then on, it became customary for all new abbots to make the trip to Edo to perform

Ome-mie — a ceremony that might be compared to an ambassador's presentation of credentials — with the Tokugawa shoguns. The Great Lecture Hall of Mount Hiko was rebuilt, sumptuously, in 1616.

Thus, by the beginning of the Edo period, Shugendō had become a religious, military, economic, and political force to reckon with. This helps explain why it was subjected in 1613 to systematic control by the Tokugawa shogunate, which divided it into two groups through the promulgation of a policy that established control along sectarian lines: the Shōgo-in of Kyoto controlled the Tendai branches (called *Honzan-ha*), while the Daigo-ji's Sambō-in controlled the Shingon branches, called *Tōzan-ha*. As a consequence, the Shōgo-in renewed its claim over Mount Hiko and treated it as a mere subtemple. Mount Hiko, as might be expected, resisted the shogunate's policy. Haguro Mountain, in the northern part of Japan, was the first to free itself of central control, gaining independent status (*bekkaku honzan*) in 1677, while Mount Hiko gained that status in 1696. In 1710 the *yamabushi* village of Mount Hiko had 637 houses and a population of 3,015 people.

A list of ritual assemblies of the Hiko multiplex, dated 1445, provides some information on the social organization of the mountain community. This framework, which probably originated during the thirteenth century and basically remained the same up to the end of the nineteenth century, established three socio-religious groups whose members specialized in the preparation and performance of separate rituals. The first group, consisting of *yamabushi* (*gyōja-gata*), organized the three courses in spring, summer, and fall. The second, *shito-gata*, emphasized Buddhist rites: the *Nehan-e* (Nirvana ritual assembly) on the fifteenth day of the second month, the *Tanjō-e* (Birth of the Buddha ritual assembly), and the *Nefu-e* (Copying of the Lotus Sutra ritual assembly). The third group, *sō-gata*, emphasized Shinto rites, that is, rites dedicated to local *kami*. This group consisted of two sub-groups, the *iro-shi* and the *katana-shi*, who performed the *Matsu-e* and *Onta-sai* ritual festivities.[24]

These social groups were distinct (though related) at all levels of their existence, and the social status of the *shito-gata* was superior to those of the *gyōja-gata* and the *sō-gata*. This distinction was expressed in terms of the *honji-suijaku* theory, based on a Buddhist doctrine that was actually a framework for the ascription of doctrinal and social power. This theory, which gained wide acceptance during the Heian period, used the term *honji* (essence) to denote buddhas and bodhisattvas, while the term *suijaku* (hypostasis) was used to denote the indigenous *kami* under whose guise the buddhas and bodhisattvas manifested themselves in order to guide local populations to their lofty teachings. In other words, Buddhism presented itself, to the Japanese of the time, not only as a desirable alternative to pre-existing schemata for the interpretation of reality, but as a framework of interpretation that included native divine entitites, while reducing them to a lower status as local, minor forms of a transcendental Buddha essence. Accordingly, on a social level, the term *honji* (essence) was applied to the *shito-gata,* who associated themselves predominantly with Buddhist temples, while the term *suijaku* (hypostasis) was applied to the *sō-gata,* who associated themselves predominantly with the native deities. In other words, the members of the community who specialized in Buddhist doctrine and rites claimed a social status higher than that of those who predominantly worshipped the *kami*, and their claim was legitimated by appeal to the more complex metaphysics of Buddhism.

In the Edo period, however, the abbots of Mount Hiko claimed that the mountain "specialized" in postulating the fundamental equality of *honji* and *suijaku*, from which we may infer that the social rank and community status of the Shinto-oriented members of the mountain community was deemed equal to that of the Buddhist prelates, scholarly priests, and their associates. This shift in social valuation was due, I would suggest, to two factors. At the local level, it was attributable to the systematic involvement of the *sō-gata* in the economic and ritual lives of the communities in which they sought economic support, and for whose members they organized pilgrimages and lodging. On a trans-local level, however, the emerging nativist studies movement (*kokugaku*) resulted in the proliferation of a new discourse on the *kami*, whose effect was the production of an anti-Buddhist representation that had actual, material and social consequences. Indeed, by the end of the eighteenth century the *sō-gata* claimed a status higher than that of the Buddhist members of their community. Their rituals were now performed first (before the seventeenth century, they had been performed last), and with greater pomp.

A need to consolidate the political and social organization of the community living on the mountain emerged at the turn of the seventeenth century for at least two reasons. First, a growing number of lay patrons came to visit the mountain at the time of ritual performances connected to the development of wetland rice agriculture, leading to a sudden population impact and, therefore, a need to protect the area. Second, as a consequence, the organization of the mountain community needed to reflect the socio-economic realities of the new political order of the times. This consolidation was achieved along two lines: a re-organization of the mountain community proper, and the promulgation of regulations that were to be observed by visitors and residents alike. Although there was some relaxation of these regulations by the end of the Edo period, observance of the demarcation between the two types of population and their activities was maintained up to the turn of the twentieth century.

The organization of the mountain community during the Edo period was as follows: The head abbot (*zasu*) supervised two administrative directors (*shitto*) and four directors of *kami* affairs (*shin-yaku bugyō*). Of these, one received the title *nemban* (yearly duty) and specialized in the formulation and control of ritual performance. Immediately below them were two "controllers of the mountain" (*yama bugyō*), one specializing in the protection of the flora and the other in its management, and two maintenance directors (*saji bugyō*) specializing in the upkeep of shrines and temples. Finally, there was a "town director" whose duty was to oversee both the city of the anchorites and the visitors and inns. Each of those administrators served a four-year term and was chosen from among the *yamabushi*. The *yama bugyō* and the *saji bugyō*, four in all, represented what we might today call environmental guardians, for their responsibility was to maintain the mountainous area in as pristine a state as possible.

The community of Mount Hiko consisted not only of its year-round residents but also of its lay patrons (of whom some 350,000 were recorded in 1875), who visited the mountain on pilgrimages in ever-growing numbers as the cult became popular, and who made the donations necessary for the maintenance of the mountain community. It is easy to imagine why regulations were required with regard to this group as well, and a legal document, signed by thirteen administrative monks and numbering thirty-six points, was issued in 1624 by the abbot and circulated widely. Here are some of its most important points:

— *Anybody caught removing wood from the designated sacred perimeter, even in as small a quantity as is needed to make a simple fan, will be condemned to forced labour.*

— *No dry wood or dead branches for fire shall be removed from the mountain. People who need firewood will have to go as far as Karagatani to the south and Reisui to the north. It is forbidden to cut wood within the mountain's perimeter, even on one's own property, in order to make furniture.*

— *It is prohibited to cultivate tea gardens outside of one's residence or to till fields next to the caves where anchorites reside permanently. Offenders against this rule will be reported to the authorities.*

— *Whoever attaches or releases horses on the access roads to the Lecture Hall will be fined three hundred copper coins.*

— *It is prohibited to scatter horse excrements along the village roads or on any of the mountain's paths.*

— *Responsibility for cleaning the access paths will rotate among the town's residents, and shall be performed every fourteenth day and every last day of the month.*[25]

* * *

The Edo period saw the emergence of a nativist discourse giving priority to indigenous divine entities, to the vernacular language, and to a new cultural identity divorced from its old Chinese and Buddhist characteristics. A number of authors wrote new doctrinal tracts on Shinto, and called for a revival of what they thought the "pure," pre-Buddhist form of their religion had been in the distant past. On the political level, the Tokugawa shogunate began to lose its hold on the country around the beginning of the nineteenth century. Movements of rebellion intensified and were often associated with calls to return the emperor to actual power and to expel foreigners. Shortly after Commodore Perry's "black ships" bombarded Japan, it became clear that radical political, social, and cultural changes had to be made. The shogunate was overthrown, and, in what is known as the Meiji Restoration, the emperor moved from Kyoto to Edo (renamed Tokyo for the occasion), assuming the direction of the country in 1868. Japan then entered the world of modern nation-states, but that entrance was marked, internally, by radical religious changes.

Indeed, in 1868, the new Japanese government ordered that all buddhas and *kami* that were worshipped together in sites of cult located all over the country be dissociated. As a result, Shinto and Buddhism became distinct entities, but this distinction did not occur peacefully: the order of separation was followed by a movement of rejection of Buddhism (*haibutsu-kishaku*), which erupted in various sites of cult around the country. It is estimated that about 60% of Japan's Buddhist temples were abolished or destroyed at the time. Statues and paintings were smashed or burnt, and a large number of Buddhist priests were forced to return to lay life. In 1872, the government issued a further decree abolishing Shugendō (*Shugen-shū haishi-ryō*) and ordered that all Shugendō temples affiliate themselves with either the Tendai or the Shingon sects.

On the eve of that Meiji upheaval, numerous Hiko *yamabushi* sided with the movements for the restoration of imperial authority. Their activities were carefully monitored by the pro-Shogunate authorities in Kokura, north of Mount Hiko,[26] who, in an attempt to control the situation, encircled Mount Hiko on 11 November 1863, arresting the abbot and twenty leading *yamabushi*. Although the abbot and a few *yamabushi* were subsequently released and returned to the mountain, six prisoners remained in Kokura and were executed, or died of disease, in 1867. A few months later, on 3 January 1868, the rescript returning the emperor to the throne was promulgated, and the Edo shogunate fell apart. On 16 September, Mount Hiko's Buddhist abbot, Kyōyū, went to the capital and met with the emperor. He then resigned the abbacy, returned to lay life, and three days later became the Shinto head-priest of Mount Hiko, which immediately set itself under the direct authority of the *Jingikan*, the newly created office of Shinto. The Kokura authorities then abandoned the siege of the mountain. In reaction, a group of youths who called themselves "*Kami* soldiers," *shimpei*, organized on the basis of a code of conduct to which they swore allegiance in 1869, began to destroy Buddhist emblems and structures on Mount Hiko. The first line of their code reads: "We will thoroughly remove (*issen*) the old habits, and [everyone] must revere the emperor and the *kami* of Heaven and Earth." The *shimpei* murdered the mothers of some Buddhist prelates; ordered all temples to slam their gates shut; destroyed the majority of buildings on Mount Hiko, leaving only some structures that were later transformed into Shinto shrines; and removed and destroyed Buddhist statues and ritual implements. Soon thereafter, the main rites of the *yamabushi* were abandoned, and the majority of the *yamabushi* left the mountain.

The lay followers of *Shugendō* in the area did not reject their beliefs so abruptly, however. They continued to provide economic support for the performance of pilgrimages and of the main ritual assemblies and festivities on the mountain. For example, the Shōen-bō temple gave lodging to 69 pilgrims in 1866, 232 pilgrims in 1870, and 213 pilgrims in 1871. Furthermore, a number of lay patrons received permission to remove various Buddhist statues and give them a proper cult in their own homes, thus precluding the disappearance of longstanding objects of cult and enhancing the potential for later material presentation of ideological resistance. Finally, some of the new Shinto priests of Mount Hiko placed screens and other devices in front of objects of cult, thus removing them from direct sight and protecting them from what would have been sure destruction.

In 1874, however, the destructions started anew, following the appointment of a Shinto priest who declared that "the order to destroy the buddhas came from the very top and cannot be defied." Bells, statues, paintings and documents that remained on the mountain were gathered and smashed to pieces. An order was issued to collect all of the objects of cult that had been located in the caves along the various courses of peregrination around the mountain peaks, and all were smashed. In 1985, only 109 houses and a population of 328 were recorded in the local census; in 1987, 16 *yamabushi* residences, 99 lay houses, and a total population of 385 people were counted. The space is now completely different: Mount Hiko is reached by train and car, pilgrimage has disappeared, and the courses through the mountain ranges have been abolished. Modernity reigns supreme over this new social, economic, and political space; it has generated a new geotype.

Conclusion

In Japan, as we have seen, sacred space was the object of various kinds of strict observances and of panoptical observation as well, and of many competing interpretations. Although the oldest geotyping of Mount Hiko may have emerged early in Japanese history, we cannot say anything about it before the appearance of detailed written documents in the thirteenth century. These documents indicate that profound changes in conceptualization and practice took place under the auspices of Buddhism, and that other geotypes appeared as social conflicts became more pronounced later on.

Sacred space is a thoroughly managed space that cannot be separated from social, economic and political conditions. It is a construct, and its formal (morphological) modalities can be classified according to various "geotypes" that range from simple space-related rituals to complex geographical understandings. The purposes of these constructs can be classified according to their philosophical contents and their social effects, and on the basis of the practices they entailed. Sacred space is an unthinkable category if it is studied separately from the communities that constructed it, challenged it, destroyed it, and provided new formulations of it over time. It is better seen, I would argue, in relation to the conflicts these successive constructs generated, and in relation to the economy that thse constructs reflected, generated, or opposed. Finally, sacred space *is* territory, even if map is not.

Notes

1. Shugendō has been little studied in the West. See G. Renondeau, *Le Shugendō: Histoire, doctrine et rites des anachorètes dits Yamabushi*, Paris 1965; H. Rotermund, *Die Yamabushi: Aspekte ihres Glaubens, Lebens und ihrer Sozialen Funktion im Japanischen Mittlealter*, Hamburg 1968; B. Earhart, *A Religious Study of the Mount Haguro Sect of Shugendō*, Tokyo 1970; and I. Averbuch, *Yamabushi Kagura: A Study of a Traditional Ritual Dance in Contemporary Japan*, Ithaca, N.Y., 1996. There are also a few articles on discrete aspects of Shugendō. Of the studies mentioned above, Renondeau grants Mount Hiko twenty-two lines; and Rotermund and Earhart both mention it just twice.
2. For a definition of these terms see Kuroda T., *Jisha seiryoku*, Tokyo 1980; see also A. Grapard, *The Protocol of the Gods: A Study of the Kasuga Cult in Japanese History*, Berkeley, Calif., 1992.
3. See A. Grapard, "Japan's Ignored Cultural Revolution: The Meiji Separation of Shinto and Buddhist Divinities (*shimbutsu bunri*) and a Case Study: Tōnomine," in *History of Religions* (1984), pp. 240–265. See also J. Ketelaar, *Of Heretics and Martyrs in Meiji Japan: Buddhism and Its Persecution*, Princeton 1990.
4. See M. Foucault, "Technologies of the Self," in L.H. Martin, H. Gutman & P.H. Hutton (eds.), *Technologies of the Self*, Amherst 1988, pp. 16–49.

5. Hōren is discussed in some detail by Japan's pre-eminent historian of the Usa Hachiman cult, Nakano H., in *Hachiman shinkō-shi no kenkyū*, Tokyo 1975, vol. 2, pp. 504–511.
6. The term *kami* refers to usually native entities given a cult in shrines. These shrines are today called "Shinto" shrines, but I refrain from using this term because it refers to religious movements that appeared during the medieval period, and to the post-1868 religion that has only some relation to the past. "*Kami* cults," then, were of great variety, tended to be highly local, and varied with the social classes celebrating them. When Buddhism was introduced into Japan, it had to deal with those cults wherever it went, and developed longstanding associations with them, up to 1868, when the government separated them.
7. See Nagano T., *Hikosan Shugendō no rekishi-chirigaku-teki kenkyū*, Tokyo 1987; Hirowatari M., *Hiko-san shinkōshi no kenkyū*, Fukuoka 1994; Hirose M. & Fukuoka Komonjo wo Yomu Kai (eds.), *Hiko-san nemban nikki*, Fukuoka 1994; Kawazoe S. & Hirose M. (eds.), *Hiko-san hennenshiryō — kodai, chūsei — hen*, Fukuoka 1987; see also Tagawa Kyōdo Kenkyūkai (ed.), *Hiko-san*, Fukuoka 1979.
8. See *Engi-shiki: The Procedures of the Engi Era* (English transl. by F. Bock), Tokyo 1970–1972.
9. *Hikosan ruki*, in Gorai S. (ed.), *Sangaku shūkyō-shi kenkyū sōsho*, Tokyo 1984, vol. 18, pp. 463–474.
10. Akyū-bō Sokuden has never been the object of a formal study, though he may have been Shugendō's most important historical figure. His works are scattered in various collections.
11. These mineral posts, still visible on the southern slopes of Mount Hiko, are remnants of ancient volcanic activity, and were thought to be supranatural signs. They look very much like the "Devil's Posts" one sees in various National Parks in the United States.
12. *Hikosan ruki* (above, note 9), p. 463.
13. I borrow the term "chronotype" from J. Bender and D.E. Wellbery, editors of *Chronotypes: The Construction of Time* (Stanford 1991), who modified Bakhtin's term "chronotype," itself borrowed from Einstein. I use the term "geotype," which I have not seen before, to refer to a structurally related concept on the spatial level.
14. *Hikosan ruki* (above, note 9), p. 465.
15. In Takakusu J. & Watanabe K. (eds.), *Taishō Shinshū Daizōkyō*, Tokyo 1924–1932, vol. 19, no. 1000a.
16. The version I use is presented in an unpublished study by Misaki R., "Jichin oshō to hokke — hō-Kyōto Shōren-in Kissui-zō 'Hokke becchō-shi' wo chūshin toshite," presented at the Third International Conference on the Lotus Sutra in Japanese Culture, held in Honolulu, Hawaii, in January 1992.
17. Takeuchi Rizō (ed.), *Usa Jingū-shi*, Beppu, Japan, 1988, vol. 5, p. 12.
18. In Nakano T. (ed.), *Dai Nihon zokuzōkyō*, Kyoto 1905–1912, vols. 7 & 19.
19. This issue is discussed in more detail in A. Grapard, "Visions of Excess and Excesses of Vision — Women and Transgression in Japanese Mythology," *Japanese Journal of Religious Studies*, XVIII (1991), pp. 3–22; and "Geosophia, Geognosis, and Geopiety: Orders of Significance in Japanese Representations of Place," in

D. Boden and R. Friedland (eds.), *NowHere: Space, Time and Modernity*, Berkeley, Calif., 1994, pp. 372–401.

20. See A. Grapard, "Flying Mountains and Walkers of Emptiness: Toward a Definition of Sacred Space in Japanese Religion," in *History of Religions* (1982), pp. 195–221.
21. *Shugen shūyo hiketsu-shū*, in Matsumoto B. (ed.), *Nihon Daizōkyō*, Tokyo 1919, vol. 38, p. 248.
22. *Chinzei Hikosan engi*, in Gorai, *Sangaku* (above, note 9), pp. 474–485.
23. The new insistence on a Shinto discourse is a telling sign of the times, and indicates that Buddhism was becoming the object of fundamental criticism.
24. See the early eighteenth-century painted scroll describing these festivities in Murakami T., *Hiko-san Shugendō Emaki*, Kyoto 1995.
25. In Nagano T., *"Hikosan sei-iki (shizen) wo hogoshita Shugendō,"* in Tagawa Kyōdo Kenkyūkai (ed.), *Kyōdo Tagawa*, XXXII (1990), p. 40.
26. The information given in the following discussion is based on Nagano T., "Hikosan Shugendō ni okeru shimbutsu bunri no juyō to teikō," in Sakurai T. (ed.), *Nihon shūkyo no seitō to ihan*, Tokyo 1989, pp. 117–148.

15
The Cult of Santa María Tonantzin, Virgin of Guadalupe in Mexico

Richard Nebel

The commemoration of the "discovery," conquest, colonisation and missionizing of the American continent by Europeans, beginning some 500 years ago, is a fitting time for pondering the themes of Christianization and the mixing of cultures and religions in that part of the world.

Our starting point is the Acontecimiento Guadalupano, the "Guadalupan event." Following the capture of the Aztec capital city México-Tenochtitlán by Hernán Cortés in 1521, there began, according to the account of Fray Bernardino de Sahagún OFM,[1] a cult of veneration of Our Lady of Guadalupe by the indigenous population at the place where a shrine to the deity Tonantzin Cihuacóatl (Our Venerated Mother Lady Snake) had formerly stood. This veneration drew its inspiration from what came subsequently to be known as the "Guadalupan event," though "events" might be a more accurate designation. These consisted of four apparitions (from the 9th to the 12th of December 1531) of the Virgin of Guadalupe on the hill of Tepeyac to the north of the former Aztec capital, which today lies within the boundaries of Mexico City; the message conveyed by the Virgin Mary to the recipient of the vision, a Christianized Indian called Juan Diego, and transmitted by him to the first bishop of México, Fray Juan de Zumárraga OFM, together with her request that a church be built in her honour at the place of her apparition; the "miracle of the flower" on Tepeyac hill; the virgin's appearance before the visionary's sick uncle and the latter's recovery; the "miracle" that took place in the presence of the bishop, in which the image of the Blessed Virgin was impressed on the cloak (*tilma*) of Juan Diego; and, finally, the unique historical role played by this scarcely verifiable series of events, which, after four hundred years, is still imbued with an aura of the wonderful and the miraculous. Its social, cultural and religious influence on the development of the colony of "New Spain" and, later, of independent Mexico was profound. Above all, the "Guadalupan message" has spurred a variety of developments in the church, theology and society of both Americas, including: theologies of liberation, the Bishops' conference at Puebla in 1979, the "New Evangelization" of America, and various religious, social and political movements in Nicaragua, Brazil, the southwestern United States and other countries. The shrine to "Our Lady of Guadalupe," situated in the megalopolis of Mexico City, with its population of twenty-two million, is today one of the most frequented Christian places of pilgrimage in the world, and it continues to gain in significance.

Of the available literature on Guadalupe, much is of a sensational nature. Very little serious research has been carried out on the subject, partly for political reasons and partly as a consequence of the overwhelming wealth of material. Mention must be made here of the pioneering works of Francisco de la Maza (1953),[2] Jacques Lafaye (1974),[3] Ernesto de la Torre Villar and Ramiro Navarro de Anda (1982),[4] Edmundo O'Gorman (1986)[5] and Francisco J. Noguez Ramírez (1987).[6]

The Guadalupan phenomenon should be considered first of all against the devotional and doctrinal background of the cult of Mary, especially in Spain, and the origin and development in the thirteenth and fourteenth centuries of the pilgrimage site known as "Nuestra Señora Santa María de Guadalupe" of Villuercas in Spanish Extremadura.[7] We should also bear in mind the many Spanish accounts of apparitions of the Virgin Mary of Guadalupe in Extremadura, and the arrangement and reconstruction of these accounts in Roman-Christian antiquity, under the influence of Judaism and Islam and in the European medieval tradition.[8] This Spanish Guadalupe ("Wolf river") became, at the time of the Catholic monarchs and in the period of Spanish colonial expansion in Africa, Asia and above all, America, a symbol of Hispanicism.[9]

The traditions that began to spread after the capture of the Aztec capital México-Tenochtitlán (1519–1521) also contained autochtonous Mexican, that is, especially Otomí-Toltec-Aztec, elements.[10] In view of the character of our source material, it is difficult to speak with certainty about the origins of the Guadalupan event or to identify historically indisputable records and testimonies.[11] We may assume that in the 1530s — perhaps even at the outset of the evangelization of central Mexico in the year 1523 — a chapel in honour of the Virgin Mary, named "Our Lady of Guadalupe," was built on the hill of Tepeyac. Only in the second half of that century, however, did the location become the focus of an active cult of the Virgin, and from the seventeenth and eighteenth centuries onward it exercised a far-reaching and politically significant influence, in particular as a centre of the Creole movement for independence from Spain.[12]

With all due scepticism regarding the historicity of the apparitions of the Mother of God, the extraordinary impact of the Guadalupan event on all sectors of Mexican society and culture may be described as unparallelled. It permitted the descendants of the peoples and cultures of Central America to lay claim to a legitimate place within the imposed social system of colonial New Spain. In the apparition of the Virgin to a representative of the indigenous peoples, they, the conquered, the Indios, the marginalized, discovered their human dignity, their capacity for "acceptance" of the Christian faith and their cultural equality. The Virgin of Tepeyac, the "Morenita," thus increasingly became a powerful symbol, pregnant with hope and life, and ultimately a signal for the people to throw off the Spanish yoke, with God's approval. They all felt themselves to be *hijos de Guadalupe* (children of Guadalupe). This applied both to the Indians and to the *mestizos*, the growing population of mixed Spanish-indigenous parentage and culture, which was in process of developing self-confidence and independence with respect to the Spaniards and Europeans.[13]

In its literary manifestations, the Guadalupan event represents a transculturation of Christianity. Its character is clearly evident in the text of the *Nican Mopohua* (Here is told), a document of singular importance to the development of a genuine Mexican theology and to theological praxis and church policies in present-day Mexico, with its approximately 10% Indian and 70% *mestizo* population.

The *Nican Mopohua*, in the 1649 version in Náhuatl by Lasso de la Vega,[14] is an impressive narrative of the apparitions and message of the Virgin Mary, known as the "Guadalupe," to the Nahua Juan Diego. It is a Spanish-Aztec "fusion of two worlds" which poses a whole series of difficult, and largely still unresolved questions regarding its content and transmission and its literary-critical, textual, linguistic and editorial analysis. It is a theologically-conceived narrative[15] which became, as it were, a "Gospel-in-culture." Structurally, it demonstrates great structural similarities to the Extremaduran legend of the fourteenth century,[16] while simultaneously inculcating the basic truths of the Christian gospel and belief, and evincing in the process an anthropologically determined theology. On the other hand, it is written in classical Náhuatl, the language of the Aztecs, rich in metaphors. Its language and content reflect the spirit of Toltec-Aztec philosophy, mythology and theology.[17] The question of the authorship of the *Nican Mopohua*, which may have been formulated and recorded in the sixteenth century by one or several students within the circle of Fray Bernardino de Sahagún OFM (Colegio de Santa Cruz de Santiago Tlatelolco), remains unsolved. The search for the original has as yet been unrewarded. In all probability, however, we can assume that the text, which emerged from the dialectics of Spanish-Occidental as well as early Mexican culture and society, was given its existing poetic-artistic form by a final editor. In this transformational process, the character given to the story by its Spanish-Christian provenance was modified by the influence of the Nahua culture in a similar way to that which occurred in the case of the "Cantares Mexicanas,"[18] religious poetry of the early colonial period, or in that of the religious discourses of the first twelve Franciscan friars with the Aztec scholars in the year 1524.[19]

An investigation of the theological significance of the *Nican Mopohua* from a linguistic, anthropological and cultural point of view indicates that, within the context of the Christian Guadalupan message, a new interpretation and orientation of early Mexican values and beliefs took place, which the four seventeenth-century "Mexican evangelists" — Miguel Sánchez,[20] Francisco de Florencia Sg,[21] Luis Lasso de la Vega,[22] and Becerra Tanco[23] — made an integral part of the Christian process of salvation. Thus, the *Nican Mopohua* should not be viewed as a historical account, but rather as a theological message that opened up a new perspective in relation to the changed historical situation of Mexico, or, more precisely, New

Spain. Adhering closely both to historical events and to legends, the message was directed towards bringing about a state of harmony between different peoples, cultures and religions, in order that, during a period of radical change, new possibilities of coexistence could be envisaged.[24]

The "Guadalupan event" has had continuing theological repercussions, as attempts are made to forge links between past and present and to emphasize the implications of the phenomenon for present-day Mexico, the Americas and the whole of Christendom. Both the Guadalupan image and the Guadalupan message, together with the popular religious manifestations which have resulted, have provided cues for theological reflection. There have been three different theological approaches to the theological interpretation of the image. The historical-prophetic interpretation, initiated by Miguel Sánchez in 1648, saw in the twelfth chapter of the Book of Revelation a confirmation of the authenticity of the apparition of the Virgin on the hill of Tepeyac and a preview of Mexico's later history.[25] The historical-nationalistic interpretation, first espoused by Fray Servando Teresa de Mier (1765–1827) and later by major public figures, claimed that Mexico had to follow its own political, economic, cultural and religious direction.[26] Finally, the conceptionistic-Guadalupan interpretation saw the Guadalupana as the key figure in a particularly Mexican conception of Roman Catholic belief.[27]

In recent decades, it has been less the image than the Guadalupan message, as expressed in the *Nican Mopohua*, that has been the focus of interest. One approach, concerned with morality and dogma, finds a confirmation in this text of fundamental Christian teachings regarding God and the Virgin and of the moral values of the Gospel.[28] A second approach, concerned with social ethics, evaluates the document in terms of its significance for marginalized, indigenous groups in the population, drawing upon it for liberation theology and feminist concerns.[29] A third approach stresses the exemplary character of the *Nican Mopohua* with regard to evangelization and "inculturation" in a Mexican, or, rather, indigenous context. It provides a basic model of a "Gospel-in-culture," a classic example of the Mexican realization of Christian belief, theology and living, and a paradigm for the resolution of social tensions and injustices.[30] This approach points in the direction of traditional Mexican Catholicism, centred on devotion to Jesus Christ as a self-sacrificing man of sorrows, as well as to the Mother of God, the consoling Morenita of Tepeyac. In this conception, the Indio sees the suffering figure of Christ as a reflection of his own tragic past and present. He seeks consolation and refuge in his mother, the Virgin Mary, and above all in the Virgin of Guadalupe. This devotion is expressed in various ways, in prayers, poetry and songs, as well as in a highly developed folk art.[31]

As a result of a general revaluation of popular religiosity by Christian theologians and by the Church, the Guadalupanismo of the various ethnic groups is experiencing a revival. It has been passed into the service of liberating trends in pedgagogy, catechesis and the pastorate in the Mexican church, and in other states of the American continent. The influence of this kind of Guadalupanismo appears, for example, among Chicano theologians in the United States[32] as well as in the spiritual approach adopted by Mexican dioceses that follow the basic principle of "Evangelización Indígena por Indígena" (EVIPI)[33] — that is, evangelization of Indians by Indians, in accord with the model of the *Nican Mopohua*, and not by missionaries dispatched from the diocese or from Europe.

Present-day Guadalupanismo, then, is no more a relic of the past. Firmly embedded in social realities, it continues to develop and to open up perspectives for the future, thus becoming a source of religious, cultural, social and political inspiration.[34]

The interpretational models of Guadalupanismo which have emerged in the course of history are extremely varied. They reflect both the clash of different cultures and religions and the struggle to integrate Christian, Spanish and Nahua cultures and to adapt and transform Christian and Toltec-Aztec traditions, each in its own particular way. Each interpretational model bears within it historical conflicts inherited from the past that still persist and are expressed, for example, in Indigenism, Hispanicism or Mexicanism.

Indigenism — the glorification and revitalization of the great pre-Hispanic Mexican past — is alive in the Guadalupe phenomenon, which radiates a force creative of identity. The cult of the Virgin has been regarded from the beginning as part of the Indians' particular religiosity, expressing the religious substance of their cultural identity. One consequence of this movement has been anticolonialism, expressed in polemics against Spanish colonization and missionary work and in the rejection of "Western" culture as a form of "alienation." Here, "Guadalupe" has been used for the purposes of self-assertion, serving as an answer to the ideology that has sought to justify colonialism (or rather its modern manifestations) by maintaining that it has been the task of the "progressive" nations to transform underdeveloped, uncivilized peoples, hardly distinguishable from children, into civilized, mature, fully-developed human beings.

Hispanicism, which regards Mexico as a colonial "branch" of Spain and Europe, also finds inspiration in "Guadalupe." Proponents of Hispanicism tend to glorify the civilizing and cultural mission of the Conquista and colonization (or rather industrialization and modernization along Western lines), which enabled Mexico to participate in universal culture and "development." This cultural Hispanicization (or Westernization) implies the acceptance of European systems of values and norms, as well as ideologies, and their internalization within the framework of the educational system. Hispanicism tends to monopolize the Guadalupe as representing a Spanish or European variety of Christianity.

"Guadalupe" has also contributed to the creation and development of a "Mexicanidad" or "Mexicanism" characterized by a balanced view of the Conquista, recognizing Mexico as a *mestizo* nation, a product of the meeting of European and autochtonous peoples and cultures. Mexicanism seeks a dialogue between the countries of Europe and other continents on the basis of a renewed national consciousness. In the realm of religion and theology, the phenomenon of the "Morenita de Guadalupe" is relevant to both past and present, representing as it does the *mestizaje*, in the sense of a successful synthesis through cultural integration.

Santa María Tonantzin, Virgen de Guadalupe, so familiar and present in Mexican life, is a source of inspiration and tradition, created by centuries of cultural intermingling between Orient and Occident, Europe and America, Spain and Mexico. She is an expression of a nation's identity and of the soul of the Mexican people, a symbol of national unity transcending racial barriers, and of the rights and dignity of the people. The *Imago Guadalupana* is both reality and transcendence, truth and utopia. This reality is literal and allegorical at the same time. It is a forever-intensified reality, reason and imagination in equal measure — an image with a thousand facets, in which individuals find intimacy and companionship, so that, together with other *hijos de Guadalupe*, they may search for their own history and mould their future.

Notes

1. Fray Bernardino de Sahagún, *Historia General de las Cosas de Nueva España*, Mexico City (Editorial Porrúa) 1956, 1982[5], I, 1, chap. 6, nos. 1–7, pp. 32–33 and III, 11, chap. 12, Appendix, no. 7, pp. 704–705.
2. F. de la Maza, *El Guadalupanismo Mexicano*, Mexico City 1953 (reprinted 1981).
3. J. Lafaye, *Quetzalcóatl et Guadalupe*, Paris 1974; in Spanish: Mexico City 1977.
4. E. de la Torre Villar & R. Navarro de Anda, *Testimonios Históricos Guadalupanos*, Mexico City 1982.
5. E. O'Gorman, *Destierro de Sombras*, Mexico City 1986.
6. F.J. Noguez Ramírez, *The Apparition and the Early Cult of the Virgin of Guadalupe in Tepeyac, Mexico City: A Study of Native and Spanish Sources Written in the Sixteenth and Seventeenth Centuries*, Ann Arbor, Michigan, 1987.
7. G. Rubio, *Historia de Ntra. Sra. de Guadalupe*, Barcelona 1926; A. Alvarez, *Guadalupe: Arte, Historia y Devoción Mariana*, Madrid 1964.
8. W.A. Cristian, Jr., *Apparitions in Late Medieval and Renaissance Spain*, Princeton, N.J., 1981; Fray Diego de Ecija, *Libro de la Invención de esta Santa Imagen de Guadalupe ...*, Cáceres 1953.
9. C.G. Villacampa, *La Virgen de la Hispanidad o Santa María de Guadalupe en América*, Seville 1942; Fray Francisco de San Joseph, *Historia Universal de la Primitiva, y Milagrosa Imagen de N.ra Señora de Guadalupe...*, Madrid 1743.
10. R. Nebel, *Altmexikanische Religion und Christliche Heilsbotschaft: Mexiko zwischen Quetzalcóatl und Christus*, Immensee 1983, 1990[2]; J. Baumgartner, *Mission und Liturgie in Mexiko*, I-II, Schöneck-Beckenried 1971.
11. P. Feliciano Velázquez, *La Aparición de Santa María de Guadalupe*, Mexico City 1931 (reprinted 1981); Noguez Ramírez, *The Apparition* (above, note 6).
12. W. Jiménez Moreno, "La Crisis del Siglo XVII y la Conciencía Nacional en Nueva España," *Revista de Indias*, XL (1980), nos. 159–162, pp. 415–423; De la Torre Villar & Navarro de Anda, *Testimonios Históricos* (above, note 4); Lafaye, *Quetzalcóatl* (above, note 3).
13. Francisco Javier Clavijero, *Breve ragguaglio della prodigiosa e rinomata imagine della Madonna di Guadalupe del Messico ...*, Cesena 1782; Cayetano de Cabrera y Quintero, *Escudo de Armas de México ...*, Madrid 1785; de la Torre Villar & Navarro de Anda, *Testimonios Históricos* (above, note 4).
14. Luis Lasso de la Vega, *Hvei Tlamahviçoltica ...*, Mexico City 1649; idem, *Nican Mopohua* (Traducción... por el Prespítero Mario Rojas Sánchez de la Diócesis de Huejutla), Mexico City 1978.
15. Cf. A. Siller, "La Evangelización Guadalupana," *Estudios Indígenas*, I (1984), pp. 1–140.
16. A.-B. Hellborn, "Las Apariciones de la Virgen de Guadalupe en México y en España," *Ethnos*, XXIX (1964), nos. 1–2, pp. 58–72.

17. M. León-Portilla, *La Filosofía Náhuatl*, Mexico City 1956, 1976^{4}.
18. J. Bierhorst, *Cantares Mexicanos ...*, Stanford, 1985.
19. W. Lehmann, *Sterbende Götter und christliche Heilsbotschaft ... "Coloquios y doctrina cristiana" des Fray Bernardino de Sahagún aus dem Jahre 1564 ...*, Stuttgart 1949; M. León-Portilla, *Coloquios y Doctrina Cristiana ...*, Mexico City 1986.
20. Miguel Sánchez, *Imagen de la Virgen María ...*, Mexico City 1648.
21. Francisco de Florencia, *La Estrella de el Norte ...*, Mexico City 1688, Madrid 1785.
22. Lasso de la Vega, *Hvei Tlamahviçoltica*, (above, note 14).
23. Luis Becerra Tanco, *Origen milagroso del Santuario de Nuestra Señora de Guadalupe ...*, Mexico City 1666.
24. G. Schulenburg Prado (ed.), *450° Aniversario 1531–1981*, Mexico City 1983.
25. Sánchez, *Imagen* (above, note 20); Lasso de la Vega, *Hvei Tlamahviçoltica*, (above, note 14); de Florencia, *La Estrella* (above, note 21); Becerra Tanco, *Origen* (above, note 23).
26. J. Servando Teresa de Mier Noriego y Guerra, *Obras Completas*, I–III, Mexico City 1981; G. Grajales, *Nacionalismo Incipiente en los Historiadores Coloniales*, Mexico City 1961; de Cabrera y Quintero, *Escudo de Armas* (above, note 13), Lafaye, *Quetzalcóatl* (above, note 3).
27. Schulenburg Prado, *450° Aniversario* (above, note 24); A. Alcalá Alvarado, *Santuario de Guadalupe ...*, Bogotá 1986.
28. A. María Garibay Kintana, "The Guadalupan Message," *Mexico Quarterly Review*, III (1968), pp. 54–60; Schulenburg Prado, *450° Aniversario* (above, note 24).
29. L. Boff, "María, Mulher Profética e Libertadora," *Revista Eclesiástica Brasileira*, XXXVIII (1978), fasc. 149, pp. 59–72; V. Elizondo, *La Morenita: Evangelizer of the Americas*, San Antonio, Tex., 1980.
30. J. Ignacio Echeagaray et al. (eds.), *Album Conmemorativo del 450 Aniversario de las Apariciones de Nuestra Señora de Guadalupe*, Mexico City 1981.
31. Nebel, *Altmexikanische Religion* (above, note 10).
32. A.G. Guerrero, *The Significance of Nuestra Señora de Guadalupe and la Raza Cósmica in the Development of a Chicano Theology of Liberation*, Boston 1984; idem, *A Chicano Theology*, Maryknoll, N.Y., 1987.
33. R. Nebel, *Santa María Tonantzin, Virgen de Guadalupe: Religiöse Kontinuität und Transformation in Mexiko*, Immensee 1992, pp. 255–263. This work contains an extensive bibliography on the theme of Guadalupe; in Spanish: Mexico City 1995.
34. O. Paz, *El laberinto de la Soledad*, Mexico City 1950; R. Bartra, *La Jaula de la Melancolía*, Mexico City–Barcelona–Buenos Aires 1987; F. González Pineda, *El Mexicano: Dinámica Psicosocial*, Mexico City 1973^{5}.

16

The Muslim Holy Cities as Foci of Islamic Revivalism in the Eighteenth Century

Nehemia Levtzion and Gideon Weigert

The Wahhābiyya and Other Reform Movements

In 1744, a concordat between the *shaykh* Muḥammad Ibn 'Abd al-Wahhāb and the *amīr* Muḥammad Ibn Sa'ūd gave rise to the Wahhābiyya movement. Because of the centrality of Arabia and the militancy of the Wahhābiyya, some historians believed that other Islamic reform movements of the eighteenth century were ramifications of the Wahhābiyya. In this way they could also explain the simultaneous appearance of Islamic reform movements in places as distant from the centre as China, Indonesia and West Africa.

Recent research, however, has shown that the Wahhābiyya could not have influenced other movements directly, because only the Wahhābiyya rejected Sufism, whereas all the other movements developed within *sūfī ṭuruq*. Nevertheless, all these reform movements, including the Wahhābiyya, developed out of the internal dynamics of late medieval Islam. An awareness of the discrepancy between the ideals of Islam and the realities of Muslim life created a cyclical drive for renewal and reform (*tajdīd wa-iṣlaḥ*). However, while the phenomenon of reform in Islam may be explained in this way, the simultaneous rise of different reform movements in the eighteenth century may not.

The key may perhaps be found in the sprawling scholastic networks of masters and disciples through which the teaching of *ḥadīth* and *taṣawwuf* (mysticism) was transmitted. Almost all the leaders of the reform movements, including Muḥammad b. 'Abd al-Wahhāb, were connected to these networks. Their hub was in the Ḥaramayn, the holy cities of Mecca and Medina, where scholars from all over the Muslim world converged to create a cosmopolitan intellectual community.[1]

The Pilgrim-Scholars

The pilgrimage to Mecca and Medina provided the Muslim world with a centre, which helped maintain a measure of unity and conformity within the diversity of regional forms of Islam. From biographies of *'ulamā'*, one gets the impression that the number of scholars and Sufis who performed the pilgrimage increased in the eighteenth century.[2]

Pilgrimage from India and Southeast Asia was always by sea. Until the end of the fifteenth century, shipping in the Indian Ocean was completely in the hands of Muslims. The aggressive intrusion of the Portuguese into the Indian Ocean and their hostile relations with the Muslim powers must have adversely influenced the movement of pilgrims. In the middle of the seventeenth century, the fleets of Oman and Muscat challenged the sea power of the Portuguese and drove them out of the Persian Gulf, and Arab ships again had a greater share in the trade between India and the Arabian Peninsula.[3]

In the eighteenth century, the Dutch controlled the trade of Southeast Asia, while the British gradually eliminated Muslim and European competitors in the trade along the shores of India. By then, both the British and the Dutch had larger ships with improved sails, which made navigation in the Indian Ocean faster and safer. In 1763, the Danish traveller Niebuhr reported that passengers on small Arab ships sailing between India and Arabia were exposed to pirates, and that it was much safer to take the larger European ships.[4] Surat in Gujarat was the major port for Indian trade, and contemporary documents mention pilgrims waiting there to embark on ships to Mokha and Muscat.[5] It was thus on board European ships that most pilgrim-scholars from Indonesia and India came to Mecca. In this way, quite paradoxically, the growing maritime power of Europe contributed to Islamic revivalism.

In the West, the Mediterranean was infested with Muslim and Christian pirates during the sixteenth and seventeenth centuries. By the eighteenth century, the superiority of European warships had put an end to the terror of the pirates, and it encouraged the growth of shipping, especially European, in the Mediterranean.[6] There are records of Muslim travellers who made the voyage from Tunisia to Egypt by sea in order to avoid the long, hard, dangerous overland routes, and in particular the treks across deserts.[7] Niebuhr even made the passage from Rosetta to Cairo by boat on the Nile, because it was safer than travelling by land. He then sailed from Suez to Jedda with pilgrims. Their number, however, was limited, because there were not enough Arab boats on the Red Sea, and European ships were not allowed to sail beyond Jedda.[8]

The majority of pilgrims from the Maghreb continued to travel to Egypt, and from there to Mecca, with the regular pilgrim caravans. The individuals who travelled by sea were mainly the pilgrim-scholars, whose pilgrimages were also journeys in search of knowledge (*fī ṭalb al-'ilm*). They travelled by themselves and stopped in the major towns on the way to associate and study with prominent scholars. Hence, whatever influence better shipping facilities may have had on the pilgrimage in general, they undoubtedly contributed to the growth in the number of pilgrim-scholars and to the development of the Ḥaramayn into important centres of learning.

Though we assume that the eighteenth century saw an increase in the number of pilgrims from most parts of the Muslim world, regional circumstances varied, and absolute figures and comparative data on trends over the course of centuries are not readily available. We shall probably have to be satisfied with circumstantial evidence, not only with regard to pilgrim-scholars, but also concerning the numbers of those who remained in the Ḥaramayn for the rest of their lives as *mujawirun*. Thus, if the number of *'ulamā' mujawirun* did increase in the eighteenth century, more resources must have been required to support scholarly activities in the Ḥaramayn. In order to substantiate this, we would have to investigate the flow of gifts to the Ḥaramayn in the eighteenth century compared to earlier centuries, and in particular the revenues from *awqāf* all over the Muslim world that were dedicated to the Ḥaramayn.

The Intellectual Milieu of the Ḥaramayn

Pilgrim-scholars from North and West Africa stopped in Cairo on their way to the Haramayn; Damascus was the base for the caravans of pilgrims from the Ottoman Empire; and pilgrims from India and Indonesia often landed in one of the ports of the Yemen, staying in Zabīd before proceeding to Mecca. In this way, Zabīd, Damascus and Cairo, as gateways to the Ḥaramayn, became important centres of learning in their own right for scholars and students on their way to Mecca. With Mecca and Medina, they formed the "inner circle."

In most Muslim centres of learning, the majority of teachers and students were of local origin, and they all belonged to the same *madhhab* (e.g., Mālikī in North Africa, Ḥanafī in Turkey and India, Shāfiʿī in Sumatra). But in the Ḥaramayn, teachers and students of different legal schools came together to participate in the thriving study of *ḥadīth*, which is common to all the *madhāhib*. To be sure, the level of scholarship in the Ḥaramayn did not reach that of Cairo, Damascus and Fez, and individual scholars from the Ḥijāz went to Cairo for advanced studies. The intellectual creativity that made the Ḥaramayn the foci for Islamic revivalism is therefore explainable only as an outcome of the convergence there of different traditions of *ḥadīth* studies and of different streams of Sufism, from North Africa, Egypt and India.[9]

There was no conformity in the ideational content of the scholastic networks. A student was influenced by several teachers, and students of the same teacher followed different tracks. Nevertheless, the fusion of *ḥadīth* and *taṣawwuf*, the exoteric and esoteric sciences, freed scholars from the fetters of a strict adherence to past legal precedents (*taqlīd*), and re-oriented Sufism towards a more rigorous observance of *sharīʿa*.

The Scholarly Network

Our review of those who contributed to scholarly life in the Ḥaramayn begins with two contemporaneous *'ulamā'*: Muḥammad Ṣafī al-Dīn al-Qushāshī (1602–1660), a Mālikī native of Medina, and Muḥammad al-Bābilī (1591–1666), a Shāfiʿī Egyptian who spent ten years in Mecca.[10] A whole generation of scholars in the Ḥaramayn were students of al-Qushāshī and al-Bābilī. Five of their students, in particular, represented the core of the scholarly network. They reappear in the *asānīd* of prominent scholars in the Ḥaramayn and of others from places like Syria and Yemen who had studied *ḥadīth* in the Ḥaramayn. Three of them were natives of Mecca: Ḥasan b.

'Alī al-'Ujaymī (c. 1639–1702),[11] Aḥmad b. Muḥammad al-Nakhlī (c. 1634–1717),[12] and 'Abdallāh b. Sālim al-Baṣrī (1638–1722).[13] The other two were *mujāwirun*: Ibrāhīm b. Ḥasan al-Kūrānī (1616–1690) from Kurdistan and Muḥammad b. Muḥammad b. Sulaymān al-Maghribī (c. 1627–1683) from Fez in Morocco.[14]

Among those who studied with both al-Qushāshī and al-Bābilī, the most influential in our network was Ibrāhīm al-Kūrānī, a Shāfi'ī. He studied with al-Qushāshī in Medina and with al-Bābilī in Egypt. Al-Kūrānī, who had already belonged to the Sufi order of the Naqshabandiyya, was initiated into the Shaṭṭāriyya order as well by al-Qushāshī, and succeeded him as head of that order in Medina.[15]

Among al-Kūrānī's most prominent students was Muḥammad b. 'Abd al-Rasūl al-Barzanjī (1630–1691), who was born in al-Kūrānī's native town of Shahrazūr in Kurdistan. Al-Barzanjī, twenty-four years younger than al-Kūrānī, followed his master to Medina and studied with him there.[16] In 1682, an *istiftā'*, a request for a legal opinion, was sent from the *'ulamā'* of India to the *'ulamā'* of the Ḥaramayn, concerning the writings of Aḥmad Sirhindī (1564–1624). The letter was addressed particularly to Ibrāhīm al-Kūrānī, who asked al-Barzanjī to reply. The latter wrote an entire treatise, which received the full support of al-Kūrānī, in which he declared Sirhindī's ideas to be unbelief.[17]

Ibrāhīm al-Kūrānī had a special relationship with scholars from Sumatra, foremost among whom was 'Abd al-Ra'ūf al-Sinkilī (c. 1620–after 1693). 'Abd al-Ra'ūf lived in Medina for twenty-one years, between 1640 and 1661, and studied there with al-Qushāshī and al-Kūrānī. On his return to Acheh in northern Sumatra, he was designated *khalīfa* of the Shaṭṭāriyya order, which became very popular there. Following al-Kūrānī's teachings, he emphasized the search for inner mystical significance, without, however, exempting the believer from the duty of observing the *sharī'a.* The Shaṭṭāriyya was thus a reform Sufi order that combined mysticism with scripturalism, in contrast to the pantheistic mysticism that had prevailed in Acheh. Significantly, most of the leaders of the Padri reform movement in the late eighteenth century came from the Shaṭṭāriyya. For thirty years, 'Abd al-Ra'ūf exchanged letters with Ibrāhīm al-Kūrānī across the Indian Ocean. He rendered major works of Islam into Malay, including *Tafsīr al-Jalālayn*, as well as some of al-Kūrānī's own works.[18]

Another distinguished student of al-Kūrānī was al-Zayn b. Muḥammad 'Abd al-Bāqī al-Mizjājī (1643–1725). Members of the Mizjājī family were prominent scholars in their native town of Zabīd, the most important centre of learning in Yemen in the eighteenth century. Relations between the Kūrānī and the Mizjājī families continued into the next generation, when Abu'l-Ṭāhir Muḥammad (1670–1733), son of Ibrāhīm al-Kūrānī, became the teacher of 'Abd al-Khālik b. al-Zayn al-Mizjājī (c. 1705–1740).[19] The latter initiated Ma Ming-Hsin (1719–1781), who visited Zabīd on his pilgrimage to Mecca, into the Naqshabandiyya. Ma Ming-Hsin was the founder and spiritual leader of the "New Teaching," a reformist movement that swept Northwest China in the second half of the eighteenth century.[20]

Muḥammad b. Ibrāhīm al-Kūrānī was born in Medina and became the Shāfi'ī muftī there. He studied with his father and with the other leading scholars of the network, Ḥasan al-'Ujaymī, Aḥmad al-Nakhlī, 'Abdallāh al-Baṣrī and Muḥammad al-Maghribī.[21]

Muḥammad b. Ibrāhīm was the teacher of Shāh Walī Allāh (1702–1762), the leader of Islamic reformism in India in the eighteenth century. Shāh Walī Allāh came to the Ḥaramayn in 1731 and for fourteen months concentrated on the study of *ḥadīth* collections beyond the standard six books. He was particularly influenced by the *al-Muwaṭṭa'* of al-Mālik, and emphasized its importance when he taught *ḥadīth* in India, after his return from the Ḥaramayn. John Voll has pointed this out as yet another illustration of the cross-fertilization which took place between different traditions of Islamic scholarship, in this case those of the Ḥanafī in India and of the Mālikī in the Maghreb.[22] Shāh Walī Allāh himself mentioned in one of his writings that it was in the Ḥaramayn that he had visions of the Prophet and his two grandsons, al-Ḥasan and al-Ḥusayn, who ordered him to initiate his reform movement.[23]

Within the scholarly community of Medina, the most prominent student of Muḥammad b. Ibrāhīm al-Kūrānī was Muḥammad Ḥayāt al-Sindī, an Indian scholar who settled in Medina and died there in 1750. The eighteenth-century Muslim historian al-Murādī called Ḥayāt al-Sindī "the bearer of the banner of the *sunna* in Medina." Ḥayāt al-Sindī also studied with 'Abdallāh b. Sālim al-Baṣrī and Ḥasan b. 'Alī al-'Ujaymī.[24] But Ḥayat al-Sindī's greatest debt was to another *mujāwir* from India, Abu'l-Ḥasan Muḥammad b. 'Abd al-Hādī al-Sindī (d. 1726). Abu'l-Ḥasan himself studied with Ibrāhīm al-Kūrānī and with Muḥammad al-Barzanjī.[25]

A detailed analysis of the teachers and students of Ḥayāt al-Sindī by John Voll presents a microcosm of the world of learning that radiated out of the Ḥaramayn.[26] The network reached as far as the region of present-day northern Nigeria, where 'Uthmān dan Fodio (1754–1817) began his *jihād* in 1804. In 1786 'Uthmān dan Fodio had studied *ḥadīth* with his uncle Muḥammad Rāj, who made the pilgrimage some time before 1773 and studied in Medina with Abu'l-Ḥasan al-Saghīr, a student of Muḥammad Ḥayāt al-Sindī.[27]

Muḥammad Ibn 'Abd-Wahhāb

Ḥayāt al-Sindī, as a prominent scholar of *ḥadīth,* had at least two Ḥanbali students. One of them was Muḥammad b. Aḥmad al-Saffārīnī from Nablus (1702–1774), who met Ḥayāt al-Sindī when he made the pilgrimage in 1736. Before that, he had studied in Syria and Palestine with two great Sufi mentors, 'Abd al-Ghanī al-Nāblusī (1641–1731) and Musṭafā al-Bakrī (1688–1749). The Muslim historian al-Jabartī described al-Saffārīnī as a Sufi and an ascetic, but also as a radical "who defended the *sunna* and suppressed *bid'a.*"[28]

Muḥammad Ibn 'Abd al-Wahhāb was introduced to Ḥayāt al-Sindī by 'Abdallāh b. Ibrāhīm b. Ṣayf, a Ḥanbali from an important Najdi family. 'Abdallāh b. Ibrāhīm believed in reform through education, as is suggested by the anecdote relating that he showed Ibn 'Abd al-Wahhāb a collection of books which he described as "weapons I have prepared for Majma'a" (his native town in Najd). Ibn 'Abd al-Wahhāb studied *ḥadīth* with Ḥayāt al-Sindī. It is said that one day Ibn 'Abd al-Wahhāb called the attention of Ḥayāt al-Sindī to those who arrived at the Prophet's tomb seeking intercession. Ḥayāt al-Sindī condemned the practice as non-Islamic.[29] This anecdote, according to John Voll, illustrates his argument that the study of *ḥadīth* in Medina "did not remain a quiet intellectual pursuit, [but] was utilized to provide a standard of judging current practices among Muslims."[30]

The brief period that Ibn 'Abd al-Wahhāb stayed in Medina, and in particular his study of *ḥadīth* with Ḥayāt al-Sindī, may have been a source of inspiration for him. Ibn 'Abd al-Wahhāb told his grandson 'Abd al-Raḥmān that it was only when he studied *ḥadīth* and *tafsīr* that he realized how far Muslims had strayed from belief in the unity of Allah (*tawḥīd al-uluhiyya*).[31] Ibn 'Abd al-Wahhāb's teachers in Medina, 'Abdallāh b. Ibrāhīm and Ḥayāt al-Sindī, represented the spirit of revivalism, which was then current in the Ḥaramayn. But they were quietists and could not have been responsible for Ibn 'Abd al-Wahhāb's militant docrines, and in particular his pronouncement of anathema on other Muslims (*takfīr*).

In his search for the sources of Ibn 'Abd al-Wahhāb's doctrines, Michael Cook found that he did not acknowledge any near-contemporary scholar as an authority. As he himself said in one of his epistles, "I did not know the meaning of 'there is no God but Allāh,' nor did I know the religion of Islam, before this blessing (*khayr*) which God vouchsafed to me. Likewise, not one among my teachers knew it." Ibn 'Abd al-Wahhāb insinuates here that he received the truth by revelation. Michael Cook concluded that the sources of his doctrines were literary and included especially the writings of the two great Ḥanbali scholars of the fourteenth century, Ibn Taymiyya and Ibn Qayyim al-Jawziyya.[32]

Indeed, Muḥammad b. Ismā'īl Ibn al-Amīr al-Ṣan'ānī (1688–c. 1768), a militant Yemeni reformist, thought that Ibn 'Abd al-Wahhāb was poorly educated, because he had not studied under the guidance of scholars; hence his naive interpretation, as al-Ṣan'ānī saw it, of the works of Ibn Taymiyya and Ibn Qayyim al-Jawziyya. Ibn al-Amīr was twenty-five years older than Ibn 'Abd al-Wahhāb, but we do not know whether there were personal contacts between the two. Ibn al-Amīr at first approved the activities of Ibn 'Abd al-Wahhāb, but he changed his mind after examining some of the latter's works.[33]

The Circulation of Reformist Ideas

Ibn al-Amīr al-Ṣan'ānī studied in the Ḥaramayn with Muḥammad b. Ibrāhīm al-Kūrānī, 'Abdallāh al-Baṣrī and Abu'l-Ḥasan al-Sindī. The latter, according to some sources, influenced al-Ṣan'ānī by directing him to the study of *ḥadīth*. It was after al-Ṣan'ānī had returned from Medina in 1720 that he began to call for a reform of society and government in Yemen.[34] A copy of his treatise on "the purification of the faith" (*Taṭhir al-i'tiqād 'an adran al-ilḥād*) was found bound together with a book by Ibn 'Abd al-Wahhāb, indicating that al-Ṣan'ānī's work, which condemned the veneration of tombs and asserted that people in Yemen, Syria and Najd were full of *shirk*, may have been studied by the Wahhābis.[35]

Reformist ideas circulated in and out of the Ḥaramayn. Ṣāliḥ al-Fullānī came to Medina from Fūtā Jallon in West Africa, which had experienced an earlier *jihād* movement in 1725. Al-Fullānī seems to have formulated his ideas during his studies in his native Mauritania and in Morocco. He came to Medina in 1774 and was one of the most infuential teachers there for thirty years, until his death in 1803. He opposed *taqlīd* and called for a strict adherence to the Koran and the *sunna*. Though he does not seem openly to have advocated *ijtihād*, he certainly was against partisanship of a single *madhhab*.[36]

Aḥmad Ibn Idrīs al-Fāsī (1749–1837) held similar views. When he came to Mecca in 1799 he met with the hostility of the *'ulamā'* there, because he preferred the text of the *ḥadīth* to the ruling of the *madhhab*. His views may have been formed during his studies between 1770 and 1797 in Fez, which was permeated with reformist ideas during the reigns of Sīdī Muḥammad b. 'Abdallāh (1757–1790) and his son Mawlay Sulayman (1793–1822).[37]

Ibn Idrīs stayed in Mecca after the Wahhābi conquest in 1803 and was treated with respect by the Wahhābīs. He conducted theological disputations with their *'ulamā'*, continued to follow his Sufi way, and even read Ibn 'Arabī, whose teachings were considered unbelief by the Wahhābīs. He left Mecca in 1803, after the Wahhābīs had been driven out, and returned only in 1817. After conducting acrimonious debates with the *'ulamā'*, he left Mecca again, or was expelled, in 1827, and he spent the last ten years of his life, until his death in 1837, first in Yemen and later in 'Asīr, which was then under the rule of the Wahhābīs.[38]

Ibn Idrīs preferred Yemen, because he was closer to its scholars, particularly Muḥammad b. 'Alī al-Shawkānī (1760–1834), in his attitude towards *madhhab* partisanship. Al-Shawkānī, the most celebrated Zaydi scholar of the eighteenth century, studied with Yemeni Sunni *'ulamā'*, members of the Mizjājī and Aḥdal families. He was also directly connected to our network through a certain 'Alī b. Ibrāhīm, a student of Muḥammad Ḥayāt al-Sindī. His debt to the study of *ḥadīth* in the Ḥaramayn is evident in his major book on *ḥadīth*, *Itḥāf al-kabīr bi-isnād al-dafātīr*, a collection of *asānīd* in which he relies heavily on the *asānīd* of al-Bābilī, Ibrāhīm al-Kūrānī, al-Nakhlī, 'Abdallāh al-Baṣrī and Muḥammad Ibn al-Ṭayyib (1698–1756).[39]

A Sufi Network

By the end of the seventeenth century, the Naqshabandiyya was firmly established in the Ḥaramayn and included among its affiliates most of the key figures in our network, such as Ibrāhīm al-Kūrānī, Aḥmad al-Nakhlī, Ḥasan al-'Ujaymī and Muḥammad Ḥayāt al-Sindī.[40] The eighteenth century saw a transition among *ṣūfi ṭuruq* from devotional paths, sets of *adhkār* and *awrād*, to corporate social organizations.[41] Pilgrims were initiated in the Ḥaramayn into new *ṭuruq*, and carried back to their homelands not only new ideas but also the nuclei for more cohesive and structurally organized *ṭuruq*.

A contemporary collection of biographies of scholars in Medina gives information about Sufi affiliation in only four or five entries. One may suggest that although almost all the scholars were affiliated with at least one *ṭarīqa*, few became famous primarily as mystics. One of them was Muḥammad b. 'Abd al-Karīm b. Ḥasan al-Sammān (1718–1776). He was initiated by Musṭ̣afā b. Kamāl al-Dīn al-Bakrī (1688–1749) into the Khalwatiyya (also referred to as *al-ṭarīqa al-Bakriyya*). Although Musṭ̣afā al-Bakrī himself had been initiated into several *ṭurūq* earlier in his life, he demanded from his disciples exclusive affiliation with his *ṭarīqa*. Indeed, the biographies of al-Sammān seem to emphasize the latter's full commitment to al-Bakrī's *ṭarīqa*.[42]

Al-Sammān's fame as a Sufi attracted distinguished visitors, such as the leading Moroccan scholar al-Tawūdī Ibn Sūda (in 1769),[43] and Aḥmad al-Tijānī, the founder of the Tijāniyya (in 1774). Al-Tijānī, who was actively searching for a devotional path, had already been initiated twice into the Khalwatiyya, by Muḥammad b. 'Abd al-Raḥman al-Azharī in Algeria and by Maḥmūd al-Kurdī in Cairo. According to al-Tijānī's biographer, he was directed to al-Sammān by the recluse *shaykh* Abu'l-'Abbās Sīdī Aḥmad b. 'Abdallāh al-Hindī, a resident of Mecca. Al-Tijānī communicated with al-Hindī without actually meeting him, through the medium of his servant. The Indian *shaykh* declared that al-Tijānī was the heir to his knowledge, secrets and gifts. He then directed him to al-Sammān, calling him "my successor as *quṭb*." From Mecca al-Tijānī continued to Medina, where he met al-Sammān. Although al-Tijānī refused to enter into a *khalwa*, al-Sammān taught him the holy names, thus reinforcing al-Tijānī's adherence to the Khalwatiyya.[44]

Two of al-Sammān's disciples spread a *ṭarīqa*, called al-Sammāniyya after him, to Sumatra and to the Sudan. 'Abd al-Ṣamad al-Palimbānī (c. 1703–c. 1788) spent most of his working life in Arabia, and was initiated by al-Sammān into his *ṭarīqa*, presumably the Khalwatiyya. 'Abd al-Ṣamad, in his turn, initiated students from Sumatra, who had come to study with him in Mecca, into the *ṭarīqa* that he named after his master, *al-ṭarīqa al-Sammāniyya*. On their return to Sumatra, they spread the new *ṭarīqa* in Palembang in south Sumatra. That the Sammāniyya became rooted in Sumatra already in the lifetime of its founder is demonstrated by the appearance there in 1781, only six years after al-Sammān's death, of a hagiography of him, and this hagiography mentions an even earlier account of miracles performed by al-Sammān.[45]

From his residence in the Ḥaramayn, 'Abd al-Ṣamad served as a guide and teacher to scholars in Sumatra. He maintained links with his homeland by correspondence, inspiring resistance to the Dutch through the messages he communicated thereby. In 1772 he wrote letters from Mecca on behalf of two returning pilgrims to three princes in Central Java. Two of the letters urged defence of the faith, while the third spoke of the virtues of a holy war. In 1774 he wrote a treatise on *Imān*, including a section on holy war. It became popular in Acheh and a century later inspired fighters against the Dutch in the Acheh war of 1873–1910. He also wrote an Arabic *ratīb*, a poetic composition for *dhikr* recitation. In 1818 a revolt broke out against the Dutch, set off by a scuffle between several returning pilgrims who were reciting a *ratīb* and a group of inquisitive Dutch soldiers. Perhaps this was a *ratīb* of the Sammāniyya.

Reform of *ṣūfī ṭuruq* in the eighteenth century was associated with a renewed interest in the doctrines of al-Ghazālī. Between 1779 and 1788 'Abd al-Ṣamad rendered into Malay the *Lubab ihyā' 'ulūm al-dīn*, an abridgement of al-Ghazālī's *Ihyā' 'ulūm al-dīn*. Like the Malay rendering of *Tafsīr al-Jalalayn* by 'Abd al-Ra'ūf, this work remained very popular. Both 'Abd al-Ra'ūf, the student of Ibrāhīm al-Kūrānī, and 'Abd al-Ṣamad, the student of al-Sammān, enriched the Islamic religious literature in Malay, thus contributing to the radicalization of Islam, as happened in several parts of the Muslim world in the eighteenth century.[46]

The Sammāniyya was introduced into the Sudan by Aḥmad al-Ṭayyib b. al-Bashīr, who had been initiated by al-Sammān in Medina. He returned to the Sudan in 1800 and spread the Sammāniyya there until his death in 1823. The Sammāniyya as a reformed *ṭarīqa*, organized on a wider geographical and societal scale and with a central hierarchical authority, expanded at the expense of the two older *ṭuruq*, the Qādiriyya and the Shādhiliyya, which had been adapted to the local parochial pattern of "holy families."[47] The Sammāniyya contributed to Islamic militancy in the Sudan through the affiliation of Muḥammad Aḥmad, the Mahdi. He was a member of the Sammāniyya for ten years (1861–1871) as a disciple of Muḥammad al-Sharīf, the grandson of Aḥmad al-Ṭayyib al-Bashīr.[48]

Some Characteristics of the Network

Tarājim a'yan al-Madīna al-munāwwara fi'l-qarn al-thānī 'ashar, an anonymous collection of biographies of scholars active in Medina in the twelfth century of the Muslim era, written after 1786 (1201), provides us with a rare opportunity to study that scholarly community. Out of more than 80 biographical entries, 24 concern *mujāwirūn*: 7 of these came to Medina from the Maghreb, 5 from Sind (India), 4 from Kurdistan, 3 from the central Ottoman Empire, 2 from Uzbekistan, and one each from Aleppo, West Africa and Daghestan. Evidently, scholars from the areas of the Maghreb, Sind, Kurdistan and the central lands of the Ottoman Empire, which made up "the intermediate region" between the "inner circle" and the farther lands of Islam, made a special contribution to intellectual life in the Ḥaramayn.

We can identify the *madhhab* affiliation of 73 scholars, among whom 47 were Ḥanafīs, 16 were Shāfi'īs, 8 were Mālikīs and 2 were Ḥanbalīs. Thirty of the Ḥanafīs belonged to seven families that produced at least four scholars each who held the offices of *qāḍī, nā'ib* and *mufti*. Six other Ḥanafīs came from Sind, and two were Uzbeks. Among the Shāfi'īs, five were members of Ibrāhīm al-Kūrānī's family, and four were members of the Samhūdī family. There were also three other Kurds and one Daghestanī. All the

Mālikīs were Maghribīs, except for the West African Ṣāliḥ al-Fullānī.

A comparison between Medina and Mecca suggests that more *mujāwirūn* preferred to study and teach in Medina, where the scholarly community seems to have been more cosmopolitan. This would be in line with a more general pattern noted by W. Ende:

> Many pious Muslims considered *mujāwara* in Medina, at the tomb of the Prophet and the resting-place of many of his companions, as even more meritorious than that in Mecca. This opinion was, among other things, influenced by the fact that apparently none of the Companions of the Prophet had expressed the wish to remain in Mecca as a *mujāwir* after having performed the smaller or greater pilgrimage.[49]

It is significant that Arab scholars from the countries of the "inner circle" — from Egypt (like al-Bābilī and Ḥasan al-Jabartī, 1698–1774), from Syria and Palestine (such as al-Saffārinī),[50] and many more from Yemen — studied and taught for many years in Mecca and Medina, but returned to their native countries.

Among the pilgrim-scholars from the farther lands of Islam, only one, Ṣāliḥ al-Fullānī, became a *mujāwir* and a teacher in the Ḥaramayn. Other pilgrims from the "outer circle" stayed for some time in the Ḥaramayn, went on to study in Zabīd or in Cairo, and returned to their homelands — to Southeast Asia ('Abd al-Ra'ūf and 'Abd al-Ṣamad), China (Ma Ming-Hsin), Agades (Jibrīl b. 'Umar) and Hausaland (Muḥammad Rāj). Some of them were inspired by the spirit of revivalism in the "inner circle," and they or their disciples (like 'Uthmān dan Fodio) became leaders of reformist movements.

Eyewitness Reports: Mecca under the Wahhābīs

The first eyewitness report on Mecca was by 'Alī Bey al-'Abbāsī, pseudonym of the Spanish (some say Jewish) traveller Domingo Badia y Leblich, who visited Mecca in 1807 dressed as an Arab. At that time Mecca was under the rule of the Wahhābīs, and the number of pilgrims was only a fraction of what it had been. Though it could accommodate over one hundred thousand souls, there were only some sixteen to eighteen thousand at that time. Almost two-thirds of the buildings in Mecca stood empty. These had been hostels for pilgrims, and in their absence the houses were not maintained and became half ruined. Scholarship in Mecca was poor; only a handful of *ṭalaba* gave lessons to an audience of a dozen in the main mosque. 'Alī Bey found the copies of the Koran produced in Mecca to be full of mistakes that revealed the ignorance of the copyists.[51]

John Lewis Burckhardt visited Mecca in 1814, after the city had been liberated from the Wahhābīs and was being ruled by a governor in the name of Muḥammad Alī. Mecca had begun to recover, but was still only a shadow of its former self. The city could have accommodated three times the number of its residents in 1814. Apart from Hijāzī Beduins who had settled in Mecca, all the other residents were foreigners or the descendants of foreigners, who adopted the local language and customs, except for the Indians, who continued to maintain their own as well. The following excerpts from Burckhardt's report speak for themselves:

> I think I have sufficient reason for affirming that Mecca is at present much inferior even in Muhammedan learning to any town of equal population in Syria or Egypt. It probably was not so when the many public schools or Medreses were built, which are now converted into private lodgings for pilgrims.[52]
>
> In the mosques, after prayers, chiefly in the afternoon, some learned olemas explain a few religious books to a very thin audience, consisting principally of Indians, Malays, Negroes and a few natives of Hadramaut and Yemen, who, attracted by the great name of Mekka, remain here a few years, until they think themselves sufficiently instructed to pass at home for learned men. The Mekkawys themselves, who wish to improve science, go to Damascus or to Cairo.[53]
>
> There is no public library attached to the mosque; the ancient libraries, of which I have already spoken, have all disappeared. Mekka is equally destitute of private libraries, with the exception of those of the rich merchants, who exhibit a few books to distinguish them from the vulgar; or of the olemas, of whom some possess such as are necessary for their daily reference in matters of law. The Wahhābys, according to a report, carried off many loads of books; but they were also said to have paid for every thing they took ... They told me that bookdealers used formerly to come here with the Hadj from Yemen, and sell

valuable books ... There are no copyists at Mekka to replace the books that have been exported.[54]

These eyewitness reports illustrate the consequences of the Wahhābī conquest of Mecca in 1803. The holy city became deserted and impoverished, as the pilgrimage stopped almost completely, as well as the flow of annual gifts from Istanbul, Cairo and other Muslim capitals. The changing fortunes of the holy city and pilgrim centre were similar, it seems, to those of commercial cities in parallel circumstances. Commercial cities had a core of native inhabitants, but their prosperity depended on the floating population of traders. Among the latter, some became residents while others were seasonal visitors. But when conditions changed as a result of wars or the diversion of trade routes, the foreign traders, even those who had been resident for years or generations, deserted the commercial city, which was left only with its native inhabitants.[55]

Mecca had a floating population of scholars and pilgrims, as well as of those who provided them with services. 'Alī Bey's report about the poor scholarship in Mecca suggests that the leading *'ulamā'*, who considered the Wahhābīs sectarians or even heretics, had left the city. It seems that some of those who had made their living from catering to the pilgrims had also left Mecca.

We do not have similar eyewitness reports for Medina, which had been more cosmopolitan than Mecca. Perhaps Medina was not as heavily affected as Mecca by the Wahhābī conquest, allowing greater continuity with the recent past.

The rehabilitation of the foreign scholarly community was slow, but in 1826 Muḥammad b. 'Alī al-Sanūsī found some teachers of prominence in Mecca and Medina. Some of these were linked by scholastic and mystical chains (*salāsil*) to the great scholars of earlier generations. Ṣāliḥ al-Fullānī appears more often than others in these *salāsil*. The proportion of natives of Mecca among the scholars seems to have been larger than before the Wahhābī conquest, when many of the prominent scholars had been immigrants to Mecca or their descendants.[56]

The spirit of reform in the Ḥaramayn came to an end as a result of the conquest by the Wahhābiyya. In Egypt, the revival of the Khalwatiyya had run its course by the beginning of the nineteenth century, as a result of the upheavals caused by the French conquest and the rise of Muḥammad 'Alī. In Morocco, the reformist thrust ceased after Mawlāy Sulaymān, whose reign ended with a revolt of the anti-reform forces.[57] Elsewhere in the Islamic world, however, the reform movements of the nineteenth century that changed the character of Islam in the farther lands, and particularly in Africa, were directly linked to the networks of *ḥadīth* scholars and Sufis with their centre in the Ḥaramayn, as well as to the Khalwati *shaykhs* in Egypt and to the reformist milieu of Fez.

Notes

1. See the Introduction to N. Levtzion & J.O. Voll (eds.), *Eighteenth Century Renewal and Reform in Islam*, Syracuse 1987, pp. 3–20.
2. For Morocco, see N. Levtzion & G. Weigert, "Religious Reform in Morocco in the Eighteenth Century," *North African, Arabic and Islamic Studies in Honor of Pesach Shinar, Jerusalem Studies in Arabic and Islam*, XIII (1995), pp. 173–197.
3. C.R. Boxer, *The Portuguese Seaborne Empire, 1415–1825*, London 1969; R.B. Serjeant, *The Portuguese off the South Arabian Coast*, Oxford 1963; and N. Steensgaard, *The Asian Trade Revolution of the Seventeenth Century*, Chicago 1973.
4. M. Niebuhr, *Travels through Arabia and Other Countries in the East*, London 1792, pp. 153, 417–418.
5. Ashir Dan Gupta, "Trade and Politics in Eighteenth Century India," in D.S. Richards (ed.), *Islam and the Trade of Asia: A Colloquium*, Oxford 1970, 181–214.
6. G. Fisher, *Barbary Legend*, Oxford 1957; P. Mason, *Histoire de l'établissements et du commerce français dans l'Afrique barbaresque, 1560–1793*, Paris 1903.
7. Abu'l-Qasim al-Zayyānī, *Al-Turjamāna al-kubrā fi akhbār al-ma'mūr barran wa-baḥran*, Rabat 1967, pp. 58–60, 83–86, 379–380; 'Alī Ḥarazm, *Jawāhir al-ma'ānī wa-bulūgh al-amānī*, Cairo 1929, I, p. 39.
8. Niebuhr, *Travels through Arabia* (above, note 4), pp. 40–44, 177, 221, 236; on travelling by boat between Suez and Jedda see also al-Zayyānī, *al-Turjamāna al-kubrā* (above, note 7), p. 215.
9. J.O. Voll, "*Ḥadīth* Scholars and *Ṭarīqahs*: An *'Ulamā'* Group in Eighteenth Century Ḥaramayn and Their Impact on the Muslim World," *Journal of Asian and African Studies*, XV (1980), pp. 264–273, particularly p. 266.
10. Muḥammad Amīn al-Muḥibbī, *Khulāṣat al-athār fi a'yān al-qarn al-ḥadī 'ashar*, Beirut 1966, IV, pp. 39–42.
11. 'Abd al-Raḥmān al-Jabartī, *'Ajā'ib al-athār fi'l-tarājim wa'l-Akhbār*, ed. Ḥasan Muḥammad Jawhār et al., Cairo, 1957–1968, I, p. 177.
12. *Ibid.*, I, p. 213; Muḥammad Khalīl al-Murādī, *Silk al-durar fī a'yān al-qarn al-thānī 'ashar*, Baghdad 1301/1883f, I, pp. 171–172.
13. Al-Jabartī, *'Ajā'ib al-athār* (above, note 11), I, pp. 208–209; J.O Voll, " 'Abdallāh ibn Sālim al-Baṣrī and 18th-Century Ḥadīth Scholarship," paper presented to MESA meeting in Baltimore, November 1987.
14. Al-Muhibbī, *Khulāṣat al-athār* (above, note 10), IV, p. 207.
15. Al-Murādī, *Silk al-durar* (above, note 12), II, pp. 5–6; al-Jabartī, *'Ajā'ib al-athār*,

I, p. 171; A.H. Johns, *EI*[2], V, cols. 432–433, s.v. *Al-Kūrānī*, and col. 525, s.v. *al-Kushāshī*.

16. Al-Murādī, *Silk al-durar* (above, note 12), IV, pp. 65–66.
17. Y. Friedmann, *Shaykh Aḥmad Sirhindi: An Outline of His Thought and a Study of His Image in the Eyes of Posterity*, Montreal 1971, pp. 8, 96–101, 119.
18. A.H. Johns, "Islam in Southeast Asia: Problems and Perspectives," in C.D. Cowan & O.W. Wolters (eds.), *Southeast Asian History and Historiography*, Ithaca, N.Y., 1976, pp. 304–320.
19. J.O. Voll, "Linking Groups in the Networks of Eighteenth-Century Revivalist Scholars: The Mizjājī Family in the Yemen," in Levtzion & Voll, *Eighteenth Century Renewal* (above, note 1), pp. 69–92. When Niebuhr visited Zabīd in 1763, the town was in economic decline after its thriving commerce had shifted to Mokha. However, it was still full of religious scholars, who drained more than half of the town's revenues. See *Travels through Arabia* (above, note 4), pp. 282–284.
20. J. Fletcher, "Les voies (*turuq*) soufies en Chine," in A. Popovic & G. Veinstein (eds.), *Les Ordres mystiques de l'Islam*, Paris 1986, pp. 14–26.
21. Al-Murādī, *Silk al-durar* (above, note 12), IV, p. 27.
22. Voll, "*Ḥadīth* scholars" (above, note 9), p. 266. In the same period, the reformist Moroccan sultan Sīdī Muḥammad b. 'Abdallāh broadened the scope of *ḥadīth* studies by introducing the study of *ḥadīth* collections other than Mālik's *al-Muwaṭṭa'*. See Levtzion & Weigert, "Religious Reform in Morocco" (above, note 2).
23. Mohamed A. Al-Freih, "The Historical Background of the Emergence of Muḥammad Ibn 'Abd al-Wahhāb and His Movement," Ph.D. Dissertation, UCLA, 1990, pp. 333–334; and S.A.A. Rizvi, *Shāh Walī Allāh and his Times*, Canberra 1980, pp. 215–216, 225, 295, 396–397.
24. Al-Murādī, *Silk al-durar* (above, note 12), IV, p. 34.
25. *Ibid.*, p. 66.
26. J.O. Voll, "Muḥammad Ḥayāt al-Sindī and Muḥammad ibn 'Abd al-Wahhāb: An Analysis of an Intellectual Group in Eighteenth Century Madina," *Bulletin SOAS*, xv (1980), pp. 32–39.
27. 'Abdallāh ibn Fūdī, *Tazyīn al-waraqāt*, ed. and English transl. by M. Hiskett, Ibadan 1963, p. 38; transl., p. 95. Ḥayāt al-Sindī studied with Abu'l-Ḥasan al-Kabīr and taught Abu'l-Ḥasan al-Saghīr. The latter, the teacher of Muḥammad Rāj, was Abu'l-Ḥasan Muḥammad b. Muḥammad Ṣadīq al-Sindī. He was born in Sind in 1713, came to Medina in 1747, and died there in or after 1773. See *Tarājim a'yān al-madīna al-munawwara fi'l-qarn al-thānī 'ashar* (author unknown), ed. Muḥammad al-Tawunjī, Jedda 1984, p. 59.
28. Al-Muradī, *Silk al-durar* (above, note 12), IV, pp. 31–32; al-Jabartī, *'Ajā'ib al-athār* (above, note 11), III, pp. 106–110.
29. Ibn Bishr, *'Unwān al-majd fī ta'rīkh Najd*, Beirut, n.d., p. 17; 'Abdallāh Ṣāliḥ al-'Uthaymin, "Muḥammad ibn 'Abd al-Wahhāb: The Man and His Works," Ph.D. Dissertation, Edinburgh, 1972, pp. 68–74; Al-Freih, "Historical Background of Ibn 'Abd al-Wahhāb" (above, note 23), p. 337; M. Cook, "On the Origins of Wahhābism," *Journal of the Royal Asiatic Society*, Series 3, II (1992), p. 192.

30. Voll, "*Ḥadīth* Scholars," (above, note 9), p. 267.
31. Al-Freih, "Historical Background of Ibn 'Abd al-Wahhāb" (above, note 23), p. 338, quoting Ibn Ḥasan, *al-Maqamāt*, fol. 7.
32. Cook, "Origins of Wahhābism" (above, note 29), pp. 198–202.
33. *Ibid.*, p. 200.
34. Al-Freih, "Historical Background of Ibn 'Abd al-Wahhāb," p. 334 (above, note 23, quoting Qāsim Aḥmad, *Ibn al-Amīr wa-'aṣruhu*, n.d., p. 128, and 'Abd al-Raḥmān Ba'kar, *Musliḥ al-Yaman*, 1988, p. 70).
35. M. Cook, personal communication.
36. J.O. Hunwick, "Ṣāliḥ al-Fullānī of Futa Jallon: an Eighteenth-Century Scholar and *mujaddid*," *Bulletin IFAN*, XL (1978), pp. 879–885; idem, "Sāliḥ al-Fullānī (1752/3–1803); The Career and Teaching of a West African *'Ālim* in Medina," in A.H. Green (ed.), *In Quest of Islamic Humanism: Arabic and Islamic Studies in Memory of Mohamed al-Nowaihi*, Cairo 1984, pp. 139–154.
37. Levtzion & Weigert, "Religious Reform in Morocco" (above, note 2).
38. R.S. O'Fahey, *Enigmatic Saint: Aḥmad Ibn Idris and the Idrisi Tradition*, Evanston 1990, pp. 58–80.
39. Ḥusayn b. 'Abdallāh al-'Amrī, *The Yemen in the 18th & 19th Centuries: A Political and Intellectual History*, London 1985, pp. 106–114.
40. Voll, "*Ḥadīth* Scholars," p. 268.
41. Levtzion & Voll (eds.), Introduction to *Eighteenth Century Renewal and Reform* (above, note 1), pp. 9–10. In the older pattern of Sufism, scholars were affiliated with several *ṭuruq* simultaneously, as was the case with a scholar of Medina, Muḥammad Badr al-Dīn b. Naṣr al-Dīn al-Bukhārī al-Ḥanafī, born in 1752. He studied with Ismā'īl b. 'Abdallāh al-Uskudārī (c. 1707–c. 1768), who was *shaykh al-ṭā'ifa al-Naqshabandiyya* in Medina. He was initiated into the *al-ṭarīqa al-Bakriyya* by Muḥammad al-Sammān, and into the Naqshabandiyya by his father and also by al-Khawāja Raḥmatallāh al-Naqshabandī, by correspondence from India (*bi'l-murāsala min al-Hind*). He was initiated by Abū Sa'īd al-Ḥasanī in Medina into the Naqshabandiyya, the Qādiriyya and the Ḥusayniyya. See *Tarājim a'yān al-Madīna* (above, note 27), pp. 61, 109–110.
42. *Tarājim a'yān al-Madīna* (above, note 27), p. 95: "*akhadha al-ṭarīqa wa-awradahu wa-intafa'a bihi*," and al-Murādī, *Silk al-durar* (above, note 12), IV, pp. 60–61: "*waqāma 'alā waẓā'if al-awrād wa'l-adhkār*." On Muṣṭafā al-Bakrī's call for exclusivity, see G. Weigert, "The Khalwatiyya in Egypt in the Eighteenth Century," Ph.D. Dissertation, The Hebrew University of Jerusalem, 1989, pp. 107–108, quoting al-Jabartī, *'Ajā'ib al-athār* (above, note 11), IV, p. 66.
43. Al-Jabartī, *'Ajā'ib al-athār* (above, note 11), II, p. 243.
44. 'Alī Ḥarazm, *Jawāhir al-ma'ānī* (above, note 7), I, pp. 40–41.
45. This information about 'Abd al-Ṣamad is based on an unpublished paper by A.H. Johns, "Enriching the Language of the Tribe: The Works of Jawi 'Ulamā' in the 17–19 Centuries," presented to the Conference on Eighteenth Century Renewal and Reform in Islam, Jerusalem, 1985. Johns cited G.W.J. Drewes, "Directions for Travellers on the Mystic Path," *VKI: Verhandlingen van het koninklijk Instituut voot Taal-, Landen volkenkunde*, LXXXI (1977).

46. N. Levtzion, "The Eighteenth Century: Background to the Islamic Revolutions in West Africa," in Levtzion & Voll, *Eighteenth Century Renewal and Reform* (above, note 1), pp. 26–28.
47. Aḥmad 'Alī al-Bashīr, *Al-Adab al-ṣūfī fi'l-Sūdān*, Cairo 1970, p. 43; P.M. Holt, "Holy Families and Islam in the Sudan," *Princeton Near East Papers*, IV (1967).
48. Na'ūm Shuqayr, *Jughrāfiyya wa-ta'rikh al-Sūdān*, Cairo 1903–1904, III, 113–118.
49. W. Ende, EI^2, VII, s.v. *Mujāwir*, cols. 293–294.
50. Al-Murādī, *Silk al-durar* (above, note 12) has many references to Syrian scholars who studied for some time in the Ḥaramayn; see, e.g., III, pp. 63–64, 220–221.
51. *Voyages d'Ali Bey El-Abessī en Afrique et en Asie pendant les annees 1803, 1804, 1805, 1806 et 1807*, Paris 1814, II, pp. 392–398, 423.
52. J.L. Burckhardt, *Travels in Arabia*, London 1829, I, p. 389.
53. *Ibid.*, pp. 390.
54. *Ibid.*, pp. 392–4.
55. An example of a trading town that was deserted in the wake of a civil war and the diversion of its trade route was Salaga in the northern region of Ghana, toward the end of the nineteenth century; see N. Levtzion, *Muslims and Chiefs in West Africa*, Oxford 1968, pp. 26–48.
56. K. Vikor, "Sufi and Scholar on the Desert Edge: Muḥammad b. 'Alī al-Sanūsī (1787–1859)," Ph.D. Dissertation, University of Bergen, 1991, pp. 92–99.
57. Weigert, "The Khalwatiyya" (above, note 42), pp. 156–160, 186; Levtzion & Weigert, "Religious Reform in Morocco" (above, note 2).

17

Hallowed Land in the Theory and Practice of Modern Nationalism

Hedva Ben-Israel

The Holy Land, Holy Russia, Holy Ireland, the Promised Land of America. How did lands become holy in the vocabulary of nationalism? Rhetoric, as we know, constitutes power. We at once suspect manipulation. The problem is whether this potential of land to be regarded as holy in the discourse of nationalism is embedded in the structure of the concept of nationalism, or emanates from the strategies of states, churches or national movements, or from other sources such as human nature.

To explain the territorial imperative or orientation in nationalism, one type of answer looks to the influence of Scripture. Because God's gift consecrated the Land of Israel for the Jewish people, other lands could be declared to be sacred for other nations. An apparently opposite theory, looking not up to heaven, but down to animals, claims a territorial instinct. Just as animals mark territories and later defend them to the death, so do humans. This theory, first posed by the Austrian biologist Konrad Lorenz in 1940,[1] and taken up by others,[2] holds man to be a "territorial species." "We defend our homes and our homelands for biological reasons, not because we choose but because we must," wrote Robert Ardrey. This school holds that the territorial imperative is blind and commands beyond logic, eliciting both patriotism and xenophobia. It would seem that we have here the sublime and the ridiculous. God's gift, on the one hand, and the fatherland as a biological instinct, on the other.

Some theories combine sacredness and impulse. Writing on the "inherent sacredness of sovereign power," Clifford Geertz asserts that "the gravity of high politics and the solemnity of high worship spring from like impulses." When a sovereign journeys round his realm, he marks it, "like some wolf or tiger spreading his scent through his territory." Tracing the stories of three royal peregrinations, Geertz shows how the cults of monarchs and their authority over the land are promoted through hallowing the land and through the transformation of authority into moral or aesthetic ideas.[3] An early anthropologist, A. van Gennep, in a work published at the beginning of the century entitled *The Rites of Passage,* demonstrated the magico-religious origin of frontiers and passports. Natural boundaries of all kinds could be crossed only at the risk of supernatural sanctions.[4]

A recent theoretical analysis of *Human Territoriality* by R.D. Sack classifies many kinds of human orientations towards territoriality. Nationalism, according to Sack, arises from the combination of two categories, reification and displacement. This combination can result in a mystical perspective which attributes authority to the territory. This, says Sack, occurs within religious uses of space, when worshippers are made to believe that structures emanate power, and also in nationalism. "The territory is a physical manifestation of the state's authority, and yet allegiance to territory or homeland makes the territory appear as a source of authority."[5]

If Geertz and van Gennep are right, land belongs to the sphere of political theology or even magic, and if Sack is right, it is the taxonomy of orientations towards land which explains the mystic powers attributed to land as a source of authority. Either way, the human/land nexus is surely one of history's most ancient and enigmatic themes, and it has a special significance within the framework of nationalism. I am not certain, however, that there is just one explanation for the phenomena of national space, authoritative space and sacred national space. We may have become over-addicted to the search for recurring patterns. My search for historical examples has produced a variety of orientations towards land, the conditions for which cannot, I think, be perfectly systematized.

This paper is part of a series of studies on aspects of nationalism to which I now wish to add a consideration of territoriality. Because the concept of nationalism is notorious for its multiple definitions, I must begin by stating briefly my framework of assumptions. I define nationalism not as an emotion like patriotism, nor as an attitude of mind, but as a political principle which holds that the nation, the cultural society, should by right be coterminous with the territorial nation-state.

Nationalism also relies on pre-existent patriotic feelings, but it could make its appearance as a political principle only in the wake of two modern notions: (1) the idea that political philosophies can be guides for action; and (2) the idea that sovereignty resides in the people. Sovereignty could only be attibuted to a recognizable group, and this meant that modern nationalism, from its very inception in the French Revolution, proclaimed the right to liberty of the pre-existing historical nation, claiming common ethnic descent. This leads to another basic assumption, which disputes the theory that there are two kinds of nationalism: that of self-determination, that is, free-choice nationalism, supposedly typical of France, and that of ethnic, cultural, and historically determined nationalism, supposedly created in Germany as a reaction against the former. I hold, on the contrary, that as soon as nationalism appeared as a popular movement, it was grounded in the historical and cultural nation, rooted in myths of common descent. Collective sovereignty and ethnicity were there together right from the beginning, and all apparent variations of nationalism are due to different historical circumstances.

I have argued all this at length elsewhere.[6] My purpose here is to build upon that construct the notion of territoriality and to ask questions about it — mainly, how it acquired attributes that have to do with holiness. The materials for such a study are scarce. In the midst of a surge of writings on nationalism, the territorial aspect is somewhat neglected. The present trend in studies of nationalism is to relegate it to the sphere of imagined narrative and invented traditions.[7] Homeland, however, cannot be charmed away into thin air, or into a purely symbolic existence, however brilliant the argumentation. While the role of sacred places in nationalism is properly recognized and studied — shrines, cemeteries, battlefields, monuments and museums are temples of nationalism, as Mosse,[8] Inglis[9] and others have shown — the role of homeland is neglected. It could be that the question of national land is avoided for the same reason that ethnicity was shunned for so long, as an unaesthetic subject. Ethnicity and land, the atavistic roots of nationalism, are also its *terra firma*, or its feet of clay.

Since ancient times, rule over land has made the difference between life and death, mastery and slavery. In the individual mind and in the international arena, it is both the material and the symbolic value of territory and the ethnic character of a population which create internal cohesiveness and external friction. Nationalist rhetoric muses at ease about culture and tradition, heroes and forefathers, but it is in the end over land that wars are fought and men die. A recent book on *Personal Identity, National Identity and International Relations*[10] attempts to connect psychology with international relations, but not on the basis of commonsense assumptions about human nature, such as, for example, that kinship arouses feelings of solidarity or that readiness to fight for borders is an extention of love for the homestead. Instead, there is an attempt to construct an identity theory to the effect that individuals, through shared identification, are linked in a shared psychological syndrome and will act together to defend their common identity. To me, the conclusions of the theoretical and empirical approaches in this case seem very similar. In either case, they explain the psychological origin of defensive and patriotic reactions, but not the abstract commitment to the principle of nationalism, which is an ideology of change, as well as of preservation.

My first point on territoriality in nationalism is that the very transfer of the country from being the possession of the king to being the birthright of the nation at once invested it with a sublime aura. Just as popular sovereignty had to be lodged in a given ethnic collectivity, so it had to be geographically delimited. Indeed, it is arguable that, historically, the substance of the territorial claims made on behalf of the nation preceded and generated the abstract formulation of the right to have sovereignty over the national land. Logically, however, the sequence is as follows: The rights of persons become the rights of the nation. The nation takes over the state, along with its frontiers. As demonstrated in the French Revolution, the territorial base of the nation-state became central in the new nationalism, especially since the frontiers had at once to be defended, extended, verified by plebiscites, and so on. Without any overt sanctification as yet, the territory, by becoming the domain of the nation, was no longer mere property, but a question of right. The right to property is inherently more solemn and sublime than property itself. Kings could dispose of their real estate with no compunctions.

Nations cannot as easily give up national territory. Claiming the land on behalf of the nation imbued it with a transcendent authority over past, present and future. With that claim, the first step was taken towards the sanctification of national land.

This transformation took place in the course of the French Revolution. Responses to the partitions of Poland, at about the same time, exemplified the new attitudes. Now that the idea of the nation and of national land was abroad, the partitions were seen, unlike previous appropriations of regions and populations, as the dismemberment of a live body. The reciprocal relationship between nation and territory had already been exercising some of the best minds of the Enlightenment, such as Montesquieu, who theorized on nation-building in certain physical environments, and Rousseau, who wrote: "The mountains, seas and rivers form the frontiers for the nations living in Europe, and it is clear that nature itself has determined the number and greatness of nations." Enlightened men like Mirabeau condemned the partitions of Poland. Mallet du Pan called them "the horror of our age." Burke wrote, "The Empress of Russia has breakfasted, where will she dine?" Macaulay later spoke of a shameful crime, and Carlyle used the already-common surgical metaphor. While most Poles in high positions acquiesced in 1773, there was one who declared that he would rather cut off his hand than sign the sentence passed on his fatherland. By the time of the 1794 uprising which preceded the final elimination of Poland, a new concept had entered the vocabulary and the mobilization tactics of the national leaders. In the Act of Insurrection, Kosciuszko, its leader, swore to the integrity of the frontiers, and the words inscribed on the seal were "liberty, integrity, independence." The new concept of territorial integrity had definitely arrived, even for Poland, which had no natural frontiers and whose spheres of influence had waxed and waned throughout her history. The partitioning powers, aware of the new winds of nationalism, signed a secret article suppressing the very name of Poland "from the present and forever."[11]

The metaphors of surgery and dismemberment had to do with the idea of the organic nation and organic land. Of course, the new nationalism that came into being also reflected modern and structural developments in social and economic life. But the language in which it was couched had to be borrowed from cultural sources. The sanctity of human life was transferred to the nation and its land. The principle of national land was expressed in grandiloquent or divine terms, borrowing from existing models of sacred places, shrines, graves, trees, and so on, which were merged with the notion of the Holy Land. In its entry on "Holiness," the *Encyclopaedia of Religion and Ethics* names "inanimate things or places such as Jerusalem, the Temple, the inner sanctuary, the Scriptures, the Mount of Transfiguration ... spoken of as holy by virtue of their special association with God." Hallowed materials could be incorporated under the aegis of nationalism to express and produce the effects that were required, for instance, for perpetrating the new phenomenon of national wars.[12]

What I am pointing out here is that the emergence of nationalism as an ideology called forth appropriate strategies of mobilization. We can trace the process whereby the concept of the sovereign nation became, so to speak, rooted in the ground, in ethnicity and geography; once there, however, it appealed to moral and religious metaphors to refine and sublimate it. This is not necessarily a question of attributing manipulative intentions to named actors, political, literary or military. It is a course rooted at once in reality and in the imagination. The theorists of nationalism, including Herder and Rousseau, had already pointed to ancient Israel as the prototype of a nation. It had a national territory designated by God, a common religion, a sense of mission, a unique culture and God-given laws and institutions. Rousseau had pointed these out to the Poles in his advice to them on how to preserve their own nation.[13] The natural borders proclaimed by the French in wartime were later transformed into divine borders. Mazzini wrote that God created nations, each complete with its own natural frontiers, each in fact complete with its own promised land. Once nationalism made frontiers a value, maps began to be used, like flags and anthems, as symbols to evoke emotions.[14]

Religious symbols were effective for buttressing nationalism, as they had been for patriotism, which was nurtured as part of the religion of monarchy. Previously, in France's wars, chaplains had preached on the eves of battles that those who fought against Catholic France fought against the Holy Land.[15] The memory of Joan of Arc, in which the fusion of religion and patriotism was visible to all, was often invoked. Later, the new principle of nationalism also had to appear sacred. What chance would it otherwise have had against the devotees of either Catholic or enlightened universalism? Historically, nationalism could thrive only because religious belief declined. It re-established the barriers between nations which Christianity had rejected. It was an alternative creed.[16] The demands it made on the individual were absolute. How could secular nationalism, disparaged by great minds such as Goethe's as base, selfish and crude, be made uplifting? To overcome and succeed both religion and universalism, secular nationalism had to appropriate the same religious symbols whose potency had long been proven.

Furet and Richet have established the novelty of the notion of the Rhine as the natural frontier of France at the time of the French Revolution.[17] Of course, the ancient texts giving Caesar's definition of Gallia had already been used to support military claims. It is only after Valmy, however, that the Rhine was claimed as a natural border by Carnot and Sieyes, on nationalist grounds. Towards the end of the nineteenth century, nationalists like Barrès, spurred by their fear for France, fused a more radical nationalism with the notion of the holiness of the French land. Barrès's nationalism, like that of Danton or Carnot, was not Catholic. It was a cult of the soil and the dead. The soil of France had generated the French race; the land and the dead were objects of worship. Barrès canonizes the mountains, calling them saints: "la montagne de Sion Vaudémont, Sainte Odile, et le Puy de Dôme." Barrès rejected both Renan's and the Catholic forms of French nationalism. His own deterministic nationalism called upon an intuitive identity emerging mysteriously from the soil.[18]

Again, we find that we cannot counterpose a "blut und boden" type of nationalism against other types of nationalism devoid of this stigma, in a typology dependent upon nationality. Race and soil were central for Barrès. In a famous debate over Alsace between the outstanding French and German historians, Fustel de Coulanges and Theodor Mommsen, the contestants seem at first to present two types of argument for nationalism, one based on the free choice of the population and the other on the determination of race. As they proceed, however, they borrow each others' grounds, arguing over whether Alsace was historically French or German.[19] Myths of descent and of sacred land appear in most nationalisms according to need and conditions which vary. Exile and an insecure hold over land enhance ascriptions of holiness. To expel strangers you appeal to ethnic arguments; to extend territory, you claim historic or religious right.

The appeal to religious image, symbol and metaphor is common to countries of different religions. Protestant countries, it is often said, are more given to nationalism because of their greater interest in the Old Testament, while Catholic countries make more of sacred places and shrines. Without even touching theology, anyone reading the texts would say that the older book is pervaded by the idea of a distinct nation, close to God who gave it a homeland, whereas the Christian Testament explicitly rejects earthly kingdoms. In the New Testament, the ideal of the Promised Land is allegorized and internationalized, and all national particularisms are dropped. The *Oxford English Dictionary* defines the term "Holy Land," among other things, as "Western Palestine or more particularly Judaea: so called as being the scene of the life and death of Jesus Christ ...; in later use, as being the scene of the development of the Jewish and Christian religion." There is an interesting distinction implied here. In Jewish tradition, more in exilic than in biblical times, the land of Israel is holy because it was given by God to his people. In Christian tradition, the land was made holy through its association with the life of Christ. The difference is perhaps analogous to that between "sacred" and "sanctified." The *Encyclopaedia of Religion and Ethics* lists holy places and things, springs, trees,.days, numbers, vows, wars and persons made holy through their association with God; "similarly Palestine, the land occupied by Jahwe's people was also holy."[20]

My purpose in stressing this distinction is to illustrate why it was a natural and unquestioned practice in the Christian world to place the Holy Land anywhere. Any place could be sanctified through association with God or with religius values. During the long period of Christian internationalism, there were also other voices, like that of the Emperor Julian, who tried to combat the Christian tendency to deprecate national peculiarities. Julian named national customs rooted in race, like the Teutons' love of freedom, the voluntary servility of the Orientals, and other "unalterable differences." However, despite the recognition of the facts of national variety even by some of the Church Fathers and in the Hellenistic monarchies,[21] and despite the political incarnations of the heavenly Jerusalem in Constantinople and in the crusaders' kingdom, it was clearly not until the sixteenth and seventeenth centuries that distinct national entities became political realities, invested with attributes of holiness. It was then, too, and this is the point, that the notion of the Promised Land descended back from heaven to earth to be taken up by the new nations.

Sermons of Bostonian preachers quote biblical promises as a basis for claiming earthly land, Indian land. This notion brought grist to the philosophers' mill. To Voltaire, says C.C. O'Brien, God was an old Jew offering real estate.[22] Nevertheless, "territorial theology" or "sacred geography" made a comeback. Biblical promises, Roman heroes and Christian martyrs together provided the perfect treasure chest for the new nations and later the new nationalisms to draw upon. In *War and Peace,* Tolstoy quotes the prayer said for the army before Borodino: "These lawless men are gathered together to overwhelm thy kingdom, to destroy thy Jerusalem, thy beloved Russia."[23] For Cromwell, the interests of England and Christianity were one and the same thing, as they were for Milton. In the New World, America began to see itself, nation and land, as a sacred object, "the kingdom of God identified with the New England pattern of life," in the words of Yehoshua Arieli.[24] A new book by A. Zakai shows that the Puritans migrating to the New World consciously rejected the notion of England as God's elect country and conferred that title upon America.[25] The notion that America was the Promised Land survived ethnic diversification, as if Providence resided in the land and in the culture. Analogies of this conception evidently exist in other cultures as well. A recent study on "Espace mythique et territoire nationale" shows that the story of the Creation in Shinto belief, taught in Japanese schools until 1945, is that the Japanese archipelago was literally carved out of the bodies of the gods. This story was taught all the more intensively after contact with the West was forced upon Japan. It was probably calculated to foster the same sense of organic kinship between gods, people and land as was current in that age of nationalism, in other places.[26]

Appeals to the Promised Land idea were not only Protestant or Orthodox. New nationalities like those of the Canadians and the South Africans, which had not existed before their encounter with a new physical environment forged them into nationhood, seemed to be highly sensitive to the surrounding natural environment. The process of nation-building in a certain landscape was telescoped for the settlers into a lifetime's experience. The confrontation with mountainous waterways, arid velds or deserts against a religious background made pioneer settlers and their descendants all the more receptive to the notion of God's guiding hand. The identification of the Calvinist Afrikaans "Voortrekkers" of the 1830s with the tribes of Israel wandering in the desert in search of the Promised Land is documented in their diaries, as were the parallel experiences of Champlain and Cartier in Canada. Why is it, wrote a French Canadian Catholic priest in the 1860s, that God allotted to certain French families "a particular territory wherein to grow and develop a national identity?" His answer comes from the Bible. God created the nations, assigned them territories and guided their migrations. Just as he sent Abraham to Canaan, which had been defiled by its inhabitants, so he sent families out of France to bring faith to the beautiful St. Lawrence valley. Their zeal in performing their task, he adds, "is etched in blood from the mouth of the St. Lawrence right up to the banks of the Great Lakes." The French Canadians, he says, are a nation, and the St. Lawrence valley is their homeland. Cartier, climbing a hill and gazing "at the gigantic forests spreading the luxuriant growth right up to the horizon,"[27] was Abraham, and Washington was Joshua, as was Pretorius. It made no difference whether their churches were Catholic or Protestant; it was the living experience, sanctified by religious associations, which was common to them all.

Italian irredentism, the most specifically territorial form of nationalism, invested with a name laden with biblical associations, is also the product of a Catholic country. I have argued in another study that the force of irredentism has historically been mobilized more for territorial than for ethnic reasons.[28] Irredentism, in Italy, Greece[29] or Israel, appears as a state strategy for expansion which legitimates itself on grounds of national territory, hallowed by history or religion. The choice of rhetoric is culture-dependent. In some contexts, we find, sovereignty over land can be discussed independently of populations, and adjectives denoting religion can be appended to land.

The intensity of Italian irredentism owes less to Mazzini than to Garibaldi. Mazzini assumed that frontiers are drawn by God. But in his numerous works elaborating his views on humanity, religion, social justice, rights and duties, there is little on land, apart from the significance of Rome. The freedom of Rome meant the freedom of the world, the victory of God over the pagan deities, of truth over falsehood.[30] But one had to fight for Venice as well, because Venice, too, belonged within Italy's divinely ordained frontiers.[31]

Italian irredentism began in 1866, after the establishment of the state and the consequent failure to complete the unification of Italy by incorporating the Trent region. Ten years later, Imbriani, a follower of Garibaldi, founded the Italia Irredenta organization. It was invented as a slogan for the expansionist war that Garibaldi was preparing to fight for the Trentino, whenever sufficient tension built up in the Balkans to make it feasible. In the 1890s Italy's European irredentism gave way to imperialist and missionary slogans in the style of Manifest Destiny. Either way, religious symbols served a territorial impulse.[32] In the twentieth century, with Corradini and D'Annunzio, the accomplishment of the synthesis of imperialist, nationalist and irredentist groups produced a new creed. D'Annunzio became the symbol of irredentism. In "Italy or Death," his defence of his participation in the battle for Fiume, he makes endless allusions to Scripture. Following the Gospel of John, he proclaims: "Fiume ... kindles our faces with her breath and says to us: Receive ye the spirit, receive the Flame."[33] In *The First Duce*, M.A. Ledeen shows just how instrumental D'Annunzio's religious rhetoric was. His mobilization speeches of 1915 were couched in the formulas of the Sermon on the Mount, and Fiume was compared to the gospels.[34] Here is an appeal to religion more elaborate than the straightforward Promised Land image. D'Annunzio evinces a similarity to Barrès and to the Irish nationalist Patrick Pearse in his wild and no-doubt sacrilegious fusion of sacred and profane.

The usurpation of the religious domain by nationalism took many forms. The popular canonization of such national heroes as Saint Joan and Saint Marat are obvious examples.[35] The most salient general forms, however, are the sanctification of land, which we have sampled, the deification of the nation and and the practice of martyrdom. By the sheer intensity of the popular feelings involved, martyrology seems to overshadow other motifs. The appeal to the sanctification of land appears in comparison almost like an excuse, a mere strategem.

Nationalist martyrdom is by far the most effective mimesis of religion. This phenomenon, once considered Christian and Catholic, has demonstrably crossed civilizations and religions.[36] In Europe, it is in Polish and Irish nationalism that the motif of martyrdom has predominated. The Polish nationalists described their nation as the Messiah, the martyr among nations; in Ireland, nationalists sacrificed themselves to save the soul of Ireland for the creed of nationalism. The martyred missionaries of Canada, so the priests taught, had paid in blood for the land. The Canadian Indian Louis Riel saw himself as the Messiah and his people, the Metis, as the chosen Hebrews. When he was led to the scaffold after his 1885 rebellion, he believed that, like Christ, he would rise again on the third day.[37]

In Poland, the deification of the nation eclipses devotion to the land. Where land was abundant, as in Eastern Europe, territories were not precisely bounded and the attitude toward them, in earlier times, was instrumental. The inroads of ideological nationalism made the land become more meaningful. Polish nationalists in the nineteenth century, influenced by Fichte, promoted the idea of the mystical union of a nation and its native soil. From the 1830s, however, martyrdom was the paramount theme of nationalist writings. In the words of Mickiewicz, "and they crucified the Polish nation, and laid it in its grave ... but the Polish nation did not die ... but on the third day the soul shall return again to the body and the nation arise and free all the peoples of Europe from slavery."[38] Walicky claims authoritatively that Polish nationalism was never merely cultural but was strongly political, invoking the frontiers of the historical state. It is nevertheless religious and emotional language that seems to dominate the rhetoric of Polish nationalism.[39]

In Ireland, too, land never attained the sacredness of nation. All national associations focussing on land in fact signified agrarian reform, freedom from starvation, anti-landlordism. The term Holy Ireland referred either to the golden age when Ireland Christianized parts of Europe or to the pagan mythological past; or it expressed feelings for the landscape, as in the writings of the Protestant Ferguson: "Oh, ye fair hills of holy Ireland!"[40] Wolfe Tone, who died on the scaffold in 1798 with the words, "I have attempted to follow the same line in which Washington succeeded and Kosciusko failed," says not a word about land.[41] For Patrick Pearse, land comes into the discourse of nationalism as a possession of the Irish people: "the soil of Ireland to the people of Ireland to have and to hold from God alone who gave it." Judging by its context, this was meant to be a socio-economic statement, borrowed from Lalor.[42] De Valera, an enemy of partition, declared that "the unity of Ireland was predetermined by the forces of history and geography." But in his statements, too, one searches in vain for the sentiment of Holy Ireland. De Valera's 1937 constitution did, on principle, contain the irredentist claim to the north. At the same time, however, he also said that were the Protestant north to be coerced by Britain into unity with the south, he would support the north. Obviously, defying Britain was more sacred than the unity of Ireland.[43] Independence through a new religion of nationalism, for Pearse, and complete independence and Catholicism, for De Valera, were immeasurably more prominent themes than land.

Pearse, in the Easter Rising of 1916, presents the most perfect example of nationalist mobilization of the masses through religious symbols. The case of the Easter Rising, which I have elsewhere analyzed in detail,[44] is one of programmed martyrdom. I use this expression not lightly, but because it best conveys the multifaceted intention, foresight and correct reading of the public mind manifested in that undertaking. The purpose was to shake Ireland free of its materialistic stupor and save its soul for the true faith of Irish nationalism, through staging the supreme act of self-sacrifice. There is a great deal of proof for this. Those who opposed the Rising argued explicitly against the strategy of planning an ulterior triumph through martyrdom, bloodshed and failure. Moreover, Pearse's own writings, from which the story of his preparations for the Rising can be reconstructed, expound the nature of Irish nationalism as a new religion and his own role as that of the nationalist saviour. The "Testament," written in a biblical blend of legal and religious style, lists the gospels and the apostles of the new faith; for example: "God spoke to Ireland through Tone, and through those who after Tone took up his testimony;" "Mitchel's is the last of the four gospels of the new testament of Irish nationality." Pearse wrote to his publisher:

> I want to ask you ... to rush these two last pamphlets through ... so timing as to have the "Sovereign People," the last of the series, on sale by Monday April 17th ... You will later appreciate the reason and regard it as sufficient.

Obviously, the "Deed" and the "Testament" were meant to be presented to the people together.[45] In Pearse's last play, *The Singer*, the nationalist leader McDara, who bears striking biographical resemblances to Pearse and expresses Pearse's own ideas, is presented as though he were an incarnation of the saviour: "I will take no pike, I will go into battle with bare hands. I will stand up before the Gall as Christ hung naked before men on the tree."[46]

The sanctification of land, nation, frontiers, heroes and forefathers was the outstanding strategy by which nationalists of all kinds, literary, philosophical or military, consciously or unconsciously imagined, narrated, and activated their nations. By now we know a great deal about the nature and meaning of nationalism. We know less about the process of mobilization whereby nationalism becomes a mass movement. I submit that mobilization through the symbols of religion was widely and successfully used by nationalist elites of all kinds. This is my answer to the questions I posed at the outset regarding the source and role of sacred land.

In summing up, I should like briefly to relate these conclusions to the present stage of studies of nationalism. Historically, nationalism began to be studied several decades ago as a body of ideas in the minds of leaders and prophets.[47] This was followed by investigations of the structural conditions for nationalism and the social and economic processes involved, a trend which conveyed an impression of the evolutionary determinism of nationalism, independent of goals or ideas.[48] The present tendency to treat nationalism in terms of invented traditions and imagined communities assigns to nationalism an instrumental role in the service of classes, elites, capitalists and politicians.[49] This new trend is not all that revolutionary; it was anticipated by Elie Kedourie's classic work,[50] in which nationalism appears as an aberration in the feverish minds of German philosophers. The new trend also admits the psychological supports for nationalism, such as the comfort of belonging to an immortal community and the security afforded by fraternity. Above all, it takes us back to the study of the images used by nationalists. In a sense, it also takes us back to the human agents, the conscious activists. It was they, after all, who spoke of reviving or awakening the past, dreaming the future, giving a new direction to history. We move back from structural to agency explanations. The human agent is back in nationalist studies, not in the old pose of prophet or hero, but as an imaginative individual, planning towards goals. The agents are sophisticated, well-versed in history, psychology and social theory, and they redeem the dismal picture of movements without actors, achievements without human drive.[51]

The flaw I find in the new theories, such as those of Gellner, Anderson, Breuilly and Hobsbawm, is that they treat the masses as having no identity and as easily manipulated. What I have tried to show is that inventive imaginations served the cause of nationalism by working within the limits set by existing or remembered realities. Those "manipulating" the masses have to reckon with religious, linguistic or cultural traditions before they can "mould" them. Patrick Pearse's plan to win the indifferent Irish masses over to separatism succeeded because he reckoned realistically with the religious images on which the Catholic nation was educated, and he knew how to play the right religious chords to produce nationalist music. Even the Church, which at first harshly condemned the Easter Rising, came round very soon after the executions, issuing a statement to the effect that nationalism and religion had never been more beautifully merged. A few years later, the new leaders of the Irish revolt, like De Valera, knew that more than the ecstatic outpourings elicited by symbols would be needed to hold the nation together permanently. This prompted De Valera to acquire the blessings of the Church, the natural leader of the people, by means of an agreement on the agenda of nationalism.

Nationalism is a political principle, but the reasons and conditions for its acceptance as a mass movement belong to the study of popular cultures, which are neither imposed nor spontaneous; they feed both on the continuous and on the contingent. Whether we can systematize the popular culture aspect of national movements, whether we can generalize and predict the particular images to which cultural groups will respond, is another matter. Are Protestant masses more susceptible to Promised Land slogans and Catholic masses to martyrology motifs? Are landless Jews and landlocked Muslims more prone to sanctify the physical environment? Can we sort out cultures bent on ethnicity? How do we quantify waves of nationalist intensity? I think that, in the long run, we will find more variety than predictable continuity. All we can say for sure is that, in the course of history, certain strategies have appeared to work, and we can try to explain why.

Notes

I am grateful to Mr. Gal Gerson for invaluable help in assembling the materials for this study.

1. K. Lorenz, "Durch Domestikation verursachte Störungen arteigenen Verhaltens," *Zeitschrift für angewandte Psychologie und Charakterkunde*, LIX (1940).
2. R. Ardrey, *The Territorial Imperative*, London 1966; D. Morris, *The Naked Ape*, London 1967; L.L. Snyder, "Nationalism and Territorial Imperative," *Canadian Review of Studies in Nationalism*, III (1975), no. 1, pp. 1–21.
3. C. Geertz, "Centers, Kings and Charisma: Reflections on the Symbolics of Power," in J. Ben-David (ed.), *Culture and Its Creators*, Chicago 1977, p. 153.
4. A. Van Gennep, *The Rites of Passage*, London 1960.
5. R.D. Sack, *Human Territoriality*, Cambridge 1986, p. 38.
6. H. Ben-Israel, "Nationalism in Historical Perspective," *Journal of International Affairs*, XLV (1991), no. 2, pp. 367–397.
7. B. Anderson, *Imagined Communities*, London 1983; E. Hobsbawm & T. Ranger (eds.), *The Invention of Tradition*, Cambridge 1983; E. Hobsbawm, *Nations and Nationalism since 1780*, New York 1990.
8. G.L. Mosse, *The Nationalization of the Masses*, New York 1975; idem, "National Cemeteries and National Revival: The Cult of Fallen Soldiers in Germany," *Journal of Contemporary History*, XIV (1979), pp. 1–20.
9. K. Inglis, "A Sacred Place: The Making of the Australian War Memorial," *War and Society*, III (1985), pp. 99–126.
10. W. Bloom, *Personal Identity, National Identity and International Relations*, Cambridge 1991.
11. N. Davies, *God's Playground*, I, Oxford 1982, pp. 523–525, 539, 542.
12. *The Encyclopaedia of Religion and Ethics*, VI, Edinburgh 1913, p. 743.
13. J.-J. Rousseau, "Considérations sur le Gouvernement de Pologne," *Oeuvres complètes*, III, Paris 1969, pp. 951–1041.
14. Anderson, *Communities* (above, note 7), pp. 174–175; P. Sorlin, "Words and Images of Nationhood," in R. Tombs (ed.), *Nationhood and Nationalism in France*, London 1991, p. 78.
15. C.C. O'Brien, *God, Land*, Cambridge, Mass., 1988.
16. G. Krumeich, "Joan of Arc between Right and Left," in Tombs, *Nationhood* (above, note 14), pp. 63–73.
17. D. Richet, "Natural Borders," in F. Furet & M. Ozouf (eds.), *A Critical Dictionary of the French Revolution*, Cambridge, Mass., 1989.
18. M. Barrès, *Amori et Dolori Sacrum*, Paris 1921, p. 271; idem, *La Colline Inspirée*, Paris 1922; idem, *Scènes et doctrines du nationalisme*, Paris n.d.
19. Fustel de Coulanges, "L'Alsace est-elle allemande ou française?" *Questions Contemporaines*, Paris 1918. I heard of this correspondence in a lecture by Professor Paul Smith of Southhampton University.
20. *The Encyclopaedia of Religion* (above, note 12), p. 758.
21. D. Mendels, *The Rise and Fall of Jewish Nationalism*, Garden City, N.Y., 1992.
22. O'Brien, *God, Land* (above, note 15), p. 7.
23. L. Tolstoy, *War and Peace*, Book 3, Part 1, Chapter 18.

24. Y. Arieli, *Individualism and Nationalism in American Ideology*, Cambridge, Mass., 1964, p. 254.
25. A. Zakai, *Exile and Kingdom*, Cambridge 1992, p. 59.
26. L. Caillet, "Espaces mythiques et territoire national," *L'Homme*, XXXI (1991), no. 3, pp. 10–33.
27. L.F.R. Lafleche, "The Providential Mission of the French Canadians," in R. Cook (ed.), *French-Canadian Nationalism*, Toronto 1969.
28. H. Ben-Israel, "Irredentism: Nationalism Reexamined," in N. Chazan (ed.), *Irredentism and International Politics*, London 1991.
29. G. Andreopolous, "State and Irredentism: Some Reflections on the Case of Greece," *Historical Journal*, XXIV (1981), pp. 949–959; G. Sabbatucci, "Il problema dell' irredentisimo e le origini del movimento nazionalista in Italia," *Storia Contemporanea*, I (1970), pp. 467–502.
30. G. Mazzini, *Scritti editi e inediti*, LXIV, Imola 1933, pp. 297–298.
31. Mazzini, *Scritti* (above, note 30), LXVI, pp. 407–415.
32. C. Seton-Watson, *Italy from Liberation to Fascism 1870–1925*, London 1967, pp. 349–365.
33. G. D'Annunzio, "Italy or Death," *Vendetta d'Italia*, 10 and 12 September 1919.
34. M.A. Ledeen, *The First Duce*, Baltimore 1977, pp. 3–16.
35. M. Ozouf, *La fête révolutionnaire 1789–1799*, Paris 1976.
36. M. Zonis & D. Brumberg (eds.), *Shi'ism, Resistance and Revolution*, Boulder, Colo., 1987.
37. T. Flanagan, *Louis "David" Riel: Prophet of the New World*, Toronto 1979.
38. Davies, *Playground* (above, note 11), II, pp. 8–9.
39. A. Walicky, *Philosophy and Romantic Nationalism*, Oxford 1982.
40. T. Flanagan, "Nationalism: The Literary Tradition," in T.E. Hachey & L.J. McCaffrey (eds.), *Perspectives on Irish Nationalism*, Lexington 1989.
41. M. Elliot, *Wolfe Tone: Prophet of Irish Independence*, New Haven 1989.
42. R. Dudley Edwards, *Patrick Pearse: The Triumph of Failure*, New York 1978, pp. 257–260.
43. J. Bowman, *De Valera and the Ulster Question 1917–1973*, Oxford 1982, pp. 147–206.
44. My study of the Easter Rising is still unpublished. I refer to it in H. Ben-Israel, "The Role of Religion in Nationalism: Some Comparative Remarks on Irish Nationalism and on Zionism," *Religion, Ideology and Nationalism in Europe and America*, Jerusalem 1986.
45. Edwards, *Pearse* (above, note 42), p. 261.
46. P.H. Pearse, *Collected Works*, Dublin 1917, pp. 1–44.
47. H. Kohn, *Prophets and Peoples*, New York 1946; C. Hayes, *The Historical Evolution of Nationalism*, New York 1931.
48. K. Deutsch, *Nationalism and Social Communications*, New York 1966; E. Gellner, *Nations and Nationalism*, Oxford 1983.
49. J. Breuilly, *Nationalism and the State*, New York 1982; P.R. Brass, *Ethnicity and Nationalism*, New Delhi 1991.
50. E. Kedourie, *Nationalism*, London 1969.
51. A.D. Smith, "The Nation: Invented, Imagined, Reconstructed?" *Millenium*, XX (1991), pp. 353–368.

18

The Role of Charismatic Dreams in the Creation of Sacred Sites in Present-Day Israel

Yoram Bilu

Following the "disenchantment of the world," dreams in modern thought have been relegated to the confines of the individual dreamer's mind.[1] In many traditional contexts, however, the epistemological ground in which the dream is located is not psychological but cosmological: dream contents may be perceived as external messages from divine or other supernatural entities.[2] As such, they are fraught with special significance which spills over to waking reality. Given this traditional conception of the dream as a possible vehicle or medium for communicating with other-worldly beings, it is not surprising that dream experiences in diverse cultural settings inspired the creation and dissemination of new religious ideas, as well as the endorsement, refutation, alteration and restoration of older ones.[3]

The peculiar features of the dream — its accessibility as a universal, spontaneously occurring phenomenon, the dramatic qualities of its visual images, the emotional overtones of its plot, the bizarre scenes and illogical twists that render its contents enigmatic and mysterious, and the strong subjective sense of reality and truth value inherent in its phenomenology[4] — all these have made the dream a prime source of religious inspiration, rejuvenation and empowerment.

On the other hand, the common occurrence and easy availability of dreams might render them suspect when they give rise to pretentious (and at time subversive) religious claims, particularly in the absence of corroborating evidence. Even in cultural settings where dream understanding is religiously based, not *every* dream is taken as a heavenly message. Since they are private events, dreams can easily be fabricated. Even if this possibility is dismissed, there is a wide, cross-cultural agreement that dreams are liable to hopeless distortions in the course of the giant leap from fuzzy and inconsistent visual images, rapidly dissipating from memory, to a coherent verbal sequence, a communicable narrative. Given these concerns, the study of visitational dreams must focus on the acceptability of the *dream-as-reported* no less than on the personal, transformative effects of the *dream-as-experienced*, or, more accurately, the *dream-as-remembered*. Where dreams spur the erection of new sacred sites, as in the case under discussion, we deal with a social phenomenon, realizable only when the dream message strikes a chord in the hearts of a following. Thus, *the social context in which the dream is related to others* (dream-telling) may be as important as the dream itself.[5]

In this paper I examine the personal and social effects of visitational dreams[6] in the context of the folk-veneration of sainted figures (*tsaddikim*). Before embarking on the central role of dreams in erecting and maintaining new sites devoted to *tsaddikim*, the ethnocultural framework within which the dreams are experienced and circulated should be presented in brief.

In recent years Israel has witnessed an impressive revival of hagiolatric traditions, particularly among immigrants from Morocco and their descendants.[7] Veneration of saints, a hallmark of Moroccan Islam, was also a major ingredient of Jewish collective identity in Morocco.[8] The saints were depicted as charismatic, pious sages who possessed a special spiritual force, akin to the Muslim *baraka*.[9] This force did not fade away after the saints had died. In most cases, in fact, it was revealed only then, transforming the tombs into pilgrimage centres and healing shrines.

The social fabric of the Moroccan Jews, including their hagiolatric practices, was ruptured following their immigration to Israel in the 1950s and 1960s. The tombs of the saints had been left behind, and this painful disengagement, together with other problems of absorption, eroded the public, collective manifestations of saint veneration. The *hillulot* (festive commemorations of the deaths of saintly persons), in particular, underwent a process of diminution and decentralization.[10] From mass pilgrimages to the sanctuaries of departed saints, they were reduced to domestic affairs, modestly celebrated at home or in the local synagogue. Once the immigrants' "travails of homecoming" had attenuated, however, hagiolatric practices were revived in force. The renaissance of Jewish Maghrebi hagiolatry in the new country was made possible by the availability and flexible employment, in four principal ways, of various compensatory substitutes for the deserted tombs.[11]

Most accessible among these alternatives were the tombs of local *tsaddikim*, mainly from the talmudic era, cherished as pilgrimage sites as early as the Middle Ages. The "Maghrebization" of these pilgrimages has been increasing continuously in recent years, particularly with regard to the popular *hillulot* of Rabbi Shim'on Bar-Yoḥai and Rabbi Meir Ba'al ha-Ness in northern Israel, which draw up to 200,000 celebrants. In addition, new pilgrimage centres have been established around the tombs of contemporary rabbis who were attributed saintly qualities during their lifetimes, or, more often, posthumously. The most celebrated of these is Rabbi Israel Abu-Ḥatseira ("Baba Sali"), a pious sage and worthy descendant of the most respected family in southern Morocco, who passed away in 1984. In the years that have elapsed since then, his sanctuary in Netivot has become a national pilgrimage centre, second only to that of Rabbi Shim'on Bar-Yoḥai in popularity.[12]

The annexation of old-time pilgrimage sites and the creation of new saints have both contributed to the preservation of hagiolatric practices under changing circumstances. Yet the function of these activities was compensatory rather than restorative, as the saints of Morocco have remained remote and practically inaccessible since the immigrants' arrival in Israel. To preserve the content rather than merely the form of Jewish Moroccan hagiolatry, a third, more straightforward and daring accommodation was required, entailing the symbolic transfer of saints from Morocco to Israel and their reinstallation in the new country. Unlike the other alternatives, this one was based on the spontaneous initiative of individuals who erected sanctuaries for Jewish Moroccan saints following inspirational dream encounters with them. A fourth pattern, very similar to the previous one, involves the renewal of a local hagiolatric tradition via dreams.[13] These dream-initiated sacred sites are the focus of the pages that follow.

It should be noted that visitational dreams were a well-established cultural genre in Morocco.[14] Dreams constituted the major means by which tombs of heretofore unknown saints were discovered, as well as an important vehicle for maintaining and solidifying the devotees' enduring linkage to their patron saints.[15] The manifestations of this dream genre among Moroccan Jews in Israel have not been limited to the third and fourth avenues for the initiation of sacred sites. Thus, in a study conducted at the old-time pilgrimage site at Meron,[16] the sanctuary of Rabbi Shim'on Bar-Yoḥai, it was found that a considerable number of pilgrims had been summoned to the *hillula* by a dream in which the *tsaddik* authoritatively called for their participation. The prevalence of this pattern, in which the pilgrim was brought to the site by a dream, highlights visitational dreams as conservative mechanisms functioning to preserve hagiolatric practices. In many other cases it was the pilgrimage that brought the pilgrim to his dream. These dreams, occurring in the precincts of the saint, appear as a contemporary version of the age-old tradition of "temple sleep" or "incubation."[17] They were actively sought by the pilgrims and had a powerful invigorating effect on the dreamers.[18]

I have chosen to focus on the symbolic transfer of saints because only in this case were dreams *critically* important to the initiation and maintenance of the sacred site. The decision to build the sanctuary was precipitated by a persistent dream message from a charismatic figure. No less important, moreover, was the role of dreams in shaping the collective response to the individual initiative. Further on, I shall highlight this dream-based dialogue between the initiator and the community by focusing on "The Gate of Paradise," one of the new sacred sites thus erected, which involves the renewal of a local tradition rather than the reinstallation of a Moroccan Jewish saint. Before that, however, I wish to touch on the role of dreams in building "The House of Rabbi David u-Moshe."

The first Israeli dream-based site was established in 1973, when Avraham, a forty-year-old afforestation worker from Safed, dedicated a small room in his modest apartment to the famous Moroccan Jewish saint, Rabbi David u-Moshe, following a dream series in which the saint appeared to him and indicated his wish to reside with him.[19] Avraham disseminated the written reports of his dreams throughout the Moroccan Jewish communities in Israel and obtained enthusiastic responses. Since then, the "House of Rabbi David u-Moshe" has become a popular pilgrimage site, strongly represented on the itineraries of visitors to the tombs of *tsaddikim* in northern Israel. On the day of the saint's *hillula*, the shrine encased in the plebeian apartment becomes the focus of a mass celebration in which many thousands of visitors from all over the country take part. The new shrine in Safed seems to have served as a source of inspiration and model for the actions of most of the other local "agents" of saints, including the founder of "The Gate of Paradise." Given this impact, it is worth reproducing Avraham's first "announcement to the public," the promulgated report of his first oneiric encounters with Rabbi David u-Moshe. This announcement was most instrumental in placing "The House of Rabbi David u-Moshe" on the holy map of Jewish hagiolatry. The popularity of the shrine has not abated in the more than twenty years that have elapsed since its erection, and it is still the most successful site among the new, dream-based shrines in Israel.

Announcement to the Public:

> I, Avraham Ben Ḥayim, who live in Canaan, Building 172, in the Holy City of Safed, have been privileged by the Lord to see wonders. And as I was ordered, I make known to you a message from our master the *tsaddik*, Rabbi David u-Moshe, may the memory of the *tsaddik* be for a blessing, who has revealed himself to me many times.
>
> In my first dream, I looked, and lo! There stood before me a man dressed in white, and the radiance of his face was like an angel's. He approached me, seized my hand, and led me to high hills. And among their huge boulders, I saw a white stretch of land. When we came to this clearing, he sat on the ground and said to me: "See, only ten people celebrate and mark my *hillula* day. And I ask you: Why have those who left Morocco forsaken me and deserted me? Where are all the thousands — my followers and believers?" I replied to him: "Do you really want them to return to Morocco from Israel to perform the *hillula*?" The man took me again by the hand, turned me around, and asked: "What place is this?" I answered him: "This is my house." The *tsaddik* continued: "In this place I want you to observe my *hillula* day each year." I asked him: "What does my lord want?" And he answered me: "I am the man who

revealed himself to those who loved me in Morocco. I am Rabbi David u-Moshe!!! I am he, the man who makes supplications and prays daily before God to preserve the soldiers of Israel, on the borders of the land! If so, why have they deserted me, those who left Morocco? Now I am here in the Holy Land, and my request is that they renew the commemoration of my *hillula*."

Two days later he again revealed himself to me in a dream, while I was tossing and turning in my bed between sleep and wakefulness. He woke me up and said to me: "My son, you made a mistake when you told people you saw me in a dream. You should have said to them that you saw me eye to eye. But never mind, I forgive you for this. And now, hear my words: I left Morocco and came here because this place is holy, and I chose you to be my servant in this holy work. And now you will do this:

(1) Establish a place for yourself where candles will be burnt in my memory, and whoever comes to pray and to make supplication for his soul will light a candle for me!
(2) Beside the place of the candles, set a collection box, and each person will make his donation in accordance with his desire and his means!
(3) Whoever approaches the place of the candles will do so with awe and love, and with his whole heart!
(4) He who enters this place must be clean in body and deed!
(5) It is forbidden to deal in or sell these candles or these memorial cups. Whoever wishes to do so will light a candle, on condition that he be clean, as stated above!
(6) The place will be open to all, night and day!
(7) On the feast of my *hillula*, there will be no distinction between great and small or between rich and poor, but all will be equal!
(8) My *hillula* will be held on the eve of the new moon of Heshvan. If the new moon of Heshvan falls on a Friday, the *hillula* will take place on the preceding Thursday!
(9) Warn your wife and the members of your household not to allow entry to a man or a woman who is unclean!
(10) Use the contributions that accumulate in the collection box to enlarge the place, so that it will be able to contain the

> thousands of people who will come here to celebrate and to pray!"
>
> After three days, the *tsaddik* again revealed himself to me at night in a dream, and this time he was accompanied by two men. He turned to me and asked: "Do you recognize these men?" I answered: "One I saw with you in the second dream, and the second one I recognize from a different dream." The *tsaddik* continued: "Do you know who they are?" I answered him: "The first is Elijah the Prophet, remembered for the good, and the second is Rabbi Ya'akov Abu-Ḥatseira, may the memory of the *tsaddik* be for a blessing." The *tsaddik* nodded to signal agreement, and he concluded his words with the admonition that I must be strict about admitting to this place only people who are clean in body and soul.
>
> As the *tsaddik* has requested, we shall hold the *hillula*, God willing, on the night of the new moon of Heshvan, this year and every year, at my home, as mentioned above.
>
> May the Lord help us for the sake of His honour and His great name.
>
> Come one and all, and may God's blessing be with us and with you!!!

The apparition of Rabbi David u-Moshe marked a dramatic transformation in Avraham's life. From then on, the saint's oneiric messages became his sole guide for action. One of the first of these messages bade him write down his dreams and distribute them among all the Moroccan synagogues in the country. This was the first step towards transforming Avraham's private vision into a public affair. The ornate rendering of the announcement, which includes Avraham's first initiation dreams, stands in sharp contrast with his plain oral recounting of the dreams. Indeed, Avraham was helped by a local rabbi in formulating the announcement, but he insisted that the written report was a true account of the saint's messages.

In the first dream, the *tsaddik*'s transfer from Morocco to Israel and his selection of Avraham's house as his new abode are portrayed straightforwardly. The saint appears as the active initiator of his own move to Safed, while the dreamer is depicted as a passive object on whom the *tsaddik*'s grace is suddenly imposed.

The saint's complaint in the first encounter — "Why have they deserted me, those who left Morocco?" — is extremely important for understanding the uncritical acceptance of the dreams. I believe that Avraham's covert sense of guilt, indicated by the deserted saint's reproach, is associated with various traumatic events in his personal history which exceed the scope of our present discussion. However, this sense of guilt resonates with the more general "Moroccan experience" in Israel, reflecting the collective frame of mind of many other ex-devotees who were dissociated from their once-cherished saints upon immigrating to Israel. Unlike his negligent followers, the saint appears attuned to the prevailing concerns of present-day Israel and prays for the safety of the soldiers on the borders.

In the second dream reported in the announcement, the saint paradoxically denies the oneiric nature of his first appearance, thus perhaps enhancing its credibility. It includes ten precepts, echoing the number of the ten commandments, which establish the rules of conduct at the new site. While most of these requirements reflect the usual decorum expected at holy sites, they also convey Avraham's vision and hope regarding the prospects of the place as a major pilgrimage centre.

In the third dream, the saint is accompanied by Elijah the Prophet and Rabbi Ya'akov Abu-Ḥatseira, two eminent figures whose appearance gives greater credence to the messages imparted in the former dreams. Although the "House of Rabbi David u-Moshe" is dedicated to the saint whose name it bears, the project is supported by other saints as well. Again, the vehicles by which these saints express their commitment to the new site are visitational dreams.[20]

Seven years after the erection of the new Safed shrine, a Moroccan-born inhabitant of Beit Shean called Yaish had a series of dreams in which Elijah the Prophet informed him that the entrance to Paradise was located in his back yard. This repeated message inspired Yaish to build a small shrine in his yard and to designate Elijah as its patron saint. "The Gate of Paradise," more pretentious but clearly less popular than the Safed shrine, has not extended its fame much beyond the boundaries of Beit Shean (a small town in the Jordan Valley), remaining a local shrine of minor importance. Let us consider this case in more detail, starting with Yaish's promulgated version of his dream-based revelation.

Announcement to the Public:

I, Yaish Oḥana who live in Beit Shean, Neighborhood D 210/2, have been privileged by the Lord to see wonders. In my first dream, a *tsaddik* appeared to me and told me to dig at the back of the yard of my house. I started digging, and suddenly a gate was uncovered. I entered the gate, and splendid things were revealed to my eyes. I saw a pool with fresh water and a lot of plants around it. I kept on walking, and I saw a wonderful garden full of all things good, and rabbis were walking around in it and enjoying the brightness of the place. One of the rabbis turned to me and said that I must keep this place because it is holy. He also told me to inform anyone who would like to enter the place that he must first purify himself.

After one week in which I did not concern myself with the dream — though the same dream recurred every day — I was again disturbed in the second week. I dreamed that I was in my yard, standing between two cypress trees, and I heard a voice calling to me with these words: "Listen, listen, listen." Three times the voice was heard. As I stood there trembling, the voice continued to call me, telling me that the place where I stood was holy, and I must preserve its holiness.

Again in the third week — this was in the month of *Ellul* — I went out on the Sabbath to pray in the synagogue. After I had prayed and returned home, I performed the *kiddush* (the ritual of sanctifying the Sabbath) and sat down to eat. Suddenly a gate was disclosed to me in the same place, with a light burning at the entrance. I stood up and looked at the place for five minutes. Again I heard the same voice calling me with the same words: "Listen, listen, listen." This time it was a reality, not a dream. I was told to build an iron gate and to clean the place, and — once I had finished — to set it in order. I was told to inform all the synagogues and the public that whoever would like to come to the place must cut his fingernails and purify himself, and make repentance.

Afterwards my wife dreamed that I came to her and told her that we must prepare a *se'uda* (festive meal) and call it after Elijah the Prophet.

And so I have done as I have been told.

That the opening passage of Yaish's written revelation is identical with the introduction to Avraham's first announcement indicates the importance of "the House of Rabbi David u-Moshe," the first and most successful of all the new sites, as a source of inspiration for the Beit Shean initiator. As in the case of Avraham, an intricate web of personal associations, too complicated to be elaborated here, connects Yaish with the site he erected. It should be noted, however, that a well-known tradition, first mentioned in the Babylonian Talmud,[21] traces the Garden of Eden in its earthly form to Beit Shean. In articulating his personal experiences or "personal myth" through the idiom of Paradise, Yaish strikes a collective chord, reviving a known myth specifically linked to his home town.

The events depicted in the announcement span three weeks in the month of Ellul during which Yaish gradually and reluctantly comes to recognize that the gate of Paradise is entombed in his back yard. His persistent disregard of the recurring nightly messages and his initial ignorance regarding the guiding saint and the unearthed site allude to the dreamer's basic innocence — a personal stance which seems to enhance one's candour and credibility. Indeed, this ignorance and innocence recur so frequently in visitational dreams as to represent a culturally patterned rhetorical device rather than a personal attribute.[22] The identity of the site is implied in the allusions to "a wonderful garden" and to "keeping" the place (cf. Gen. 2:16).

Unlike Avraham's first announcement, in which the paramount tone was passive, the tone of Yaish's announcement is double-edged. On the one hand, he presents himself as a receptacle for external messages from authoritative beings and voices. On the other hand, however, the narrative is fraught with active imagery — "I started digging ... I entered ... I kept on walking" — which bespeaks the personal and spontaneous nature of the revelation and anticipates the industrious phase of site-building. Following the first dream, Yaish is the recipient of vocal messages which repeatedly emphasize the holiness of the site, leading up to its explicit identification. These messages seem to be informed by prototypical biblical revelations, from Jacob's dream at Bethel to Moses's encounter with God at the burning bush. The association with the latter episode, based on the phonetic similarity between the words *tishma, tishma, tishma* ("listen, listen, listen") and *Moshe, Moshe* ("Moses, Moses"), may at first appear tenuous, but then the near-identical messages that ensue render it convincing: "the voice ... telling me that the place where I stood was holy" certainly echoes the voice heard by Moses, telling him that "the place where you stand is holy ground" (Ex. 3:5).

The revelatory sequence reaches its apex at the end of the third week, when the identity of the place is conveyed directly to Yaish. The fact that this peak experience takes place in wakeful reality endows it with extra validity. The timing of the revelation (a Sabbath eve in Ellul, the month of penitence that leads up to the High Holidays) and the preceding activities (evening prayer in the synagogue, the ritual of *kiddush*, the Sabbath meal) converge to produce the apposite framework for the revelation — an intersection of sacred space, sacred time and appropriate ritual activity.

As in the case of Avraham's announcement, the report ends with specific injunctions, which Yaish has pursued meticulously. The festive meal dream which seals the revelatory sequence anticipates the transition to the collective, to which I shall turn presently. The dreamer is Ḥana, Yaish's wife, but Yaish himself enjoys a privileged status here as a dream character, the emissary of the saints, who transmits vital information regarding the patron saint of the site. This putatively marginal dream is highly important, since it situates the new site within the cultural bounds of the folk-veneration of saints.

As "charismatic significants,"[23] the visitational dreams of Avraham, Yaish and other saint agents have constituted unfailing sources of inspiration and empowerment for them. However, since these personal experiences were translated into tangible activities in the public sphere — the building of new shrines and the recruitment of a following — the critical aspect in the phenomenon under discussion is the impact of the announcements on the Moroccan Jewish community in Israel. That the announcements were well received — in the case of Avraham, all over the country; in that of Yaish, within the bounds of Beit Shean — has to do with the aforementioned interweaving of private fantasy with public symbols.[24] Even though the initiatory dreams were moulded in part by the dreamers' personal histories, they were not idiosyncratically construed. Rather, they were based on a "cultural grammar" that provided the dreamers and their communities with an idiomatic common ground.[25] In this sense, Avraham, Yaish and their colleagues appear as cultural brokers who provided ex-members in the cult of the saints with new foci for cult activities, to which past hagiolatric sentiments, heretofore inchoate and amorphous, could be rechanneled. Through their projects, then, the painful disengagement from the saints could be rectified and assuaged.[26]

Judging from autobiographical accounts related elsewhere by Avraham and Yaish, their lives were accompanied by visitational dreams long before the onset of the revelations presented here. In the case of Avraham, a reconstruction of his "oneiric biography" is revealing in terms of the impressive acceptance of his project. The first saint to frequent his dreams was a family *tsaddik*, Avraham's maternal grandfather, Rabbi Shlomo Timsut, who passed away when Avraham was a child.[27] As soon as Avraham moved to Israel, however, Rabbi Shlomo, a Moroccan saint, ceased to appear in his grandson's dreams, transferring him in his last apparition to the custody of Rabbi Shim'on Bar-Yoḥai, a potent saint residing in the vicinity of Safed:

> On that night I saw the *tsaddik*, Rabbi Shlomo, in a dream. He said to me: "Listen — look who is standing next to you." I turned my face and saw Rabbi Shim'on Bar-Yoḥai. He [Rabbi Shlomo] said to me: "Here he is, standing next to you. If you need something, just come to him. He will give you." Rabbi Shim'on took a loaf of bread, handed it to me, and said: "Go, make your Sabbath; from now on you'll lack for nothing."

Later on, Avraham became particularly attached to another Moroccan Jewish saint, Rabbi Ya'akov Abu-Ḥatseira. Following a dispute in the neighborhood synagogue which made it impossible to conduct the festive meal in honour of the *tsaddik*, Avraham decided to conduct the meal in his home, using his own modest means. The saint rewarded him with a very reassuring message in the following dream:

> I saw myself walking on a plateau (full) of sand, and it was terribly hot there. Then I was running together with all those people [of the synagogue]. I was so thirsty that I almost fainted. I began to tremble all over my body. Suddenly I saw a mountain on which a rabbi was seated, holding a big book in his hand.

> All the grass around him was made of big snakes. He looked around and said: "Woe to the one who enters this place; I'll send the snakes against him!" I stood up, and he said: "No, you can come, you needn't be afraid; come on, hold this stick." All the snakes lowered their heads, and I entered. He filled a glass of water for me, and I drank it. He said: "Do you know who I am?" I said: "No." [He said:] "I am Rabbi Ya'akov Abu-Ḥatseira." Then he said: "You must proceed [on your way]. You'll lack for nothing."

These dreams refute the idea that the apparition of Rabbi David u-Moshe was a sudden, unexpected act of revelation. It appears, rather, as the product of a persistent process of active search in which a veteran member of the cult of the saints gradually shifts allegiances until he finds the "appropriate" patron saint. Thus, Rabbi Shlomo, a natural object of veneration for Avraham, is rightly his own, but his reputation among the Moroccan émigrés is meagre. Rabbi Shim'on is the most renowned saint in Israel, a core symbol of mysticism and piety, but his tradition is well established and cannot be appropriated by any single devotee, dutiful and resourceful as he may be. This also holds true of Rabbi Ya'akov, whose living descendants' claim to be his legitimate heirs cannot easily be challenged.[28] Rabbi David u-Moshe, a *tsaddik* whom Avraham claims not to have known in Morocco, seems to have been a cultural figure ready to be enshrined. Well known and highly venerated by many Jews from southern Morocco, the hagiolatric practices related to him lacked focus and coherence once his sanctuary had been left behind. In addition, as a legendary or ahistorical *tsaddik*, Rabbi David u-Moshe did not have descendants vying for his grace.

The fact that Avraham, Yaish and other saint agents succeeded in striking a collective chord in their projects is most vividly reflected in the ongoing dialogue, based on dreams, between the initiator and the community. In the cases discussed above, the new sites were validated consensually through these dream dialogues, which gave rise to what might be designated a "community of dreamers" around the site.[29] The psychological and socio-cultural functions of the new shrines for the dreamers become manifest in these dreams and account for their uncritical acceptance.

I have collected several hundred such dream reports in various settings. For the sake of brevity, I limit myself here to the analysis of two examples from the Beit Shean community of dreamers. The first dreamer, Meir, a neighbor of Yaish, is deeply involved in the development of "the Gate of Paradise."

> I am walking near Kitan Junction, on the old road to Beit Shean. There was some sort of a hut, and I saw someone there, looking like a religious kibbutz member, with a *kova tembel* [a typically Israeli hat, one of the country's national symbols in the 1940s and 1950s] on his head. He was sitting there, and I saw myself as if I were going to work [in the Kitan textile factory]. He asked me: "Shalom, Meir, how are you?" and I replied: "Shalom, what are you doing here?" And he pointed at this [Yaish's] house, towards the valley, and he indicated to me that they were working there with compressors, digging some sort of a stream. I asked him why, and he said to me: "Look, the stream as it is now, the rain always blocks it." The passage they are digging is in the direction of this [Yaish's] house. Then I asked him: "What happened?" And he said: "Look, it always overflows here, and disrupts the traffic. So we would like to dig a stream here." And he showed me how they were working.
>
> Suddenly I met another person, and he also asked how I was and so on. And it seemed to me that the place was full of trees; there were definitely trees there, and people were coming out, old-timers, like Yemenites. And a young man was standing there, like I told you before, a kibbutz member with a *kova tembel*. And I asked him: "Who are these people?" And he replied: "This is a very old *moshav* [a semi-cooperative village], and in the morning everyone is going to work." And I saw them, one with a basket, another with a bicycle. And I said: "Can I see this?" And he said yes. I entered that place, and instead of some sort of a *moshav*, I saw something like his [Yaish's] house.
>
> And I saw something like a hospital, a Sick Fund clinic, girls with white cloaks and all that. And I saw a man sitting there with three bottles of wine near him, and inside [the bottles] were myrtle sprigs. I asked him: "Tell me, are these sprigs of myrtle? ... I would like to ask a question." And this is what I asked him: "Why does not every plant thrive?" He answered me: "Look, that is a secret that I can't disclose." And I saw the

> people, like sick people, sitting there, in some sort of a Sick Fund clinic. And he told them to take some sort of arak from the bottles. As if they had thrown away ... as if they had been taking some pills or something, and now they were not taking those pills any more. And he gave them arak to drink; this was their medicine. And I asked them: "Well, how do you feel?" And they said: "All the pain that we have — with the stuff he is giving us, it's all right, it passes away."
>
> And I went on, and I saw a third man, and I asked him: "What are you planting here?" And he said: "Look, mister: Here, near the entrance to Beit Shean, we already planted something one year ago, and the inhabitants spoiled what we had planted." Then I said: "Nobody is to blame. You did not inform us, neither by letters nor through the Ministry of Religious affairs or the local municipality." Then he said: "You'll receive a letter, and then you'll know." That is what he said to me.

This dream, experienced immediately after Yaish presented his revelations in the local synagogue, elucidates the motivational basis of Meir's commitment to the site. Unlike Yaish's dreams, which occurred in a contextual vacuum, Meir's dream is embedded with places and characters from the reality of Beit Shean and its environs: Kitan Junction (a textile plant where Meir worked together with many other Beit Shean residents), a religious kibbutz member, a veteran *moshav* of Yemenite Jews, a Sick Fund clinic, and Yaish's home, where the dreamer is heading. The diversion of the stream in the direction of Yaish's home alludes to the identity of the site, since a river comes out of Eden to water the garden (Gen. 2:10). The flow of water will ensure the growth of the plant, which stands for the site. The road construction that will allow fluid, undisturbed locomotion in the direction of the site represents the dreamer's wish to see the popularity of the site grow, and perhaps also to unearth the gate (of Paradise) — the "passage" in the dream.

The sequence of characters and places in the dream indicates that, for Meir, the road to the Garden of Eden, which ends in a development town of Moroccan Jews, starts at a religious (and Ashkenazi) kibbutz and goes on through a Yemenite *moshav*. This is a highly suggestive indicator of Meir's integrative vision, entirely absent from Yaish's announcement. Indeed, in Meir's subsequent dreams the shrine is presented as a national, all-Israeli site that attracts a multitude of visitors, including President Navon, Prime Minister Begin, and Beit Shean's local hero, Minister David Levy (Meir had this dream in late 1979).

The transition in the dream from Yaish's house to the Sick Fund clinic is based on a functional similarity, as the two institutions constitute rival healing agencies. Moreover, the neighbourhood Sick Fund clinic is in fact adjacent to the shrine in Yaish's yard. In the dream, the transition not only highlights the site as a therapeutic resource, but also emphasizes the superiority of the traditional agency over the modern clinic: the arak takes the place of the modern medication as the preferred mode of healing.

The generally optimistic mood of the dream is marred by apprehension and uncertainty, epitomized by the question, "Why does not every plant thrive?" The answer is given by the third person, who appears at the end of the dream. The plant — the site — was planted a whole year ago near the entrance to the town (indeed, Yaish's house is located near the western entrance to Beit Shean), but "the inhabitants spoiled what we had planted." The dreamer's yearning for a reassuring sign regarding the success of the plant is congruent with his relentless attempts in daily reality to validate the revelation by soliciting support from celebrated rabbis and even by excavating the site. The fact that the Ministry of Religious Affairs and the local municipality have not been notified about the site may allude to their reluctance to acknowledge formally the holiness of the place without corroborating evidence. The letter promised at the end of the dream hints at the announcement to the public circulated by Yaish in Beit Shean. It might well be that Meir's dream, which he reported to Yaish, paved the way to the promulgation of the announcement.

Meir's vision situates Yaish's revelatory experiences in the very centre of the communal, collective realm, endowing them with meaning derived from the local Beit Shean setting. The dream represents the immense importance that Meir ascribes to the site as a place for rejuvenation and healing, as well as his strong ambitions to play a role in its development. Later on, Meir deepened his linkage with the site by means of an intensive dream dialogue, too lengthy to present here, with Yaish.

The second dream report was related by Rachel, a young woman who was an active participant in the Beit Shean community of dreamers.

> I dreamt that I went to Yaish's house, and there was a gate there. I knocked on the door, and a little old man wearing a hat came out. I asked him: "Where is Yaish?" He said to me: "Yaish isn't here; I've taken his place. I keep the place. What do you want? He isn't home." I say: "I came ... (because I knew that in fact, in reality, I didn't feel well, I always had problems with my pregnancies), come, give me a little bit of arak from this place." Then he asked me: "Have you bathed [in the ritual bath]?" I knew in the dream that I had to go the bath only the next day. I said: "No, I have to go only tomorrow." He said: "No, so I won't [let you in]." I said to him: "But Yaish, whenever I ask him, always says to me that you must be clean; you don't have to bathe." He said: "No!" This is how he motioned to me [gesturing]: "You won't come in. And Yaish, from this day on, should know that no woman is allowed in here without having bathed." I said all right. He didn't let me in. He was standing with me at the gate, all in the dream, standing and talking with me like that. He said to me: "Wait here, I will go and fetch you." He brought me a glass of arak and an orange, and I went home.
>
> And my mother — I lost her when I was fourteen years old — I came home, and my mother said to me: "Where did you go? I mean, where have you been all these years? I have been waiting for you for so long." I told her: "Mother, we have a place, what shall I tell you, everything [every wish] in this house is granted."
>
> I started to explain. She said: "My soul, come take me there." I took her there, to Yaish, I saw her holding a baby in her arms, giving it milk.

For Rachel, the new shrine offers a cure for all ills, and she frequents it whenever she or any member of her family faces a problem. She appears in her dreams as an intimate associate of Yaish's family, a privileged position which grants her an edge over the other supplicants. This privileged position is translated in the dreams into scenes of oral nurturance. While an exchange of food products between the saint and the dreamer is a common theme in visitational dreams,[30] in the case of Rachel it is more salient than usual and seems to represent a compensation for various deprivations, the most painful of which was the loss of her mother when she was fourteen.

The dream related above is divided into two separate though thematically related scenes. Rachel visits the site with a specific life problem (pregnancy complications). She meets with the "guardian of the site" — who represents the patron saint of the place, Elijah the Prophet. His refusal to give her free access because she has not immersed herself in the ritual bath is probably related to guilt feelings that she harboured during that period in her life regarding religious observance. Rachel, who was not religious before her marriage, had gradually become more observant, and the dream may have reflected (and reinforced) this trend. The bitter pill of being forbidden to enter is sweetened to some degree by Rachel's elevation to the role of an intermediary between the saint and Yaish. Moreover, she nevertheless obtains something from the holy place — arak and an orange — which signify that her wish will be granted and the pregnancy will end well.

In the second part of the dream, Rachel meets her long-deceased mother. The mother's question — "Where did you go? I mean, where have you been all these years? I have been waiting for you for so long" — appears as a sheer projection of the dreamer's sense of loss, following the premature death of her mother. The dynamic association between the reunification with the lost mother and "the Gate of Paradise" finds expression in the visit to the site that the two make together. The concluding scene reflects a manifest oral wish. Whether the baby represents the dreamer returning to her mother's lap, thus compensating for her painful loss, or the baby to whom Rachel is going to give birth, it seems evident that for Rachel the site constitutes a "mother surrogate" that guides and protects her. As she says: "We have a place, what shall I tell you, everything [every wish] in this house is granted."

Note that the two scenes in the dream are parallel. In both, the dreamer is confronted with a parental figure: the saint, clearly a father figure, and the mother. Both are depicted in gratifying, nurturing roles, and the resources they provide, in both cases, are directed towards the well-being of the baby, before or after birth.

The functional importance of the site for the dreamers stems from its interweaving of two cardinal religious symbols — saints and Paradise — which constitute idiomatic ground for articulating personal experiences related to unrealized wishes, disturbing problems, and painful losses or deprivations. Yaish's yearning to go back to the lost paradise of his childhood and to find himself a more satisfying, spiritual path in life, Meir's sense of calling and concern for his community, Rachel's wish to be reunited with her long-deceased mother — all these desiderata find expression in the dreams. The "therapeutic" effects of the dreams are not exhausted on the expressive-cathartic level, however. By reorganizing their inchoate experiences on the symbolic-collective level of saints and Paradise, Yaish is able to espouse a more spiritual lifestyle, and Rachel finds tangible compensation for the painful loss of her mother.

In the space where the personal concerns of each dreamer meet the cultural traditions in which beliefs in saints and Paradise are grounded, the sacred site encapsulates a set of experiences shared by all members of the community. It is not accidental that the new shrines have emerged in development towns, which are geographically and economically peripheral, or that in five of the new sites, including Yaish's and Avraham's, the event that precipitated the apparition of the saint was a nearly executed plan to move to another, more central and attractive town. In all of these cases, the appearance of the saint eventually cancelled the decision to leave and bound the initiators inextricably to their homes. Like other inhabitants of the development towns, mainly of Moroccan extraction, Yaish, Avraham, and other saint agents have walked the arduous way from the harsh years of the 1950s and 1960s to the more prosperous years of the 1970s and 1980s. Along this road, they slowly acquired a genuine sense of belonging and local identity. In this respect, the dream-based sites have symbolized and facilitated the process whereby many residents of development towns, once passive victims of arbitrary settlement policies, have become rooted in their communities and developed local patriotic sentiments.[31]

Indeed, many visitational dreams collected around the site in Beit Shean convey the idea that the shrine endows the town with holiness, thus transforming a peripheral and neglected place into a beautiful and attractive community. In one of Yaish's charismatic dreams, this transformation is represented as an alchemic process that turns black into gold:

I woke up in my dream and started digging in the place, with my bare hands, and black water started coming out. I asked in my dream: "What is this black water?" And the water was running to the place where we pray, and then it came back in the form of gold. So I said, "what is this, black water that turns to gold? This can't be." Then I entered through the gate. Inside it was sheer delight, a spring of fresh water, truly the Garden of Eden (Paradise).

Notes

1. S. Freud, *The Interpretation of Dreams*, New York 1955; C.G. Jung, *Man and His Symbols*, London 1964.
2. C.W. O'Nell, *Dreams, Culture, and the Individual*, Novato, Calif., 1976.
3. G.E. von Grunebaum & R. Caillois (eds.), *The Dream and Human Societies*, Berkeley, Calif., 1966.
4. C.S. Hall, *The Meaning of Dreams*, New York 1959.
5. G. Herdt, "Selfhood and Discourse in Sambia Dream Sharing," in B. Tedlock, *Dreaming: Anthropological and Psychological Interpretations*, Cambridge 1987, pp. 55–85.; K.T. Kernan & J.L. Turner, *It's Just a Dream: The Use of Dreams by the Mentally Retarded*, Los Angeles 1986.
6. V. Crapanzano, "Saints, Jnun, and Dreams: An Essay in Moroccan Ethnopsychiatry," *Psychiatry*, XXXVIII (1975), pp. 145–159; B. Kilborne, "Moroccan Dream Interpretation and Culturally Constituted Defense Mechanisms," *Ethos*, IX (1981), pp. 294–312; A.F.C. Wallace, "Dreams and the Wishes of the Soul," *American Anthropology*, LX (1958), pp. 234–248.
7. Y. Bilu, "Personal Motivation and Social Meaning in the Revival of Hagiolatric Traditions among Moroccan Jews in Israel," in Z. Sobel & B. Beit-Hallahmi (eds.), *Tradition, Innovation, Conflict*, Albany, N.Y., 1991; E. Ben-Ari & Y. Bilu, "Saint Sanctuaries in Israeli Development Towns: On a Mechanism of Social Transformation," *Urban Anthropology*, XVI (1987), pp. 243–272; A. Weingrod, *The Saint of Beersheba*, Albany, N.Y., 1989.
8. See I. Ben-Ami, *Saint Veneration among Moroccan Jews* (in Hebrew), Jerusalem 1984.
9. P. Rabinow, *Symbolic Domination*, Chicago 1975; E. Westermarck, *Ritual and Belief in Morocco*, London 1926, pp. 35–261.
10. I. Ben-Ami, "The Folk-Veneration of Saints among Moroccan Jews: Tradition, Continuity and Change," in S. Morag, I. Ben-Ami & N. Stillman (eds.), *Studies in Judaism and Islam*, Jerusalem 1981, pp. 283–345.
11. See Y. Bilu, "Jewish Moroccan Saint Impresarios in Israel: A Stage-Developmental Perspective," *The Psychoanalytic Study of the Child*, XVI (1990).
12. Y. Bilu & E. Ben-Ari, "The Making of Modern Saints: Manufactured Charisma and the Abu-Ḥatseiras of Israel," *American Ethnologist*, XIX (1992), pp. 29–44.
13. See Bilu, "Saint Impresarios," (above, note 11).
14. V. Crapanzano, "Saints, Jnun, and Dreams"; B. Kilborne, "Moroccan Dream Interpretation" (both above, note 6).

15. See I. Ben-Ami, *Saint Veneration*, (above, note 8).
16. See Y. Bilu & H. Abramovitch, "In Search of the Saddiq: Visitational Dreams among Moroccan Jews in Israel," *Psychiatry*, XLVIII (1985), pp. 83–92; H. Abramovitch & Y. Bilu, "Visitational Dreams and Naming Practices among Moroccan Jews Living in Israel," *Journal of Jewish Sociology*, XXVII (1985), pp. 13-21.
17. O'Nell, *Dreams, Culture* (above, note 2); L. Oppenheim, *Ancient Mesopotamia*, Chicago 1968; Von Grunebaum & Caillois, *The Dream* (above, note 3).
18. J.S. Lincoln, *The Dream in Primitive Cultures*, London 1935.
19. I. Ben-Ami, "Folk-Veneration" (above, note 10); see Y. Bilu, "Dreams and the Wishes of the Saint," in H. Goldberg (ed.), *Judaism Viewed from Within and from Without*, Albany, N.Y., 1987, pp. 285–313.
20. See Bilu, "Dreams and the Wishes" (above, note 19).
21. BT Eruvin 19a.
22. See Bilu, "In Search of the Saddiq" (above, note 16).
23. V. Lanternari, "Dreams as Charismatic Significants: Their Bearing on the Rise of New Religious Movements," in T.R. Williams (ed.), *Psychological Anthropology*, The Hague 1975, pp. 221–235.
24. G. OBeyesekere, *Medusa's Heir*, Chicago 1980; M.E. Spiro, "Collective Representations and Mental Representations in Religious Symbol Systems," in B. Kilborne & L.L. Langness (eds.), *Culture and Human Nature*, Chicago 1987, pp. 161–184.
25. B. Tedlock, *Dreaming* (above, note 5).
26. See Bilu, "Saint Impresarios" (above, note 11).
27. See I. Ben-Ami, *Saint Veneration* (above, note 8).
28. Y. Bilu & E. Ben-Ari, "The Making of Saints" (above, note 12).
29. See Bilu, "Dreams and the Wishes" (above, note 19).
30. See Bilu, "In Search of the Saddiq" (above, note 16); idem, "The Inner Limits of Communitas: A Covert Aspect of Pilgrimage Behavior," *Ethos*, XVI (1987), pp. 302-325.
31. E. Ben-Ari & Y. Bilu, "Saint Sanctuaries" (above, note 7).

19
Facing a Holy Space: Psychiatric Hospitalization of Tourists in Jerusalem

Moshe Kalian and Eliezer Witztum

Introduction

Tourism is a widespread phenomenon with a long tradition. The sociology of tourism is a growing specialty concerned with the study of tourist motivations, roles, relationships and institutions, and their impact on the tourists themselves and on the societies which receive them.[1] The scientific study of tourism is relatively new. It originated in Central Europe, and the first social scientific article on the subject was published in 1899.[2] Since 1950 there has been a steady increase in data-gathering relevant to tourism, corresponding to its growth as a major world industry. There are many approaches to tourism: the sociologist tries to construct a typology to categorize tourists; the economist treats tourism as an industry; the anthropologist tries to examine the tourist's impact on local populations, and so on. We would like to add another aspect: the psychopathology of tourists.

Recent studies on tourism have emphasized the highly heterogeneous character of the motivation to travel. Travelling is associated with curiosity, adventure, status and much more. Pearce[3] mentions phenomena as diverse as self-actualization, the desire for achievement and cognitive attribution in order to explain individual differences in motivation. These same motives are part of our daily lives, but the difference is that as tourists we alter our routines.[4] These changes of routine sometimes have a tremendous impact on mental states, especially with some types of tourists. For this article we have chosen only one field of examination, namely, the relationship between tourism and psychopathology, with a particular stress on the role of religion.

Freud wrote about the experience of travel and the associated loss of a sense of reality, in connection with his visit to the Acropolis in 1904. Writing home, he related that his experience there had surpassed anything he had ever seen or could imagine.[5] More than thirty years later, in a letter to Romain Rolland,[6] Freud described in detail this curious psychological experience, which was essentially a peculiar disbelief in the reality of what was before his eyes. He had puzzled his brother by asking him if it was true that they were on the Acropolis. He felt himself being divided into two persons, one who was in fact on the Acropolis and another who could not believe that this was the case.

There is some psychiatric literature on the issue of the psychiatric hospitalization of people who visit another country. Special mention is made of "airport wanderers" and of visitors to specific places. For example, Magherini and Zanobini[7] describe a particular kind of acute psychotic reaction arising in art-loving tourists visiting Florence. Between 1978 and 1986 they studied 107 foreign patients who were hospitalized. From the analysis of the data, it is clear that there was no relevant difference between males and females; most of the patients came from European countries; those most affected were between twenty and forty years old; and they were mainly single people travelling on their own, not in organized groups. The stay in hospital was short, the prognosis was benign, and the holiday generally was interrupted only for a short while.

Flinn[8] and Singh[9] listed some of the causes of the psychotic breakdowns of travellers. These included unfamiliar surroundings, the presence of strangers, inactivity, boredom, a sense of isolation, and the shock of cultural retransplantation. Hiatt and Spurlick[10] noted a class of patients who are on the move in order to seek a "geographical solution to internal problems."

Shapiro, working in a department of Queens New York Psychiatric Hospital, did a study of 359 psychiatric patients who were sent in from nearby Kennedy Airport. Most of the people he studied demonstrated symptoms of schizophrenia (74%). Contrary to the findings of others, who stressed the importance of phobic anxiety relating to flight or of culture shock, he found that the airport setting only gave a specific colour to pre-existing problems. The airport had a symbolic value. Separation and reunion, as major foci of disturbance, may be important factors in explaining the phenomenon of "airport wanderers." With certain groups of people, added Shapiro, "the airport can also serve to disorganize by generating degrees of overwhelming anxiety stimulated by feelings related to separation, abandonment, and hostile impulses."[11] Jauhar and Weller[12] investigated psychopathological phenomena at Heathrow Airport from the perspective of changes of time zone. They found that depression was more common in travellers journeying from east to west and hypomania in travellers in the opposite direction.

Tourism and Pilgrimage: The Phenomenology of Tourist Experience

What is the nature of a tourist experience? What drives people to travel enormous distances and enter into other cultures? Historians of tourism have pointed out that religious pilgrimages are one of the principal forerunners of modern tourism. Cohen developed a phenomenological typology of tourist experiences based on the concept of the "centre" and the "quest for the centre" described by Mircea Eliade. Eliade pointed out that every religious "cosmos" possesses a "centre" which is pre-eminently the zone of the sacred, the zone of absolute reality. This is the point "where the axis mundi penetrates the earthly sphere."[14] The centre, however, is not necessarily geographically central to the life space of the community of believers. According to Turner, its exocentric location may be meaningful in that it gives direction and structure to the pilgrimage, a sacred journey of spiritual ascent to "the centre out there."[15]

There have been several attempts to classify tourists, their behaviour and their experiences.[16] For our purpose, which is to examine the relationship between the purpose of the journey and the psychiatric breakdown, Cohen's typology[16] seems the most appropriate. In this typology, tourist experience is categorized according to the significance of the culture, social life and natural environment of others for the traveller and the degree to which his journey represents "a quest for the centre." Cohen describes five modes of tourist experiences: (1) the recreational mode; (2) the diversionary mode; (3) the experiential mode; (4) the experimental mode; and (5) the existential mode.

The first mode is typical of modern man: the trip as a recreational experience is akin to other forms of entertainment, such as television, the cinema or the theatre. It represents a movement away from the centre. The diversionary mode of travel is an escape from the boredom and meaninglessness of routine everyday existence. This mode is similar to the recreational mode but does not fulfill the recuperative function of the former. It is characteristic of alienated tourists who merely enjoy their holiday or "have a good time," without it contributing to the resumption of their roles or positions at home.

The experiential mode, characterized by a more intense searching than the preceding two, is a quest for a vicarious experience of the authentic life of others. In the experimental mode the tourist actually tries out various alternative lifestyles in an effort to discover one which he himself wishes to adopt. These people travel in order to "find themselves." The existential mode is represented by the traveller who sets out for a specific spiritual centre, and his visit to this centre is the phenomenological analogue of a pilgrimage.

Cohen[17] concludes that tourism is essentially a modern metamorphosis of the pilgrimage, after secularization has brought about the breakdown of the deep structural themes of such journeys and of much of their symbolic significance and mystical power, thus transforming their loci into mere destinations or "places of attraction." Modern pilgrimage, in contrast, may look indistinguishable from tourism; by analyzing their respective motivations, however, we can discern the difference between pilgrim-tourists, who travel toward the religious or cultural centres of their lives, and traveller-tourists who travel away from them to the periphery.

Jerusalem as a Religious Centre: Pilgrims, Millennialists and Messiahs

Jews have made pilgrimages to Jerusalem ever since Temple times, when the city drew hundreds of thousands of visitors on each of the three annual pilgrim festivals. After the destruction of the Temple, devout Jews continued to make their way to Jerusalem, despite tremendous difficulties. In modern times, the establishment of the State of Israel has strengthened Jewish travel to the region, although it has become less clear what motivates the travellers.

The late Joshua Prawer described Christianity's attitude towards Jerusalem as ambivalent and constantly changing, as a result of the historical and religious relationship between Christianity and Judaism.[18] The diminishing of the importance of the earthly Jerusalem, which gave way to the emphasis on a heavenly Jerusalem, has been an important facet of the Christian argument against Judaism. Prawer argued, however, that while the Christian theologians busied themselves with the mystical interpretation of Jerusalem as the kingdom of heaven, the Christian masses were drawn to the earthly Jerusalem.[19] Christian pilgrimage to the Holy Land began in the early days of Christianity and became an established institution from the fourth century on, continuing almost uninterrupted to the present day.

This type of pilgrimage belongs to the category that Turner calls "prototypical," that is, relating directly to the life of the founder of the religion and his intimates. Christian pilgrims to the Holy Land have never gone in expectation of miraculous cures or benefits. They go, rather, to vivify their understanding of Christianity by immersing themselves in the geographical setting of its birthplace, and to imitate Christ by retracing the steps of his life as recorded in the Gospels. Jerusalem, where they can follow in the footsteps of his last journey on the Via Dolorosa, is especially meaningful.[20]

Jerusalem, as a holy city, has always been an attractive place for some eccentric religious circles, both Jewish and Christian, who believe that the millennium, the end of the world, or the messianic era is approaching. The central element in Christian eschatology is the expectation of the Second Advent of Christ and the establishment of the kingdom of God on earth. There are those who believe that the Second Advent is imminent, and they want to be present in Jerusalem when it happens. According to Jewish eschatology, too, Jerusalem is the place where the Messiah's redemption of humankind will occur. Visitors and tourists coming to Jerusalem and presenting themselves as Messiahs or proclaiming the millennium have been reported many times in the course of history, especially in the nineteenth century — and this phenomenon continues today.

Hospitalization of Tourists in Jerusalem

Since 1979, all foreign tourists in need of psychiatric hospitalization in the Jerusalem area have been referred to the Kefar Shaul Psychiatric Hospital. During the first year, only 25 tourist-patients were admitted. Now, however, the number of referrals has reached an average of 50 patients per annum. In recent years, comprehensive statistical data have been kept on these patients. The most extensive data, on which we base our findings, were collected during 1986 and 1987. The data on this group were compared with the demographic data of another group of 177 tourists hospitalized between 1979 and 1984.[21] No significant statistical differences between the two groups were found with regard to age, sex, marital status, religion, country of origin, method of referral or the number of previous visits to Israel. We believe, therefore, that the data we present are a fair representation of hospitalized tourists in Jerusalem.

The group studied in our survey comprised 32 women and 57 men whose average age was 32.4 years; 74% were single, 15% were divorced, and only a minority — 11% — were married. 52% had received 13 or more years of education, 36% had between 8 and 12 years of education, while 7% had five years of education or less. Most of the tourists came from North America (40%) and Western Europe (44%); the remainder were from Eastern Europe, South America, South Africa or elsewhere.

The whole range of tourist objectives we have described was represented in our sample. Recreational tourism was the mode for 38% of our group; 26% came for reasons of a mystical-religious nature; about 15% were visiting relatives; and 7% came to do volunteer work. The experiential mode — that is, trying out a new lifestyle — provided the chief impetus for 11% of our group. These people came to learn and considered staying.

Examination of the behaviour of the patients before admission shows that deviant behaviour such as excessive preaching and vagrancy was found in 33% of them. Manifestations of aggression, such as physical attacks on people or threats to use weapons against them, led to the admission of 11%, while another 11% were walking around naked when apprehended and referred to hospital. 13% were admitted after attempting suicide, and 33% did not demonstrate any specific forms of deviant behaviour.

Table 1 shows the religious affiliation of the patients and their levels of religious involvement.

Table 1: Religion and level of religious observance[22]

	Observant	Strict	Non-observant	Total
Jewish	22	10	13	45
Catholic	8	5	5	18
Protestant	3	2	9	14
Other	1	0	1	2
Unknown				10
Total	34	17	28	89

There is no significant difference in the level of religious involvement of the patients belonging to the various religious groups (chi-square=7.3, p=.30).

We will now turn to the diagnosis of the patients' conditions. Psychotic episodes, which include acute psychotic episodes and acute exacerbation of chronic psychotic disorders, were by far the most important factor leading to hospitalization.

Table 2: Diagnosis[23]

Schizophrenia	49	(55%)
Acute psychosis	14	(16%)
Affective psychosis	11	(12%)
Personality disorder	7	(8%)
Dementia	2	(2%)
Other	6	(7%)

There was no correlation between the diagnosis and the religious background, sex or age of the patients, although of course the patients suffering from dementia were much older than the other patients.

To bring the connection between the religious factor and their illness into sharper focus, patients were asked to describe the nature of their experiences at the time of their admission. Thirty-six patients (40%) reported mystical experiences. Many identified with religious figures: twenty-two (25%) thought they were the Messiah; four (5%)

thought they were God; three (4%, all of them Catholic) identified with Satan; and another seven (8%) identified with biblical figures (Moses, King David, the Virgin Mary and John the Baptist). Given the near overlap (91% — see Table 3) between those who reported mystical experiences and those who identified with such figures, we may say that their mystical experiences arose from religious delusions.

Table 3: Religious delusions and mystical experiences[24]

Mystical experiences:	Yes	No
Identification with:		
Messiah	20	2
God	3	1
Satan	2	1
Other (mostly biblical figures)	6	1
No identification	5	29
Unknown		19

An interesting phenomenon is that mystical experiences were more frequent in patients from Roman Catholic backgrounds than in Jewish or Protestant patients.

On the basis of our material and that of the earlier study of Kalian et al.,[25] we can submit the following profile of tourists in Jerusalem who have required psychiatric hospitalization. In general, they are men and women of North American and European origin, in their twenties and thirties, with an above-average education. Half of them have professions, but only a quarter actually work. Psychotic phenomena are the predominant symptoms in about 80% of cases, while the rest suffer from personality disorders or other disturbances.

Our hypothesis that most people suffering acute psychotic disturbances during a journey had suffered before from psychiatric problems was confirmed: 82% of the patients in our survey had received psychiatric treatment before their hospitalization in Jerusalem. This leaves us, nonetheless, with 18% of patients who had not previously received treatment. We assumed that the latter group would differ in some way from those with a history of previous illness. However, no differences appeared in the demographic variables, or in their motives for travelling, their religious involvement, or the nature of their religious delusions.

Case Vignettes

(1) Delusional behaviour: Mr. W., an American tourist, aged 33, was referred by a court for observation. According to his history, he was the middle son in a mixed Jewish-Christian family and had received a partial academic education. He served for several years in the U.S. Air Force and worked in pottery after his discharge. He divorced his wife after five years of marriage because she had an abortion against his will. He considered himself "religious," but did not belong to any specific congregation. In the last few weeks he had become more devout and had come to Jerusalem "to help Israel fight her enemies." On the fifth day of his visit, he was "instructed by God through telepathy to cure the blind." He went to a shop in the Old City of Jerusalem and left all his clothes there in exchange for a sword. Suddenly he grabbed the sword and ran with it, naked, toward the "Golden Gate," intending "to cure the blind and fulfill his mission." He was stopped by the police.

(2) Recreational tourism: Mrs. T., a British tourist, aged 36, was referred by the staff of a general hospital emergency room on account of her violent behaviour and threats to kill herself. Upon admission she was restless, claiming that she was "carrying the son of Jesus" in her womb, and was afraid of "having another miscarriage."

Her history revealed that she was of the Christian faith, a high school teacher with an academic background, married for several years but with no children because of recurrent spontaneous miscarriages. She had had several affective episodes during the last five years, but her condition before her journey was reported to be stable. She came alone to Jerusalem, five days prior to her hospitalization, for a short vacation. She had felt exhausted from work and planned a seven-day vacation to recover. On the fifth day, she complained that she was having a miscarriage and refused to accept the doctors' conclusions that there were no positive physical findings (including pregnancy). During the psychiatric hospitalization, she experienced a state of elation and claimed she possessed supernatural powers.

She was diagnosed as having an acute exacerbation of a chronic bipolar affective disorder and was treated accordingly. When she was discharged after eight days, she insisted on having another gynecological checkup before returning home.

(3) Existential tourism: Mr. A., a Catholic tourist from Latin America, was brought in by the police and two members of his tour group on the fourth day of his visit to Jerusalem. That morning, it was reported, he had suddenly became bizarre, speaking in a strange language and producing odd voices. He avoided food and stayed in his room. When members of his group tried to approach him, he became violent.

On admission he seemed to be disoriented and subject to hallucinations, producing strange voices with incomprehensible and halting speech and bizarre words. No physical problems were detected. After about 12 hours and haloperidol treatment, he became relatively coherent and was able to give a verbal account in Spanish. According to him, he was married, his wife was pregnant and he had a daughter. He ran his own mechanics business. He reported no previous psychiatric treatment. However, during the last two years he had gradually become "closer to religion," felt that he "should study religion more profoundly," and at times believed that "God was speaking" to him in various ways. Sometimes, at night, he thought that he heard "voices."

He decided to visit the Holy Land to complete his religious searching and prepared himself carefully for the trip. Three days prior to his hospitalization he had visited the Western Wall, and since then he had felt a gradual increase both in anxiety and in the frequency of "inner voices." On the day of his hospitalization, he "experienced direct contact with God." He stayed in the hospital for four days, receiving antipsychotic medication, and then returned to his group.

(4) Identification with Jesus Christ: Mr. F., aged 41, divorced with no children, a German-speaking Protestant tourist, was brought in by the police after coming to a local police station with a strange complaint. He spoke in a quiet voice and was well behaved. He was partially cooperative and claimed that he was Jesus Christ, his mother was the Virgin Mary and his father was God. His affect was flat and inappropriate.

From the information he gave during hospitalization, it turned out that he was the youngest son of a waitress and had never known his biological father. He had a vocational high school education and had worked as a professional painter until three years before, when he was hospitalized for the first time. Since then he had had two other psychiatric hospitalizations, each lasting for about three months. He liked visiting distant places and had already toured Africa, the Far East and Eastern Europe, for what he described as "pure tourist curiosity."

His visit to Jerusalem was of a different nature. Although not very devout in his home country, he had decided to come to Jerusalem "to find his religious faith in the Holy Land, and to find the Cross." He arrived two weeks prior to his current hospitalization and stayed in a small hotel in the Old City. On the day of his hospitalization, he went to the hotel kitchen and offered his services "to improve the order there." After being refused, he went to a police station demanding to register an official complaint. He was referred to the hospital.

During hospitalization, he expressed delusions of grandeur and persecution. He was discharged after 10 days of treatment in a partial dissimulative state, and returned home.

Discussion

There are only a few psychiatric studies relating to the role of particular places in inducing or exacerbating psychopathological states in individuals. The places mentioned in the psychiatric literature have a number of common characteristics. All the places are known throughout the world and attract millions of visitors for many reasons, ordinarily without any mental morbidity. Nevertheless, the study of the psychopathology of those who do suffer mental breakdowns in a particular place has yielded important observations and deductions (just as Freud's hypotheses with regard to the psychosexual stages of normal development were deduced from the particular psychopathology of his patients).

There are works relating to the psychological significance of JFK airport, the city of Florence, the White House in Washington, D.C., and Jerusalem. Each of these places has a unique symbolic significance. JFK airport is a gigantic global crossroads, a contemporary symbol of the basic human conflict of separation and reunion. The White House — the residence of a powerful yet benevolent authority of an earthly nature — may symbolize grandiose aspirations and the desire to exercise control.[26] Florence — a shrine of the visual arts of the Renaissance — is also a place of intimacy where one might unconsciously communicate with the psyches of artists who skillfully sublimated their drives into immortal paintings and sculptures.[27]

Among all these, Jerusalem, the primal site of the pilgrimages that preceded modern tourism, with its multilevel spiritual and religious significances, has a unique status.[28]

The topic of psychogeography, or the psychology of spatial existence, has been much discussed recently. Psychogeography is the study of how issues, experiences, and processes are symbolized and expressed in a wider social and natural context, creating cultural maps which often depict the image of things belonging to one's group rather than a true reflection of the world.[29]

Thus, it has been suggested by A. Falk that, from this point of view, the city of Jerusalem could be conceptualized as an idealized mother "to whom one could come for solace or succor." In Judaism, according to Falk, the "longing for Zion was always like the longing of a child for its long-lost mother, ... while the Christian idea of the New Jerusalem came from the yearning for an ideal new world." Falk even goes so far as to associate the longing for "mother" Jerusalem with "our early development as human beings" and "the longing to return to the womb, as well as the incestuous yearnings of sons for their mothers." These primitive feelings, he argues, are repressed and "displaced to the geographic, religious and political spheres," so that "the hills and valleys of Jerusalem unconsciously remind us of the curves of the body of our mother when we were infants."[30]

We do not deny the validity of the metaphorical concept of Jerusalem as a mother-figure, or the significance of the form of representation of Jerusalem in medieval maps — where, in some cases, Jerusalem occupies most of the space of Palestine or is drawn right next to the Mediterranean, with pilgrims' ships docked in its harbour.[31] We interpret this form of representation as demonstrating the importance of the city and its imagery in the eyes of the cartographer. However, Falk's interpretation and generalizations, such as the assertion that "psychologically [this graphic description and the longing for Jerusalem] are features of a child's idealization of its depriving mother,"[32] are speculative and lack empirical support. Our approach is different, relying on phenomenological analyses of empirical data. We focus on the attempt to understand the specific cultural and religious context of the people we have described, who, in most instances, had a psychotic episode while visiting Jerusalem.

This group certainly displays some specific characteristics. Although material for comparison is scarce, there is clearly a correlation between the meaning of Jerusalem as a place central to religious experience and the nature of the psychotic episodes that we studied.

The diagnostic picture given in Table 2 above corresponds closely to that in Shapiro's study of airport wanderers.[33] Thus, we can agree with Shapiro that people who break down in the course of a journey mostly suffer from pre-existing pathological complaints and that the environment lends its specific colour to the disturbance. That specific colour shows up clearly in the 40% of our patients who reported mystical experiences, most of whom also believed that they were mystical/religious figures.

Religious ideas among psychotic patients are often mentioned in psychiatric textbooks. The best-known cases are patients who claim to be famous religious figures or adopt religious attitudes. Beit-Hallahmi and Argyle[34] summarize the literature on the connection between religious ideas and psychiatric disorders and state: "It seems that religious ideas are more likely to be connected with cases of affective disorders and cases of paranoid schizophrenia. The appearance of such religious content can be explained on the basis of differential learning and exposure to religious ideas." The relationship between religious affiliation and mental condition, however, is far from simple. Empirical studies indicate a variety of relationships between religious affiliations and mental states.[35] Bergin[36] reviewed extensive empirical literature on the subject and claimed in his meta-analysis that "there is no support for the preconception that religiousness is necessarily correlated with psychopathology but shows only slightly positive correlates of religion." Surveys examining the distribution of religious beliefs in psychiatric patients[37] show that it does not differ significantly from that in the general population.

Another notable factor was the consistency of the psychotic behaviour demonstrated by our patients. During their psychiatric crises, the tourists' behaviour was dictated by the norms associated with their particular religious explanatory models. Thus, for example, the 30% who identified with a messianic figure never walked around naked.

Notes

1. P. Pearce, *The Social Psychology of Tourist Behaviour*, Oxford 1982.
2. E. Cohen, "The Sociology of Tourism: Approaches, Issues, and Findings," *Annual Review of Sociology*, X (1984), pp. 373–392.
3. Pearce, *Social Pyschology* (above, note 1).
4. G.E. Machils & W.R Burch, "Relations between Strangers: Cycles of Structure and Meaning in Tourist Experiences," *Sociological Review*, XXII (1983), pp. 666–692.
5. E. Jones, *The Life and Work of Sigmund Freud*, II, New York 1955, p. 24.
6. S. Freud, "A Disturbance of Memory on the Acropolis," *Standard Edition*, XXII, London 1962, p. 239.
7. G. Magherini & A. Zanobini, "Eventi e psicopatologia: Il perturbante turistico: nota preliminare," *Rassegna di studi psichiatrici*, LXXIV (1987), pp. 1–14.
8. D.B. Flinn, "Transient Psychotic Reactions during Travel," *American Journal of Psychiatry*, CXIX (1962), pp. 173–174.
9. H.A. Singh, "A Case of Psychosis Precipitated by Confinement in Long Distance Travel by Train," *American Journal of Psychiatry*, CXVII (1961), pp. 936–937.
10. C.C. Hiatt & R.E. Spurlick, "Geographical Flight and Its Relation to Crisis Theory," *American Journal of Orthopsychiatry*, XL (1970), pp. 53–57.
11. S. Shapiro, "Psychiatric Symptoms and the Airport," *Aviation, Space and Environmental Medicine*, XLVIII (1977), pp. 555–557; also idem, "A Study of Psychiatric Syndromes Manifested at an International Airport," *Comprehensive Psychiatry*, XVII (1976), pp. 453–456; idem, "Airport Wandering as a Psychotic Symptom," *Psychiatria Clinica*, XV (1982), pp. 173–176.
12. P. Jauhar & M.P.I. Weller, "Psychiatric Morbidity and Time Zone Changes: A Study of Patients from Heathrow Airport," *British Journal of Psychiatry*, CXL (1982), pp. 231–235.
13. Cohen, "Sociology of Tourism" (above, note 2); idem, "A Phenomenology of Tourist Experiences," *Sociology*, XIII (1979), pp. 179–201.
14. M. Eliade, *The Myth of Eternal Return*, Princeton, N.J., 1971, p. 12.
15. V. Turner, "The Center Out There: The Pilgrim's Goal," *History of Religion*, XII (1973), pp. 191–210.
16. E. Cohen , "Pilgrimages and Tourism: Convergence and Divergence," paper presented at the conference on "Pilgrimage: The Human Quest," University of Pittsburgh, 1981.
17. Idem, "Sociology of Tourism" (above, note 2).
18. J. Prawer, "Christianity between Heavenly and Earthly Jerusalem," in idem, *Jerusalem through the Ages*, Jerusalem 1968, pp. 179–192 (in Hebrew).

19. Idem, "Jerusalem in Jewish and Christian Thought in the Early Middle Ages," *Cathedra*, XVII (1980), pp. 40–72 (in Hebrew).
20. V. Turner, *Image and Pilgrimage in Christian Culture: An Anthropological Perspective*, Oxford 1978, p. 1.
21. M. Kalian, B. Eisenberg & I. Bar-El, "Tourists Who Need Psychiatric Hospitalization: Population Characteristics and Treatment Principles," *Proceedings of the First International Congress on Hospital Laws*, Tel Aviv 1985.
22. The table is adapted from I. Bar-El, E. Witztum, M. Kalian & D. Brom, "Psychiatric Hospitalization of Tourists in Jerusalem," *Comprehensive Psychiatry*, XXXII (1991), pp. 238–244.
23. Adapted from *ibid.*; the diagnoses are defined in accordance with I.C.D.–9CM, the *International Classification of Diseases*, Ninth Revision: *Clinical Modification*, I, Second Edition, U.S. Department of Health and Human Services, 1980.
24. Adapted from Bar-El et al., "Psychiatric Hospitalization" (above, note 22).
25. Kalian et al., "Tourists" (above, note 21).
26. J.A. Sebastian & J.L. Foy, "Psychotic Visitors to the White House," *American Journal of Psychiatry*, CXXII (1965), pp. 679–686; D. Shore et al., "White House Cases: Psychiatric Patients and the Secret Service," *American Journal of Psychiatry*, CXLII (1985), pp. 308–312.
27. G. Magherini, "Psychiatric Disorders and Life Events: The Stendhal Syndrome," lecture presented at the Albert Einstein Institute, New York (1990), pp. 1–17.
28. E.J. Leed, *The Mind of the Traveler*, New York 1991, pp. 144–146.
29. H.F. Stein & W.G. Niderland (eds.), *Maps from the Mind*, Norman 1989, p. 1.
30. A. Falk, "The Meaning of Jerusalem: A Psychohistorical Viewpoint," in Stein & Niderland (eds.), *Maps* (above, note 29).
31. R. Rubin, *Jerusalem in Maps and Pictures*, Tel Aviv 1988 (in Hebrew).
32. Falk, "Meaning of Jerusalem" (above, note 30).
33. Shapiro, "Psychiatric Symptoms," "A Study" and "Airport Wandering" (all above, note 11).
34. B. Beit-Hallahmi & M. Argyle, "Religious Ideas and Psychiatric Disorders," *International Journal of Social Psychiatry*, XXIII (1977), pp. 26–30.
35. C.B. MacDonald & J.B. Luckett, "Religious Affiliation and Psychiatric Diagnosis," *Journal for the Scientific Study of Religion*, XXII (1983), pp. 15–37.
36. A.E. Bergin, "Religiosity and Mental Health : Critical Evaluation and Meta-analysis," *Professional Psychologist: Research and Practice*, XIV (1983), pp. 170–184.
37. J. Kroll & W. Sheehan, "Religious Beliefs and Practice among 52 Psychiatric Inpatients in Minnesota," *American Journal of Psychiatry*, CXLVI (1989), pp. 67–72.

List of Contributors

David Ayalon is Emeritus Professor of Islamic Studies at the Hebrew University of Jerusalem.

Hedva Ben-Israel is Emeritus Professor of History at the Hebrew University of Jerusalem.

Yoram Bilu is Associate Professor of Psychology at the Hebrew University of Jerusalem.

Allan G. Grapard is Professor of Religious Studies at the University of California at Santa Barbara.

Alfred Haverkamp is Professor of Medieval History at the University of Trier.

Sara Japhet is Professor of Bible at the Hebrew University of Jerusalem.

Moshe Kalian is District Psychiatrist of the Central Region, Israel.

Benjamin Z. Kedar is Professor of History at the Hebrew University of Jerusalem.

Nehemia Levtzion is Professor of Asian and African Studies at the Hebrew University of Jerusalem.

Abraham Malamat is Emeritus Professor of Jewish History at the Hebrew University of Jerusalem

Doron Mendels is Professor of History at the Hebrew University of Jerusalem.

Richard Nebel is Professor of Religious Studies at the University of Bamberg.

Evelyne Patlagean is Professor of History at the University of Paris X, Nanterre.

Haviva Pedaya is Lecturer in Jewish Thought in the Department of History at Ben Gurion University of the Negev, Beer Sheva.

David Shulman is Professor of Indian Studies and Comparative Religion at the Hebrew University of Jerusalem.

Itamar Singer is Professor of Ancient Near Eastern Studies at Tel Aviv University.

Jonathan Z. Smith is Professor of the History of Culture at the University of Chicago.

Kenneth R. Stow is Professor of Jewish History at the University of Haifa.

Gideon Weigert is a researcher in Islamic Studies associated with the Department of History at Ben Gurion University of the Negev, Beer Sheva.

R.J. Zwi Werblowsky is Emeritus Professor of Comparative Religion at the Hebrew University of Jerusalem.

Eliezer Witztum is Professor of Medicine at Ben Gurion University of the Negev, Beer Sheva.

INDEX OF NAMES AND PLACES